THE NARRATIVE UNITY OF LUKE-ACTS

THE NARRATIVE UNITY OF LUKE-ACTS

A Literary Interpretation

Volume 1: The Gospel according to Luke

by

ROBERT C. TANNEHILL

Fortress Press
Philadelphia

Biblical quotations are the author's own translation.

Library of Congress Cataloging in Publication Data

Tannehill, Robert C.
  The narrative unity of Luke-Acts.

  (Foundations and facets)
  Bibliography: p.
Contents: v. 1. The Gospel according to Luke.
  1. Bible. N.T. Luke—Criticism, interpretation,
etc. 2. Bible. N.T. Acts—Criticism, interpretation,
etc. I. Title. II. Series: Foundations and facets.
New Testament.
BS2589.T35   1986   226'.406   86-45224
ISBN 0-8006-2112-3 (cloth)
ISBN 0-8006-2557-9 (paper)

TYPESET ON AN IBYCUS SYSTEM AT POLEBRIDGE PRESS

Printed in the United States of America   1-2557
95   94   93   92   91   1   2   3   4   5   6   7   8   9   10

To Methesco with thanks.

Nourished by a gentle stream and caring people.

Contents

THE NARRATIVE UNITY OF LUKE-ACTS

The following study will emphasize the unity of Luke-Acts. This unity is the result of a single author working within a persistent theological perspective, but it is something more. It is a *narrative* unity, the unity appropriate to a well-formed narrative. Change and development are expected in such a narrative, yet unity is maintained because the scenes and characters contribute to a larger story that determines the significance of each part.

To be sure, our expectations of narrative unity, shaped perhaps by the modern novel, are not always fulfilled in Luke. Much of Luke shares the episodic style of the synoptic gospels in general, in which individual scenes may be vivid but their connection into story sequences is often unclear. The neglect of clear causal connections among episodes (indications that one event leads to the next) is striking when we compare the synoptic gospels with modern narrative. Our narrator is quite capable of making such connections, as major portions of Acts attest, but chose to leave the Jesus tradition in its looser form. Despite the episodic style of large portions of Luke, it traces the unfolding of a single dominant purpose. This unifies the gospel story and unites Luke with Acts, for this purpose is not only at work in the ministry of Jesus but also in the ministries of Jesus' witnesses. Luke-Acts is a unified narrative because the chief human characters (John the Baptist, Jesus, the apostles, Paul) share in a mission which expresses a single controlling purpose—the purpose of God. The individual episodes gain their significance through their relation to this controlling purpose of God, and the narrator has made efforts to clarify this relation.

Disclosures of the nature of God's purpose are highlighted at key points in the narrative as guides in interpreting the story. The disclosures at the beginning of Luke are especially important in suggesting ultimate expectations. However, conflict soon appears in the plot, for God's purpose repeatedly encounters rejection. The unity of this narrative is a unity in tension, and the last section of Luke, the crisis in Jerusalem and the ironic triumph that follows, has special importance in showing how God's purpose meets human rejection.

These disclosures of God's purpose and of how it responds to human resistance provide an interpretive context for understanding the mission of

Jesus and his witnesses. This mission is carried out in interaction with important groups encountered in the narrative. Jesus' shifting and developing relationships with these groups, or with individuals that represent them, are a significant part of the Lukan story. Special attention will be given to these relationships in the following chapters.

Foundational work for this volume began with a sabbatical leave supported by the Methodist Theological School in Ohio, the Institute for Antiquity and Christianity of the Claremont Graduate School, the Society of Biblical Literature, and the Association of Theological Schools in the United States and Canada. I hope that this volume is a suitable gift of thanks for what I have received from these supporters and from the larger community of scholars.

Robert C. Tannehill

BAGD   Bauer, Walter. *A Greek-English Lexicon of the New Testament and Other Early Christian Literature.* 2d ed. Translated, revised, and augmented by William F. Arndt, F. Wilbur Gingrich, and Frederick W. Danker. Chicago: University of Chicago Press, 1979.

BDF   Blass, F. and A. Debrunner. *A Greek Grammar of the New Testament and Other Early Christian Literature.* Translated and revised by Robert W. Funk. Chicago: University of Chicago Press, 1961.

dif.   differs from; i.e., the named gospel(s) contain(s) a passage which is generally parallel, but the Lukan version differs from the other version(s) in the feature being discussed.

ed.   edited by

ET   English translation

LXX   Septuagint

NT   New Testament

RSV   Revised Standard Version

TDNT   *Theological Dictionary of the New Testament,* edited by Gerhard Kittel and Gerhard Friedrich. Translated by Geoffrey W. Bromiley. 9 vols. Grand Rapids: Wm. B. Eerdmans, 1964–1974.

Luke-Acts is the longest and most complex narrative in the New Testament. It was written by an author of literary skill and rich imagination who had a complex vision of the significance of Jesus Christ and of the mission in which he is the central figure. This complex vision is presented in a unified literary work of two volumes.

Because of its size and complexity, it is difficult to comprehend Luke-Acts as a unified literary work. This problem has been aggravated by a lack of leading concepts which would help scholars to explore ways in which narratives achieve unity or the particular ways in which Luke-Acts may be unified. The recent development of narrative criticism of the gospels, the result of extensive borrowing from non-biblical literary criticism, opens new opportunities, of which my work hopes to take advantage. It now appears to me that the author has carefully provided disclosures of the overarching purpose which unifies the narrative and that literary clues show the importance of these disclosures. Such disclosures guide us in understanding the story.

In this work I am not concerned with developing narrative theory (a helpful task which I hope others will continue) but with using selected aspects of narrative criticism to gain new insights into Luke-Acts. Luke-Acts is very familiar to those who have studied it at length, and familiar issues have come to dominate Lukan scholarship. But I am convinced that accents will be differently placed and questions differently posed if Luke-Acts is approached as a unified narrative with the help of narrative criticism. Some aspects of this transformed understanding have already begun to emerge, and I have profited from them. I hope to carry the discussion a stage further.

A complete literary analysis of Luke-Acts would involve much that I have ignored. I have chosen to focus on major roles in the narrative, understood in the context of the comprehensive purpose which is being realized throughout the narrative. I will be standing on the borderline between character and plot, understanding character in terms of role, which is character in action and interaction within an unfolding plot. These roles express competing and conflicting purposes, from which significant plot may emerge if a dominant purpose and tendency appears.

Jesus, the central character of Luke's Gospel, has a mission which he must fulfill. This mission is shared with others (John the Baptist, the apostles, Paul) and so extends beyond the places and time of Jesus' earthly life. This mission is received from a higher source. It entails responsibility for the realization of God's purpose in the world. The author of Luke-Acts consciously understands the story as unified by the controlling purpose of God and wants readers to understand it in the same way.[1] Focusing on one or more dominant purposes is a principal way of unifying a story. The reporting of unconnected events does not make a story, for a story is more than a string of incidents. In stories of the traditional kind, events take on meaning because they reveal purposes at work and represent movement toward the fulfillment of a major purpose or obstacles which block fulfillment. Luke-Acts has a unified plot because there is a unifying purpose of God behind the events which are narrated, and the mission of Jesus and his witnesses represents that purpose being carried out through human action.

Luke-Acts discloses at particular points the nature of God's purpose which unifies the narrative. We will find the following material particularly helpful in this regard: the angelic announcements and prophetic hymns of the birth narrative; the quotations from Isaiah in Luke 3:4–6 and 4:18–19 (the latter revealing the mission which Jesus has received from God); Jesus' passion announcements and announcements of his imminent exaltation (Luke 20:17, 42–43; 22:69); and the reviews of past events and preview of coming events in Luke 24. These disclosures are meant to guide the readers in understanding the central elements of the plot and in interpreting them as part of the purpose of God.

At the end of Acts this purpose of God is only partially fulfilled. This incompleteness is not merely the result of mission fields still unharvested. It is also the result of the frequent and persistent rejection which the mission encounters. Rejection of the mission by many Jews is the most painful. Jewish rejection is repeatedly highlighted in the narrative from the first scene of Jesus' public ministry to the last scene of Acts. Attention to this important aspect of the plot shows that the mission is not a simple success. There is a persistent tension within the plot, caused by rejection of the message. The mission's triumphs are triumphs in spite of repeated rejection which seems to lead to dead ends. The discovery that these are not, in fact, dead ends comes as a comforting surprise. This strain of negativity within the plot makes the story richer and more complex. The story emerges as a dialogue between God and a recalcitrant humanity, rather than God's monologue. This negativity also makes the story more

---

[1] Repeated use of the phrase βουλὴ τοῦ θεοῦ ("purpose of God"), which is characteristic of Luke-Acts, is initial indication of this. See Luke 7:30; Acts 2:23; 4:28; 5:38–39; 13:36; 20:27.

relevant to our own experience, which includes at least as much rejection and defeat as success. Since the purpose of God is ultimately a purpose of universal salvation, according to Luke-Acts, the tension within the plot is not resolved at the end of Acts, which, in fact, dramatizes the recurrent rejection of salvation by the Jews.

My concern with Luke-Acts as a unified narrative leads me to note many internal connections among different parts of the narrative. Themes will be developed, dropped, then presented again. Characters and actions may echo characters and actions in another part of the story, as well as characters and actions of the scriptural story which preceded Luke-Acts. There are a number of significant parallels among Jesus, his predecessor John, and his witnesses in Acts. These connections provide internal commentary on the story, clarifying meanings and suggesting additional nuances. Many of the connections which I will discuss have been noted before by various scholars, but when they are drawn together, they become much more impressive. My concern with these internal connections leads to considerable movement back and forth in Luke-Acts as I discuss texts. I am concerned with a text not as an isolated datum but as a functional member of the total narrative. I am also concerned with the meanings and suggestions of meaning which emerge when we note how part interacts with related part.

Such connections are complex and could be discussed at much greater length than I have done. Theoretically, we could distinguish three levels of significant connections which contribute to this complexity: (1) Some connections are emphasized strongly and are supported by clear literary signals, such as repetition of key words and phrases, indicating either that the author consciously intended the connection or that the author's message was bound to certain controlling images which repeatedly asserted themselves in the process of writing. These connections can contribute to our understanding of a narrative's message at a primary level. (2) Reading a narrative is an imaginative process. From words on a page we must reconstruct a narrative world which probably differs from our own. This imaginative process includes a realm of free play. There are a large number of possible connections and significances which the text may suggest but not necessarily emphasize. Some of these will no doubt depart from the author's conscious intentions, but no author can completely control what readers will find in the text. If these discoveries or inventions do not obscure the text's main emphases, the author and other interpreters would do well to be tolerant. Furthermore, there is no clear boundary between these first two levels, since the one shades into the other. (3) There is a subversive process of detecting connections, a "hermeneutics of suspicion" which seeks to uncover significant connections which the author might not acknowledge. These connections reveal cultural limitations, unconscious or concealed drives which are not socially acceptable, or ideology which may not stand examination in the light of day. Such subversive interpretation is also necessary; no human work can be exempted from it.

I am seeking connections within the text primarily at level (1) and therefore will try to show that there is literary evidence to support the connection. This does not absolutely guarantee that I will never stray into level (2). I am not working at level (3), except, perhaps, in noting that any narrative employs "narrative rhetoric." Although we are usually unaware of it, the narrator is persuading us to view characters and events in particular ways. We see and hear only what the narrator wants us to see and hear, and in the way the narrator wants us to see and hear it. The narrator is always seeking to weave a spell over us, so the reader should beware. On the other hand, those who are so suspicious that they cannot play the game lose their chance for excitement.

In discussing these internal connections, I want to take Acts fully into account. I will discuss in this volume various anticipations of Acts which we find in Luke. A fuller picture of the rich connections between Luke and Acts must wait for volume two.

Connected passages may fit into a progressive sequence, a narrative line which develops toward a resolution. Or the connection may simply be iterative, i.e., the same theme or situation is repeated, with some variation but with little indication that events are moving toward a climax or resolution. There is a good deal of the latter in Luke, for it, like Matthew and Mark, is quite episodic. In most of Luke there is much less indication that scenes are related causally, one scene *leading* to another, than in most of Acts. In this respect Luke shows its debt to the synoptic tradition. Iterative scenes still contribute something to the overall narrative. The total picture of Jesus and his mission is being enriched through repeated, similar episodes, each of which adds some new variation to familiar situations and themes. Such enrichment can take place through repeated "type-scenes,"[2] which can also be a means of narrative emphasis, highlighting certain aspects of Jesus' work because of their importance to the narrator.

On the other hand, there are developments larger than the short episodes, uniting these episodes into sequences. In the story of Jesus' public ministry, such developments are most apparent in material related to the crisis in Jerusalem toward which the story moves. Some of the discussion in the chapters on "Jesus and the Crowd or People," "Jesus and

---

[2] On type-scenes see below, pp. 18, 170–71.

the Authorities," and "Jesus and the Disciples" will concern developments which unite larger segments of the narrative. Indeed, these three chapters will discuss a simultaneous, interrelated development which is artificially separated in the chapters so that we can see how it affects each group. The chapter entitled "John and Jesus Begin Their Mission" also seeks to trace a development, one that leads to Jesus' announcement of his mission in Nazareth.

The central chapters of this work are organized by narrative roles. They concern Jesus as he interacts with groups which appear repeatedly in the narrative. There are advantages and disadvantages to the approach I will use. Isolating and following the developing relations between Jesus and significant groups in the narrative, a task that, to my knowledge, has not been previously attempted in such breadth and detail, helps me to clarify some continuities and progressions that would be less clear if I simply followed the order of the material in Luke, as the standard commentary does. A great deal is going on at once, and it is easy for discussion to become fragmented. The text is like a rope with multiple strands. The continuity of each strand is not easily seen, since it winds around other strands. I have attempted to separate the strands in order to test the strength of their continuity. This is somewhat dangerous, for the strands also mingle and interact. In a single scene Jesus may be reacting to a Pharisee and also to a sinful woman, or contiguous scenes may reflect on each other, despite their different characters. We must keep these complexities in mind.

Although I may appear to jump around in the Lukan text in some of the chapters, the selection of material for discussion is not arbitrary. It is determined by the appearance of the characters that are the subject of the chapter. Within the chapters I am often following the order of relevant material in Luke, and I hope to preserve a sense of the forward movement of the story in doing so. However, it is sometimes important to point out connections with other material which may occur considerably earlier or later. Although my procedure will make it more difficult for readers to find the discussion of a particular passage, an index is provided for this purpose. I cannot provide detailed commentary on all passages nor discuss all issues in the interpretation of Luke in a work of this kind. My aim is to highlight what I believe the narrator is highlighting through the literary design of the work, especially when this leads to new perspectives in reading Luke. I hope to avoid the "flattening" effect of much commentary, in which a narrative's main interests and emphases are lost in the host of details discussed.

The preceding comments should make clear to narrative critics that the following discussion will not be an example of reader response criticism, in the sense of an attempt to record the reading process with its myriad temporary interpretations, anticipations, and adjustments. I want to be sensitive to the ways in which the text is leading the reader. But the discussion that follows is not simply an expanded reading; it is commentary. It represents part of what might be said after reading a second, third, or fourth time. It is not confined to what is happening when reading for the first time, with much of the text still unknown.

I am concerned with Luke-Acts in its finished form, not with pre-Lukan tradition. Furthermore, I do not engage in elaborate arguments to distinguish tradition from Lukan redaction of that tradition. Brief comparisons of Luke with Matthew and Mark are useful where there are parallel texts, for these comparisons help us to recognize the distinctiveness of the Lukan version. But detailed analysis of the changes and additions introduced in Luke would lead me away from my main task.[3] Moreover, all material in Luke-Acts, whether it originated as tradition or redaction, is potentially important for my task. The decision to include a unit of tradition in the work is a choice which affects the total work. Even if the wording of the traditional unit is unchanged, it has been redacted by inclusion in a new writing. This is particularly true if the literary shaping of the total work highlights this unit in some way, giving it an important function within the whole or linking it with other material and thereby suggesting that it reveals something of continuing importance. The quotation from Isaiah in Luke 4:18–19 may serve as an example. This is clearly pre-Lukan tradition, and we know its source. There are a few variations from the Septuagint text which may be due to Lukan redaction. But it is most important to note the new function which the quotation has been given within the Lukan narrative, where it reveals Jesus' commission at the beginning of his ministry. Because of this new function, its meaning in Luke must be interpreted by noting the relation of its parts to the larger portrait of Jesus' ministry, where this commission is fulfilled. This requires investigation of Luke-Acts as a unified narrative, the task which I am attempting.

I have tried to avoid technical terms of literary theory which are still not widely used by biblical scholars. A brief explanation of some of the technical terms which I do use may be helpful. Literary scholars often distinguish between "author," "implied author," and "narrator." The author is the person external to the work who, among other things, wrote

---

[3] Although I accept the view that Mark and Q were sources of Luke, this view does not greatly affect following interpretations. In many cases the point of synoptic comparisons is simply the distinctiveness of the Lukan version. If a change of a particular source is implied, my point would often hold whether that source were Q, Mark, or (as some scholars would maintain) Matthew.

the work. We can often learn about him or her through biographical information gained from other sources than the literary work. We meet the "implied author," however, by investigation of the literary work itself. The implied author is the kind of person who would write this kind of work, which affirms certain values and beliefs and follows certain norms. While there is usually a close connection between the values and beliefs of the author and of the implied author, the perspectives of the two should not be simply identified. The implied author is likely to be a purified self, more consistent and noble, or perhaps more radical, than the author in external life, and may even be an experiment in being a different sort of person. The "narrator" is an instrument used for getting the story told. The narrator is the voice telling us all that we learn in the story. Literary scholars tend to distinguish the narrator from both the implied author and the author because the narrator may be a fictional person who has a role in the story, or if not, may still have characteristics distinct from the implied author, expressing views, for instance, which are not those which the story as a whole wishes to affirm. In this case the narrator is "unreliable." However, in Luke-Acts there are no signs that we have an unreliable narrator. We can begin with the assumption that the values and beliefs affirmed by the narrator are also those of the implied author.[4] I will use the terms narrator and implied author without implying a major distinction between them. Usually I will refer to the narrator. However, references to the implied author may appear when I am discussing values and beliefs which must be indirectly inferred from the composition of the narrative.

It is not a simple matter to understand the values and beliefs of the implied author clearly and fully. The situation is simplest when a reliable narrator expresses judgments directly, as when we are told that Zechariah and Elizabeth "were both righteous before God" (Luke 1:6). But values and beliefs are pervasive in narrative even when the narrator does not express them directly. We are always perceiving characters and events in the way that the narrator presents them to us, which may imply negative or positive judgments about them and will also represent judgments about

---

[4] An interpretation of the Lukan narrator as unreliable has been proposed by James Marshall Dawsey, *Confusion and Irony in the Gospel of Luke.* I am not convinced by this interpretation. We cannot arrive at an accurate understanding of the narrator's point of view if we begin by denying to the narrator all views expressed by Jesus but not repeated in the narrator's own speech. It is a common highlighting technique of narrators to put the most important material into the direct speech of central characters. The narrator of Luke-Acts appreciated the dramatic possibilities of "showing" rather than "telling." Hence the key function of characters' speeches in this narrative. We should assume that Jesus' words are understood and accepted by the narrator who is presenting them to us unless there are convincing indications to the contrary. I am not convinced by the cases of conflict between the views of Jesus and the narrator presented by Dawsey.

what is important. Furthermore, the views of the implied author may be shared through the voices of characters within the story. When a character is presented as perceptive and authoritative, we should suspect that the views expressed by this character also represent those of the implied author—unless our initial impression is undermined by events later in the story. When the views of a character do mirror those of the implied author, we have "reliable commentary."[5]

Telling a story involves "narrative rhetoric." The narrator constructs a narrative world which readers are invited to inhabit imaginatively, a world constructed according to certain values and beliefs. These values and beliefs are intended to be appealing and convincing. This is especially true of a story as serious as a gospel. We may speak of narrative rhetoric both because the story is constructed to influence its readers and because there are particular literary techniques used for this purpose. A gospel story exercises influence in a much richer way than through theological statements, which might be presented in an essay. Readers are led to believe or to reaffirm their belief in the central character, Jesus, and are thereby influenced in complex ways—in their attitudes, controlling images, patterns of action, feelings, etc. Seeking for a Lukan theology within Luke-Acts tends to divorce theological themes from the larger purpose of the work. Instead, we should seek to understand Luke-Acts as a system of influence which may be analyzed in literary terms. The message of Luke-Acts is not a set of theological propositions but the complex reshaping of human life, in its many dimensions, which it can cause. Study of Luke-Acts as a literary system of influence should help to make that message clear and should enable modern readers to encounter this work responsibly, with their eyes open to the narrator's purposes and to the crucial life issues involved. Understanding Luke-Acts as a unified narrative is an important step in this direction.

It may be helpful to anticipate the following chapters by a brief summary of some of the results: the importance of the birth stories will be underscored when we recognize that the angelic announcements and prophetic hymns found there form one interconnected disclosure about Jesus which establishes a set of expectations about the course of the story. This set of expectations includes both the establishment of a messianic kingdom for Israel and the fulfillment of God's saving purpose universally, embracing both Jews and Gentiles. In one important respect the expectations awakened in the birth stories are not fulfilled: because Jeru-

---

[5] Further explanation of concepts in the last two paragraphs may be found in Wayne C. Booth, *The Rhetoric of Fiction*. Although these concepts were developed in the study of modern fiction, they can be applied to other types of narrative, including biblical narrative.

salem rejects its messianic king, the earthly messianic kingdom is not established. This represents a tragic turn in the story. Both of the Isaiah quotations in Luke 3:4–6 and 4:18–19 are important disclosures of God's purpose, and particular phrases from these quotations help to interpret the significance of the larger narrative. There are indications of Jesus' developing awareness and acceptance of his mission prior to his announcement in the Nazareth synagogue. Following this announcement, the narrator connects a series of scenes, scattered through chapters 5–19, by a system of literary echoes or reminders, thereby giving an impressive portrayal of Jesus' work of releasing sins. The narrator also highlights Jesus' acceptance of excluded people in a series of quest stories. The Jerusalem section of the narrative is concerned with the rejection of Jesus as king, which is a crisis in the fulfillment of Jesus' role and is accompanied by a series of statements about Jerusalem that are filled with pathos. Ironically, God is able to integrate this rejection into God's purpose, overruling human intentions and expectations. Jesus' disciples are unable to understand that he must suffer, and this failure is connected with a series of other failings: they compete for status, they have premature expectations of eschatological fulfillment because they do not reckon with Jesus' rejection, and they are unable to face the threat of death. They begin to change only when they are enlightened by the risen Christ, who explains from Scripture how God works in a resistant world. The portrait of the apostles in Luke and in Acts presents a sharp contrast, for a crucial change takes place through Easter and Pentecost.

LUKE 1:1–4

In the formal introduction to the work, the narrator explains to Theophilus that he intends "to write to you in order ($\kappa\alpha\theta\epsilon\xi\hat{\eta}s$)" (v. 3).[6] Why is the order of the writing important, and what kind of order is in mind? As Richard Dillon has emphasized, the Gospel of Luke does not, at important points in the narrative, reflect a chronological order that can be accepted as historically accurate.[7] Perhaps a historically accurate sequence was not a major concern of the author, even if it had been possible. On the other hand, the writing does not follow the order of argument and logic which would be appropriate to an essay. Since the prologue shows

---

[6] $\kappa\alpha\theta\epsilon\xi\hat{\eta}s$ probably modifies the infinitive "to write" rather than the phrase that precedes it. See Henry J. Cadbury, in *Beginnings,* part 1, vol. 2, 505. Cadbury argues that the break in the sentence must occur before $\kappa\alpha\theta\epsilon\xi\hat{\eta}s$, for "the new colon scarcely begins with the enclitic σol."

[7] Richard J. Dillon, "Previewing Luke's Project," 221–22.

the narrator's awareness of writing a narrative, the order in question may be an order appropriate to narrative.

This suggestion is supported by a comparison of v. 3 with v. 1. Luke's prologue is a balanced period in which the protasis (vv. 1–2) and the apodosis (vv. 3–4) have corresponding members.[8] "Many" corresponds with "me also" and "to set in order a narrative (ἀνατάξασθαι διήγησιν)"[9] corresponds with "to write to you in order."[10] By using the phrase "it seemed good to me also," the author is joining this new undertaking to its predecessors as an effort of the same type, which can be designated "narrative (διήγησιν)." A διήγησις is a longer narrative composed of a number of events, differing from a διήγημα, which concerns a single event.[11] In a longer narrative the question of proper order becomes more difficult. Unity must be maintained through a series of events by the display of major developments and patterns. The way in which this is done will determine the effect of the whole. The prologue indicates that the narrator has this challenge in mind.

The narrator undertakes this task so that Theophilus and others might "know the assurance" or "certainty" (RSV: "truth") concerning matters of which they have already been informed (v. 4). For some reason narrating "in order" should lead to "assurance." It should have a convincing and faith-supporting function. Such assurance is not produced by simply arranging events according to an objective chronology (or some other supposedly objective principle of order). There is no single chronological order in human experience. Different people learn of events in different order, and this order may affect the significance of events for them. Furthermore, control of time is an important interpretive technique in narrative. Narrators have frequently found it useful to guide readers by allowing them to anticipate certain events in advance and by encouraging them to reflect on them afterwards, thereby making possible a richer experience of these events than a strictly chronological account would provide. The narrator also controls what we experience and the speed with which we experience it. The narrative will pause for detailed description of one scene, then summarize many events in a few sentences.

---

[8] See BDF, no. 464.

[9] It is possible that ἀνατάσσομαι is synonymous with συντάσσομαι ("compile," with emphasis on bringing *together* in proper order), but the prefix ἀνα may have been chosen with a view to the *repeated* efforts of the "many."

[10] See H. Cadbury, *Beginnings,* part 1, vol. 2, 495: "It is rather for the sake of variety than to express a difference that Luke does not repeat of himself in verses 3 and 4 the exact words applied to others in verses 1 and 2. καθεξῆς γράψαι may mean no more and no less than ἀνατάξασθαι διήγησιν."

[11] So Hermogenes, Progymnasmata 2. See Leonhard von Spengel, *Rhetores graeci,* vol. 2. This point was called to my attention by Erhardt Güttgemanns, "In welchem Sinne ist Lukas 'Historiker'?" 14–15.

Narrative is always selective, based on some interpretation of what is important. A completely objective chronology would not only be bound to clock time but would also have to devote equal attention to each minute of the day, which no narrator does. Nor would we listen long to such an account.[12]

Martin Völkel noted that Acts 11:4 is the closest Lukan parallel for the use of καθεξῆς in Luke 1:3,[13] since both passages refer to narration. In response to criticism of his eating with Gentiles in the house of Cornelius, Peter "was setting forth" the matter "to them in order (καθεξῆς)." What follows is a narrative of the recent events that led to the baptism of Gentiles and table fellowship with them. This narrative is designed to be persuasive. Peter is trying to convince his hearers that he did what was right and necessary, and he succeeds by means of the narrative. Here in a brief scene we may have a suggestive parallel to the author's strategy for the whole work, as explained in the prologue.

Why is a narrative necessary in order to change the minds of Peter's Jerusalem critics? Viewed in isolation, an event may seem to have a particular meaning, but when it is placed in a narrative context, its meaning can change. Viewed in isolation, the Jewish believers in Jerusalem saw Peter's behavior as a violation of God's law. In the narrative context which Peter supplies, the baptism of Gentiles and table fellowship with them climax a whole series of remarkable events which reveal God's will in a new way. One must understand how these actions are linked to previous events which led up to them in order to judge their significance. So Peter sets forth the matter "in order." This does not mean that he follows an objective chronology. The order of narration in Peter's report to Jerusalem is in some respects different than the order in which the same events were narrated in Acts 10. For instance, in Peter's report we do not learn about Cornelius' encounter with the angel until 11:13, while the narration in Acts 10 begins with this event. That is because Peter in his report is following the order of his own experience. He tells about Cornelius' vision as he learned about it in Cornelius' home. In Acts 11 the story is being told from Peter's point of view. The hearers experience everything just as Peter did. This contributes to the persuasive power of the narrative. Peter's hearers are like Peter in important ways. Peter began with the same commitment to the Jewish way of life as his hearers. They also share a common experience of baptism with the Holy Spirit. Since his hearers share so much with Peter, Peter's new experience is best able to lead them to a new understanding of God's will. By explaining his

---

[12] On the narrator's control of time see Gérard Genette, *Narrative Discourse*, 33–160.
[13] See "Exegetische Erwägungen zum Verständnis des Begriffs καθεξῆς," 293.

own change "in order," Peter is able to lead the Jewish believers along the same path.

While Peter is relating his own experience, according to Acts 11, the narrator of Luke must tell a larger story and rely upon the early church's traditions for materials (Luke 1:2). Nevertheless, a personal vision of the meaning of Jesus and his witnesses is being shared, a vision which is expected to bring assurance to others because it also brings assurance to the narrator.

Peter narrates a whole series of charismatic experiences which point, he believes, in a common direction. In a similar way, the narrator of Luke-Acts believes that events are moving in a single direction (although the path may not be straight and the direction obvious) toward the fulfillment of God's purpose of inclusive salvation. Narrating in proper order, then, must include clarification of this movement and direction, which unify the whole and give it meaning. As Richard Dillon has emphasized (borrowing from Martin Dibelius), the narrator sought a narrative order which would bring out the "*Richtungssinn*, or 'directional thrust'" of the material which was being presented.[14] Through revealing this sort of order in the narrative—an order which nourishes faith because it discloses a saving purpose behind events—the narrator sought to create "assurance."

This assurance is supported by the contour and patterns of the whole narrative when it is interpreted in the light of certain key scenes of disclosure. It would not be adequate assurance if it ignored the resistance, conflict, and disappointment which believers were encountering in the author's time and have encountered since. Luke-Acts does not ignore these unsettling experiences. Gerhard Schneider has argued that the needed "assurance" in Luke 1:4 refers especially to the reliability of the promises made in Scripture and by Jesus.[15] This fits with the strong Lukan emphasis on certain scriptural promises as disclosures of the saving purpose of God for Jew and Gentile through Jesus Messiah. The reliability of these promises would be an issue in light of the strong "counter-current in the flow of the narrative"—the repeated emphasis on rejection —to which David Tiede rightly points.[16] As part of its strategy of bringing assurance through story, the Lukan narrative highlights this rejection so that it may show how resistance, conflict, and disappointment are being absorbed into a larger pattern which points toward God's victory—an ironic victory because the forces of rejection and experiences of suffering are themselves becoming the means by which God's purpose is accomplished in the world.

---

[14] R. Dillon, "Previewing Luke's Project," 223.
[15] See "Der Zweck des lukanischen Doppelwerks," 53.
[16] See *Prophecy and History*, 14–16.

Chapter One

PREVIEWS OF SALVATION

The Lukan birth narrative is a carefully composed literary unit. It is united both by an elaborate pattern of repetition and by a sequence of increasing disclosure of God's purpose in Jesus. Its dominant tone is joy at the fulfillment of Old Testament prophecies of salvation, but comparison with subsequent events indicates that there is also a subtle tone of pathos.

THE REPETITIVE PATTERN
IN THE BIRTH NARRATIVE

The parallels between John the Baptist and Jesus in Luke 1–2 have been widely recognized and discussed.[1] These parallels are most obvious in the annunciations to Zechariah and Mary. The same angel, Gabriel, appears to John's father and to Jesus' mother, followed by a similar sequence of events. Both parents are "troubled" by the encounter with the angel (1:12, 29). The angel responds, "Do not fear," announces the unexpected birth of a son, determines the child's name, indicates that he "will be great," connects the child's conception or fetal life with the Holy Spirit, and announces the child's future role in God's saving purpose (1:13–17, 30–35). Both Zechariah and Mary respond with a question which emphasizes that this birth is not possible by normal human power, and the angel gives each an additional sign, which in Zechariah's case involves temporary punishment for his disbelief (1:18–20, 34–38).

These annunciation scenes are not only similar to each other but also recall similar scenes in the Old Testament.[2] Indeed, part of their purpose is to recall past sacred occasions when God disclosed an important birth, especially of a person like Isaac, through whom God's covenant faithfulness to Abraham was manifested. But the annunciations of the births of John and Jesus first of all invite comparison with each other. The annunciation to Mary directly follows the annunciation to Zechariah, and they

---

[1] For summary of various analyses of these parallels, see Raymond E. Brown, *The Birth of the Messiah*, 248–53, 292–98, 408–10. See also Joseph A. Fitzmyer, *Luke I–IX*, 313–15.

[2] See the divine announcements of the births of Ishmael (Gen 16:7–13), Isaac (Gen 17:1–3, 15–21; 18:1–2, 10–15), and Samson (Judges 13:2–23). See also the discussion of this story pattern by R. Brown, *The Birth of the Messiah*, 156–59.

are especially close in features and wording. This similarity suggests that
John and Jesus are part of a single divine purpose, which is developing
according to the same biblical pattern. It also highlights any differences
which may appear within the pattern of similarities.

The two birth stories, with accompanying scenes disclosing God's
purpose for these two children, are also parallel. Here the pattern is more
flexible. A common repertoire of story elements is used in the two cases,
but the narrator exercises the option of dramatic expansion of different
elements in the two cases. The common repertoire of elements preserves a
sense of recurrence in the story, which is heightened by some repetitions
close enough in wording to act as refrains that remind the reader of the
repetitive pattern.

In both cases we are told of the birth, circumcision, and naming of the
child, accompanied by scenes of recognition and celebration (including a
canticle), and the sequence closes with a refrain of growth and strengthening (1:80; 2:40). The births of John and Jesus are expressed in similar
words (1:57; 2:6–7). However, John's birth is told briefly, and attention
focuses instead on the expanded scene of circumcision and naming. In
contrast, Jesus' birth scene is expanded by the disclosure to the shepherds,
while his circumcision and naming occupy only one verse (2:21). The
recognition and celebration at the circumcision of John is balanced by the
presentation of Jesus in the temple, with the words of Simeon and Anna.
Inclusion of the presentation in the temple in this flexible repetitive
pattern is indicated by the relation between the two canticles in 1:68–79
and 2:29–32, which are Spirit-inspired celebrations of God's salvation,
both introduced by the theme of blessing God (1:64, 68; 2:28). It is also
indicated by the placement of the refrain of growth at 2:40, after the
presentation in the temple. Placement of some of the common story
elements depends on which scenes are dramatically expanded. In the case
of John, both the canticle and the statements about spread of the news and
placing these matters "in the heart" (1:65–66) are part of the expanded
circumcision and naming scene. In the case of Jesus, the latter elements
occur right after the birth (2:17–19), while the canticle is reserved for the
presentation in the temple. Simeon's canticle is relatively short compared
to Zechariah's Benedictus, but the Nunc Dimittis is supplemented by
other revelatory statements concerning the significance of Jesus' birth
(2:10–11, 14, 34–35, 38).

The story of the twelve year old Jesus in the temple (2:41–52) repeats
and develops certain themes from the infancy narratives, but it no longer
deals with Jesus as an infant nor is there any corresponding scene
concerning John. I do not regard it as part of the repetitive pattern. On the
other hand, the visitation scene in 1:39–56 does have a role within this

pattern. This scene might be regarded as an additional, complementary scene corresponding to 2:41–52.[3] However, our previous observation that the narrator can expand or contract story elements should alert us to the fact that the brief notice of Elizabeth's reaction to her pregnancy in 1:24–25 corresponds to the visitation scene, particularly to the first part of the Magnificat (1:47–49). Both 1:25 and 1:48–49 refer to what the Lord "has done" for the mother when God "looked upon" her despised or humble station.[4]

The imbalance between the brief statement in 1:24–25 and the visitation scene with its canticle has significance for the narrative. The visitation scene unifies the two story lines through a meeting of the two mothers. However, both the words of Elizabeth and Mary show the surpassing importance of Mary and her baby in comparison to Elizabeth and John, a significant emphasis after the parallels in the annunciation scenes. The imbalance also underscores the contrast between Zechariah's doubt and Mary's faith. Zechariah's encounter with the angel ends when Zechariah is struck dumb because he did not believe the angel's words (1:20, 22); Mary's encounter with the angel ends with her submission to her appointed role as mother of the Messiah (1:38), an act of acceptance which reveals her faith (1:45). Zechariah will bless God for God's saving work which begins with John's birth, but he cannot express his praise of God immediately after the angel's message. He is prevented by doubt and dumbness. Elizabeth cannot substitute for her husband in expressing God's praise, for she did not receive the angel's message interpreting her baby's role. The Magnificat and the Benedictus correspond to each other as canticles in praise of God by parents of the two boys. But the Magnificat comes first, in a scene immediately following the angel's message to Mary, highlighting her ready faith. Zechariah must be disciplined to accept and respond to God's saving work. Therefore, his hymn comes at the very end of John's birth narrative. The visitation scene portrays the human response to God's saving work which the angelic messages should create but which is significantly missing in the case of Zechariah until his tongue is released.

The repetitive pattern which has been discussed does not compete with but rather contributes to the forward movement of the story. Before discussing this further, however, it is important to consider how thor-

---

[3] So J. Fitzmyer, *Luke I–IX*, 314.

[4] This correspondence creates a difficulty for the theory of Raymond Brown, who sees a parallel between 1:24–25 and the visitation scene without the Magnificat, which he regards as a later addition by the author that disturbs the parallelism. Actually, part of the Magnificat is the closest parallel to 1:25. See R. Brown, *The Birth of the Messiah*, 251–52, 297, 339–40.

oughly the Lukan birth narrative is permeated with the Old Testament hope and celebrates its fulfillment. In an important sense the Gospel of Luke begins in mid-story and immediately makes us aware of that fact. We cannot understand what the excitement is about unless we realize that ancient hopes, treasured in the hearts of the Jewish people, are coming to fulfillment. The "narrative world" which the reader must comprehend in order to appreciate the literary work does not begin with "the days of Herod the king," mentioned in 1:5, but stretches back at least to God's promise to Abraham.[5] Plotted time begins with the days of Herod mentioned in 1:5, but story time begins much earlier.[6] The skill with which the narrator moves the plot forward while continually reminding us of the ancient past is striking. The fact that the narrator breaks into story time at the moment when Israel's hopes begin to be fulfilled gives the scenes of the birth narrative their special poignancy.

The birth narratives in Luke are permeated by the narrative patterns and language of the narrator's Scripture. We have already noted that the annunciations to Zechariah and Mary follow the pattern of Old Testament annunciations of the birth of a child.[7] The Old Testament pattern functions as a "type-scene" which can be freely imitated in shaping scenes which the narrator feels to be similar.[8] Important elements in the births of both John and Jesus also appear to be borrowed from the birth of Samuel in 1 Samuel 1-2. Elizabeth resembles Hannah, Samuel's mother, a barren woman who is granted a child by God after prayer (1 Sam 1:10–11; see Luke 1:13), but in the Magnificat Mary describes herself like Hannah (1 Sam 1:11; Luke 1:48), and her hymn resembles Hannah's hymn. Furthermore, the presentation of Jesus in the temple may parallel Hannah's presentation and gift of her son at the sanctuary. The refrain which describes the growth of John and Jesus (1:80; 2:40, 52) resembles statements about the growth of Samuel (1 Sam 2:21, 26). The multiple use of the Samuel material suggests free play of the imagination with Scripture rather than an attempt to rigidly define scriptural types for Jesus.

---

[5] On the imaginative world created by a story and the temporal extent of this "narrative world," see Norman Petersen, *Literary Criticism*, 40, 50–52.

[6] Plotted time concerns the order in which events are presented to the reader. Story time concerns the chronological order in which all events mentioned in the story supposedly happened. When plotted time deviates from story time, as it often does, it is often useful to ask why the narrator has introduced such deviations. See N. Petersen, *Literary Criticism*, 47, and G. Genette, *Narrative Discourse*, 33–85. Genette calls such deviations "anachronies."

[7] See above, p. 15.

[8] On biblical type-scenes, see Robert Alter, *Art of Biblical Narrative*, 47–62. A type-scene is a basic situation which appears several times in narration. There is a set of similar characteristics which persists despite variations and additions. For further discussion of type-scenes in Luke, see pp. 170–71.

In addition to these narrative patterns which recall Old Testament stories, the Lukan birth story borrows heavily from the language of the Old Testament, especially in the annunciations to the parents and in the canticles,[9] but not only there.[10] Apart from the reference to the Gentiles in 2:31–32, John and Jesus are presented as the fulfillment of hopes for the redemption of Israel and Jerusalem. Jesus is the Davidic Messiah (1:32–33, 68–69), who will bring political freedom to the Jewish people (1:71, 73–74). The strongly Jewish atmosphere of the birth story is also apparent from its settings and characters. It begins and ends with scenes in the temple. The central characters are described as devoted to the law and to the hope for Israel's redemption (1:6: Zechariah and Elizabeth; 2:23–24, 27: Mary and Joseph; 2:25: Simeon; 2:37–38: Anna). Thus the birth story is not only steeped in the Old Testament but also takes a very positive attitude toward the Torah obedience and hope of pious Jews.[11] The story is shaped to attract our sympathy to devoted men and women who have waited long for the fulfillment of Israel's hopes and who now are told that the time of fulfillment has come.

This fulfillment is celebrated through the repetitive patterns which we have noted. The use of extensive repetitive patterns is not unusual in Luke-Acts. Augustin George has compared the parallels between John and Jesus in the birth narratives to the parallels between Peter and Paul in Acts.[12] Since these parallels are widely scattered in Acts, an even closer comparison may be the repetitive pattern of arrests, examinations before the Sanhedrin, and releases in Acts 4–5, or the similarity suggested between the rejection of Moses, Jesus, and Stephen in Stephen's speech and death scene (Acts 7:23–60).[13] Each of these patterns must be examined for its own sake. For the present, we must ask what the repetitive pattern in the birth narrative contributes to Luke as a literary work with a religious message.

As Augustin George has pointed out,[14] the parallels between John and Jesus emphasize the unity of their task. They share roles in a single design of God which is working itself out in a consistent way. At the same time, the comparisons between John and Jesus suggested by the parallels will

---

[9] For details, see R. Brown, *The Birth of the Messiah*, 272–78, 309–12, 358–60, 386–89, 457–59.

[10] Cp. Luke 1:25 with Gen 30:23; Luke 1:41 with Gen 25:22 LXX; Luke 1:42 with Judg 5:24; Luke 2:25 with Isa 40:1, 49:13; Luke 2:38 with Isa 52:9.

[11] This is true despite 2:34–35, which I will discuss below.

[12] See *Études sur l'oeuvre de Luc*, 54–58.

[13] On these passages, see vol. 2. In Acts 7 the pattern of similarity involves Moses as well as Jesus and Stephen. In Luke 1–2 there are also Old Testament precedents for the pattern of experience shared by the parents of John and Jesus.

[14] *Études sur l'oeuvre de Luc*, 64–65.

show the superiority of Jesus over John, as will become clearer below. Repetitive pattern heightens awareness of both similarities and differences, for it guides the reader in making comparisons.[15] The multiple possibilities of comparison suggested by the pattern of repetition promote a complex interaction of narrative elements with an enriching background. This interaction reaches beyond the single episode and awakens echoes from more distant parts of the narrative, or from other stories. In this way overtones resound which add suggestive richness to the narrative and actively engage the imagination of the reader in the exploration of associations. The multiplication of associations makes more and more available to the reader for such imaginative work. As readers become actively engaged in the exploration of the narrative's symbolic world, central symbols expand in significance, enticing us to give full attention to their mysteries and meanings. Repetitive pattern can contribute to deepening disclosure as new associations are suggested, guiding readers in the discovery of expanding symbols with hidden residues of meaning.[16]

THE ANGELIC AND PROPHETIC DISCLOSURES IN THE BIRTH NARRATIVE

The repetitive pattern discussed so far provides a framework which holds together a series of disclosures concerning the roles of John and Jesus in God's saving purpose. I am referring to the angels' messages and to the canticles, each of which is the central element in the scene in which it occurs. These disclosures contain repetitive elements that invite comparison. However, they not only repeat but progress. Viewed together, they reemphasize and enrich central themes and also progressively reveal new aspects of God's saving purpose. They are the chief media for the central expanding symbols of the birth narrative.

These angelic and prophetic disclosures have both theological and narrative importance. Theologically, they disclose the narrator's insights and assumptions with regard to God's purpose in Jesus. In terms of narrative composition, they are the narrator's clues for the readers concerning the overarching purpose which holds the story together and in terms of which subsequent events are to be understood. These statements

---

[15] See Roman Jakobson, "Closing Statement," 368–69. He notes that "parallelism" (i.e., repetitive pattern) prompts "one of the two correlative experiences which Hopkins neatly defines as 'comparison for likeness' sake' and 'comparison for unlikeness' sake.'"

[16] See E. K. Brown, *Rhythm in the Novel,* 33–59. According to Brown, "the expanding symbol is repetition balanced by variation, and that variation is in progressively deepening disclosure" (p. 57).

imply, of course, that the birth narrative, whether based on pre-Lukan sources or not, is no foreign body tacked on to the front of Luke in spite of tensions with the Lukan outlook. Paul Minear has argued persuasively against such a division of the birth narrative from the rest of Luke-Acts,[17] and my discussion below will support his position.

The episodes in Luke-Acts are parts of a unitary story because they are related to a unifying purpose, the purpose of God ($\beta o u \lambda \dot{\eta} \ \tau o \hat{v} \ \theta \epsilon o \hat{v}$), to which the writing refers with some frequency (Luke 7:30; Acts 2:23; 4:28; 5:38–39; 13:36; 20:27). Luke-Acts has a particular understanding of this purpose, which the narrator shares with the readers in key scenes. In relation to this purpose individual incidents take on meaning: they represent steps in the realization of this purpose or portray human resistance to it.

If we are to understand the narrative in its unity, we must pay attention to disclosures of this overarching purpose in light of which individual events take on meaning. In this regard, four types of material in Luke-Acts have special importance: previews and reviews, repeated or highlighted scriptural references, commission statements, and interpretive statements by reliable characters. I will discuss each of these briefly.

First, recent theoretical discussions of narrative have noted that the sequential experience of events in the story may be controlled by disclosing information out of chronological order. There may be previews of coming events and reviews of past events, often in a way that interprets these events from some perspective.[18] The birth narrative contains a heavy concentration of previews of God's purpose which is to be realized through Jesus and his witnesses in the following story.

Second, the narrator finds God's purpose revealed in Scripture, particularly in certain key texts of the Septuagint which appear repeatedly in Luke-Acts or are given a prominent position in it. Jesus' quotation from Isaiah in Luke 4:18–19 is an obvious example. These scriptural passages not only show in a general way that the law and the prophets are fulfilled in Jesus. They express a particular understanding of God's purpose and are programs for action. The discerning reader will ask whether and how this purpose is being realized in the narrative. The angelic and prophetic disclosures in the birth narratives are filled with scriptural language. Words and phrases which reappear later in Luke-Acts should be given special importance in understanding the story.

Third, God's purpose is realized through chosen instruments, persons commissioned by God to carry out some aspect of this purpose. At various

---

[17] See "Luke's Use of the Birth Stories," 111–30.
[18] See G. Genette, *Narrative Discourse*, 33–85, who speaks of "prolepses" and "analepses."

points in Luke-Acts there are statements of the commission which has been received by Jesus, the twelve, Paul, etc. These commission statements are also disclosures of divine purpose, programs for action by particular characters, and keys to the plot.[19] The angelic and prophetic disclosures in the birth narratives have important things to say about the future roles or commissions of John and Jesus.

Fourth, we must also consider what reliable characters within the story have to say about God's purpose and the meaning of the events being narrated. It is common for an author to present one or more characters as especially reliable in their judgments and perceptive in their statements. These characters are likely to become spokespersons for the author in interpreting events of the story.[20] So statements by Jesus in the gospel, and by Peter, Stephen, and Paul in Acts, may be important for interpreting the narrative as a whole. As we consider the birth narrative further, we must ask whether the angelic and prophetic disclosures in it are reliable interpretations of the purpose of God which unifies and gives meaning to the Lukan narrative. We can scarcely doubt that angels are reliable messengers for God within the Lukan world view. The indications that Elizabeth, Zechariah, and Simeon speak under the inspiration of the Holy Spirit (1:41, 67; 2:25–27), and the description of Anna as a "prophetess" (2:36), would seem to indicate that they, too, are reliable spokespersons for God. However, this conclusion must be verified by comparing what they say with the subsequent course of the narrative, and this comparison may raise some questions, especially with regard to the strong statements of salvation for Israel in some of these prophetic utterances.

The four types of material overlap, for a scriptural quotation may also be a preview or a commission statement, etc. Mentioning them in series, however, provides some idea of the range of material in which we are likely to find clues to the divine purpose which unifies the story. This will be helpful to us not only in discussing the birth narrative but also in the interpretation of other key scenes in Luke-Acts.[21]

Charles Talbert has discussed Luke's use of recognized means of

---

[19] A unified narrative sequence results from the acceptance of a commission by a story character and the attempt to fulfill this commission. See Robert C. Tannehill, "The Gospel of Mark as Narrative Christology," 60–61. My term "commission" is similar to the term "mandate" in some structural analysis of narrative. See Jean Calloud, *Structural Analysis of Narrative,* 17, 25, 27; Daniel Patte, *What Is Structural Exegesis?* 37–44.

[20] See W. Booth, *The Rhetoric of Fiction,* 18: "The author is present in every speech given by any character who has had conferred upon him, in whatever manner, the badge of reliability."

[21] The last seven paragraphs repeat ideas originally published in my article "Israel in Luke-Acts: A Tragic Story," *Journal of Biblical Literature* 104 (1985): 69–70, copyright © 1985 by the Society of Biblical Literature. Used by permission.

legitimating religious and political leaders in presenting Jesus, thus speaking persuasively to people in the ancient Mediterranean world. Among these means is the appeal to prophecy and its fulfillment.[22] Talbert's discussions are helpful, but I think Luke-Acts has a further persuasive effect, in which Scripture and other prophecies have a major role. Insofar as the narrator, through selective use of Scripture and other prophecies, is able to present a vision of God's purpose and the world's destiny which seems great and good, worthy of God and creation, this vision would be attractive to many readers. Probably this remains true today. One possible benefit of the present study may be in helping modern readers comprehend the breadth and depth of this Lukan vision so that they can decide whether it is still attractive to them.

The Annunciations to Zechariah and Mary

The announcement of the angel to Zechariah in 1:13–17 actually combines all four of the significant types of material just noted. It is an interpretive preview of what will happen later in the story, it uses scriptural references which play a further role in Luke-Acts, it reveals the future mission of John, and it is made by Gabriel, God's messenger. A number of points indicate the close connection between Gabriel's words and the later Lukan narrative. The angel's promise of joy for Zechariah and for many begins to be fulfilled within the birth narrative itself (1:58, 64, 68–79). This is also true of the promise that the baby would be filled with the Holy Spirit while still in the womb, for the unborn John gives a prophetic sign to his mother (1:41, 44). The statement that John will be "great" agrees with Jesus' later statement about him in 7:28.[23]

The final statements of Gabriel about John in 1:16–17 express, partly in borrowed, biblical imagery, central themes in the Lukan understanding of John's role. Twice we are told that John will cause people to turn, employing the verb ἐπιστρέφω, commonly used in the sense of repent or convert in Luke-Acts.[24] When John begins his ministry, he will preach a baptism of repentance (Luke 3:3; Acts 13:24), and a sample of his call to repentance is given in Luke 3:7–14. It is also John's role to "go before" the Lord (1:17), a theme which is closely linked with the idea of preparing the Lord's way, as the combination of these phrases in 1:76 shows. Apart from 1:76, John is connected with preparing the way of the Lord in scriptural quotations applied to him in 3:4 and 7:27. The two verbs for "prepare" in these two quotations (ἑτοιμάζω, κατασκευάζω) appear together in 1:17.

[22] See *Reading Luke*, 234–40, and "Promise and Fulfillment," 91–103.
[23] So R. Brown, *The Birth of the Messiah*, 273.
[24] So used in Luke 22:32; Acts 3:19; 9:35; 11:21; 14:15; 15:19; 26:18; 26:20; 28:27.

The point in 1:17 seems at first to be different. Instead of preparing the Lord's way, John is to "prepare (ἑτοιμάσαι) for the Lord a people made ready (κατεσκευασμένον)." However, the tasks of preparing a way and preparing a people are very closely related, if not identical. This is suggested not only by a comparison of 1:17 with 3:4 and 7:27, but also by 1:76–77, the section of the Benedictus which clearly refers to John. Here there seems to be at least a partial parallelism between John's call "to prepare his ways" and "to give knowledge of salvation to his people in forgiveness of their sins." Note also the combination of repentance for the people and preparation of Jesus' way in Acts 13:24: John proclaimed "a baptism of repentance for all the people of Israel before the face of his entering" (εἴσοδος, literally, "way in"). John prepares the Lord's way by preparing a repentant people, whose hearts have turned and who are ready to receive their Lord.

The statement that John will go before the Lord "in the spirit and power of Elijah" is not contrary to Lukan ideas.[25] While the Gospel of Luke suggests parallels between Jesus and Elijah,[26] this does not prevent the narrator from suggesting that John fulfills some of the functions of the eschatological Elijah.[27] The narrator not only refers to Elijah in describing John's mission in 1:17 but also attributes to John Elijah's function of turning the hearts of fathers, mentioned in Mal 3:22–23 (4:5–6 ET).

When Zechariah's tongue is loosed so that he can bless God, he repeats and elaborates, with prophetic insight, on the angel's message concerning his son (1:76–77). His words to his son are virtually a summary of key themes in the introduction of John's ministry in 3:1–6 and in Jesus' later statement about John in 7:26–27. In 3:1–6 John is presented as a prophet by dating his prophetic call in the manner of Old Testament prophetic writings.[28] He preaches a "baptism of repentance for forgiveness of sins," and he cries that the people must "prepare the way of the Lord," for "all flesh will see the salvation of God." The themes of prophet, preparing ways, salvation, and forgiveness of sins all appear in 1:76–77. The themes of prophet and preparing the way return in 7:26–27. Zechariah's words, plus the emphasis on preparing the people through repentance in 1:16–17, provide an accurate preview of John's role in Luke. We will note later that John's ministry is not sharply contrasted with that of Jesus and his followers, for the salvation through forgiveness of sins offered by Jesus

---

[25] Here I agree with Paul Minear, *To Heal and to Reveal*, 95–97, rather than Hans Conzelmann, *The Theology of St. Luke*, 22, 24.

[26] See below, pp. 72, 87–88, 97.

[27] Recall that both Elizabeth and Mary are associated with Hannah, the mother of Samuel. One association does not exclude another.

[28] See below, pp. 47–48.

and his witnesses is already part of John's message, and John's call to repentance never ceases to be part of the message of Jesus and his witnesses.[29]

Gabriel's announcement to Mary also contains a preview of the baby's future role. The disclosure of Jesus' role begins with the statement, "He will be great" (1:32), which parallels a previous statement about John (1:15). This is followed, however, by clear indications of the superiority of Jesus over John. While John "will be called prophet of the Most High" (1:76), Jesus "will be called Son of the Most High" and will reign as king (1:32–33). While John will be filled with the Holy Spirit while still in his mother's womb (1:15), Jesus will be conceived through the Spirit's agency (1:35). The special importance of Jesus' birth will be emphasized further in the visitation scene which follows, in which Elizabeth will address Mary as "the mother of my Lord" and bless her and her offspring (1:42–43).

Gabriel's description of Jesus' destiny indicates that he will be named "Son of the Most High," will inherit "the throne of David his father," and "will reign over the house of Jacob forever" (1:32–33). This combination of themes recalls Nathan's oracle to David in 2 Sam 7:12–16, where David's successor is called God's son and God promises that his "throne" will be established "forever."[30] To be sure, 1:35 indicates that the title Son of God belongs to Jesus in light of his wondrous conception, a motif which goes beyond the Old Testament idea of the king as God's son. However, this does not mean that the traditional royal Messiah is being replaced with a different sort of Son of God. Jesus as Davidic Messiah and fulfiller of Israel's hope for a messianic king has greater continuing importance in Luke-Acts than the virgin birth does. For the author, the virgin birth is an indication of God's purpose and power at the very beginning of Jesus' life, and this wondrous beginning does not compete with the view that he is Son of God as Davidic king but attributes his kingship to prevenient divine action.

The importance of the Davidic Messiah in Luke's understanding of God's promise to Israel will become clearer as we go along. At this point I will simply note that the title Son of God is not only associated with the Davidic Messiah in Gabriel's words to Mary but also in later passages of Luke-Acts, which serve as reminders of this special sense of Son of God. In Luke 4:41 the cry of the demons, "You are the Son of God," is taken as indication that "they knew that he was the Messiah" (dif.[31] Matthew,

---

[29] See below, pp. 48–53, 233–35.
[30] The promise concerning David's throne is also important in the Pentecost speech. See Acts 2:30.
[31] This abbreviation will be used repeatedly with the following meaning: the named gospel(s)

Mark). Following Jesus' ambiguous answer to the Sanhedrin's question whether he is the Christ, they repeat their question in this form: "Then are you the Son of God?" (22:67–70). In Acts 9:20–22 Paul's preaching in Damascus is summarized twice in quick succession, first "this one [Jesus] is the Son of God," then "this one is the Messiah," and in his major speech at Antioch of Pisidia Paul declares that God has fulfilled the promise to David by raising Jesus and declaring, "You are my Son" (Acts 13:22–23, 32–34). The connection of divine sonship and kingship also appears in Jesus' statement at the last supper that "my Father has conferred on me royal rule (βασιλείαν)" (Luke 22:29).[32]

The hope for Israel's promised king, who will succeed to David's throne, is not confined to Gabriel's words to Mary. This hope has thematic importance in the birth stories and will reappear later also. It is developed in the Benedictus, which makes clear that this hope implies rescue from foreign oppressors (1:69–71). These previews interpret in advance the meaning of the angels' announcement of the birth "in David's city" of "a savior who is Messiah Lord" (2:11). Even in Acts 13:22–23 Jesus is "savior" as David's offspring and successor to the throne. Furthermore, "salvation" in Luke 1:71 has clear connotations of political freedom. To suppose that the author could not be thinking in such political terms because all would know that Israel did not become an independent state with its own king ignores the tragic line of the story: the story is presenting a real possibility and a valid hope which was tragically rejected at the moment of fulfillment.[33]

The Magnificat

Before the significance of Jesus as Davidic Messiah is developed further in the Benedictus, additional themes, also to be developed later, are introduced in the Magnificat. The poetic structure of the Magnificat is important to its interpretation. This poem can be understood as a traditional hymn of praise, beginning with an introductory statement of praise of God (1:47), followed by a series of reasons for this praise.[34] However, an additional pattern emerges from the repeated use of strong action verbs at the beginning of clauses. The following rather literal translation

---

contain(s) a passage which is generally parallel, but the Lukan version differs from other version(s) in the feature being discussed.

[32] Noted by A. George, *Études sur l'oeuvre de Luc,* 230. George also interprets Jesus' statement in 10:22, "All things have been delivered to me by my Father," as "an investiture of messianic powers" (p. 225). It is noteworthy that the following saying speaks of the present fulfillment of the hopes of "prophets and *kings*" (dif. Matthew), a probable allusion to the hope for the reestablishment of the Davidic kingdom.

[33] See R. Tannehill, "Israel in Luke-Acts," 69–85.

[34] See R. Brown, *The Birth of the Messiah,* 355–56.

attempts to highlight this and other features, preserving the word order of
the Greek even when this violates the rules of good English.

46 *Magnifies*/my soul/the Lord
47 And *has found gladness*/my spirit/in God/my Savior
48 For *he has regarded*/the humble state/of his slave girl
    For behold henceforth/will call me blessed/all generations
49 For *has done* for me/great things/the mighty one
        And holy/his name
50   And his mercy/to generations/and generations/
          for those who fear him.

51 *He has done*/ a mighty deed/with his arm
    He has scattered/proud people/in thoughts/of their heart
52 *He has put down*/mighty rulers/from thrones
    And *has exalted*/humble people
53 Hungry people/*he has filled*/with good things
    And rich people/*he has sent out* / empty
54 *He has helped*/Israel/his servant
       To remember/mercy
55   As he spoke/to our fathers/to Abraham/and to his seed/
          forever.

The italicized phrases translate the strong action verbs that repeatedly
begin the lines (after a conjunction, in some cases). This pattern of initial
verbs helps to mark off the lines and puts great stress on God's action, to
which all the italicized verbs refer after the first two lines. In each case the
italicized English phrase translates one Greek word. The divisions within
the lines indicate that there is also a rhythm of phrases or words in the
poem. This does not involve counting accents or long and short syllables
but is simply the natural rhythm of reading when the voice emphasizes the
important words of the line. Each marked section of the line (a "foot" in
this type of rhythm) contains one major Greek word or one major word
and dependent minor words.[35] When we note where the strong action
verbs are dominant and where they are not, the poem divides into two
stanzas or strophes. The division is marked by the two concluding lines of
each strophe, which contrast with what precedes them but resemble each
other. Verses 49b–50 and 54b–55 resemble each other in both thought and
form. They contrast with the lines preceding them by shifting from the
pattern of initial verbs in independent clauses and by a change in the

---

[35] On the theory of rhythm being followed here, see Robert C. Tannehill, *Sword of His
Mouth*, 46–49 and n. 9. See also Tannehill, "The Magnificat as Poem," 269–71.

rhythm (a short, two foot line followed by an unusually long line). They also resemble each other by interpreting God's intervention as mercy (ἔλεος) shown in faithfulness to the covenant people, placing this in the perspective of Israel's history. Syntax becomes looser in the final lines of each stanza, the sense of dramatic action recedes, and the long final lines in vv. 50 and 55 create a sense of pause.

Just as there is a connection in thought between the final lines of the two strophes, there is also a connection between vv. 48a, 49a of strophe one and vv. 51–53 of strophe two. Verse 51a repeats the verb of v. 49a and begins to develop the thought. The Magnificat goes through the same pattern twice. However, there is this difference: In strophe one the reason for the thanksgiving is very personal; the mighty God has done something great for a particular humble woman. In strophe two the scope of God's action expands. We hear again of the mighty God and the humble, but now whole societies are involved. Furthermore, a new group is introduced. People who are proud, mighty, and rich are contrasted with those who are humble and hungry. The similarities and contrasts are highlighted by repeated use of word roots: "humble state . . . humble people (ταπείνωσιν . . . ταπεινούς)," "the mighty one . . . mighty rulers (ὁ δυνατός . . . δυνάστας)." We have moved from a bipolar contrast between the mighty God and a humble woman to a triangular tension involving two wonders: The mighty God exalts the lowly, those who do not share God's might. The mighty God also puts down the rulers who have a might that looks like God's.

Verses 51–53 contain the most powerful language of the poem and are therefore its climax. Not only does the thought expand as just indicated, but also strong, graphic words are used (God's "arm," "scattered," etc.). These strong words are emphasized and the pace of the poem quickened by the elimination of all articles and most conjunctions. Most important is the strong contrast built into these verses, based on the words mighty, humble, hungry, rich in an a-b-b-a pattern, with accompanying contrasting verbs. There is even a rhyme pattern in vv. 52–53, which also emphasizes the contrast.[36] Content and form mesh: the mighty God's reversal of the existing order is proclaimed in strong language full of sharp reversals.

The patterns of repetition and contrast within the Magnificat increase the interaction among words, helping to give them resonance and poetic power. In particular, the implied, but never prosaically stated, connection

---

[36] In v. 53 the words "hungry" and "rich" carry the contrast. This explains why they are placed in emphatic position at the beginning of the lines, displacing the verbs which normally come first.

between the mighty God's favor to one humble woman (in strophe one) and God's intervention for the humble and poor in general makes God's grace to Mary an emblem or paradigm of God's saving work which is now beginning. The reversal proclaimed in v. 52 with images of descent and ascent anticipate Simeon's words in 2:34 about the "fall and rising of many in Israel," and vv. 51–53 as a whole anticipate Jesus' words of comfort to the poor and warnings to the rich, his invitation to the outcast and his denunciations of the religious establishment.[37] The social reversal which Mary celebrates will be realized concretely through Jesus' ministry and through his witnesses who continue to "upset the world" (Acts 17:6).[38]

It is finally the plan or purpose of God which gives shape and meaning to the story of Jesus and his witnesses. To this extent God functions as a character in the plot, though hidden from human view. We should pay close attention, then, to any disclosures of God's purpose and to the way in which God is characterized within the story. One of the important functions of the Magnificat is to provide an initial characterization of the God whose purpose shapes the following story. The Magnificat consists primarily of third person statements about God. As Jacques Dupont has pointed out,[39] most of the descriptions of God collect into two semantic fields: those of mercy and of power. On the one hand, God is described as "my savior," one who has "looked upon" a woman of humble station and has "helped Israel his servant," remembering mercy. On the other hand, God is the Lord of this "slave woman ($\delta o\acute{u}\lambda\eta$)," the "mighty one" who has done "great things," the one who has "done a mighty deed with his arm," scattering and putting down humans who claim to be mighty. The two types of description come together in the climactic reversal pattern in 1:52–53. There God's mercy for the humble and poor appears in the mighty overthrow of the powerful and rich who oppress them. This is viewed as an act of faithfulness to Israel.

Mary's hymn suggests a set of expectations about God's character and

---

[37] David Peter Seccombe understands the poor and the humble people of 1:51–53 to refer to Israel, while the rich are Gentile oppressors of Israel. See *Possessions and the Poor*, 74–81. An application to oppressed Israel need not be excluded, but we should also recognize the connection of 1:51–53 with the reference to an upheaval *within* Israel in 2:34 and with Jesus' sharp words to proud and rich Jews (16:14–15; 18:9–14, 18–25).

[38] The discussion of the Magnificat above is a summary of my article "The Magnificat as Poem," *Journal of Biblical Literature* 93 (1974): 263–75, copyright © 1974 by the Society of Biblical Literature. Used by permission. I have also adapted material from my article "Homiletical Resources: Gospel Lections for Advent," *Quarterly Review: A Scholarly Journal for Reflection on Ministry* 2 (Fall 1982) 34–36. Used by permission of The United Methodist Publishing House and the United Methodist Board of Higher Education and Ministry, copyright © 1982.

[39] See "Le Magnificat," 339–42.

purpose which guide the reader in understanding what is most important in the subsequent story. We will note below the importance of the description of God as "savior" (1:47) and as merciful to Israel in fulfillment of the promise to Abraham (1:54–55), since these themes link the Magnificat with the following canticles. At this point I will focus on the description of God as one who puts down the mighty and rich, exalting the lowly and poor in their place. Variations on this reversal motif have an important place in Luke. Not only is Jesus described in advance by Simeon as one who causes the "fall and rising of many in Israel" (2:34), but Jesus himself will speak of the reversal of the poor and the rich, the hated and the favored (6:20–26), the wise and the babes (10:21), those who come from far and those in whose streets Jesus taught, the last and the first (13:25–30). Furthermore, the scribes and Pharisees are portrayed as people who seek both status (11:43; 20:46–47) and money (16:14), like the proud and the rich in 1:51–53. Jesus responds with aphorisms and parables which proclaim the humiliation of those who exalt themselves (14:7–11, 16–24; 16:15, 19–31; 18:9–14). The disciples are also warned with sharp sayings which emphasize the reversal which God is working through Jesus (9:24, 46–48; 12:1–3; 22:24–27).

Jesus not only speaks of reversal but the author of Luke-Acts shows us surprising reversals as the plot unfolds. In a series of clashes between divine and human power, God appears not merely as ruler but as the *over*ruler of human authority and purpose. This is already signaled in 1:51–53. It is developed most emphatically in connection with the death and resurrection of Jesus, as we see in the Psalm quotation in Luke 20:17 and in the Acts sermons which emphasize that Jerusalem killed its Messiah but God raised him up (Acts 2:23–24, 36; 3:15; 4:10; 5:30). Political rulers, too, try to oppose God's will and end up serving it (Acts 4:25–28). Paul the persecutor is overruled by the Lord Jesus. The repeated rescues from prison (Acts 5:17–26; 12:1–19; 16:19–40) also show God overruling human threats. The theme of human opposition which does not stop the mission but contributes to its spread is important in Luke-Acts and contributes to its picture of the overruling God (Luke 4:16–37; Acts 8:1–8; 11:19–21; 13:44–48; 18:6; 28:25–28). Luke's portrayal of the overruling God produces a number of ironic situations in the plot: blind disciples on the road to Emmaus explain to Jesus about Jesus' death (Luke 24:15–24); guards stand watch before a prison from which the prisoners have already escaped (Acts 5:17–26).

While the author believes that God's purpose will ultimately triumph, God is not the only actor in the story, a situation that would remove conflict, drama, and narrative interest. God's purpose must be achieved by overruling, by reversal, by twists in the plot which surprise human actors.

Such reversals in the plot have central positions in Luke's story. Mary's hymn of praise begins to make clear that the story deals with a God who works in human life by overturning the presumption of the powerful and the resignation of the weak. Since the outcome of events repeatedly conflicts with human calculations, the signature of this God appears in the human experience of irony.[40]

Not only does Luke's story presuppose the conflict of human and divine purposes, but one might argue that there is tension between the "revolutionary" and the "conservative" aspects of Luke's characterization of God. God is the God of reversal, and so a revolutionary, but Luke-Acts also proclaims God's faithfulness to Israel, as in Luke 1:54–55, and concern with God's promise to Israel does not diminish toward the end of the work (see Acts 26:6–7). Since it is hard to understand how both of these characteristics of God can come to expression, especially when much of Israel rejects its Messiah and finds itself on the downward side of a reversal, there is tension in the story which even the author, perhaps, has not resolved.

The Magnificat is like an aria in opera; the action almost stops so that the situation may be savored more deeply. At the same time, this savored meaning contributes to the flow of the narrative, for Mary's song both develops a mood which has already been established and opens perspectives that will be more fully developed in the following canticles. The first three verses, the most personal section of the poem, contribute to the parallel portraits of the parents of John and Jesus rejoicing at God's salvation which is to be brought through their sons. Certain repeated theme words contribute to this portrait. Gabriel told Zechariah concerning his son, "He will be joy for you and exultation ($\dot{\alpha}\gamma\alpha\lambda\lambda\acute{\iota}\alpha\sigma\iota\varsigma$)" (1:14). This exultation actually begins with Elizabeth and the unborn John (see 1:44, where the same word is repeated), but Mary immediately joins in, "My spirit has exulted ($\dot{\eta}\gamma\alpha\lambda\lambda\acute{\iota}\alpha\sigma\epsilon\nu$) in God my savior" (1:47). Similarly, Mary "magnifies ($\mu\epsilon\gamma\alpha\lambda\acute{\upsilon}\nu\epsilon\iota$)" the Lord, and the word is later repeated in John's birth scene (though now of God's action), for neighbors and kin heard that "the Lord was magnifying his mercy with" Elizabeth (1:58). In addition, Elizabeth had said that the Lord "looked upon ($\dot{\epsilon}\pi\epsilon\hat{\iota}\delta\epsilon\nu$)" her to take away her reproach (1:25), and in parallel Mary states, "He looked upon ($\dot{\epsilon}\pi\acute{\epsilon}\beta\lambda\epsilon\psi\epsilon\nu$) the humble state of his slave girl" (1:48). Zechariah, of course, will belatedly match Mary's hymn with a hymn of his own. Other key words in the early part of the Magnificat are linked to the preceding narrative: Mary as the Lord's "slave girl" (1:38, 48); God as the "mighty one ($\dot{o}$ $\delta\upsilon\nu\alpha\tau\acute{o}\varsigma$)" (1:49; see the references to God's power in 1:35

---

[40] On the God of Luke-Acts as a God of irony, see pp. 282–84, 288–89.

[δύναμις] and 1:37 [οὐκ ἀδυνατήσει]); God as the one who does "great things" (1:49; both of the promised sons will be "great" according to 1:15, 32). Furthermore, Mary's statement that "all generations will call me blessed" in 1:48 is a direct response to Elizabeth doing that very thing in 1:45.

Even more important are elements in the Magnificat which prepare themes to be more fully developed in the rest of the birth narrative and beyond. The description of God as "my savior" in 1:47 anticipates the emphasis on salvation in Zechariah's and Simeon's words (1:69, 71, 77; 2:30), as well as in the angels' announcement of the birth of a savior (2:11). The Benedictus combines a synonym for salvation with a verb twice used of God in the Magnificat when it states, "He has done redemption (ἐποίησεν λύτρωσιν)" (1:68; see 1:49, 51). The emphasis on a royal heir to David's throne in the annunciation to Mary is missing in the Magnificat, although the reference to mighty ones being "put down from thrones" in 1:52 may indicate what happens when the Messiah ascends *his* throne. The Magnificat refers to the promise to Abraham instead of the promise to David. It is important to note, however, that the Benedictus will incorporate both promises into a unified statement of praise. The close connection of 1:54–55 with 1:72–73 is shown by a remarkable string of shared terms: "mercy," "to remember," "our fathers," "Abraham." The last two verses of the Magnificat move from the parallelism of short sentences which characterizes most of the poem to a looser syntax with an infinitive, a syntax characteristic of the Benedictus. These verses also share the phrases "his servant (παιδὸς αὐτοῦ)" and "as he spoke (καθὼς ἐλάλησεν)" with the Benedictus (1:69–70).[41] As previously noted, the metaphors of descent and ascent in 1:52 anticipate Simeon's oracle of conflict, in which he says that Jesus "is destined for the fall and rising of many in Israel" (2:34). Simeon's statement that "thoughts (διαλογισμοί) of many hearts" will be revealed (2:35) may also be related to 1:51: "proud in the thought (διανοίᾳ) of their heart." This connection would suggest that the thoughts of the proud are among those that will be exposed.

The Benedictus

In its setting, the Benedictus is related to both the Magnificat and the Nunc Dimittis. Like the Magnificat, it expresses the thanksgiving of a parent for the salvation which will come through the birth of the two babies. Like the Nunc Dimittis, it follows the birth, circumcision, and

---

[41] In the speech of Peter where Luke 1:70 is repeated, Jesus is also called God's "servant (παῖδα αὐτοῦ)." See Acts 3:13, 21, 26.

naming of the baby, disclosing his future role and also revealing the larger purpose of God of which he will be a part. Only one canticle is connected with the birth of John, but it is relatively long because it pulls together themes from the two annunciations and the Magnificat and opens some new themes which will be developed in the angels' words to the shepherds and in Simeon's words in the temple. We have already noted that the words addressed specifically to the baby John in 1:76–77 summarize the message of the angel about John in 1:17 and also relate closely to aspects of John's ministry as described in 3:1–6 and 7:26–27.[42] The rest of the Benedictus does not refer specifically to John but celebrates God's act of salvation for Israel of which John will be a part. In doing so, it unites the emphasis on the restoration of David's kingdom, which we find in the annunciation to Mary (1:32–33), with the emphasis on the fulfillment of the promise to Abraham, found in the Magnificat (1:54–55). Furthermore, the implications for Israel of both the promise to David and to Abraham are clarified by significant explanatory additions.

Couplet parallelism, which is relatively strong in the Magnificat, is not characteristic of the Benedictus, although vv. 68b–69 and 72 appear to be two couplets which mark the beginning of the two sections on David and Abraham. In most cases, however, we do not have synonymous or antithetical lines but a long string of clauses, often introduced by infinitives, which expand the initial statement that God "has visited and done redemption for his people." While the Benedictus lacks repetition in couplets, with its poetic effect of emphasis and enrichment, the successive clauses may nevertheless emphasize and enrich earlier material, for there is considerable repetition of theme words. For instance, "salvation" in v. 71 picks up "salvation" in v. 69; "oath" in v. 73 picks up "covenant" in v. 72. Since repetition of theme words emphasizes them and deepens their meaning by using them in several contexts, it has some of the poetic effect of parallelism. Synonymous words may also be substituted.

Pierre Auffret detects a chiastic pattern of theme words within the Benedictus.[43] In my opinion, the desire to find strict chiasm can lead us to overlook and misconstrue some of the data. While there is an inclination toward chiasm, the basic phenomenon is the strong tendency to reuse theme words in order to emphasize them and expand their significance, whether the repeated use falls into a chiastic pattern or not. The end of the Benedictus does return to theme words of the beginning, as shown by the repetition of "visit ($\dot{\epsilon}\pi\iota\sigma\kappa\dot{\epsilon}\pi\tau\omega\mu\alpha\iota$)" in 1:68, 78[44] and the close connection

---

[42] See above, pp. 23–24.

[43] See "Note sur la structure littéraire," 248–58.

[44] Eduard Schweizer adds this to Auffret's chiasm. See "Zum Aufbau von Lukas 1 und 2," 331, n. 20.

of "redemption for his people . . . salvation for us" in 1:68–69 with "salvation for his people" in 1:77. But 1:77–79 also repeats theme words from other parts of the Benedictus, thereby tying the various parts of the hymn together and relating these themes to the light imagery which is newly introduced at the end. The section on the covenant with Abraham begins with a reference to "mercy" (1:72), and this word is repeated in 1:78. The statement to John in 1:76 refers to preparing "ways," and this word returns in 1:79, where the ways of the Lord become "a way of peace."[45] The earlier repetition of "enemies" and "hand" in 1:71, 74 is also significant, for this helps to give remarkable emphasis to salvation as political freedom, connecting it both to the promise to David and to Abraham.

In 1:68–69 Zechariah celebrates God's act of "redemption for his people" through raising up "a horn of salvation for us in the house of David." The redemption for which God is praised is distinctly a redemption for Israel and will come through the appearance of the Davidic king of whom Gabriel spoke in 1:32–33. This king, promised by the prophets in Scripture, will bring "salvation from our enemies and from the hand of all who hate us" (1:71). Similarly, God's fulfillment of the oath to Abraham will mean that Israel will be free to "serve" God "without fear, having been delivered from the hand of enemies" (1:74). The enemies who might cause such fear are oppressors like Antiochus Epiphanes, who attempted to exterminate the Jewish religion, and the Romans, with whom there was repeated danger of conflict over the rights of Jews in the practice of their faith. Understanding salvation to include political freedom for the Jewish homeland does not conflict with the dominant theology of Luke-Acts. It only appears to do so when we fail to understand its function within the total story: fulfillment of this hope for freedom is anticipated here in order to prepare for and heighten the effect of the tragic turn which will take place when the leaders of Israel reject the king who could fulfill this promise. The narrator understands the Scriptures to promise a messianic kingdom for Israel which will be a time of peace and freedom from oppressors. This promise is acknowledged as valid—if only Israel would accept its Messiah.

The first readers of Luke would read these happy words in a historical context which gives them a tinge of pathos. They could already, at this early point in the story, begin to sense that Israel's story will be presented as a tragedy. Zechariah's words are full of joy, but the first readers were

---

[45] Auffret regards the repeated "mercy" as part of a second chiasm which involves not the whole Benedictus but vv. 71–79. The repeated use of "way" in vv. 76 and 79 does not fit either chiasm.

aware that the future did not bring "salvation from our enemies" to Israel. Furthermore, the Lukan story will place special emphasis on the destruction of Jerusalem which climaxes the Roman defeat of the Jewish rebellion (see the interconnected statements by Jesus in 13:34–35; 19:41–44; 21:20–24; 23:27–31). Zechariah, inspired by the Holy Spirit, rightly understands the saving purpose for Israel behind the birth of John and Jesus and rightly reacts with joy. But he does not know that much of Israel will reject its king and that this rejection will be prolonged, blocking fulfillment of the hope for Israel's freedom.[46] Thus there are already suggestions of tragic irony in the story. Readers who recognize this may well begin to feel sympathetic pity for persons like Zechariah whose deeply felt joy and hope will be disappointed.

Thematic connections between the Benedictus and later sections of Luke-Acts support the interpretation just given. The words "redemption ($\lambda \acute{v} \tau \rho \omega \sigma \iota \varsigma$)" and "redeem ($\lambda v \tau \rho \acute{o} o \mu \alpha \iota$)" are not common in Luke-Acts, but they occur in two significant places in addition to 1:68. Anna is a female counterpart of Zechariah and Simeon. Like them she praises God, and she speaks of Jesus "to all those awaiting the redemption of Jerusalem" (2:38). This recalls Zechariah's words about redemption, but with "Jerusalem" substituted for "his people." This change is significant in light of the emphasis placed on the destruction of Jerusalem in Luke. Anna's expectation is expressed in a way that will make its later negation sharp and clear. The theme of redemption returns in Luke 24:21 as the disappointed disciples, after the death of Jesus, say, "We were hoping that he was the one who is going to redeem Israel." Again it is a question of *Israel's* redemption. This hope is revived by Jesus' resurrection, which leads the disciples to ask, "Are you at this time restoring the kingdom to Israel?" (Acts 1:6). Here the hope for Israel's messianic kingdom, strongly expressed in the birth narratives, reappears. This question does not merely show the blindness of followers who have not yet received the Spirit. Jesus corrects their curiosity about times, but he does not reject the possibility of a restored kingdom for Israel, and Peter, after receiving the Spirit, still holds out the hope of the "restoration of all the things which God spoke through the mouth of his holy prophets from of old" (Acts 3:21), provided the people of Jerusalem repent. Both Acts 1:6 (connected to 3:21 by the theme of restoration) and Luke 1:69–70 indicate that the

---

[46] To this extent, Zechariah is an unreliable interpreter of the story, but he expresses what should have been and would have been apart from rejection. Furthermore, there are some indications in Luke-Acts that the narrator has not given up hope of a messianic kingdom for Israel with Jesus as king, although this kingdom has been postponed. On this continuing hope, see R. Tannehill, "Israel in Luke-Acts," 81–85.

messianic kingdom is among the things promised by God "through the mouth of his holy prophets from of old" (a long and solemn phrase shared by Luke 1:70 and Acts 3:21).

When Jesus weeps over Jerusalem at his arrival, his words are reminiscent of the Benedictus. However, Zechariah's joy is replaced by Jesus' mourning. The mood changes drastically because of the failure of the city to recognize and accept the fulfillment of its hopes. Zechariah twice uses the unusual word "visit"[47] to describe God's redeeming concern for Israel (1:68, 78); Jesus mourns because "you did not know the time of your visitation"[48] (19:44). Israel's "enemies," mentioned in 1:71, 74, are also mentioned by Jesus (19:43), and he is clearly referring to the Roman troops who will destroy Jerusalem. The Benedictus ends by speaking of Israel's feet being guided "into a way of peace" (1:79); Jesus mourns because Jerusalem does not know "the things that lead to peace" (19:42). The repeated statements that Jerusalem does not *know* what is crucial to its welfare—the things that lead to peace and the time of its visitation— should also be compared with the reference to giving "knowledge of salvation to his people" in 1:77.[49] Furthermore, Jesus' approach to Jerusalem, which immediately precedes Jesus' weeping over the city, has been modified in ways which recall the hopes of the birth story. The disciples describe Jesus as "the king" (19:38; dif. Matthew, Mark), while Gabriel before his birth spoke of his kingdom (1:33). "In heaven peace, and glory in the highest places" (19:38; dif. Matthew, Mark) echoes the angels' words in 2:14, with a significant difference, however, for the angels said, "On earth peace." Jerusalem will not recognize "the things that lead to peace"; therefore, the hope of peace on earth is not being realized for it. The approaching tragic turn in the narrative is forcefully expressed through repeating language of the birth story while Jesus makes clear that the salvation anticipated at the beginning will not be realized now for Jerusalem.

The Benedictus takes on new significance when we understand its relation to the rest of Luke's story. It arouses conflicting emotions: joy and hope but also sorrow and pity. The joy is valid in the context of the total story, for some of the promises are indeed being realized for some people. But Luke's joyful birth story has a hidden lining of sadness. Great expectations contribute to a sense of tragedy if the expected happiness is

---

[47] ἐπισκέπτομαι, used once more in Luke, four times in Acts, four times in the rest of the New Testament.

[48] ἐπισκοπή, used once more in Luke-Acts, twice in the rest of the New Testament.

[49] The theme of peace continues in the birth story in 2:14, 29, and the latter verse is followed by Simeon's statement, "My eyes have seen your salvation." Cp. 19:42: the things that lead to peace "are hid from your eyes."

lost. Part of the function of the birth story is to awaken a lively sense of great expectations so that readers will feel the tragic loss more vividly.

In 1:72–75 words already associated with the promise to Abraham in 1:54–55 are repeated, but the explanation of the oath to Abraham is new. This was an oath that God would "give to us, having been delivered from the hand of enemies, without fear to serve [or "worship"][50] him in holiness and righteousness." This interpretation of the promise to Abraham as a promise of freedom from oppression for the sake of unhindered service of God is remarkable. It agrees, however, with the presentation of the promise to Abraham in Stephen's speech. In Acts 7:5–7 God promises Abraham the land for his descendants but also speaks of the enslavement of the people in Egypt. God will judge the enslavers of Abraham's offspring, "and after these things they will go out and will serve (λατρεύ-σουσιν) me in this place." Freedom from slavery leads to the worship and service of God. The quoted words draw upon Exod 3:12, which, however, says, "You will serve God at this mountain." In Stephen's speech the promise no longer applies to the temporary service of God at the encampment of Sinai but to the continual service of God in the promised land. This is also central in the promise to Abraham as expressed in Luke 1:73–75.

We have already noted that 1:77–79 repeats a number of important words from the earlier parts of the Benedictus.[51] This section also touches on themes that will receive further development later in Luke-Acts. While 1:69 relates salvation to the messianic kingdom, 1:77 makes clear that this salvation will require the renewal of the people through the "release of sins." Giving knowledge of salvation to the people through release of their sins is here the task of John the Baptist, but Peter and Paul will later take over this role of making known salvation and release of sins (see Acts 4:10–12; 5:31; 13:26, 38).[52] The theme of salvation continues to be important in Luke 2. In 2:11 the angels' announcement of the birth of a "savior" is again a reference to the Davidic Messiah ("Messiah Lord" born "in the city of David"). Simeon's vision of salvation for all peoples in 2:30–32 will significantly expand this messianic hope without negating it. The closing reference to peace in 1:79 will also be reemphasized in 2:14, 29, and Jesus Messiah will again be associated with peace when the meaning of his ministry is summarized in Acts 10:36.

Light imagery is introduced in the last two verses of the Benedictus. In

---

[50] λατρεύω is often used of the religious service which a worshiper offers to God.
[51] See above, pp. 33–34.
[52] The connection of Luke 1:77 with these Acts texts is noted by R. Brown, *The Birth of the Messiah*, 390, n. 36. There are other similarities between the ministry of John and the ministry of Jesus' followers. See below, pp. 48–53, 233–35.

this context, the "rising from on high" refers primarily to a rising light, like the sun or a star, although ἀνατολή can also refer to the prophesied Davidic "shoot."[53] This rising light will appear to those sitting in darkness and will guide them in finding the path of peace. Simeon will also relate salvation and light (2:30–32). Later, light imagery will be associated with Paul, not only in the narratives of his call but also in descriptions of his commission (see Acts 13:47; 26:17–18). Thus Paul will have an important role in fulfilling the prophetic words of Zechariah and Simeon.

The Annunciation to the Shepherds and Simeon's Oracles

In 2:8–14 we have a third annunciation scene, which follows the same pattern as the previous two: the appearance of an angel, a response of fear, the command not to fear, the announcement of a birth that brings joy. In this case, however, the announcement is not to a parent of the child to be born, for this birth is not just a family affair. Indeed, the angel stresses that he brings a message of "great joy which shall be for all the people" (2:10). The parents were instructed how to name their children. This would be inappropriate for shepherds, who have nothing to do with naming this baby. Nevertheless, a name is given by the angel: "Messiah Lord (χριστὸς κύριος)." The title Messiah, which appears here for the first time, should be interpreted in light of what has already been said to Mary and by Zechariah about salvation for the Jewish people through the reestablishment of the Davidic kingdom. The reference to the birth "in David's city" supports this connection. The unusual combination "Messiah Lord" appears only here in Luke-Acts without the name Jesus,[54] but it is closely related to Acts 2:36, where, on the basis of scriptural argument, Peter concludes that God made Jesus "both Lord and Messiah."[55] The angel anticipates Peter's proclamation.[56]

Two important oracles concerning the baby Jesus are spoken by Simeon in the temple. The location is one of several examples of significant settings which enhance major scenes (see Jesus in the Nazareth synagogue in Luke 4:16–30; the temple and the chambers of the Sanhedrin in Acts 3–5; Paul in the agora of Athens and before the Areopagus in Acts 17:16–34). Simeon also fits a character type which we repeatedly encounter in the birth stories and, to a lesser degree, elsewhere in Luke-

---

[53] See R. Brown, *The Birth of the Messiah*, 373–74.

[54] "The Lord Jesus Messiah" or "our Lord Jesus Messiah" appears in Acts 11:17, 15:26, 28:31, and as a significant variant reading in Acts 4:33, 20:21.

[55] A relation noted by Christoph Burger, *Jesus als Davidssohn*, 137.

[56] Peter's statement, which seems to be based on Jesus' resurrection, may appear to conflict with the angel's announcement, which proclaims Jesus as Messiah and Lord already at birth. This issue must be postponed until we consider the Pentecost speech.

Acts. Simeon and his female counterpart Anna are prophets who are inspired by the Spirit. They are deeply devoted to their Jewish faith (Simeon is "righteous and devoted" in 2:25; Anna does not leave the temple, "serving [λατρεύουσα] with fasts and prayers day and night" in 2:37). As part of this devotion, they expectantly await (expressed with προσδέχομαι) the "consolation of Israel" and the "redemption of Jerusalem" (2:25, 38). And they are old. The promise that he would see the Lord's Messiah is evidently the only thing holding Simeon to life (2:26, 29), and a considerable point is made of Anna's age (2:36–37). They are expectantly waiting and have waited long. They represent the long history of an expectant people, nourished by God's promise. Zechariah and Elizabeth also fit this character type. They, too, are righteous, careful observers of the law (1:6), old (1:7), and filled with the prophetic Spirit when they recognize the fulfillment of God's promise (1:41, 67). These people represent their faith at its best, according to the values of the implied author, even though Zechariah has temporary doubts. To them the coming of the long awaited salvation is revealed.

Variations on this character type will appear later in the story. Joseph of Arimathea is also described as one who "was awaiting (προσεδέχετο) the reign of God" and a "good and righteous man" (23:50–51). Paul presents himself as a Jew of the same type, saying, "I serve (λατρεύω) the God of the forefathers, believing all the things prescribed by the law and written in the prophets, having a hope in God which these [Jewish accusers] themselves expectantly await (προσδέχονται)" (Acts 24:14–15). Paul also recognizes that the twelve tribes of Israel are characterized by their devoted "worshiping [or "serving (λατρεῦον)"] night and day" in hope of obtaining the fulfillment of the promise to the fathers, only distinguishing himself from the many other Jews who share this hope because they fail to recognize that the fulfillment has come (Acts 26:6–7). The description of the earnest worship and hope of the twelve tribes in Acts 26:6–7 is very close to the description of Anna in Luke 2:37–38. Near the end of the second volume the author is still wrestling with the hopes and fate of such devoted and expectant worshipers of God. This hope is expressed powerfully in the birth narrative, but with a poignant touch of pathos, through the figures of Zechariah and Elizabeth, Simeon and Anna.

Simeon's two prophetic utterances contrast sharply in mood. In the first he blesses God (2:28), as did Zechariah (1:68), and joyfully acknowledges the fulfillment of God's promise that he would see the Messiah. He refers to himself as God's "slave (δοῦλος)," as Mary did previously (1:38, 48), and speaks of God's dismissal of him from his long watch "in peace," which probably indicates Simeon's share in the messianic peace celebrated in 1:79 and 2:14. As in the Magnificat and Benedictus, a "for (ὅτι)" clause follows the introductory statement. The words in 2:30–32 paraphrase themes from Second Isaiah,[57] forming them into a new poetic statement which expresses the universal scope of God's saving purpose. It is this universal saving purpose of God which is the chief moving force behind this story of Jesus and his witnesses. Simeon discloses to the readers the hidden purpose which unites the narrative and constitutes its central meaning.

The scriptural basis of this understanding of God's purpose appears clearly in Simeon's reference to seeing God's "salvation," using σωτήριον, a neuter form which is rare in the New Testament (used four times, including three times in Luke-Acts). This neuter form is frequent in Isaiah 40–66. It will occur again in Luke 3:6 as part of a quotation of Isa 40:3–5 which has been extended beyond the parallel quotation in Matthew and Mark to include the statement, "All flesh will see the salvation (σωτήριον) of God." This quotation will reinforce what Simeon is saying, for it, like Simeon, refers to *seeing* God's *salvation*, which will appear to and for *all*. Isa 40:5 is one of the scriptural roots of the narrator's vision of God's saving purpose. The continuing importance of the statements in Luke 2:30–32 and 3:6 is shown by the final words of Paul quoted in Acts, which refer again to "this salvation (σωτήριον) of God" (Acts 28:28). This is the only other use of this neuter form in Luke-Acts. Jacques Dupont, noting these connections, states, "Luke seems to be inviting us to recall the allusion early in his first volume to 'the salvation of God' which, according to Isaiah, was to be revealed 'to all flesh'."[58] The end of the work reminds us of the divine purpose which was disclosed at the beginning and which remains central throughout. But these words of Paul follow quotation of a bitter passage from Isa 6:9–10, which speaks of eyes that do not see and ears that do not hear. The result is emphasis on the disappointment of the scriptural promise cited in Luke 3:6, for now readers can compare two statements from Isaiah about seeing. On the one hand, Isa 40:5 proclaims, "All flesh will see the salvation of God." On the other hand, Isa 6:9–10 states, "Looking they will look, yet certainly not see, for . . . they have closed their eyes, lest they see with their eyes." When Paul applies the latter text rather than the former to the Roman Jews (who are only the latest of a series of Jewish groups to reject Jesus), it becomes clear that the promise of all flesh seeing the salvation of God has not been realized for them and those like them. The story that begins by

---

[57] R. Brown, *The Birth of the Messiah*, 458, lists Isa 40:5; 42:6; 46:13; 49:6; 52:9–10.
[58] See *Salvation of the Gentiles*, 16.

proclaiming that "all flesh will see the salvation of God" ends on a tragic note. All flesh has not seen God's salvation.[59]

More than the fate of the Roman Jews is at stake. God's promise in Scripture, which the narrator presented to us as a key to understanding God's purpose in history, has not been fulfilled. Here is a theological problem that the narrator does not solve, for the narrative ends with an unresolved tension between promise and reality. Nevertheless, the narrative helps to prevent despair by believers who are living without a solution, for rejection and suffering are incorporated into a story in which a lively hope in God's promise persists, in spite of all. This persistent hope appears in at least the following features of the story: (1) The promise that "all flesh will see the salvation of God" is not trimmed back because there is no clear way in which it can be realized. On the contrary, the narrator has chosen to highlight this promise as a disclosure of the ultimate purpose of the God who will, somehow, finally triumph. (2) There are significant events which are partial fulfillments of the promise, and the narrator focuses our attention upon them. A hope that has been buffeted need not become weak or detached from life so long as there are events in experience that nourish it because they represent significant breakthroughs in moving toward the ultimate goal. Luke-Acts celebrates significant breakthroughs toward inclusive salvation when narrating Jesus' mission to the outcasts of Israel and the early church's surge into the Gentile world. The promise gives these developments special significance, while these developments help to keep the promise alive and relevant. (3) There are some indications that the author has not given up hope for the Jews who have rejected the church's message.[60] (4) The end of Acts encourages the church by balancing the negative result among many Jews with the continuing opportunity among Gentiles and by providing a model of endurance in adversity, for the final verses speak of Paul steadfastly continuing the mission in spite of Jewish rejection and Roman imprisonment.

Simeon has seen God's salvation, present in the form of this baby, but he understands himself as only the watchman who first spots what will affect all. This salvation has been "prepared in the presence of ($\kappa\alpha\tau\grave{\alpha}$ $\pi\rho\acute{o}\sigma\omega\pi o\nu$) all the peoples" in order that they, too, might behold it and

---

[59] Seeing God's salvation means recognizing it and responding to it, which shades over into personal participation in it. Lack of response is expressed as a failure of proper seeing and hearing in Acts 28:26–27. When Paul says that the Gentiles, in contrast to the Roman Jews, "will hear," he means that they will respond to and share in "this salvation of God" (28:28). The reference to seeing in Luke 3:6 should be understood in a similar way. See also Acts 26:18, where the opening of eyes clearly has a salvific effect.

[60] See R. Tannehill, "Israel in Luke-Acts," 81–85.

share in it. This thought is developed through parallel clauses which speak of a light which will be saving illumination for both the Gentiles and Israel.[61] We are explicitly told that "all the peoples" means both the Gentiles and Israel. Both must see and share God's salvation in order to fulfill the prophecy in Isa 40:5, "All flesh will see the salvation of God." Anything less is a tragic restriction of God's saving purpose.

The narrator may never have carefully considered whether "all flesh" in this passage means every single individual.[62] The narrator is concerned not with this issue but with the fate of Israel. The severest challenge to the promise that "all flesh will see the salvation of God" is the rejection of salvation through Jesus by a major segment of the Jewish people. This problem begins to appear in Simeon's second oracle.

From Simeon's words we can look back to the light imagery in the final

Connecting Themes in the Angelic Announcements and Prophetic Hymns
of the Birth Narrative (and in Luke 3:1–6).
A Progressive Disclosure of the Significance of John and Jesus in God's Purpose.

	1:14–17	1:32–33, 35	1:46–55
joy, exultation	1:14		1:47
John as prophet	1:15, 17		
turning, repentance	1:16, 17		
go before, prepare	1:17		
the Davidic king		1:32–33	
God's power		1:35	1:49, 51
Lord/slave			1:46–48
savior, salvation			1:47
God's mercy			1:50, 54
overturn of society			1:51–53
remember, our fathers, Abraham			1:54–55
his servant, as he spoke			1:54–55
redemption			
forgiveness of sins			
dawning, light			
peace			
all peoples, all flesh			

[61] The syntax of 2:32 is ambiguous. "Glory" may either be another object of the preposition "for (εἰς)" ("light for revelation . . . and for glory"), or it may be in synonymous parallelism with "light," which would emphasize its associations with brightness and shining. In either case, both the Gentiles and Israel are the recipients of light, which is a metaphor for the "salvation" in v. 30. The same equation of light and salvation occurs in central statements about the mission in Acts 13:47; 26:18, 23.

[62] The reference to "as many as were ordained to eternal life" in Acts 13:48 suggests that salvation of all individuals is not assumed.

lines of the Benedictus and recognize that the "rising" or "dawning from on high" is meant to illumine both Jews and Gentiles. Simeon's reference to "light for revelation of Gentiles" in 2:32 relates to Isa 49:6, which will be a key text for the interpretation of the mission in Acts, being quoted in 13:47 and, in fragmentary form ("to the end of the earth"), in 1:8.

Simeon speaks again to Mary in 2:34–35, and these words contrast sharply in tone with his vision of God's salvation. Jesus is destined to be "a sign provoking contradiction (σημεῖον ἀντιλεγόμενον)." He will cause an upheaval in Israel. Through his overturn of Jewish society and the resistance which he provokes, "thoughts from many hearts" will be revealed. Thus the saving revelation mentioned in 2:32 also exposes the hidden attitudes which oppose God's purpose.

These words provide a clear preview of the resistance which Jesus will

1:68–79	2:10–12, 14	2:29–32, 34–35	3:1–6
	2:10		
1:76			3:2
			3:3
1:76			3:4
1:69–71	2:11		
		2:29	
1:69, 71, 77	2:11	2:30	3:6
1:72, 78			
		2:34	3:5
1:72–73			
1:69–70			
1:68		(cf. 2:38)	
1:77			3:3
1:78–79	(cf. 2:9)	2:32	
1:79	2:14	2:29	
		2:31–32	3:6

encounter during his ministry. The revelation of the "thoughts (δια-λογισμοί)" of "hearts" plays a role in the resulting conflicts, for Jesus is repeatedly presented as one who exposes the thoughts of opponents and weak disciples. In the healing of the paralytic, Jesus recognizes the negative "thoughts (διαλογισμούς)" of the scribes and Pharisees and immediately challenges them by questioning the thinking in their "hearts"

(5:21–22). Luke shares with the parallel in Mark 2:6–8 the use of the verb διαλογίζομαι, but Luke alone has the noun form. In the healing of the man with the withered hand, Luke alone has the statement, "He knew their thoughts (διαλογισμούς)" (6:8). Again Jesus responds by challenging the thoughts of the scribes and Pharisees. Luke 6:8 appears to be an echo of 5:22, tying these scenes more closely together and reinforcing the picture of Jesus as one who recognizes and exposes the hidden negative attitudes of his opponents. With the disciples also, Jesus knows and challenges "the thought (διαλογισμόν) of their heart" when they have a false attitude (9:46–47). The parallel in Mark 9:33–34 uses the verb διαλογίζομαι, but Luke alone has the noun and adds "of their heart." Luke alone uses the verb διαλογίζομαι of the plot of the wicked tenant farmers who kill the owner's son (20:14). This is significant because Jesus is using the parable to expose the attitude of the scribes and high priests toward himself. Finally, the risen Jesus immediately recognizes and challenges the "doubts (διαλογισμοί)" in the "heart" of his followers when he appears to them (24:38). Thus Jesus, in discerning the resistance to his mission by both critics and disciples, fulfills the prophecy of Simeon that he will be "a sign provoking contradiction, . . . in order that thoughts of many hearts might be revealed."

Simeon's words add important new perspectives to the previews of salvation in the previous canticles and angelic announcements. He discloses the comprehensive scope of God's work of salvation, which must embrace both Israel and the Gentiles. He also reveals that the story will be full of conflict and tension. Already readers can anticipate that the story will concern God's comprehensive saving purpose as it encounters human resistance. A problem is beginning to appear which will give the story dramatic interest and allow struggling humans to recognize in it a reflection of their own experience. It remains to be seen whether and how God's saving purpose can be realized in the face of human resistance.

Chapter Two

JOHN AND JESUS
BEGIN THEIR MISSION

THE MISSION OF JOHN (LUKE 3:1–20)

The divine purpose disclosed in the birth narrative begins to be fulfilled as John the Baptist begins his ministry. We were told that John would be a prophet (1:76) who would "prepare" the Lord's "ways" or "go before" the Lord (1:17, 76), causing many "to turn to the Lord their God" (a way of speaking of repentance), and giving the people "knowledge of salvation . . . in release of their sins" (1:77).[1] All of these things begin to happen as the narrator relates the ministry of John the Baptist. We also hear again of God's comprehensive "salvation ($\sigma\omega\tau\eta\rho\iota\nu$)," previously mentioned by Simeon (2:30–32).

The references in the birth narrative to preparing the Lord's ways and to God's salvation for all peoples were anticipations (in the order of the narrative) and reminiscences (for those acquainted with Scripture) of the Isaiah quotation in Luke 3:4–6. The importance of this quotation to the narrator is shown by the anticipations of it in the birth narrative. The importance of the last line is shown by the fact that Luke alone continues the quote to include it, while Matthew and Mark end with "make straight his paths." This quotation from Isaiah not only interprets John's special mission but reveals the purpose of God which underlies the whole narrative of Luke-Acts.[2]

In agreement with the birth narrative, John is presented as a prophet. This is indicated by the elaborate introduction in 3:1–2, which serves not only as a historical reference point for a major new departure in the narrative but also mimics the opening lines of many of the prophetic books in the Old Testament.[3] The narrative begins with a reference to the coming of the word of God, which is thus presented as the moving force behind John's ministry. God's word turns John into a prophetic preacher

---

[1] See above, pp. 23–24.

[2] See the previous discussion of Luke 3:6, pp. 40–42.

[3] See Hosea, Micah, Joel, Jonah, Zephaniah, Haggai, Zechariah, Jeremiah. These introductions to prophetic books use λόγος κυρίου (but ῥῆμα τοῦ θεοῦ in Jeremiah) and some form of γίνομαι, the name of the prophet, and usually the name of his father and a date by reference to one or more kings.

of repentance for the release of sins, as had been predicted in the birth narrative (1:16–17, 77).

John's message is summarized as "a baptism of repentance for release of sins" just before the Isaiah quotation. Following the quotation, we are given a sample of John's call to repentance. Thus the quotation is framed by John's preaching of repentance and is partly interpreted by this context. Preparing the Lord's way means preparing the people through repentance, as 1:17 indicated ("to turn hearts . . . , to prepare for the Lord a people made ready"). The images of road building in Isaiah become images of repentance. Height and depth are to be leveled; the crooked and rough are to be made straight and smooth. This drastic transformation of a terrain that obstructs travel becomes a symbol of the repentance that the Lord's coming requires. Some of this imagery is used elsewhere in similar ways. Valleys filled in and mountains brought low (using ταπεινόω) may recall the lowering and raising proclaimed in 1:52: "He has put down the mighty from thrones and has exalted the lowly (ταπεινούς)." The images of crooked and straight, repeating words used in Luke 3:4–5, reappear in Acts in contexts where repentance, or hardened opposition to the message of repentance, is important (Acts 2:40; 8:21; 13:10). The connection in the last case is especially clear, for in the phrase "the straight ways of the Lord," Paul repeats three words from Luke 3:4–5.

It is important to note that John the Baptist is the preparer of the way and forerunner not only in the sense that he bears witness to Jesus, the stronger one who is coming (3:16), but also in the sense that he prepares a repentant people, a people ready to receive the Lord because they have passed through the drastic leveling and straightening that Isaiah described. Furthermore, the description of the divine purpose being realized through John already has the final goal, the revelation of God's salvation to all flesh, firmly in view. John initiates a mission that will continue throughout Luke-Acts and reach out to the whole world. Moreover, John's role does not become obsolete when Jesus appears on the scene. John performs a function that has lasting importance. He begins something that continues and grows.

Jesus and his witnesses, in fact, take over and continue the message of John the Baptist, and the narrator sometimes uses phrases which remind us of this fact. The task of "proclaiming . . . repentance for release of sins" (3:3) remains central throughout Luke-Acts. In Nazareth Jesus indicates that he has been called to "proclaim release" (4:18),[4] and the scenes in 5:17–32 in which Jesus asserts his authority to "release sins" and defends his mission "to call . . . sinners to repentance" (dif. Matthew, Mark) are

---

[4] See below, pp. 65–66.

linked by the narrator to a series of later scenes which keep this important aspect of Jesus' mission before the reader.[5] In 24:47 the mission of proclaiming "repentance for release of sins" (the same words used of John in 3:3, again dependent on the verb κηρύσσω)[6] is given by the risen Jesus to his followers, and this mission is carried out in Acts.

More striking is the fact that other phrases used to describe the mission of John the Baptist are reused in describing the work of Jesus' followers, suggesting that they are continuing the work of John. In 7:27 John's function of preparing the Lord's way is associated with a second quotation from Scripture, which includes the statement, "Behold, I send my messenger (ἄγγελον) before your face." When the journey to Jerusalem begins, the function of Jesus' followers is described in the same words: Jesus "sent messengers (ἀγγέλους) before his face" (9:52), and again, "He sent them . . . before his face" (10:1). The scriptural task of preparing the way, which was originally John's according to 3:4 and 7:27, is continued by Jesus' followers. The preachers in Acts also continue John's work. At the end of Peter's first sermon, the hearers ask,[7] "*What should we do?*" (Acts 2:37), repeating the crowd's response to John (Luke 3:10), and Peter replies, "*Repent* and be *baptized . . . for release* of your *sins*" (Acts 2:38; cf. Luke 3:3). He later adds, "Be *saved* from this *crooked* (σκολιᾶς) generation" (Acts 2:40; cf. Luke 3:5–6). Paul, too, when he summarizes his past preaching, asserts that his message has consistently been "to *repent* and to turn to God, doing works *worthy of repentance*" (Acts 26:20; cf. Luke 3:8: "Make fruits worthy of repentance"). Jesus' witnesses, like John, are prophetic preachers of repentance. What John began, they continue, for John's call to repentance remains important. The narrator's portrait of John has continuing significance for the narrative, for in significant ways John is a "prototype of the Christian evangelist."[8]

The continuing significance of John the Baptist is also indicated by speeches in Acts which explicitly recall his work. John's baptism is used to date the beginning of Jesus' ministry (Acts 1:22; 10:37). This is not simply because Jesus' baptism is important. Acts 10:37 speaks of "the baptism which John proclaimed," combining baptism with the verb κηρύσσω as in Luke 3:3 and indicating that John's whole mission of calling people to repentance through baptism is important. This is even

---

[5] See below, pp. 103–9.

[6] Many manuscripts read "and" instead of "for (εἰς)" in 24:47, but the latter reading is strongly supported by the combination of Sinaiticus, Vaticanus, and P75.

[7] In the rest of the paragraph, words in Acts which repeat word roots in Luke 3:3–10 are italicized.

[8] C. Talbert, *Reading Luke*, 27.

clearer in Acts 13:24–25. The Acts speeches refer to the ministry of Jesus prior to his passion only briefly. When they do, as in 10:38, the opportunity is used to recall special Lukan emphases in the presentation of Jesus' ministry. The portrait of John in Luke receives the same treatment in Acts 13:24–25. This brief statement contains specific features which reflect what was previously said in Luke. Again John's "baptism of repentance" is something that he proclaimed (using the compound form προκηρύσσω). This baptism of repentance was for "all the people of Israel," which agrees with the rather surprising statements in Luke that "all the people" (excepting the Pharisees and lawyers) were baptized by John (3:21; 7:29–30). The phrase "before the face of his entrance" (or, more literally, "way in [εἴσοδος]") paraphrases the description of John in the scriptural quotation in Luke 7:27: "I send my messenger before your face, who will prepare your way (ὁδός) before you." Acts 13:25 paraphrases Luke 3:15–16, in which John declares his unworthiness in comparison to the coming one.[9] That John made this statement when he "was finishing the course" agrees with the close connection between John's witness to the coming one and his imprisonment in Luke 3:15–20. Thus John's work and words are of sufficient importance to be recalled in the Acts sermons, where Jesus' ministry receives only brief mention. In recalling John, not only his witness to the one coming after him is noted but also his proclamation of a baptism of repentance for release of sins for all the people. The preachers in Acts continue to call for repentance and to offer release of sins.

Not only the general proclamation of repentance but also more specific aspects of John's preaching sound themes that will be developed later in the narrative. John's words to the crowds are remarkably harsh in light of the fact that they have come to be baptized.[10] John does not greet them in friendly fashion but warns them that only complete repentance is adequate. He warns in 3:8 against substituting an appeal to Abraham as father and declares that "God from these stones is able to raise up children for Abraham." Later in Luke a rich man will appeal to "father Abraham," to no avail (16:24, 27, 30), while others who seem to have renounced their place in Abraham's family are declared to be children of Abraham (19:9). The fact that the rich man who appeals to Abraham did not share with the poor ties this passage more closely to John's warnings, for John will emphasize that one of the fruits of repentance is sharing clothing and food with those in need (3:11). The vivid warning that a tree which does not

---

[9] The author commonly prefers paraphrase to exact repetition. See Henry J. Cadbury, "Four Features of Lucan Style," 91–97.

[10] In Matt 3:7–10 the same words are addressed not to the crowds but to the Pharisees and Sadducees.

bear good fruit will be cut down is developed in Jesus' parable of the barren fig tree (13:6–9; see also 6:43–44). John's instruction to the crowd to share clothing and food with the needy will be echoed by various commandments of Jesus (see 6:30; 12:33; 14:12–14; 16:9; 18:22) as part of his extensive teaching on the dangers and right use of possessions. The commands to both the toll collectors and the soldiers in 3:12–14 are related to 19:8, where the problem of extortion by those with power is recognized in Zacchaeus' offer to make restitution "if I have extorted (ἐσυκο-φάντησα)[11] anything from anyone."

We have already noted the connection between Luke 3:8a and Acts 26:20, and between Luke 3:15–16 and Acts 13:25. Even more important are John's words about baptism in Holy Spirit in Luke 3:16, for the narrator traces a progressive fulfillment, in several stages, of this promise. John's prophecy of the coming of the stronger one finds immediate fulfillment as Jesus appears in 3:21–22. These verses also report the descent of the Holy Spirit, but on Jesus alone. John's promise that "he will baptize you in Holy Spirit" remains unfulfilled during Luke's Gospel. At the beginning of Acts, however, the risen Jesus, in anticipation of Pentecost, repeats the promise of baptism in Holy Spirit, contrasting it with John's baptism as John did, and states that the promise will soon be fulfilled (Acts 1:5). The contrast with John's baptism is retained, even though Jesus does not indicate that he is repeating John's own words. The coming of the Spirit to Jesus' followers at Pentecost is only the beginning of the fulfillment of this promise. As the mission spreads, the reception of the Spirit by new groups is reported, and when the Gentiles of Cornelius' household receive the Spirit, the same promise is recalled, now as a "word of the Lord" (11:16). The promised baptism in Holy Spirit, which sur-passes John's water baptism, has spread to the Gentiles. The contrast between John's baptism and receiving the Spirit through Jesus appears once more in Acts 19:1–7, where Paul encounters a group of "disciples" who have been baptized into John's baptism but have not received the Spirit. In 19:4 the narrator has Paul paraphrase the description of John's baptism and John's words about the coming one in Luke 3:3, 16. Then, through Paul, this group is included in the growing community of those who have received the promised Holy Spirit. Thus the words of John about baptism in Holy Spirit anticipate major developments in Acts, for they are repeated by the risen Jesus and are progressively fulfilled, as is brought out especially at two key points: the beginning of the mission at Pentecost and the first inclusion of Gentiles in the mission.

The mission of Jesus and his witnesses both parallels and surpasses the

---

[11] Luke 3:14 and 19:8 are the only occurrences of this verb in the NT.

mission of John the Baptist. John acknowledges his unworthiness in comparison with the stronger one who is coming and speaks of the baptism in Holy Spirit which will surpass his water baptism (Luke 3:16). But we have also noted that there is continuity between the mission of John and the mission of Jesus and his followers. What is initiated by the word of God to John continues through the rest of the narrative. This applies especially to the proclamation of repentance for release of sins, but there is also continuity between specific aspects of John's preaching in 3:7–17 and the preaching of Jesus, as we have seen. Furthermore, the way in which John's mission is introduced is formally parallel to the way in which the narrator introduces the missions of Jesus, Peter and the apostles, and Paul. There is a sermon by each of these figures near the beginning of the story segment that will concentrate on his work, and this sermon either includes or is accompanied by a scriptural quotation which reveals the divine purpose behind the mission which is beginning. These scriptural quotations have significance beyond the scenes in which they appear. They provide clues to God's purpose as it is being realized through the entire missions of Jesus, the apostles, and Paul. Thus the quotation from Isaiah in 3:4–6 is matched by the Isaiah quotation which introduces Jesus' ministry in 4:18–19, the quotation from Joel in Peter's Pentecost sermon (Acts 2:17–21), and the quotation from Isa 49:6 which follows Paul's major speech in Antioch of Pisidia (Acts 13:47). Since the quotation in Luke 3:4–6 relates John's work of preparing the way to the revelation of God's salvation for all flesh, his work receives a place in the divine purpose which underlies the whole narrative of Luke-Acts.

The observations in the previous paragraph count against Hans Conzelmann's interpretation of John the Baptist in Luke. Conzelmann believes that Luke, by his editorial work, has placed John in the epoch of Israel, separating him from the period of Jesus.[12] Instead, we find that there are many links between John's mission and the mission that follows. The segmentation of the narrative also counts against this view. While there is a subordinate division at 3:21, where the narrative begins to focus on Jesus rather than John, the references there to baptism maintain continuity with the preceding section, which spoke of John's baptism. On the other hand, 3:1–2 marks a major new segment of the narrative. Rather than establishing continuity with the previous episode, the narrator introduces a new character performing a new activity in a new place and time. The major shift in time is marked by an elaborate dating. If the narrator had wished to make a distinct break between the periods of John and of Jesus, this could have been done by placing the dating at the beginning of

---

[12] See *The Theology of St. Luke*, 22–27.

Jesus' ministry rather than in its present position. As it is, the ministries of John and Jesus are presented as a continuous series of events that have their beginning with the coming of the word of God to John in the fifteenth year of the rule of Tiberius.[13]

The reference to the imprisonment of John in 3:19–20, which Luke alone introduces at this point, does round off the section on John in the Lukan narrative, although the break is not comparable to that created by 3:1–2. One effect of the rounding off is to give John greater importance as a prophetic figure in his own right, for his career is not simply used to introduce Jesus' baptism. The reference to John's imprisonment also suggests a further parallel between John and Jesus. Both will suffer as rejected prophets. Jesus' and the disciples' share in the fate of the rejected prophets will later be highlighted in a series of passages (Luke 4:24; 6:22–23; 11:49–51; 13:33–34; Acts 7:52). John's fate at the hands of Herod anticipates this emphasis. Thus the parallels between John and Jesus which characterize the birth narrative continue beyond Luke 2. The section on John's ministry begins with a rather lengthy scriptural quotation and ends with an arrest that will lead to death. Jesus' ministry will begin and end in the same way.

JESUS DISCOVERS HIS MISSION
(LUKE 2:41–52, 3:21–4:13)

Jesus first takes an active role in 2:41–52, the story of the boy Jesus in the temple. This scene foreshadows Jesus' future greatness, shows Jesus' developing awareness of his special relation to God and of the obligations which that entails, and is linked with following scenes in Luke 3–4 which together present Jesus, through prayer and struggle, arriving at a clear understanding of his mission and accepting it as the task which he must fulfill.

Charles Talbert compares Luke 1:5–4:15 with similar material in Greco-Roman biographies and comments,[14]

The biographical tradition used a combination of birth, family, and boyhood stories to give anticipations about the future life of the hero. . . . All of these components functioned also as prophecies of the character

---

[13] For further criticism of Conzelmann's view of John, see Walter Wink, *John the Baptist*, 46–57. Among other points, Wink notes that Luke describes John as "preaching good news (εὐηγγελίζετο)" (3:18). Wink argues that this verb has "the full force of its use elsewhere as the key term for describing the Christian message" (p. 53).

[14] See "Prophecies of Future Greatness," 137.

of the public career of the subject of the biography. If this was their purpose in the Greco-Roman biographies, then this is how a reader/ hearer of Luke would most probably have taken the material of a similar nature in Luke 1:5–4:15.

Virtually the totality of the material about Jesus in Luke 1:5–4:15 would have been regarded as an anticipation of his later public greatness. . . . [This material] would combine to foretell/foreshadow the type of person Jesus would be in his public ministry which began at Luke 4:16–30.

The scene of the boy Jesus in the temple anticipates Jesus' public ministry by presenting to the reader a twelve year old with precocious understanding of religious questions and with a developing sense of his own special destiny. His actions are controlled by his recognition that he "must be ἐν τοῖς τοῦ πατρός μου" (literally, "in the things of my Father"). The phrase is ambiguous, perhaps deliberately so. Jesus is reproaching his parents for not knowing where he would be, so the context suggests that this phrase refers to a place, "the house of my Father," which is a possible translation. But this need not exclude a second meaning, "(involved) in my Father's affairs," which is appropriate because it anticipates Jesus' entire mission, whether in Jerusalem or elsewhere.[15] The fact that his parents do not understand the saying (2:50) suggests such complexity of meaning[16] and also highlights the fact that Jesus is following a higher destiny, which will cause his life to conflict with the expectations and practises of ordinary life. Jesus already senses a divine purpose for his life which places him under obligation. This is indicated by the appearance in 2:49, for the first time in Luke, of the impersonal verb δεῖ ("it is necessary," "must"), which will be used repeatedly to refer to the divine purpose which Jesus must fulfill in his preaching and suffering (4:43; 9:22; 13:33; 17:25; 22:37; 24:7, 26, 44). The failure of Jesus' parents to understand what "must" be anticipates a similar failure of Jesus' disciples which will be emphasized later (9:22, 44–45; 17:25; 18:31–34; 24:25–26).[17]

Jesus' sense of special destiny and obligation is related to his recog-

---

[15] On the possible meanings of ἐν τοῖς τοῦ πατρός μου, see J. Fitzmyer, *Luke I–IX*, 443–44. See also Henk de Jonge, "Sonship, Wisdom, Infancy," 331–37, who argues that, while these words may refer to God's house, they are an unnatural expression if one wishes to refer *only* to the temple. He concludes that "Luke deliberately chose an enigmatic expression in order to profit from its ambivalence" (p. 333).

[16] See Heinz Schürmann, *Das Lukasevangelium,* 137: "The nonunderstanding of the parents characterizes Jesus' word as a secret word, which reaches into great depths."

[17] See Geoffrey F. Nuttall, *The Moment of Recognition,* 13–14.

nition of God as "my Father." Here we find Jesus recognizing and affirming that he is God's Son, as the angel said before his birth (1:32–35). There the title Son of God was associated with Jesus' future role as messianic king. That association will persist, as the equivalence between "Son of God" and "Messiah" in 4:41 (dif. Matthew, Mark) indicates. The titles "Son" and "Father," used of Jesus and God, also form a repeated theme which ties together scenes between the annunciation to Mary and Jesus' ministry in Capernaum. Some of these scenes present steps in Jesus' recognition and affirmation of his special relationship to God and the mission which it entails. What the angel prophesied to Mary, the boy Jesus has begun to recognize as he speaks to his parents in the temple. This is reaffirmed as God says directly to Jesus, "You are my Son," following his baptism (3:22). We are also reminded that Jesus is a descendant of Adam, the first Son of God, in the genealogy (3:23–38),[18] and the temptation scene involves a debate with the devil over what it means for Jesus to be Son of God (4:3, 9). After that conflict is settled, the people of Nazareth show their lack of understanding by speaking of Jesus as "son of Joseph" (4:22). But the demons see more clearly, and Jesus is confessed as Son of God as he begins his mature ministry (4:41). This concentration of references to Jesus as God's Son and to God as Father is not typical of all parts of Luke.[19] In this section of the narrative, the narrator shows a special interest in gradually disclosing what it means for Jesus to be Son of God.

It should also be noted that references to the Spirit connect 3:22 with 4:1, 14, 18, and that the general descriptions of Jesus as one on whom God's "grace" or "favor ($\chi\acute{\alpha}\rho\iota\varsigma$)" rests, and as advancing "in favor with God and humans" (2:40, 52), are demonstrated concretely by the "words of grace" which Jesus is able to utter in the Nazareth synagogue (4:22). These are further indications of the narrator's concern to form the series of scenes into a unified narrative.

It may seem doubtful that an ancient author would present one who is the Son of God as recognizing that relationship gradually through a process of development. However, the frame within which the narrator places the episode of the boy Jesus in the temple supports this interpretation. Summary statements about the growth of the child follow the birth

---

[18] While it may be significant to the narrator that Jesus' human genealogy includes David, Abraham, and Adam, the genealogy's importance is relativized at the beginning by the clause "being son, as was supposed, of Joseph" (3:23). The verb $\nu o\mu\acute{\iota}\zeta\omega$ ("think," "suppose") is almost always used in Luke-Acts of cases where there is contrast between the supposition and the truth. Acts 16:13 seems to be the only exception. Thus the narrator implies that Jesus is Son of God in a more direct sense than through descent from Adam.

[19] At the most, comparable concentrations occur in 9:26–11:13 and 22:29–24:49.

narratives of John and Jesus (1:80; 2:40). In Jesus' case, however, there is
a second refrain of growth (2:52) after the boy Jesus speaks in the temple
about his Father. In both cases there is reference to Jesus growing and
"being filled with wisdom" or "advancing in wisdom." In the temple the
boy Jesus demonstrates wisdom both in his dialogue with the teachers
(2:47)[20] and in his recognition of where he must be and what his main
concern must be as God's Son. The scene of the boy Jesus in the temple is
meant to be a demonstration of Jesus' growing wisdom and of the special
favor of God which rests upon him. That being so, we should note that the
second refrain of growth *follows* this scene. The boy's budding wisdom in
the temple is only a first step in a process of growth that continues
thereafter ("was advancing," a translation of a Greek imperfect, implies
continuous or repeated action). We should consider, then, whether some
of the following scenes which speak of Jesus as God's Son imply a
deepening understanding of the implications of this special position. In
2:49 Jesus only demonstrates that he recognizes God as his Father and
that this relationship determines what he must do and where he must be.
Perhaps there is more to be learned about the mission of God's Son.[21]

Jesus next appears in 3:21–22. This brief scene does not focus on Jesus'
baptism, which is mentioned only in a participle, but on the descent of the
Spirit upon Jesus and the voice from heaven to him. Furthermore, Luke,
unlike Matthew and Mark, indicates that these events took place while
Jesus was praying. In Luke-Acts times of prayer and worship are frequently the occasions for divine revelations to characters in the story. This
is true of Zechariah (Luke 1:9–11), Anna (2:37–38), Cornelius (Acts
10:2–6), Peter (10:9–16), Paul (9:11–12; 22:17–21), and the prophets and
teachers of the church in Antioch (13:2). This is true also of Jesus. Jesus'
choice of the twelve is preceded by prayer, indeed, prayer through the
whole night (dif. Matthew, Mark), in which Jesus is evidently seeking
divine guidance for the choice (6:12). The transfiguration also takes place
while Jesus is praying (dif. Matthew, Mark). Luke alone has the added
detail that Jesus was conversing with Moses and Elijah about Jesus'
"exodus, which he was going to fulfill in Jerusalem" (9:31). The specific
content of this conversation is conveyed neither to the disciples nor the
readers. We are left to assume that the communication was meant primarily for Jesus, who is receiving a revelation concerning the significance
of his divinely ordained way. In 22:40–46 also, if vv. 43–44 are an original

---

[20] The word σύνεσις is used in 2:47, while in 2:40, 52 we find σοφία. J. Fitzmyer points out,
however, that σοφία and σύνεσις are often used together in the LXX. See *Luke I–IX*, 442.

[21] For a partially similar view of the Lukan Jesus, asserting that the Evangelist depicts the
earthly life of Jesus "in developmental terms," see Charles Talbert, "The Way of the Lukan
Jesus," 237–49.

part of the text, Jesus prays concerning his mission and receives a response through a vision of a strengthening angel. Luke's description of the descent of the Spirit and the divine voice during prayer in 3:21-22 fits with these other scenes in which revelation and divine direction come during prayer and worship.[22]

While Jesus is praying, the Holy Spirit descends upon him. The narrator will carefully connect the following sequence of events to this descent of the Spirit. The descent of the Spirit has a narrative effect; it initiates a sequence of events. In the introduction to the temptations, the narrator not only tells us that Jesus was "full of Holy Spirit" but also that "he was being led by the Spirit in the wilderness" (4:1). After the temptations "Jesus returned in the power of the Spirit into Galilee" (4:14; dif. Matthew, Mark), and in the next scene he publicly announces that "the Spirit of the Lord is upon me" (4:18) in a statement which describes his mission (dif. Matthew, Mark). Thus the Holy Spirit is connected with each of the narrative segments between 3:22 and 4:18 (excluding the genealogy, which interrupts the narrative sequence) and is directly related to Jesus' mission. The Spirit is the divine power active in his mission. The temptations, too, can be understood as a result of the Spirit leading Jesus to mission, for the temptations involve a necessary struggle to clarify the meaning of this mission. This connection between the descent of the Spirit and the beginning of Jesus' mission parallels the course of events at the end of Luke and the beginning of Acts. The risen Jesus connects the beginning of the apostles' mission with the coming of the Spirit upon them (Luke 24:46-49; Acts 1:8), and the Pentecost scene shows that the coming of the Spirit leads immediately to the first preaching and expansion of the community. Thus in both Luke and Acts the descent of the Spirit initiates the central sequences of events which dominate these writings. The coming of the Spirit to Jesus following his baptism is a crucial beginning point in the narrative whose consequences unfold as Jesus' mission develops.

The descent of the Spirit is accompanied by the voice from heaven, "You are my beloved Son; in you I have taken pleasure" (Luke 3:22). Both Jesus and the readers are already aware that Jesus is God's Son, but this statement at this point still has importance. It is a statement in which God directly addresses Jesus, which makes it an especially strong affirmation of their unique relationship. Jesus' position as God's Son is also related to the descent of the Spirit, which means empowerment for mission, in this

---

[22] H. Conzelmann points to "the motif of Jesus at prayer" as an indication of Jesus' "subordinate position" in relation to God. See *The Theology of St. Luke*, 175. In other words, the frequent references to Jesus praying indicate that he must repeatedly turn to God for guidance as his mission unfolds.

scene. Being God's Son will have narrative consequences, for it entails a mission which must be fulfilled, as the following narrative makes clear. After struggling with a false understanding of what it means to be God's Son (4:1–13), Jesus announces the true understanding of his mission in the Nazareth synagogue in an explicit statement of what he has been sent to do (4:18–19). The Scripture quotation in 4:18–19 contains no reference to Son of God. This gap is filled by 4:41, where readers are reminded that the mission of teaching and healing in Capernaum is being performed by the Son of God/Messiah. The announcement in 4:18 does clearly refer to the scene in 3:22, however. Within the narrative sequence, the statement, "The Spirit of the Lord is upon me because he has anointed me," is a clear reference to the previous descent of the Spirit, and the rest of Jesus' announcement in Nazareth interprets that event as a call to a particular mission. We can understand 3:22 in the Lukan perspective only if we attend to the interpretation of this event as a call to the mission described in 4:18–19. Through 4:18–19 the descent of the Spirit and the divine declaration of sonship are understood as an anointing for the mission described in Isa 61:1–2, which thus becomes an important disclosure of what it means for Jesus to be God's Son. In the temptation scene, where we find explicit reference to Jesus as God's Son (4:3, 9), the devil introduces false understandings of Jesus' Sonship. In contrast, the announcement in the Nazareth synagogue reveals the true understanding.

In 4:18 the descent of the Spirit on Jesus is interpreted as an event in which God "anointed (ἔχρισεν)" Jesus. This feature is important to the narrator, for it is repeated in Acts 10:38, where Peter declares, "God anointed him with Holy Spirit and power." The narrator is also aware of the connection between anointing and the title χριστός ("Anointed One," "Messiah"), as the shift from this title to the description of Jesus as the one "whom you anointed (ἔχρισας)" in Acts 4:26–27 shows. These passages suggest that the anointing with Holy Spirit is to be understood as testimony to Jesus as the Messiah.[23] If this is so, 3:22 and 4:18 continue to focus on the fulfillment of the hope for the successor to David's throne, a hope that was strongly expressed in the birth narrative. In discussing this hope, we noted that there are a series of passages in Luke-Acts which suggest the close connection, or equivalence, of the titles "Son of God" and "Messiah," or connect Jesus' position as Son with kingship.[24] The probable connection between "you are my Son" in 3:22 and Ps 2:7, a psalm about Israel's king which in Acts is applied to Jesus as Messiah, the one

---

[23] On the expectation that the Messiah will receive the Spirit, see Erik Sjöberg and Eduard Schweizer, *TDNT* 6:384, 400.

[24] See above, pp. 25–26, 55.

who fulfills the promise of a successor to David (Acts 4:25–27; 13:23, 32–34), is further support for the messianic implications of Jesus' anointing with Holy Spirit. Thus Jesus' anointing with the Spirit and designation as God's Son can be understood as a stage in the establishment of Jesus' kingship in fulfillment of the messianic promise to Israel.

I have emphasized that Jesus' announcement of his mission in 4:18–19 is an interpretation of the descent of the Spirit in 3:22. We must assume, therefore, that this understanding of his mission arose sometime between the descent of the Spirit and Jesus' arrival in Nazareth. The only event narrated with any scenic detail between 3:22 and 4:16 is the temptation in the wilderness, and this scene is connected with 3:22 both by references to the Spirit and to Jesus' role as Son of God (4:1, 3, 9). The sequence of events suggests, then, that the clear understanding of his mission revealed in Nazareth is at least partly worked out through Jesus' struggles with the devil, who wishes to instill a false understanding of what it means to be the Son of God who is anointed with the Spirit.

Jesus is tempted by the devil to a false use of his power and a false understanding of his role. As we noted earlier, the narrator is not reluctant to speak of Jesus as growing in wisdom. The temptation scene is an occasion for growth in Jesus' understanding of his mission through struggle. It is linked to the Spirit anointing and divine recognition in 3:22, and the devil presents one interpretation of the meaning of that event. It precedes the announcement in Nazareth, which presents another interpretation of 3:22. The rejection of the first interpretation and the affirmation of the second marks the progress that Jesus has made in understanding his mission following his anointing with the Spirit.

The mission which Jesus claims in 4:18–19 can only be fulfilled when the devil's temptations are silenced. It is a mission in which Jesus' anointing with the Spirit is for the sake of the poor, the prisoners, the blind. But the devil tempts Jesus to use his Spirit-power[25] as Son of God to serve his own needs and self-centered desires by satisfying his own hunger, seeking complete protection from harm, and gaining ruling authority, even if bought at the price of false worship. The goal of authority over all the kingdoms of the world may not in itself be wrong, since Jesus will become "Lord of all" (Acts 10:36) and authority over the nations is promised to the messianic king (cf. Ps 2:8). But it matters greatly from whom this authority is received (Luke 4:6–8; contrast 22:29, where Jesus speaks of the "royal rule" which he has received from "my Father").

The order of the temptations in Luke differs from the parallel in

---

[25] The coming of the Spirit confers power. See 4:14.

Matthew, the suggestion that Jesus throw himself down from the temple being placed last. This temptation may come last because it most closely resembles the renewed period of intense temptation in the passion story. The setting of the last temptation is Jerusalem, and it concerns using God as a guarantee of rescue from death. The one with divine Spirit-power is tempted to use that power to make himself invulnerable. Leaping from a pinnacle of the temple would demonstrate such invulnerability in an extreme situation. This temptation returns through human tempters at the crucifixion, for Jesus is repeatedly challenged to "save" himself (23:35, 37, 39). These tempters, like the devil in 4:3, 9, base their temptations on the power which Jesus should have as Messiah, using an "if" clause (23:35, 37).[26] But Jesus overcomes this temptation, allowing God to work through his death rather than attempting to bend God's will for personal rescue. The concluding remark of the temptation scene, which indicates that "the devil withdrew from him until an opportune time" (4:13), need not point exclusively to the passion. At the Last Supper Jesus looks back on his past ministry as the time of "my trials" or "temptations" (22:28). But the passion is peculiarly the time of Satan's activity (22:3, 31, 53).

In the temptation scene Jesus' dedication to God's purpose, rather than his own desires, is tested. The successful outcome of this test requires the rejection of one understanding of what it means to be the Son of God anointed with the Spirit and the acceptance of another understanding. Through this process Jesus is prepared to begin his ministry.

Jesus Announces His Mission
(Luke 4:14–21)

Luke 4:14–44 is a major narrative segment, bound together by the framing summaries of Jesus' teaching and preaching in 4:14–15 and 4:44 and by the reminder of 4:18 in 4:43. This arrangement encourages comparison between Jesus in Nazareth and in Capernaum. I will discuss the relation between 4:14–30 and 4:31–44 later,[27] while concentrating at present on 4:14–30.

In 4:15 the narrator reports a repeated activity which stretches over some time: "He was teaching in their synagogues" (imperfect tense in Greek). The temporal relationship between this summary remark and the following scene in Nazareth is unclear. The reader can either assume that

---

[26] Frederick Danker notes that the mockery on the cross is "a temptation akin to the type expressed in 4:1–13." See *Luke,* 38, 40.

[27] See below, pp. 82–83.

the announcement in Nazareth is a new departure or that Jesus has been saying such things for some time, although the narrator chooses to omit or postpone such material in order to focus on Nazareth. In either case, the Nazareth episode has been highlighted as the first episode reported with scenic detail in Jesus' public ministry (dif. Matthew, Mark). Its importance is further indicated by the general statement about Jesus' mission which it contains and the dramatic conflict which results. This scene becomes the primary illustration of what Jesus was saying when teaching in the synagogues, it interprets his ministry as a whole, and it anticipates his later rejection. That Jesus' teaching in the synagogues continues to reflect the announcement made in Nazareth is indicated by 4:43–44, which deliberately picks up the wording of this announcement in describing his continuing preaching (dif. Mark). As audience reaction to Jesus' teaching is very favorable according to the summary in 4:15, so the initial reaction to Jesus' teaching is positive in Nazareth (4:22). But then there is a drastic change.

I previously stated that important clues to what is central in the narrative, giving it continuity, can be found in four types of material: major Old Testament quotations, statements of the commission which an important character has received from God, previews and reviews of the course of the narrative, and disclosures of God's purpose by characters presented as reliable.[28] The quotation from Isaiah which Jesus reads in the Nazareth synagogue fits all four of these categories. As Scripture, it is viewed as testimony to God's purpose. As a statement by Jesus, it comes from the human character of highest authority within the narrative. It is a statement of what the Lord has sent Jesus to do, i.e., a statement of Jesus' commission, which should lead us to expect that it is also a preview of what Jesus will in fact be doing in the following narrative.

There are some uncertainties about the syntax and structure of this poetic quotation. H. J. B. Combrink detects a chiastic structure, which begins with "to preach good news" and continues through the rest of the quotation.[29] However, the chiastic relation between the lines which refer to "release ($\overset{\text{'}}{\alpha}\phi\epsilon\sigma\iota\varsigma$)"[30] is clearer than the relation between the lines which precede and follow them. Perhaps we should emphasize instead that certain words and grammatical forms are repeated with a rhythmic effect at the beginning and end of short phrases. "Me" ($\dot{\epsilon}\mu\dot{\epsilon}$ or $\mu\epsilon$) occurs three times in the first half of the quotation. Later "release" occurs twice, and there is a series of four infinitives, three of them referring to preaching.

---

[28] See above, pp. 21–22.
[29] See "The Structure and Significance of Luke 4:16–30," 29, 31.
[30] The RSV translates this word as "liberty" in its second occurrence in 4:18.

These repetitions mark rhythmic phrases which correspond to short poetic lines, for the repetitions indicate that something which has already been said is being picked up and repeated but also enriched and expanded through new expression. Thus there is a pulsating series of overlapping phrases which poetically develop a single thought. This can be clarified visually by arranging the text as follows:[31]

> Spirit of the Lord is upon me,
>> Because he anointed me;
> To preach good news to the poor he has sent me,
>> To proclaim to the captives release
>>> And to the blind new sight,
>> To send forth the broken in release,
>> To proclaim the Lord's acceptable year.

The last five lines depend on a single main verb ("has sent"), which binds them closely together.[32] They are closely related in form and meaning. Four of the five lines begin with infinitives[33] which describe the nature of Jesus' mission. The overlapping phrases emphasize a mission of preaching or proclaiming which has "release" as its goal. The repeated "me" in the first three lines relates this mission emphatically and specifically to the speaker.

The quotation from Isaiah is a public disclosure of Jesus' commission from God which functions as a guide to the reader in understanding the following story of Jesus' ministry. If this is so, the ways in which Jesus and his ministry are described in other parts of Luke-Acts should fit this disclosure. The full extent to which central themes in the Lukan portrait of Jesus are embedded in this quotation will only become clear later, when we are able to trace some of these themes through the gospel as a whole.[34] However, an initial discussion of the connections between this quotation and the Lukan narrative must be given here.

We have already seen that the narrator carefully constructs a bridge between the descent of the Spirit in 3:22 and the opening statement in 4:18 ("Spirit of the Lord is upon me"), for there are repeated references to the Spirit at the beginning of narrative segments that lead up to the Nazareth scene (4:1, 14). While references to the Holy Spirit are less frequent in the

---

[31] It is well to keep in mind that we are dealing primarily with an *oral* phenomenon. The breaks between small sense units become the natural places for a speaker to pause when reciting. These breaks are suggested by syntax but also by patterns of repetition which convey emphasis.

[32] Luke 4:43 supports the view that "to preach good news," like the following infinitives, depends on "he has sent." This is noted by H. Schürmann, *Das Lukasevangelium,* 230.

[33] "And to the blind new sight" presupposes, of course, the infinitive in the previous line.

[34] See especially pp. 77–85, 103–9, 127–32.

rest of the gospel, the renewed emphasis on the Spirit in Acts (a gift mediated through Jesus according to Acts 2:33) shows its continuing importance. Furthermore, summaries of Jesus' ministry in the Acts sermons continue to emphasize that God "anointed" Jesus "with Holy Spirit" (Acts 10:38), or, as alternatives, that "God was with him" or was acting through him (Acts 2:22; 10:38). Indeed, Jesus provides the model for the Spirit-inspired preachers and healers of Acts.

We have also noted that the narrator recognizes the connection between being "anointed" and being the "Anointed One," the royal Messiah.[35] This need not exclude the idea that Jesus, anointed with the Spirit, is a prophet, for 4:24–27 will bring out his prophetic role. However, it speaks against Joseph Fitzmyer's view that the anointing in this passage is a prophetic and not a royal anointing.[36] This interpretation would isolate the text from the preceding references to Jesus as Davidic Messiah and Son of God (a title with messianic associations in Luke-Acts). As I previously indicated, 4:18–19 functions as a disclosure of what it means for Jesus to be Son of God, for it refers back to the moment when the Spirit descends on him and the divine voice declares him to be God's Son (3:22). Furthermore, at his birth Jesus was declared to be Son of God who will reign over the house of Jacob, and his birth was initiated by the Holy Spirit (1:32–35). The previous connections established between the Spirit and Jesus' role as Son and king should not be forgotten when we interpret the significance for Luke of Jesus' anointing with the Spirit.[37] We should also note that the "Lord's acceptable year" which Jesus is sent to proclaim is closely connected with the "reign ($\beta\alpha\sigma\iota\lambda\epsilon\iota\alpha$) of God" (see 4:43) within which Jesus has been granted royal authority by his Father (22:29–30).

Jesus announces that he has been sent "to preach good news" and "to proclaim." This fits the description of Jesus' ministry in the following narrative, for, as will be detailed below,[38] the verb "preach good news ($\epsilon\dot{\nu}\alpha\gamma\gamma\epsilon\lambda\dot{\iota}\zeta o\mu\alpha\iota$)" is used repeatedly in summaries of Jesus' activity (dif. Matthew, Mark) and the verb "proclaim ($\kappa\eta\rho\dot{\nu}\sigma\sigma\omega$)" will reappear as its synonym. These later summaries indicate that Jesus is continually doing what he was sent to do, according to his declaration in the Nazareth synagogue. The quotation lists a series of groups to whom this good news or proclamation is directed. The language is from Isaiah, and some words are not used again in Luke-Acts. Nevertheless, later description of Jesus' ministry gives us some idea of how this commission is fulfilled.

---

[35] See above, p. 58.
[36] See *Luke I–IX*, 529–30.
[37] These connections correspond to Jewish expectations that the Messiah will possess the Spirit. See E. Sjöberg, *TDNT* 6:384.
[38] See below, pp. 77–82.

Jesus has been sent to preach good news to the poor. In the following lines of the quotation, the words "captives," "blind," and "broken" probably have some metaphorical range. They are not restricted to their literal sense (although they may include people who cannot see physically, etc.). "Poor" may also have such metaphorical range. However, it has first of all a concrete application to people without economic resources, for these people receive special attention elsewhere in Luke. The description of Jesus' message as good news to the poor fits into a larger picture, for Jesus is fulfilling the purpose of a God who is especially concerned with helping the poor and hungry. The good news is an eschatological promise to the poor, but it is accompanied by an ethical challenge to those with resources, asking them to share now with the poor in order to relieve their situation. These themes have already been sounded before Jesus' announcement in Nazareth. Mary declared God's intervention for the hungry in the Magnificat (1:52–53). John the Baptist made clear that preparation for the time of salvation requires sharing with those in need (3:10–11). In the Nazareth synagogue Jesus begins to spread the good news for the poor and to expand John's challenge to respond to what God is doing on behalf of the poor. At the beginning of the sermon in Luke 6, Jesus preaches good news to the poor through the beatitudes for the poor and hungry (6:20–21). These beatitudes apply to the disciples, as well as other poor people,[39] because the disciples have voluntarily made themselves poor by "leaving all" and following Jesus (5:11, 28; 18:28–30). The good news to the poor applies both to those who had no choice and to those who have chosen poverty by leaving home and livelihood or by responding to Jesus' command to "sell your goods and give charity" (12:33).

In 7:22 Jesus, summarizing his ministry for John the Baptist, declares that "the poor have good news preached to them," repeating words of Isaiah quoted in Luke 4:18. In 7:22 the poor are listed beside the blind, lame, and others being healed by Jesus. Jesus' work of healing is part of his good news to the poor, since disabled persons would generally be poor beggars in the ancient world. In the parable of the great banquet, the poor are again listed with the blind and lame (as well as the crippled). These people, surprisingly, end up at the dinner party in the parable; they are also the people who should be invited by the rich when they give dinner parties (14:13, 21). The parable of the great banquet reflects on what is happening in Jesus' ministry, where the poor are receiving the surprising good news of an invitation to God's banquet. Thus Jesus' announcement in Nazareth that he has been sent to preach good news to the poor both

---

[39] On the addressees of the beatitudes, see pp. 206–8.

picks up a theme from the earlier chapters of Luke and prepares for an important aspect of Jesus' following ministry.[40]

Jesus has also been sent to bring "release ($\overset{\text{v}}{\alpha}\phi\epsilon\sigma\iota\varsigma$)" to the "captives" and the "broken." The importance of the proclamation and realization of release is indicated by the double use of this word. Indeed, the line in which "release" is used for the second time is found in Isa 58:6, not Isa 61:1–2, the source of the rest of the quotation, and its insertion is best explained by the desire to reemphasize this word "release."[41] In seeking to understand its meaning in the context of Luke-Acts, we need to keep the following factors in mind:

(1) It occurs here right after the reference to good news to the poor, and the successive lines may be partially synonymous. This would suggest that the captives would include those economically oppressed, those enslaved because of debts, etc.

(2) Various sorts of physical and mental disorders are understood to be caused by demonic possession, which in certain passages is described as bondage to Satan. Thus in a summary of Jesus' ministry which clearly recalls Luke 4:18–19, Peter speaks of Jesus "healing all those oppressed ($\kappa\alpha\tau\alpha\delta\upsilon\nu\alpha\sigma\tau\epsilon\upsilon o\mu\acute{\epsilon}\nu o\upsilon\varsigma$) by the devil" (Acts 10:38), and Jesus describes a crippled woman as one "whom Satan bound" (Luke 13:16). Indeed, the images of bondage and release are central to the healing story in 13:10–17. Jesus declares that the woman must "be released from this bond" of Satan (13:16), and there are further references to release in 13:12, 15 (using $\grave{\alpha}\pi o\lambda\acute{\upsilon}\omega$ or $\lambda\acute{\upsilon}\omega\;\grave{\alpha}\pi\acute{o}$). The argument from analogy in 13:15 refers to the release of animals which are tied in place, differing in this respect from the similar arguments in Sabbath controversies in Matt 12:11 and Luke 14:5. Since the woman was held in Satan's bondage, the relevant analogy is the loosing of a tied animal, not raising one that has fallen into a well. This story develops with some clarity the manner of thinking behind the brief references to those "oppressed by the devil" (Acts 10:38) and the "prisoners" (Luke 4:18), to whom Jesus brings release. It is probably significant, then, that there is considerable emphasis on Jesus' triumph over demons when he leaves Nazareth and goes to Capernaum, where a woman is also released from a fever.[42] Jesus' healings and exorcisms are an important aspect of his mission of bringing "release."

(3) The word $\overset{\text{v}}{\alpha}\phi\epsilon\sigma\iota\varsigma$ appears elsewhere in Luke-Acts only in the phrase $\overset{\text{v}}{\alpha}\phi\epsilon\sigma\iota\varsigma\;(\tau\hat{\omega}\nu)\;\grave{\alpha}\mu\alpha\rho\tau\iota\hat{\omega}\nu$ ("release of sins," but usually translated

---

[40] On the poor and the rich in Luke, see further pp. 127–32.

[41] The catchword connection is present in the LXX but not in the Hebrew. On the significance of this insertion from Isa 58:6, see further Robert C. Tannehill, "The Mission of Jesus," 66, 70–71.

[42] See below, pp. 83–85.

"forgiveness of sins"). This phrase appears in passages of clear theological importance, the speeches in Acts (2:38; 5:31; 10:43; 13:38; 26:18) and the mission charge at the end of Luke (24:47). The release of sins is important not only in the ministry of John the Baptist (Luke 1:77; 3:3) and of Jesus' witnesses but also in the ministry of Jesus himself. This will become especially clear when we see that the narrator gives the episodes of the healing of the paralytic and the meal with tax collectors and sinners (5:17–32) special importance. These two scenes, which occur early in the story of Jesus' ministry and emphasize his mission of releasing sins and calling sinners, are repeatedly recalled by a system of echoes in later episodes, resulting in an interconnected series of scenes highlighting this important aspect of Jesus' ministry.[43] Moreover, the idea of bondage to evil or to Satan occurs in contexts that concern repentance and forgiveness as well as demonic possession. Note the reference to the "bond of iniquity ($\sigma\acute{v}\nu\delta\epsilon\sigma\mu o\nu$ $\mathring{a}\delta\iota\kappa\acute{\iota}as$)" in Acts 8:22–23 and the reference to the "authority of Satan" in Acts 26:18. The former phrase is found in Isa 58:6, a verse which is the source of part of Luke 4:18.[44]

When Jesus speaks of new sight for the blind, he may be referring, in part, to his work of healing. This sense is supported by the reference to the blind receiving their sight as the first of a list of Jesus' healing activities in his reply to John the Baptist (7:22). As a physical ailment, blindness need have no special importance; one type of physical problem can stand for all. However, seeing and light also function metaphorically in Luke-Acts, and Isaiah is an important source of these metaphors. Sharon Ringe has noted that Isa 61:1–2 is connected with a series of other passages in Isaiah, with the granting of light or sight to the blind as one of the connecting themes.[45] Some of these other passages have also influenced Luke-Acts, and it is likely that they would affect the author's understanding of what it means for Jesus to be sent to give sight to the blind. The command to "send forth the broken in release" in Isa 58:6 is followed by the promise of light rising in the darkness (Isa 58:8, 10).[46] The reference to "a light of the nations" and "salvation to the end of the earth" in Isa 49:6 is quoted in Acts 13:47 (cf. 1:8), but "a light of the nations" is also mentioned in Isa 42:6–7, where it is followed by a reference to opening the eyes of the blind: "I have given you for a covenant of the people, for a light of the nations, to open eyes of

---

[43] See below, pp. 103–9.

[44] Noted by Robert B. Sloan, Jr., *The Favorable Year of the Lord,* 119–20.

[45] Sharon H. Ringe, *The Jubilee Proclamation,* 61–69. See also James A. Sanders, "From Isaiah 61 to Luke 4," 80–83. Sanders regards Isaiah 61 as a midrash on Leviticus 25 and traditions in Second Isaiah.

[46] Cp. $\tau\acute{o}\tau\epsilon$ $\mathring{a}\nu\alpha\tau\epsilon\lambda\epsilon\hat{\iota}$ $\mathring{\epsilon}\nu$ $\tau\hat{\omega}$ $\sigma\kappa\acute{o}\tau\epsilon\iota$ $\tau\grave{o}$ $\phi\hat{\omega}s$ σov (Isa 58:10) with Luke 1:78–79.

the blind (ἀνοῖξαι ὀφθαλμοὺς τυφλῶν), to lead out those bound from their bonds and from a house of prison those sitting in darkness."[47]

It appears that interrelated passages from Isaiah function as a group in expressing for the narrator of Luke-Acts the divine promise which is being realized through Jesus and his witnesses. In these passages opening the eyes of the blind is related to "a light of the nations," and it is clear that this promise of light plays an important role in Luke-Acts (Luke 2:32; Acts 13:47). Within the context of Luke-Acts, then, the reference to sight for the blind in Luke 4:18 can also suggest the perception of divine revelation and salvation, merging into the theme of light and seeing developed on the basis of Isaiah in Luke 1:78-79, 2:30-32, and 3:6. The importance of these themes is confirmed when they return in Paul's last major speech, which contains a retrospective summary of his mission. There the risen Christ is described as the one who "is about to proclaim light both to the people and to the nations" (Acts 26:23), and Paul's own mission is described in terms of bringing the people and the nations to the light (26:18). More strikingly, Paul summarizes his mission in words that seem to paraphrase Jesus' description of his mission in Luke 4:18. In Acts 26:17-18 Paul presents his commission from the risen Christ in these terms: ". . . the people and the nations, to whom I send you [cf. Luke 4:18: "He has sent me"] to open their eyes, [cf. Luke 4:18: "to proclaim . . . to the blind new sight"] so as to turn from darkness to light and from the authority of Satan [cf. the "prisoners" who need "release" in Luke 4:18] to God, so that they might receive release of sins" (cf. "release" in Luke 4:18). Here the reference to opening eyes is connected with turning from darkness to light, from the authority of Satan to God, and so clearly is not limited to enabling blind people to see physical objects. Rather, it is equivalent to revealing God's salvation to the world, as in Luke 3:6 (=Isa 40:5).

Finally, Jesus has been sent "to proclaim the Lord's acceptable year," that is, the time of salvation characterized by good news for the poor, release for captives, sight for the blind. Sharon Ringe and Robert Sloan have discussed the connection between Isa 61:1-2 and the law of the Jubilee year in Leviticus 25, as well as the significance of Jubilee themes for Jesus and Luke.[48] In Leviticus the Jubilee year is the "year of release" (ἐνιαυτὸς ἀφέσεως—Lev 25:10), a time of release and return of family property which has been sold and release of Israelites who have become indentured servants. Deuteronomy 15 also commands the release of debts

---

[47] With "light of the nations" see also Luke 2:32. With "those sitting in darkness" see Luke 1:79.

[48] See Sharon Ringe, *The Jubilee Proclamation*; Ringe, *Jesus, Liberation, and the Biblical Jubilee*; Robert Sloan, *The Favorable Year of the Lord*.

every seven years. While it seems clear that Isa 61:1-2 develops themes from the Jubilee year, it is not so clear that the author of Luke-Acts was aware of the connection between this passage and the law of Jubilee. This remains a possibility but has not yet been proved.[49] This is not to deny that the social concern expressed in the Jubilee law is also present in Luke, for the "good news to the poor" does reflect a concern for economic justice, as Jesus' later teaching will make clear.[50]

Some other possible connections of "the Lord's acceptable year" should be noted. In 4:43 Jesus states that he has been "sent" to "preach good news of the reign of God," repeating two key verbs from the quotation in 4:18 but adding that the good news concerns "God's reign" or "kingdom." This verse integrates the mission of Jesus as presented in 4:18-19 with his later preaching of God's reign and suggests that the two ways of describing the contents of Jesus' preaching—"the Lord's acceptable year" and "God's reign"—are closely related, if not synonymous. It may also be significant that the narrative later refers to the time of Jesus' encounter with his hearers as the "time of your visitation" (19:44; see also the emphasis on "this time" in 12:56). This is a time of special opportunity but also of fateful decision. Within Luke-Acts "the Lord's acceptable year" may refer to this same special time.

THE CONFLICT WITH THE NAZARENES
(LUKE 4:22–30)

When Jesus claims that Isa 61:1-2 is fulfilled "today" because it is a description of his own mission, the initial reaction of the people of Nazareth is favorable.[51] Their question, "Is this not Joseph's son?" does reveal their limited understanding of Jesus, for prior to this the readers of Luke have been repeatedly told that Jesus is *God's* Son, and when the genealogy was introduced, it began with the significant qualification "being son, as was supposed, of Joseph" (3:23). This question is part of their wonderment and shows that the Nazarenes do not really grasp Jesus' importance, but it does not indicate hostility.[52] Therefore, there

---

[49] R. Sloan asserts that "it is . . . not merely the very important Is. 61 that finds programmatic expression in Luke's gospel, but it is primarily the notion of *jubilee*" (emphasis by Sloan). See *The Favorable Year of the Lord*, 146. However, he has failed to prove his case, too quickly assuming that Luke would recognize the "jubilary" connections of the themes being used and that the connection with the law of Jubilee remained significant for him.

[50] See below, pp. 127-32, 207-8.

[51] Joachim Jeremias, to be sure, has argued that 4:22 expresses an unfavorable reaction. See *Jesus' Promise to the Nations*, 44-45. Against Jeremias' view see R. Tannehill, "The Mission of Jesus," 53-54.

[52] Fearghus Ó Fearghail agrees that "they were bearing witness" indicates a positive reaction

seems to be no cause in their words or expressed attitudes for Jesus' harsh words which follow. Jesus, after voicing the "words of grace" from Isaiah, seems to be remarkably ungracious in his response to the Nazarenes, and this response appears to be unmotivated.

This surprising turn is functional if the narrative is suggesting that Jesus' response is not the normal human response to what his people have been saying but a response to hidden factors apparent only to those endowed by the Spirit with prophetic insight. There are similar cases in Luke-Acts: Simeon, in the Spirit, recognizes the truth about the baby Jesus (2:27–32), while Paul, filled with Holy Spirit, recognizes Elymas as a "son of the devil" (Acts 13:9–10). We can also say that the scene in Nazareth is an example of "thoughts of many hearts" being "revealed," as Simeon prophesied (Luke 2:35). Simeon's words are not a passing remark in Luke, for, as I showed above,[53] Jesus repeatedly recognizes and reveals the thoughts of others' hearts in concrete situations (5:21–22; 6:8; 9:46–47; 24:38). The scene in Nazareth appears to be an additional case.[54]

Hidden in the hearts of his townsfolk are attitudes of which they, perhaps, are not yet conscious: resistance to God's purpose combined with jealous possessiveness. When they come to understand more fully the nature of Jesus' mission, he will not be acceptable to them. The present case will follow the general rule: "No prophet is acceptable in his homeland" (4:24). Prophets are directed by a different voice than the voices of neighbors, and they see in their neighbors things which people wish to hide. Prophets' missions are not controlled by the desires of relatives and chums. The mission which Jesus begins will turn to the excluded and the strangers in a widening circle. This will provoke the jealousy of the homefolk, whose concerns are centered on themselves, not on the vision of salvation for all flesh.

Jesus' sharp response to the Nazarenes, who were so favorably impressed with his statement of his mission, may still seem strange. If so, a comparison with the presentation of John's preaching in 3:7–9 may be helpful. We have already noted that the missions of both John and Jesus

---

to Jesus (a reaction based on their past acquaintance with him) but interprets the rest of the verse as astonishment, coupled with criticism and rejection, at the message just delivered. See "Rejection in Nazareth," 60–72. However, too much is forced from the remark about Joseph's son when it is understood not only as a sign of inadequate understanding but also a sign of rejection. In light of v. 23, it can even be understood as excited anticipation that Nazareth is about to reap the benefits of being close to a hometown boy who makes good. Ó Fearghail believes that only a negative reaction in v. 22 can explain Jesus' harsh words that follow. I am about to offer a different explanation.

[53] See pp. 43–44.

[54] There need be nothing miraculous about this case, since Jesus has known the people of his hometown for a long time, but the narrator does assume that Jesus is a person of insight who can accurately predict their attitudes before they have been openly expressed.

are introduced by extensive quotations from Isaiah. There are further similarities in what follows these quotations. The response of the people to both of these prophets is favorable. In John's case, this is shown by the fact that crowds come out to be baptized (3:7). But John greets them with scorching words: "offspring of vipers!" John does not confuse superficial religion with real repentance, and Jesus does not confuse wondering admiration with openness to his mission. Jesus abruptly rejects a claim to benefits on the basis of sharing a common "fatherland ($\pi\alpha\tau\rho\acute{\iota}s$)." John just as roughly rejects any claim on God based on the assertion that "we have Abraham as father ($\pi\alpha\tau\acute{\epsilon}\rho\alpha$)."

The relation between the statements in 4:23 and 24 is ambiguous and probably complex. First, v. 23 indicates that the Nazarenes expect Jesus to perform healings in his hometown, and v. 24 indicates that this will not be the case. Verse 24 also suggests a reason for this lack of healings: he will not be able to work in Nazareth because he will be rejected there. This fits the course of the story. Jesus is rejected in Nazareth, and this appears to be a permanent break, for there is no indication that he returns later. However, a second thought may also be implied: v. 23 indicates that the Nazarenes feel slighted,[55] especially in comparison with Capernaum, and think Jesus should concentrate more on his old neighbors. Jesus may announce that he is unacceptable at home because he knows that he cannot accommodate the jealous possessiveness which is indicated by v. 23 and underscored by the angry reaction to vv. 25–27. Serving this jealous possessiveness would conflict with serving the God who intends to reveal salvation for all flesh. From this perspective, the jealous attitude expressed in v. 23 is part of the reason for the conflict between prophet and hometown expressed in v. 24. Thus the conflict between prophet and homeland which first surfaces in v. 24 may be understood as the result of Jesus' resistance to the false desires expressed in v. 23, but this conflict also leads to the final frustration of those desires as the benefits that the Nazarenes·might have received from Jesus are lost, because they react with anger and try to kill him.

The reference to prophets who benefit Gentiles rather than Jews in vv. 25–27 may seem out of place at this point in the story. However, the narrator evidently did not think so, which suggests that it can be understood on two levels. On the one hand, Elijah and Elisha provide extreme examples of prophets who do not fulfill the desires of those wanting healing for their own homeland. They even healed Gentiles instead of Israelites. Their examples support rejection of the request in v. 23. Elijah,

---

[55] Or will feel slighted, if the future form $\acute{\epsilon}\rho\epsilon\hat{\iota}\tau\epsilon$ ("you will say") refers to their attitude at a later point in the story. In that case, Jesus is responding to a tendency that is still latent.

at least, may also be an example of a prophet not acceptable in his homeland, since the Elijah narrative is dominated by this prophet's conflict with the king and queen of Israel and by a sense of widespread apostasy among the people (see Elijah's despair in 1 Kgs 19:10, mitigated somewhat by 19:18). Thus Elijah and Elisha provide scriptural witness to the inevitable conflict between God's purpose and the human desire to make special claims to God's salvation or place limits on its scope. These scriptural examples demonstrate God's independence—and therefore the prophet's independence—of these claims and limits, correcting the attitudes in Nazareth uncovered by Jesus' remark in v. 23. The angry reaction of the people in the synagogue indicates that Jesus has struck a tender spot in the self-image of this group.

On the other hand, the emphasis on Elijah and Elisha's ministry among Gentiles rather than Jews foreshadows the development of the Gentile mission in Acts. In this context, the reference to Gentiles has special significance; it indicates a major group toward which the mission is moving. This reference is not out of place when we view the scene from the larger Lukan perspective. We have already been told that God's saving purpose includes the Gentiles (2:30–32; 3:6), and the rejection at Nazareth begins a geographical movement which will include a number of rejections and turnings to new groups and areas. In Acts, Gentiles are repeatedly the beneficiaries of these turns in the mission. Thus Nazareth and the Gentile mission in Acts are the beginning and maturing of one development marked by events of similar character: when the prophetic witnesses are not accepted, they turn to a new group or area, and the mission moves forward in spite of rejection.[56] The inclusion of a contrast between Gentiles and Jews in a series of remarks that begins with a contrast between Nazareth and Capernaum is eased by the ambiguity of the term πατρίς ("fatherland," "homeland"—4:23, 24), which can refer either to Jesus' hometown or to the homeland of the Jewish people.

At the point in Acts where the mission begins to spread to the Gentiles, the Nazareth scene is recalled (Acts 10:36–38; note especially the reference to Jesus being anointed with Holy Spirit). This connection supports the view that the ministry to Gentiles in Luke 4:25–27 is more than a good example of prophetic independence. Furthermore, Acts 10:34–35 borrows a key word of Luke 4:19, 24 to proclaim the acceptance of Gentiles. In Nazareth Jesus announces "the Lord's acceptable (δεκτόν) year," but, in an ironic reversal of the harmony that this seems to imply,

---

[56] See R. Tannehill, "The Mission of Jesus," 62–63. With the Nazareth scene compare especially Acts 13:14–52, where the rejection and turning is preceded by a speech in a synagogue setting similar to the Nazareth setting.

also declares that he will not be "acceptable (δεκτός)" to the people of his homeland. The only other use of this adjective in Luke-Acts is in Acts 10:35, at the beginning of the speech which contains further references to the Nazareth scene. There the circle of those "acceptable" to God is declared to include people "in every nation." At this point the relevance of God's word "sent to the sons of Israel" through Jesus is being deliberately enlarged. The proclamation of "the Lord's acceptable year" is now to be understood as a proclamation to people of every nation. This is preceded by the assertion that God is not a προσωπολήμπτης, i.e., one who plays favorites or shows partiality to certain individuals or groups. Because God refuses to treat people in this way, Jesus must resist the people in his own homeland who are jealous of attention to outsiders and feel that his saving work should be directed especially toward them.

Luke 4:25–27 has a further function in the narrative. Elijah and Elisha are scriptural models for Jesus' healing ministry. Jesus' raising of the widow's son in 7:11–17 clearly recalls Elijah's raising of a widow's son,[57] and Larrimore Crockett believes that the healing performed for a foreign officer in 7:1–10 parallels Elisha's healing of Naaman. These are the two incidents mentioned by Jesus in 4:25–27. Indeed, there may be a whole series of parallels between 4:14–30 and 7:2–23, for the two mighty acts at the beginning of chapter 7 are followed by Jesus' answer to John the Baptist, which again relates Jesus' ministry to Isaiah 61 and ends with a warning against taking offense at him (as the Nazarenes did).[58] The narrator is apparently interested in Jesus as a prophet on the model of Elijah-Elisha both because he is a great miracle-working prophet (see 7:16) and because of the ministry to outsiders suggested by the incidents cited in 4:25–27.

The angry reaction of the people shows the truth of Jesus' statement in 4:24: now that they have been reminded of the way that prophets behave, Jesus is indeed unacceptable to them. In other situations also, a prediction or warning of rejection precedes the actual rejection, showing the speaker's insight into human tendencies (see Acts 3:23 with 4:1–3; 13:40–41 with 13:44–46). The attempt of the angry Nazarenes to kill Jesus fails, for Jesus simply passes through their midst and goes his way. This is mysterious. There is no indication of how Jesus could escape a crowd that

---

[57] See below, pp. 87–88.
[58] See Larrimore Crockett, *The Old Testament in the Gospel of Luke*, 138–40. See also Crockett, "Luke 4:25–27 and Jewish-Gentile Relations," 181–82. However, I am not convinced by Crockett's assertion that 4:25–27 is "a prolepsis . . . of Jewish-gentile *reconciliation*" ("Luke 4:25–27 and Jewish-Gentile Relations," 183, Crockett's emphasis). This ignores the strong negative tone of these verses: "Many widows . . . in Israel, and to none of them was Elijah sent. . . ."

was intent on his death. The narrator is content to let the readers wonder about this. This mysterious event may convey the impression that a purpose is at work here which will not be blocked by human resistance.[59] The statement that "they threw him out of the city" foreshadows later situations in which a group either attempts to kill or succeeds in killing one of the prophetic preachers in Luke-Acts. Anticipating his own death, Jesus tells of the tenants' treatment of the beloved son of the vineyard owner: "Throwing him out of the vineyard, they killed him" (Luke 20:15). The report of Stephen's death is similar: "Throwing him out of the city, they were stoning him" (Acts 7:58). See also Acts 14:19: "Having stoned Paul, they were dragging him out of the city, supposing him to be dead." As the repeated image of throwing or dragging shows, killing is part of violent removal, forceful separation from the place of mission by people who regard the prophet as an abomination.

Thus in the first scene in the narrative of Jesus' mission, Jesus announces "words of grace" but encounters the violent rejection which prophets can expect in their homeland. The good news which Jesus preaches is already shadowed by a conflict that will persist to the end of Acts.

As we study Jesus' ministry in Luke, we will notice specific reminders that Jesus is fulfilling the commission announced in the Nazareth synagogue. The story of Jesus develops as Jesus interacts with various groups. The following chapters will focus on characteristic features of Jesus' mission which emerge through these interactions and on significant developments in Jesus' relationships with these groups.

---

[59] H. Schürmann, *Das Lukasevangelium*, 240, suggests that 4:30 shows the divine protection, promised in Psalm 91, which the devil tried to get Jesus to demonstrate in Luke 4:9–11. This is possible but is not strongly indicated. If we make this connection, we must also say that Jesus expects and receives the promised divine protection only as he obediently fulfills his mission. That mission will include suffering and death.

Chapter Three

JESUS AS PREACHER AND HEALER

Some of the summaries of Jesus' work mention both his preaching and his healing (Luke 5:17; 6:18; 9:11; see also 5:15), and 4:16–44, which the narrator has carefully united through repetition of key words, seems designed to balance emphasis on Jesus' message and his healing.[1] The importance attached to both of these activities also appears in the narrator's summary of Luke as an account of what "Jesus began both to do and to teach" (Acts 1:1; compare Luke 24:19: Jesus was a man "powerful in work and word"). Later in this chapter we will consider Jesus' work as healer and exorcist, but first we will discuss the summary descriptions of Jesus as preacher which recall his commission in 4:18 to "preach good news" and "proclaim."

JESUS AS PREACHER OF GOOD NEWS

The narrator presents a basic understanding of Jesus' ministry in the brief summaries of Jesus' work as preacher, which are scattered through much of the gospel narrative. These summaries fit Jesus' announcement in 4:18–19 that he has been sent to preach good news to the poor and to proclaim release, for we are repeatedly told that Jesus was preaching good news and proclaiming. At key points this is done in language which is especially close to the statement of Jesus' commission in 4:18–19. Thus Jesus is presented as continually carrying out the mission of preaching and proclaiming described in 4:18–19, and particular scenes in the narrative take their place within the context of this basic activity.

After a day and night of teaching and healing in Capernaum, the crowd attempts to prevent Jesus from leaving. In response, Jesus restates his mission, "Also in the other cities I must preach the good news ($\epsilon\dot{v}a\gamma\gamma\epsilon\lambda\dot{\iota}\sigma a\sigma\theta a\iota$) of God's reign, because for this I was sent ($\dot{a}\pi\epsilon\sigma\tau\dot{a}\lambda\eta\nu$)" (4:43). This statement differs significantly from the Markan parallel in repeating two key words ("preach good news," "sent") from the Isaiah quotation in 4:18. A third repeated word follows in 4:44: "And he was

---

[1] See below, pp. 82–85. On word and deed as a formulaic pair in Greco-Roman thought and in Luke-Acts, see Frederick W. Danker, *Benefactor*, 339–42.

proclaiming (κηρύσσων) in the synagogues of the Jewish land." These observations allow some important conclusions: (1) The narrator is making clear that the mission which Jesus announced in Nazareth is his continuing mission which he must perform "in the other cities also," indeed, in the whole Jewish land.[2] (2) The verb εὐαγγελίζομαι ("preach good news") is a key term in the narrator's description of Jesus' mission. This is supported by a comparison of Luke with Matthew and Mark. The noun εὐαγγέλιον is never used in Luke and only twice in Acts, while the verb εὐαγγελίζομαι is frequent. In contrast, Matthew and Mark use the noun fairly frequently, while the verb occurs only once (Matt 11:5). Lukan usage may show the influence of Isa 61:1 LXX and other passages in Isaiah 40–66.[3] (3) Telling the people of Capernaum that he must preach good news "also in the other cities" implies that he has already preached good news in Capernaum. This gives us some idea of the content of Jesus' "teaching" there, which made such a strong impression (4:31–32). (4) The narrator shifts from "preach good news (εὐαγγελίσασθαι)" to "proclaiming (κηρύσσων)" in 4:43–44 and has already referred to the same activity as "teaching (διδάσκων)" in 4:31. Therefore, these three terms are virtual synonyms. This conclusion is supported by their use in the rest of Luke-Acts.[4] (5) When we compare 4:43 with 4:18–19, we see that an important new phrase has been introduced: "God's reign." Thus Isaiah's time of "release," the "acceptable year of the Lord," is closely associated in the narrator's mind with the reign of God, a theme which will be important in the rest of Luke-Acts.

After characterizing Jesus' message as preaching good news to the poor, proclaiming release to captives, and preaching good news of God's reign, the narrator provides brief reminders of Jesus' repeated involvement in this preaching task. These are to be understood in light of Luke 4:18–19, 43–44. Immediately after 4:43–44 we learn that a crowd was

---

[2] The term Ἰουδαία in 4:44 means the whole country of the Jews, not Judea in distinction from Galilee. It is used in this comprehensive sense in Luke 6:17; 7:17; 23:5; Acts 10:37. Cf. H. Schürmann, *Das Lukasevangelium*, 256; J. Fitzmyer, *Luke I–IX*, 557–58.

[3] See Isa 40:9; 52:7; 60:6. These four Isaiah passages use the verbal stem, while the noun εὐαγγέλιον does not occur in Isaiah LXX and is rare in the LXX as a whole. Not only Isa 61:1 but also 52:7 may be important to the narrator, for Acts 10:36 seems to be influenced by it.

[4] Εὐαγγελίζομαι and κηρύσσω are used together in Luke 4:43–44; 8:1; 9:2, 6; Acts 8:4–5. Both have God's reign as content (Luke 4:43; 8:1; 9:2; 16:16; Acts 8:12; 20:25; 28:31) and, in Acts, also have Jesus or the Messiah as content (Acts 5:42; 8:5, 35; 9:20; 11:20; 17:18; 19:13). Διδάσκω is also used with one of the other two verbs to describe a single action (Luke 20:1; Acts 5:42; 15:35; 28:31), and the preaching of the missionary message is often called "teaching" in Acts (4:2, 18; 5:21, 25, 28, 42; 15:35; 18:11; 28:31). In general summaries of Jesus' activity we are told both that Jesus "was teaching in the synagogues" (Luke 4:15) and that he "was proclaiming in the synagogues" (4:44). Similarly, as he traveled on his way through cities and villages, he was both "proclaiming and preaching good news" (8:1) and "teaching" (13:22).

"hearing the word of God" and that Jesus "was teaching" them (5:1, 3). The healing story in 5:12–14 begins by locating Jesus "in one of the cities," a reference back to Jesus' statement in 4:43 that he must preach "also in the other cities." The similar phrase "on one of the days" in 5:17 probably means one of the days of Jesus' itinerant preaching ministry announced in 4:43–44. That ministry also involved proclaiming or teaching "in the synagogues" (4:15, 31–33, 44), and, as opportunity arises, the narrator repeats these references to synagogue teaching (6:6; 13:10).

It would be easy to lose sight of the connection of Jesus' preaching with the themes of 4:18–19, 43 since many of the references to Jesus' preaching and teaching are brief and vague. However, we encounter more specific reminders in 7:22 and 8:1. In 7:22 Jesus responds to the question of John the Baptist with a rhythmic series of short sentences which summarize his work. These words have been shaped with a precise sense of form. While they are intentionally reminiscent of the Old Testament, especially Isaiah, they follow their own formal rule, which unifies them, while requiring reformulation of the words from Isaiah. There is a series of two word sentences with noun subjects first, always masculine plural, followed by present tense verbs. This repetitive pattern gives the words a distinct rhythm, which is emphasized in Luke's version by the absence of conjunctions.[5] H. Schürmann rightly calls this a "celebration of salvation (Heilsjubel)," not just a collection of citations.[6] Nevertheless, the connection with Old Testament promises deepens our understanding of the reason for celebration, for the events which Jesus recites are viewed as signs of the promised time of salvation. Especially important is a group of texts in Isaiah which list in a *series* some of the *same* disabilities as in Luke 7:22 and proclaim that they will be removed.[7] Isa 61:1 is clearly one of the passages in mind in this celebration of the fulfillment of Old Testament hope, for none of the other texts which show some affinity to Luke 7:22 connects "poor" with the verb "preach good news." If this word combination reflects Isa 61:1, then the reference to the blind receiving sight probably does also.

Furthermore, the poor and the blind, the two groups that relate to Isa 61:1, have positions of emphasis at the beginning and the end of the rhythmic series. There are several indications that the narrator is aware of

---

[5] Except, perhaps, for one καί about which there is some textual uncertainty. Its inclusion is supported by good witnesses.

[6] *Das Lukasevangelium*, 411.

[7] Isa 29:18–19: deaf, blind, poor; 35:5–6: blind, deaf, lame; 42:18: deaf, blind. Isa 26:19 refers to the resurrection of the dead. However, the raising of the dead and cleansing of lepers may relate to the miracles of Elijah and Elisha. See Luke 4:25–27 and the similarities between Luke 7:11–17 and Elijah's raising of the widow's son in 1 Kgs 17:17–24.

such fine details. While the parallel in Matt 11:4 reads, "Report to John what you hear and see," Luke 7:22 has "what you saw and heard." The order of the two verbs of perception in Luke reflects the order of the rhythmic series, for it is primarily the *last* element, the preaching of good news to the poor, which has been *heard*. The narrator also shows special interest in the first element, for in v. 21 (not found in Matthew) the narrator takes special note, in a separate sentence, of Jesus granting sight to many blind people. In contrast, there is no specific reference to healing the deaf, either in 7:21 or in previous accounts of Jesus' healing. While the fulfillment in Jesus of other prophecies of salvation is important, the fulfillment of Isa 61:1 is especially important.

The question of John the Baptist provides the opportunity for comprehensive reflection on the implications of the narrative to this point. John's question is motivated by his disciples' report "about all these things" (7:18), i.e., all the things that Jesus has been doing and saying, and 7:22 is a summary of Jesus' preaching and healing ministry from its beginning. This scene also has specific ties to earlier scenes. John's question concerning "the coming one" in 7:19 is related to his prophecy concerning the "stronger one" who "is coming" in 3:16.[8] John, who to this point has made no confession of Jesus as the fulfillment of his prophecy, is now raising that possibility. In 3:15–16 John's statement concerning the coming "stronger one" was caused by the people's speculation concerning the Messiah, and the phrase "the coming one" returns in 19:38 with the title "king." These connections suggest that John's question concerns the Messiah. Jesus answers by pointing to the fulfillment of Isaiah's prophecies of salvation for the needy, including the physically needy, thereby making these prophecies central to his role. This answer helps to integrate Jesus' role as healer into his messianic role.

Furthermore, 7:22 recalls Jesus' commission in 4:18–19 and emphasizes that this commission, also drawn from Isaiah, is being fulfilled. The fulfillment of this commission was affirmed in an anticipatory way in 4:21; now it can be affirmed on the basis of many deeds and words reported in the subsequent narrative. Moreover, the sudden shift from rhythmic words of joyous fulfillment in 7:22 to a warning about taking offense in 7:23 parallels a similar shift from joyous announcement to rejection in the Nazareth scene. Jesus offended the people of Nazareth, and it remains true that he can only be accepted as the coming one by those who can face and accept his offensiveness. Jesus' answer to John in 7:18–

---

[8] The two passages are also related through the repetition of the verb προσδοκάω ("wait for," "expect") in 3:15; 7:19–20. There is a parallel in Matt 11:3 to the latter passage, but there is no parallel to Luke 3:15. The verb is characteristic of Luke-Acts.

23 makes clear that themes in 4:16–30 remain central for understanding the rest of Jesus' ministry, which is the fulfillment of what was announced and foreshadowed in Nazareth.[9]

The announcement of Jesus' mission in 4:18–19 was followed in 4:43–44 by a summary statement of Jesus' mission linking themes from the Nazareth scene to Jesus' itinerant ministry of preaching God's reign in the cities of the Jewish land. The reminder of 4:18–19 in Jesus' response to John the Baptist is followed in 8:1 by a summary statement of Jesus' ministry which is reminiscent of 4:43–44. In 8:1 we are told that Jesus was "preaching good news of God's reign," as he said he must do in 4:43; he was also "proclaiming ($\kappa\eta\rho\acute{v}\sigma\sigma\omega\nu$)," as in 4:44; and the statement that he was traveling "from one city and village to another ($\kappa\alpha\tau\grave{\alpha}$ $\pi\acute{o}\lambda\iota\nu$ $\kappa\alpha\grave{\iota}$ $\kappa\acute{\omega}\mu\eta\nu$)" broadens the reference to "the other cities" in 4:43.[10] The additional notice that the twelve were with him reflects the appointment of the twelve in 6:12–16 and prepares for their role as partners in Jesus' mission in 9:1–6. Jesus' mission is extended by the twelve, who, according to 9:2, 6, also "proclaim God's reign," "preach good news," and "heal." Shortly afterwards we are told again that Jesus was "speaking about God's reign" and healing (9:11).

The importance of 4:18–19, 43–44 for understanding Jesus' ministry as a whole is also indicated by 16:16: "The law and the prophets were until John. From then on God's reign is being preached as good news ($\epsilon\grave{v}\alpha\gamma\gamma\epsilon\lambda\acute{\iota}\zeta\epsilon\tau\alpha\iota$)." Here preaching the good news of God's reign is presented as the key factor which sets off the new time, the time of Jesus' ministry, from the old time of the law and the prophets. The emphasis on preaching good news of God's reign agrees with 4:43 but differs from Matthew's parallel to 16:16 (Matt 11:12–13). Finally, in Jerusalem Jesus is still "teaching . . . and preaching good news" (20:1). The controversies in the temple are challenges which occur in the midst of a continuing preaching ministry characteristic of Jesus since his announcement in Nazareth.

The importance of 4:18–19, 43–44 for understanding Jesus' ministry as a whole has been confirmed by the narrator's repeated indications that Jesus is carrying out his task of preaching good news and proclaiming, disclosed first in these passages. The summary of Jesus' ministry in Acts 10:36–38 also confirms the importance of these passages and their themes. While using language which clearly recalls Luke 4:18 ("how God

---

[9] Sharon Ringe argues that there are additional resemblances between Luke 4:16–30 and 7:1–50, the larger context in which 7:18–23 is found. See *The Jubilee Proclamation*, 172–73 and *Jesus, Liberation, and the Biblical Jubilee*, 47–48.

[10] The addition of villages in 8:1 may suggest that Jesus is now covering the population more thoroughly. Cf. Ulrich Busse, *Die Wunder des Propheten Jesus*, 194, 467.

anointed him with Holy Spirit," Acts 10:38) and reflects the same geographical perspective on Jesus' ministry as Luke 4:43–44 ("throughout
the whole of the Jewish land, beginning from Galilee," Acts 10:37), Peter
summarizes God's message through Jesus in the phrase "preaching good
news of peace (εὐαγγελιζόμενος εἰρήνην)" (Acts 10:36).[11]

Peter's summary of Jesus' ministry not only highlights the preaching of
good news but also emphasizes Jesus' work of healing. Isa 61:1, as quoted
in Luke 4:18–19, is also influential in describing Jesus as healer, for the
familiar reference to Jesus being anointed by God with Holy Spirit leads
directly to a description of Jesus' activity in these terms: Jesus "went
about doing good and healing all those oppressed by the devil, for God was
with him." That Jesus healed those caught in the devil's oppressive power
fits with the emphasis on "release" in Luke 4:18.[12] The Spirit and power
are associated in Luke 4:14, the summary statement which introduces the
Nazareth scene, as they are in Acts 10:38. The healing work results from
the anointing with Spirit and power, a connection which is supported by
the repeated references to power in relation to healings and exorcisms in
the gospel (see Luke 4:36; 5:17; 6:19; 8:46; 9:1). Thus Acts 10:38 confirms
that Jesus' healings are an important part of the task which Jesus was
empowered to perform in fulfillment of the commission announced in
Luke 4:18–19. We must now consider the Lukan portrait of Jesus as
healer more carefully.

JESUS' MIGHTY ACTS IN CAPERNAUM
(LUKE 4:31–43)

The events in 4:31–43 are bound closely together by unity of place and
time. The narrator presents a rapid sequence of events taking place in the
same place and during a brief time (a Sabbath day, the following evening,
and the next morning). There are indications of connections with preceding material. The narrator is beginning to fill out the summary report
about Jesus' activity in 4:14–15 by narrating specific incidents.[13] As in
4:14–15, we are told that Jesus was teaching in the synagogue (4:31, 33),
making a strong, favorable impression so that his fame spread throughout

---

[11] The combination of preaching good news with peace probably reflects Isa 52:7, but the
following reference to anointing with Holy Spirit indicates that the good news of Isa 61:1 is
also in mind.

[12] See above, p. 65.

[13] Ulrich Busse, in discussing the relation of Luke 4:16–30 to 4:14–15, speaks of Luke's
"narrative technique of illustrating a summary notice with a concrete example." Cf. *Das
Nazareth-Manifest Jesu*, 31.

the surrounding area (4:32, 37), and the reference to "the power of the Spirit" in 4:14 is developed by emphasis on Jesus' "authority and power" in 4:32, 36. There are also connections with the scene in Nazareth, which begins with the same pattern of Jesus speaking in a synagogue and receiving at first a favorable response (4:22). As we have seen,[14] the Capernaum events end in 4:43 with a restatement of Jesus' mission which recalls 4:18, followed by a summary statement of Jesus' preaching in the synagogues (4:44). In other words, 4:14–15, 18 and 4:43–44 are related and form a frame around the intervening material,[15] which suggests the unity of this material as an initial portrayal of Jesus' mission in its two aspects of word and deed. The events in Capernaum should not be viewed in isolation from the Nazareth scene which immediately precedes. Rather, in Capernaum Jesus is carrying out the commission which he announced in Nazareth, and there is special emphasis on the part of his commission which he did not carry out in his hometown, his work as healer and exorcist. Thus there is both narrative continuity and thematic balance between the scenes in Nazareth and Capernaum.

The events in Capernaum begin to show that the "power of the Spirit" which rests on Jesus according to 4:14 and 18 will manifest itself in a ministry of healing and exorcism. There are several indications that the readers of the gospel are being introduced to a general role of Jesus. In 4:33–34 the "spirit of an unclean demon" responds to Jesus by asking, "Have you come to destroy us?" The plural pronoun suggests that the present confrontation is only an illustration of a larger purpose: the destruction of demonic powers in general. Furthermore, the sequence of events in Capernaum suggests something of the scope of Jesus' work of exorcism and healing. Jesus first helps a man, then a woman. Then there is a report of many other healings and exorcisms similar to the two narrated in detail (4:40–41), with emphasis on the extensiveness of Jesus' healing work ("*all* who had people sick with *various kinds* of diseases").

In Acts 10:38 and Luke 13:10–17[16] sickness and demonic possession are viewed as oppressive constraint, bondage, from which one must be freed. Thus Jesus' healings can be understood as "release for prisoners" (4:18).[17] This perspective explains some of the differences between 4:38–39 and the parallel accounts of the healing of Simon's mother-in-law. In contrast to Matthew and Mark, Luke 4:38 indicates that Simon's mother-

---

[14] See above, pp. 77–78.

[15] See U. Busse, *Das Nazareth-Manifest Jesu*, 13–14, and S. Ringe, *Jesus, Liberation, and the Biblical Jubilee*, 37–38.

[16] On this scene see p. 65.

[17] U. Busse notes that "the Evangelist favors the imprisonment metaphor" in describing the sick. Cf. *Die Wunder des Propheten Jesus*, 433.

in-law was "seized," "oppressed," or "ruled" (συνεχομένη) by a great fever, implying confinement or constraint.[18] Then Jesus "rebuked (ἐπετί-μησεν) the fever" (dif. Matthew, Mark). The same verb was used of Jesus' commanding word to the unclean spirit in 4:35, and encounters with such spirits are a repeated context for the use of this verb. This observation suggests that the fever is viewed as a personal force, like a demon. As a result of Jesus' command, the fever "released her." While the verb ἀφῆκεν ("released") is shared with the parallel accounts, in Luke it is placed in a context where it has the full force of release from an oppressive confinement and illustrates the "release (ἄφεσιν) for captives" of which Jesus spoke in 4:18.[19]

In Capernaum the demons recognize Jesus, and their recognition provides an opportunity to remind the reader of Jesus' special status through repetition of some of the titles applied to Jesus in the introductory chapters of the gospel. The repetition of these titles helps unite the portrait of Jesus up through 4:13 with the first accounts of Jesus' preaching and healing. The demons know that Jesus is "the Holy One of God" (4:34), "the Son of God," and "the Messiah" (4:41). The readers of the gospel were told similar things about Jesus in such passages as 1:35; 2:11, 26, and the title "Son of God" is particularly prominent in Luke 1–4 (1:32, 35; 3:22; 4:3, 9). Now these titles are being associated with Jesus' active ministry, but Jesus does not reveal himself in these terms nor is he recognized by humans.

There is strong emphasis on the authority and power of Jesus' word in the Capernaum sequence. This emphasis is indicated not only by the statements in 4:32, 36 but also by the repeated use of the verb ἐπιτιμάω (RSV: "rebuke," 4:35, 39, 41), which according to Howard Kee and Joseph Fitzmyer[20] implies, in the context of exorcism, the pronouncement of a commanding word. However, it is not just Jesus' commanding word

---

[18] Helmut Koester, *TDNT* 7:877–79, 883, indicates that, apart from the sense "'to hold together' so that something is maintained in good order," the basic meanings of συνέχω are "'to enclose,' 'lock up,' . . . 'to take or hold captive,'" and, developing out of these meanings, "'to oppress,' 'overpower,' 'rule.'" The meaning "'to oppress,' 'overpower,' 'rule,'" is often found in the passive with the reason in the dative, and this meaning applies when some illness is the cause.

[19] George E. Rice understands 4:31–6:11 as a systematic portrayal of Jesus' work of release announced in 4:18. Luke is portraying release from Satan's power (4:31–44), the power of sin (5:1–32), and cultic traditions (5:33–6:11). His views are presented in three short articles: "Luke's Thematic Use of the Call to Discipleship"; "Luke 4:31–44: Release for the Captives"; "Luke 5:33–6:11: Release from Cultic Tradition." I agree that the theme of release appears in 4:31–44 and 5:1–32, and I will discuss later the special importance of 5:17–32 in portraying Jesus' work of releasing sins (see pp. 103–8.). I do not find sufficient evidence of an emphasis on release in 5:33–6:11.

[20] Cf. Howard Clark Kee, "The Terminology of Mark's Exorcism Stories," 232–46; and J. Fitzmyer, *Luke I–IX*, 546.

to demons which shows his authority and power. The narrator notes that the people recognized the same authority in Jesus' teaching (4:32). Indeed, when we consider 4:16–44 as a whole, we see that the narrator has balanced emphasis on Jesus' message with emphasis on his healing and exorcism, the Nazareth scene focusing on the message, the Capernaum sequence on healing and exorcism, although it begins and ends with references to Jesus' message (4:31–32, 43–44). The importance of Jesus' message is further indicated by the repeated use of λόγος ("word," 4:22, 32, 36; 5:1), in all cases except 4:36 in connection with Jesus' preaching or teaching. Thus 4:16–44 provides a first impression both of Jesus' message and of his healing work, with emphasis on Jesus' authoritative word in both activities.

The immediate proximity of the scenes in Nazareth and Capernaum (differing from Mark's order), the reference to events in Capernaum in the Nazareth scene (4:23), and the similarity in the way in which the scenes begin, with Jesus speaking on the Sabbath in a synagogue, invite readers to compare the events in the two towns for similarities and differences. There is a difference in that Jesus, anticipating a request for healing, rejects this request in Nazareth (4:23–27), while he does heal in Capernaum. However, there is continuity in that the "release" which Jesus has been sent to proclaim, according to his announcement in Nazareth, is becoming a reality for the people of Capernaum through release from demonic possession and disease. There is contrast between Nazareth and Capernaum in that the former town turns in anger against Jesus, while the latter is so favorably impressed by Jesus that the people want him to stay (4:42). Nevertheless, both Nazareth and Capernaum show that they want to keep Jesus' benefits for *themselves* (4:23–28, 42), a desire which Jesus rejects. Furthermore, the negative judgment on Capernaum in 10:13–15 suggests that this town's enthusiasm for Jesus' mighty acts proved to be an inadequate response to his mission. Finally, Jesus' message is essentially the same in both towns. While the introductory statement about Jesus' teaching in Capernaum (4:31–32) does not make this clear, in 4:43 Jesus restates the mission which he must fulfill throughout the cities and does so in terms that recall the announcement of his commission in 4:18–19. Wherever Jesus goes, he will be preaching the same good news.

Jesus' amazing healings and exorcisms contribute to the very rapid spread of his fame. Comparison of the following statements shows how the narrator conveys an impression of rapidly growing fame: After the exorcism in the synagogue of Capernaum, "a report about him was going out to every place of the neighboring area" (4:37). After the healing of the leper, "the word about him was spreading more" (5:15). In the next scene

Pharisees and teachers of the law[21] are present "from every village of Galilee and Judea and Jerusalem" (5:17). This is surpassed in 6:17–18, where we hear of "a great multitude of the people from all the Jewish land and Jerusalem and the seacoast of Tyre and Sidon, who had come to hear him and be healed." We reach the climax of this development in 7:17: "And this statement about him went out in the whole Jewish country and all the neighboring region." The fame of Jesus as healer is presupposed in Acts, for in his sermons Peter assumes that his hearers already know about Jesus' mighty acts, even when he is speaking to Gentiles in Caesarea (Acts 2:22; 10:37–38). After Luke 7:17 the emphasis shifts. Instead of emphasizing the spread of Jesus' fame, the narrator presents the response of various groups to "all" Jesus' works. In other words, the response is now evoked not only by a healing which may have just taken place but by all of Jesus' amazing works to that point in the narrative (see 7:18; 9:43; 13:17; 19:37).

Jesus' Mighty Acts as Manifestations of God's Promised Salvation

Paul Achtemeier has rightly observed that there is a positive relationship in Luke-Acts between seeing Jesus' and his followers' healing power and coming to faith.[22] However, this does not mean that faith is merely belief in miracles and trust in miracle workers. When the mighty acts of Jesus and his followers are seen within the broad context of God's purpose and Jesus' commission as presented in Luke-Acts, the faith prompted by mighty acts becomes faith in God's saving purpose and power for the world. People recognize in Jesus an extraordinary authority and power (4:36), but they also recognize that God is the source of this power. In the healing work of Jesus, God is actively engaged in bringing salvation to the people. There is strong emphasis in the Lukan healing stories on God as the true source of healing and therefore the one to whom praise is due. We are repeatedly told following healings that either the person healed or the crowd (or both) glorifies or praises God—see 5:25–26 (by both; only by the crowd in Mark and Matthew); 7:16 (story unique to Luke); 13:13 (story unique to Luke); 17:15, 18 (story unique to Luke); 18:43 (dif. Mark, Matthew); 19:37 (dif. Mark, Matthew). The implications of this motif are clarified when less stereotyped language is used. According to

---

[21] These two groups are mentioned instead of the crowd in order to prepare for the conflict in this scene.

[22] "The Lukan Perspective on the Miracles," 553–56.

9:43 "all were amazed at the grandeur of God," and in 7:16 the crowd not only glorifies God but also says, "God has visited his people." The idea of God's "visitation" (using the verb ἐπισκέπτομαι or the noun ἐπισκοπή) plays a significant role in Luke's Gospel.[23] In 1:68, 78 God's visitation is associated with the redemption, salvation, and dawning from on high which fulfill the messianic hope and the promise to Abraham. God has "visited" the people in order to bring the salvation to Israel promised long ago. Therefore, when Jerusalem does not recognize "the time of your visitation," it is cause for weeping (19:44). According to 7:16 the crowd responds to Jesus' resurrection of the widow's son by recognizing what Zechariah recognized in 1:68–79, that God has begun to give active attention to Israel in order to fulfill the promised redemption. The *theo*logical perspective on Jesus' mighty acts, in which they are viewed as manifestations of *God's* redemptive activity, continues in Acts. These were mighty acts "which God did through him" (2:22) or which Jesus was able to do "because God was with him" (10:38).

Thus Jesus' mighty acts are signs that God is at work to bring about the fulfillment of a comprehensive hope for Israel and the world, long planned and long prophesied in Scripture. In light of the importance and broad meaning of the nouns σωτηρία, σωτήριον ("salvation") in Luke-Acts, the use of σώζω ("save," "heal") in healing stories (Luke 6:9; 8:36, 48, 50; 17:19; 18:42) already suggests a connection between healing and God's redemptive purpose in all its aspects. Even clearer is the emphasis placed on the fulfillment through Jesus' mighty works of scriptural visions of promised salvation. The quotation from Isaiah in Luke 4:18–19, with its promise of release for captives and sight for the blind, the summary of Jesus' healings in 7:22 in words that recall prophecies of salvation,[24] and Jesus' declaration (after a report of exorcisms) that the disciples are witnessing the fulfillment of what many prophets and kings longed to see (10:23–24) show the stress on the fulfillment of scriptural hope. Jesus is the one through whom God is working for divine purposes announced long ago by the prophets, and the overcoming of physical suffering is an integral part of God's redemptive plan for the world. Placing Jesus' and the disciples' healing work in the context of this large hope, rooted in God's purpose revealed in Scripture, is an important function of Luke 4:18–19, 7:22, and 10:23–24. These passages are supported by allusions to events and persons of Israel's story that provide precedents and interpretive models for understanding Jesus' mighty acts. Elijah's raising of

---

[23] See also ἐπιβλέπω in Luke 1:48; 9:38.
[24] On 7:22 see pp. 79–80.

the widow's son is especially important,[25] but the reference to "the finger of God" in Luke 11:20 seems to relate Jesus to Moses in his contest with Pharaoh and his magicians.[26]

That Jesus' healing work is part of something larger—a saving purpose for the world which embraces physical as well as other dimensions of life—is confirmed by the connection between Jesus' healings and the coming of God's reign. We have already seen that Jesus is "preaching good news of God's reign," as is made clear in 4:43 and in summaries of Jesus' preaching thereafter. Since 4:43 refers back to and interprets 4:18–19, preaching good news of God's reign must include the proclamation of release to captives and sight to the blind, a proclamation which takes effect through Jesus' exorcisms and healings. Thus proclaiming the reign of God and healing, mentioned together in summaries of Jesus' and the apostles' work in 9:2, 6, 11, are related tasks. The healings are concrete realizations for needy persons of the salvation which the preachers announce in preaching good news of God's reign.

Jesus' words to the seventy-two in 10:1–24 repeat and expand his instructions to the twelve in 9:1–5, and the implications of passages like 9:2, 11, which relate healing and proclaiming God's reign, are clarified in this second mission scene. The pairs of missioners are to "heal the sick" in each town "and say to them, 'God's reign has come near to you'" (10:9; cf. 10:11). The announcement accompanies the healing and interprets the meaning of the healing as the powerful and saving approach of God's reign. Since the mighty acts are manifestations of God's nearness in royal power, the proper response to them would be repentance, as 10:13–15 makes clear. The subjection of demons by the missioners is a cause of great joy, for it shows that they have authority over Satan, who has fallen from power (10:17–20). Exorcism of demons demonstrates that Satan's rule is collapsing as God's rule draws near, thereby fulfilling the hopes of "many prophets and kings" (10:23–24).

The same connections among expulsion of demons, the coming of God's reign, and the conquest of Satan are found in Luke 11:14–22. In reply to the charge that he casts out demons by Beelzebul, Jesus constructs a

---

[25] In the story of Jesus raising the widow's son at Nain, compare the encounter at the gate of the city (Luke 7:12) with 3 Kgdms 17:10 LXX (=1 Kgs 17:10), the young man's speaking as a sign of returned life (Luke 7:15) with 3 Kgdms 17:22, and the literal repetition in Luke 7:15 of the sentence "And he gave him to his mother" from 3 Kgdms 17:23. The confession in Luke 7:16 that Jesus is a "great prophet" relates in general to Elijah's role as a miracle working prophet and perhaps specifically to the widow's confession that Elijah is a "man of God" in 3 Kgdms 17:24. Furthermore, details reminiscent of 3 Kgdms 17:17, 21, 23 occur in Luke 8:55 and 9:42 (dif. Matthew, Mark), and there is explicit reference to Elijah and the widow in 4:25–26.

[26] For discussion of both the Elijah and Moses parallels see A. George, *Études sur l'oeuvre de Luc*, 79–84, 127–32.

dilemma: If, as the opponents charge, Jesus is acting by Beelzebul, Satan's rule is over, since a divided kingdom will not stand. If, on the other hand, one admits that Jesus is acting "by the finger of God . . . , then God's reign has come upon you." In either case Satan's power is broken and God's reign is at hand. The strong man Satan has been conquered by a stronger one. Thus the exorcisms are signs of a massive shift in the power which controls human life and destiny, as God's promised salvation approaches.

Finally, the parable of the great supper indicates that it is not the exorcisms alone which witness to the nearness of God's reign. In dealing with the issue of who will eat bread in God's reign (14:15), Jesus tells a story in which "the poor and crippled and blind and lame" are unexpectedly invited to a banquet (14:21). This list of people who share in the banquet of God's reign is similar to the list in 7:22 of those being healed and helped by Jesus, in fulfillment of prophecy. Jesus' healing occurs within the context of his proclamation of God's reign. The healings and exorcisms are signs that God's reign is at hand, and those healed are being invited to share in the banquet which marks its coming.

We have noted the strong emphasis in Luke on healings and exorcisms as signs of God's power. We have also noted the connections of Jesus' healings with the fulfillment of scriptural hope for a time of salvation, as well as with the proclamation of God's reign. Jesus' healings in Luke are not demonstrations of personal power but signs that a comprehensive saving purpose, which embraces the physical as well as other dimensions of life, is being realized in the world.

ROLES IN LUKAN EXORCISM AND HEALING STORIES

The exorcism stories differ in the degree to which they develop Jesus' interaction with the demon, on the one hand, and with the possessed person, on the other hand. We will first consider briefly Jesus' interaction with the demons. Jesus' relation to demons is highlighted in the exorcism in the Capernaum synagogue (4:33–37) and in the story of the Gerasene demoniac (8:26–39), where, however, the role of the possessed man is also developed. In these stories there is emphasis on the qualitative distinction between Jesus and the demon, expressed by $\tau\acute{\iota}\ \dot{\eta}\mu\hat{\iota}\nu\ \kappa\alpha\grave{\iota}\ \sigma o\acute{\iota}$ (freely, "What have you to do with us?" 4:34; cf. 8:28) and by the contrast between "the holy one of God" and the "unclean spirit" (4:33–34). Jesus and the demons are opposites and adversaries. The demons want to preserve distance and be left alone. They immediately recognize Jesus, having a capacity to recognize the holy not shared by the people with whom Jesus mingles (4:34, 41; 8:28; see the devil's words to Jesus in 4:3, 9). Nevertheless, the demons must submit to Jesus' authoritative command, which prevents them from working further harm to their victims. While Mark 1:26 and 9:26 depict the frightening and possibly dangerous effects of the demon *after* Jesus' exorcising command, the parallels in Luke 4:35 and 9:42 make clear, in the one case, that the man was not harmed and, in the other case, that the convulsion took place *before* Jesus' command. Luke 8:28 presents a stronger picture of the demons' impotent groveling when they respond to Jesus with "I beg you" instead of Mark's "I adjure you by God."

It is more typical of the narrator to focus on Jesus' significance for the needy person. This is true of the healing stories and even of some of the exorcisms. Jesus' significance for the victims of demonic possession is brought out in the stories of the Gerasene demoniac (8:26–39) and of the father with the demoniac son (9:37–43). The rather full description of the Gerasene demoniac's behavior before and after the exorcism emphasizes the great change that Jesus has made in his existence. In 9:37–43 there is no dialogue with the demon, only the statement that Jesus rebuked the unclean spirit, but there is a dialogue between Jesus and the father, who speaks for himself and his son, the victim. Here the significance of Jesus for the father and the son is heightened and given emotional force by elements of pathos. There is vivid description of the boy's plight in 9:39, 42. Furthermore, he is his father's "only" son (9:38; dif. Mark), and the father's emotional ties to his son are again recognized in the statement "He gave him back to his father" (9:42; dif. Mark). These features of the story encourage the reader to sympathize with the plight of father and son and to rejoice when they find help through Jesus.

In Acts 10:38 we are told that Jesus "went about doing good (εὐεργετῶν) and healing all those oppressed by the devil." Jesus the healer is a benefactor of needy humanity.[27] This role is broadly developed in a series of healing stories in which Jesus responds to persons with physical needs or their representatives by helping them. The relation between Jesus and these persons will now be explored. Here I will focus on the movement from physical need to the fulfillment of that need which is the central core of these stories in so far as they are *healing* stories. This will require us to consider the way in which the narrator presents the interaction between Jesus as healer and the person with a physical need.

---

[27] "Doing good and healing" is a hendiadys, as is shown by the application of εὐεργεσία to a healing in Acts 4:9. On the use of the benefactor motif in Luke-Acts and its relation to Hellenistic-Roman ideas concerning the benefactor (εὐεργέτης) see Georg Bertram, *TDNT* 2:654–55; U. Busse, *Die Wunder des Propheten Jesus*, 434–37; F. Danker, *Luke*, 6–17; Danker, *Benefactor*.

In addition, a supplicant, one who expresses the need and requests help, is sometimes present as a separate person.[28]

The simple episodes that we are considering can be analyzed in terms of the "moves" in each of them. A "move" comprises the development from a need or lack through the effort to overcome that need or lack and ends when that effort terminates.[29] A move is an arc of tension between a need and the resolution of that need or the final renunciation of all efforts to resolve it. Even the brief episodes in the gospels may contain more than one move, and these moves may combine in various ways. However, we are concerned with the move which arises from a physical need and finds its resolution in an act of healing by Jesus.

In order to create interest in what is happening, the narrator must bring the need into focus. This results in giving a prominent role in the episode to someone other than Jesus. While in the gospel as a whole the fulfillment of Jesus' commission gives shape to the story, in the individual healing episodes it is the physical need of a person which has this role; the need calls for action and determines when the episode may successfully close. The narrator controls the readers' experience in part through deciding what needs and tasks will be the center of attention in a story. If an individual's physical need is the primary focus of attention, we tend to react to events in light of the afflicted person's need, for it is his or her problem that creates tension, sets things moving, and gives events meaning as success or failure. This tends to create sympathy for the afflicted person, unless counterbalanced by negative description.

The narrator of Luke has various ways of increasing this sympathy and adding suspense, thereby heightening interest in the afflicted person's fate. A supplicant, either the needy person or someone related to the needy person, may appear in the story and request help. In these cases we have a tension of desire in addition to the tension of need, i.e., someone not only needs something but wants something. The narrator may report a dialogue between the supplicant and Jesus, which is a way of focusing attention on this desire and Jesus' response, for the narrator has chosen to expand this aspect of the narrative into a detailed scene rather than using summary narration.[30] That is, the flow of the narrative has been slowed to

---

[28] The following discussion will focus on some emphasized aspects of healing stories in Luke. More complete and detailed discussion of the form of NT healing stories may be found in Gerd Theissen, *Miracle Stories in the Early Christian Tradition*; Antoinette Clark Wire, "Gospel Miracle Stories and Their Tellers," 83–113; Robert W. Funk, "The New Testament Healing Miracle Story," 57–96.

[29] This insight is borrowed from Vladimir Propp, *Morphology of the Folktale*, especially 92–94.

[30] For discussion of scene and summary, as well as other variations in narrative tempo, see G. Genette, *Narrative Discourse*, 86–112.

approximate the speed of actual events through attention to the characters' words, rather than briefly summarizing the outcome. Furthermore, the narrator of Luke has a taste for pathos and uses pathetic touches to increase sympathy for those whom Jesus heals. The sense of need is increased by indicating that the problem was of long duration (8:43: twelve years; 13:11: eighteen years), by vivid description of a demoniac's wild behavior (8:27, 29), and by specifying that the *right* hand of a man was withered (6:6; dif. Matthew, Mark). The love of parent for child adds pathos to three different scenes,[31] and in all three cases pathos is heightened by specifying that the child is an *only* son or daughter (7:12: a scene unique to Luke; 8:42, dif. Matthew, Mark; 9:38, dif. Matthew, Mark). The raising of the widow's son in 7:11–17 is an especially good example of the use of pathos. The dead man is the only son of a widowed mother. Not only has the mother already lost her husband, but presumably she both loves her son and is dependent economically on him. We are presented with a funeral scene with a large crowd of mourners. Although the narrator seldom indicates the emotions of Jesus,[32] we are told here that "the Lord was moved with compassion (ἐσπλαγχνίσθη)" on seeing the widow, and after bringing the son back to life, we are told that Jesus "gave him to his mother," which not only recalls Elijah's raising of a widow's son (see 1 Kgs 17:23) but also reemphasizes the son's importance to his mother.

Interest in and concern for the needy person's success in finding a cure are increased when obstacles appear which must be surmounted by decisive action. These add to suspense and therefore to the readers' involvement in the needy person's problem and efforts to find a solution. In Luke 5:17–26 the paralytic and his friends not only encounter the obstacle of the crowd, forcing them to lower the paralytic through the roof, but also a second obstacle in the objection of the scribes and Pharisees, an obstacle which Jesus overcomes for them.[33] An apparent obstacle appears when Jesus is delayed on the way to heal Jairus' daughter and the girl dies before he arrives (8:41–56). The crowd at the house underscores this obstacle, for it is mourning the girl when Jesus arrives and then laughs at his claim that the girl is sleeping. The blind beggar, shouting for Jesus' attention, is first rebuked by the crowd, but his persistence in spite of this obstacle leads to a cure (18:35–43). When Jesus overcomes the obstacle,

---

[31] 7:2 is a further variation on this: the centurion's slave was "precious to him."

[32] See J. Fitzmyer, *Luke I–IX*, 95.

[33] This objection introduces a second "move" into the story, since there is now another kind of tension which must be resolved. The story not only concerns whether a man will be healed but how Jesus can defend his work of releasing sins. However, for the paralytic and his friends the objection of the scribes and Pharisees is another obstacle in finding a cure.

this emphasizes his authority and power, but these obstacles also increase the readers' involvement in the experience of the person in need, adding interest and suspense to the development from need to solution which is basic to these healing stories.

In one group of stories, the social and religious status of the needy person is a potential obstacle, adding suspense by raising the question of how Jesus will react to such people. In each case there is some indication that there might be a problem. In the story of the leper in 5:12–16, the leper is confident that Jesus is *able* to cleanse him but is unsure if he will *want* to (5:12). Although the leper is socially ostracized and religiously unclean, Jesus is willing to touch and heal him (5:13). In the story of the centurion in 7:2–10, it is the centurion himself who declares that, as a Gentile, he is "not worthy" to have Jesus enter his house or to meet Jesus directly. The woman with the "flow of blood" (8:43–48) is unclean because of this.[34] Her behavior after touching Jesus' clothing and being cured shows that her uncleanness is a factor in the story, for she is fearful how Jesus will respond to her contact with him. She hides as long as possible and finally approaches "trembling." Here the suspense of the story concerns not so much the healing as Jesus' response to being touched by an unclean woman.[35] In 17:12–19, the story of the ten lepers, we are told as the scene comes to a climax that the leper who returned to Jesus was a Samaritan. The importance of this fact is underscored when Jesus refers to him as "this foreigner." In each case Jesus refuses to recognize any social or religious barrier to his healing work and explicitly affirms the right of the needy person to share in it, in the case of the first leper by responding "I do want to" (5:13), in the other three cases by giving his approval to the suspect persons who have sought his help by describing their behavior as "faith." Of these four stories, only the last is unique to Luke. Nevertheless, their importance in Luke is indicated by the fact that they fit a larger Lukan emphasis on Jesus' ministry to the neglected and excluded.[36]

Robert Alter, in discussing "the techniques of repetition" in the Hebrew Bible, indicates that repetition of word-motifs is used "in larger narrative units, to sustain a thematic development and to establish instructive connections between seemingly disparate episodes."[37] When we compare

---

[34] See Lev 15:19–30 and Marla J. Selvidge, "Mark 5:25–34 and Leviticus 15:19–20," 619–23.

[35] Cures through touching Jesus have already been reported in Luke 6:19. There is no indication that there is anything wrong in an ordinary person seeking to be cured in this way.

[36] See chap. 4. On the centurion, the woman with the flow of blood, and the Samaritan leper, see pp. 114–16, 118–20, 136.

[37] *Art of Biblical Narrative*, 94.

the various healing and exorcism stories in Luke, we discover that there are a series of repetitions not only of word-motifs but of whole sentences. These repetitions should remind the reader that a basic kind of relationship between Jesus and a character type has returned. The repetition not only indicates the importance of this relationship but also enriches the readers' experience of it, for each scene will express the relationship in an individual way, with some scenes developing a special aspect of the relationship. Thus the words, "What do you have to do with me?" in 8:28 recall the almost identical response of the demon in 4:34. This is verbal indication that a basic situation—a demon sensing the threatening presence of Jesus—has returned. After the similarity is established, the story in 8:26–33 develops the encounter of Jesus with the demon at greater length and in a unique way. In another set of scenes, two kinds of verbal repetition recall a situation which the narrator evidently regards as especially impressive and useful. A situation of extreme need within a family is indicated three times by referring to a mother or father's "only (μονο-γενής)" son or daughter (7:12; 8:42; 9:38), and on two of these occasions the cure is followed by the statement, "And he gave him [or "gave him back"] to his mother" or "father" (7:15; 9:42). In other respects there is variation. One scene involves a mother and a son, another a father and a daughter, another a father and a son. Two involve resurrection, while the third is an exorcism. In spite of these variations, the repeated words remind readers of the return of a situation which has special interest for the narrator, who may regard it as particularly revelatory of Jesus' significance as benefactor of those in extreme need. The last two healings on the trip to Jerusalem both contain the cry, "Jesus . . . , have mercy on us" or "me" (17:13; 18:38, 39), an entreaty which is not found elsewhere in Luke's healing stories. In this case, the repetition may emphasize that Jesus shows mercy both on a Samaritan and on a Jew (see the blind beggar's repeated use of the distinctly Jewish title "Son of David" in 18:38, 39). In both these cases Jesus' final response is the declaration, "Your faith has saved you" (17:19; 18:42), a sentence which is exactly repeated in two other places (7:50, not a healing story; 8:48).

In each of these four cases, Jesus is commending a particular person by describing his or her behavior as "faith" and is attributing a crucial role to this faith in each person's successful search for wholeness. Those who are commended by Jesus for their faith become examples to others, and the series of episodes in which faith is demonstrated builds up a composite picture of the way faith shows itself. In addition to the stories already mentioned, faith is attributed to the paralytic and his friends in 5:20 and to the centurion in 7:9, while Jairus is urged to have faith in 8:50. Those who are commended for their faith have done something extraordinary.

They have shown unusual boldness or persistence in approaching Jesus, undeterred by crowds and religious barriers (the paralytic and his friends, the centurion, the hemorrhaging woman, the Samaritan leper, the blind beggar; also the sinful woman in 7:36–50). They have shown unusual humility and trust in Jesus' power (the centurion). They have shown a gratitude for what Jesus has done that contrasts with the attitude of others (the sinful woman, the Samaritan leper). The boldness of these persons suggests that their faith involves an awakening of hope, a throwing off of helpless resignation through the recognition of a power outside themselves capable of meeting human need.

Three of the four stories in which Jesus declares that "your faith has saved you" show special affinities to which this repeated statement may call attention. There seems to be a clear intention to relate the first two instances, for they are less than a chapter apart and end not only with the refrain, "Your faith has saved you," but in addition, "Go in peace." In comparison with its parallels in Mark and Matthew, Luke 8:48 is phrased so as to conform more exactly to Luke 7:50. This calls attention to some similarities in the two cases, for each concerns a woman who boldly steps out of line in order to "touch" Jesus (7:39; 8:44–47), and Jesus accepts both, commending their faith. There are also similarities between the stories of the sinful woman and the Samaritan leper. Both stories are centrally concerned with the gratitude or grateful love which a socially excluded person shows to Jesus, and both stories contrast this response with the attitude of another or others. Jesus' statement to the Samaritan leper, "Your faith has saved you" (17:19), may remind the reader that the sinful woman earlier showed her faith in a similar way.

In the stories of the sinful woman and the Samaritan leper, there is interest in the relation between Jesus and the other person which may develop after that person has been helped. In 7:41–47 Jesus interprets the woman's actions as an expression of her grateful love, arising from forgiveness granted by Jesus.[38] The failure of the Pharisee to show similar love throws sharply into focus the contrasting ways in which sinners and Pharisees are responding to Jesus. The story of the Samaritan leper also presents contrasting responses to Jesus. It is clear that being healed by Jesus does not always produce a right response, for nine lepers fail to return to Jesus and give thanks. When Jesus asks, "Where are the nine?" he is faulting their behavior for not "returning to give glory to God" (17:17–18). Why must they *return* to do this? Presumably God could be thanked elsewhere. It is clear that acknowledgment of God's power,

---

[38] The fuller discussion of the story of the sinful woman on pp. 116–18 includes comment on the exegetical problem in 7:47.

transmitted through *Jesus*, is the basis for judging the lepers' behavior. The healed person's response to Jesus after the healing plays a key role in the story, just as the sinful woman's response to Jesus is emphasized in 7:36–50.[39] The emphasis on the response of gratitude to Jesus suggests that Jesus should not be forgotten once help has been received, for receiving help can and should be the start of a lasting relationship, as with Peter, who follows Jesus after the healing of his mother-in-law and the great catch of fish (5:11), and the healed women, who accompany Jesus on his journeys (8:2–3).[40] Enjoying Jesus' benefits is not sufficient; his mighty acts must be seen as signs of God's reign, as calls to repentance and invitations to participate in God's purpose through bearing fruit steadily as disciples.

In Luke's healing stories Jesus is presented as benefactor of the sick and disabled. The narrator's efforts to create sympathy for the sick, discussed above, also heighten the importance of Jesus' response to their needs. It is Jesus who is able to meet the varied needs of these pathetic sufferers. But Jesus is not a doctor who acts in his own right. In addressing the needs of the sick and disabled, he is carrying out God's purpose for the time of salvation announced in Scripture, bringing release to the captives and sight to the blind (4:18). Since God's purpose and power stand behind Jesus' healings, the crowd responds appropriately when it glorifies God.

JESUS THE PROPHET

Jesus is "a prophet mighty in work and word" (24:19) and yet is rejected and suffers a violent fate. The rejection, as well as the mighty work and word, belongs to a pattern of prophetic experience which is important for understanding the Lukan view of Jesus. This prophetic pattern enables the narrator to hold together as a meaningful unity Jesus' message, acts of power, and violent death. We distort the Lukan view of Jesus' mighty acts when we isolate them from the prophetic context which unifies these three facets of Jesus' story. To be sure, this unity is full of tension. A powerful prophet who benefits the people by saving acts should receive grateful

---

[39] On the Samaritan leper see further pp. 118–20.

[40] Discipleship motifs are also associated with the healed blind man, who "was following" Jesus after receiving his sight (18:43), and with the healed demoniac in 8:34–39, who sits "at Jesus' feet," begs to "be with" Jesus, and finally proclaims what Jesus has done. However, in the latter case the people of the area ask Jesus to leave after the exorcism, and Jesus does not permit the healed man to accompany him. This is Gentile territory, and Jesus' withdrawal fits the general Lukan view that Jesus' contacts with Gentiles were limited and exceptional. The Gentile mission comes after Jesus' mission to Israel.

recognition. However, biblical history, as understood by the narrator, indicates that it has repeatedly been otherwise.

Those who speak of Jesus as a prophet in Luke may not understand him completely, but this title does not represent a distortion to be rejected. The title prophet says something positive and important about Jesus. In particular, it enables the narrator to comprehend, through relating Jesus' life to a scriptural pattern, the combination of powerful word, mighty deed, and rejection by God's people found in the tradition about Jesus. It also illuminates the similarity and continuity among Jesus, his Old Testament predecessors, and his successors in the church's mission. The importance of Jesus as prophet is shown by the narrator's care to emphasize the parallel between Jesus' mighty acts and those of Elijah, leading to the confession, "A great prophet has arisen among us" (7:16).[41] It is also shown by the fact that Jesus himself twice indicates that his life is governed by the rule of rejection and death for prophets (4:24; 13:33).[42]

The association of Jesus' mighty acts with his role as prophet is especially clear in the raising of the widow's son (7:11–17). However, the interest in Jesus as a prophet like Elijah continues after this scene. In 7:39 a Pharisee refers to the claim that Jesus is a prophet, 9:8 and 19 report that some view Jesus as Elijah or another prophet, and reminiscences of the story of Elijah and the widow's son recur in 8:55 and 9:42. Jesus is also the promised prophet like Moses (Acts 3:22; 7:37). Moses, like Jesus, was "mighty in his words and works" (Acts 7:22; cf. Luke 24:19), did "wonders and signs" (Acts 7:36), and yet was rejected by his people (Acts 7:23–40). The references to Jesus casting out demons "by the finger of God" (Luke 11:20; cf. Exod 8:19) and to Jesus' "exodus" in Luke 9:31 (dif. Matthew, Mark) indicate that this Moses typology is also present in Luke's Gospel.[43] Since Jesus is like the miracle-working prophets Moses and Elijah, it is not surprising that in Luke 4:23–24, 13:32–33, and 24:19 Jesus is spoken of as a prophet in connection with his healings and exorcisms.

But the prophets are rejected by the people, suffer persecution, and are killed. There is an interrelated group of passages in Luke-Acts which summarize Old Testament history by saying that "their fathers" or "your fathers" persecuted or killed the prophets (Luke 6:23; 11:47–51; Acts 7:52), and Jerusalem is addressed as "the killer of the prophets" (Luke

---

[41] See above, p. 88.

[42] The role of Jesus and his witnesses as prophets is illuminated by P. Minear, *To Heal and to Reveal*, 102–47; Luke T. Johnson, *The Literary Function of Possessions*, 38–126; Richard J. Dillon, *From Eye-Witnesses*, 114–27; U. Busse, *Die Wunder des Propheten Jesus*, 372–414.

[43] On Luke's Moses typology, see further A. George, *Études sur l'oeuvre de Luc*, 128–29.

13:34).[44] These statements provide a general pattern within which the rejection and death of Jesus are understood. This application to Jesus is made clear in key previews and reviews of his death. Preview statements in Luke 4:24 and, especially, 13:33–34 reveal that his fate will fit the pattern of the rejected and murdered prophet, and in a later review of events Stephen declares that the murderers of Jesus have treated him in the same way as their fathers did the prophets (Acts 7:52). The emphasis on the rejection of Moses in Acts 7:23–40 leads up to this accusation.

The prophet Jesus, who performed mighty works for the people, is rejected and killed. This course of events seems tragic and irrational yet follows scriptural precedent. This tensive combination of mighty acts and suffering through rejection not only appears in the thematic references to the prophet already mentioned but is also expressed in connection with the Son of Man passion sayings in Luke 9. In 9:43 Jesus abruptly breaks into the amazement produced by his mighty acts to speak of his coming fate. This verse forms a tight juncture between the preceding exorcism story and the following passion announcement. While Mark separates the exorcism and the passion announcement by a private conversation between Jesus and the disciples and then by a travel notice (Mark 9:28–30), in Luke Jesus speaks to the disciples "while all were marveling at all the things which he was doing," a reaction caused by the preceding exorcism. In this situation, with everyone so impressed by Jesus' power, the sudden announcement that Jesus is going "to be handed over" seems calculated to produce shock, or, as 9:45 indicates, stupefied bewilderment, as Jesus vainly attempts to communicate with the disciples about the other side of his destined role.[45] The combination of power and suffering elsewhere associated with the prophet reappears in high tension through the editorial bridge in 9:43.

We find a similar sequence in 9:18–22. The material between the disciples' puzzled question about Jesus' identity in 8:25 and Peter's confession in 9:20 leads us to assume that Peter arrived at his new insight through witnessing Jesus' mighty acts and, through Jesus, receiving the power to heal and cast out demons himself.[46] The response of Jesus to Peter's confession is the same as his response to the marveling at miracles in 9:43: Jesus declares that the Son of Man must suffer. Here also the narrator has tightened the connection between the passion announcement and what precedes it. The passion announcement in 9:22 does not form a

---

[44] The development of this tradition of "the violent fate of the prophets" has been traced by Odil Hannes Steck, *Israel und das gewaltsame Geschick.*

[45] Note that Luke 9:44 departs from Matthew and Mark in omitting any reference to resurrection.

[46] On this point see further pp. 214–15, 218–19.

separate sentence but is attached with a participle to the preceding verse. This connection makes clear that the rebuke, the command to silence, and the passion announcement are all part of a single response by Jesus to Peter's confession. Here as in 9:43–45 the shift from recognition of Jesus' power and greatness to the announcement of his coming suffering is sudden, deliberately abrupt.

The pattern of striking conjunctions of Jesus' power and grandeur with his rejection and death noted in 9:20–22 and 9:43–45 can also be found in the transfiguration scene in Luke. When Jesus appears in glory to his disciples, Luke alone adds that Moses and Elijah were speaking to Jesus about "his exodus, which he was going to accomplish in Jerusalem" (9:31). Here Jesus' glory is tied to a task still to be accomplished, which involves rejection and death. These interesting conjunctions in Luke 9 are prepared by 7:22–23, where the joyful affirmation that the prophecies of the time of salvation are being fulfilled in Jesus' healings is abruptly followed by the warning, "Blessed is whoever is not scandalized by me." The possibility of scandal is heightened in Luke 9 when Jesus begins to speak about his coming death. Thus the excitement produced by Jesus' miracles, including Peter's confession based on Jesus' demonstrations of power, is being tempered by the passion announcements. Recognizing the grandeur of God manifest in Jesus (see 9:43) is inadequate; one must also recognize that Jesus must die rejected. There is a mystery here which the disciples will be slow to understand[47] but which is central to Jesus' role as prophet and Messiah.

---

[47] On the hiddenness and revelation of this mystery in the disciples' story, see pp. 226–27, 277–89.

Chapter Four

JESUS' MINISTRY TO THE OPPRESSED AND EXCLUDED

Jesus' Ministry to the Oppressed and Excluded

In his ministry Jesus intervenes on the side of the oppressed and excluded, assuring them that they share in God's salvation and defending them against others who want to maintain their own superiority at the expense of such people. The groups for whom Jesus intervenes are not sharply defined and delimited. They include a number of partly overlapping groups. In his ministry Jesus helps the poor, sinners, tax collectors, women, Samaritans, and Gentiles. Each of these groups was excluded or subordinated in the society to which Jesus spoke, and the Lukan narrator seems to be especially interested in Jesus' ministry to these people.

THE RELEASE OF SINS

Before dealing with other aspects of Jesus' ministry to the excluded, we will consider certain literary methods which the narrator uses to give an impressive portrayal of Jesus as the one through whom God sends the release of sins to sinners and tax collectors. We previously noted the importance given to proclaiming "release ($\H{a}\phi\epsilon\sigma\iota\varsigma$)" in the statement of Jesus' mission in 4:18. In discussing the significance of release for the captives in Jesus' mission, I suggested that it has a broad meaning which probably includes at least the following: (1) release for the poor, i.e., the economically oppressed; (2) release through healing and exorcism for those oppressed by demons and the devil; (3) "release of sins ($\H{a}\phi\epsilon\sigma\iota\varsigma$ $\H{a}\mu\alpha\rho\tau\iota\hat{\omega}\nu$)."[1] After the announcement in Nazareth the healings and exorcisms reported in 4:31–5:16 immediately give an indication of how Jesus brought the second kind of release. Beginning in 5:17 the narrator demonstrates special interest in Jesus as the proclaimer of the release of sins by taking a diverse group of stories related to this theme and artfully connecting them, even though they are separated by other material. The stories are connected because later stories repeatedly remind the reader of earlier, related stories. This contributes to the unity of the narrative. It also encourages a reading process of recall and comparison so that as each

---

[1] See above, pp. 65–66.

new episode is sounded, the related episodes resound with enriching harmonies.

Luke 5:17–26 is the first of this series of connected episodes. This story of the healing of the paralytic is Jesus' first encounter with the scribes and Pharisees and so begins the series of controversies with them. It is also the first reference to Jesus forgiving sins.[2] Luke presents the scene as a demonstration of Jesus' authority to release (or forgive)[3] sins before representatives of all Israel. While Mark indicates the presence of a large crowd and introduces "some of the scribes" only when their response affects the course of events (Mark 2:6), Luke indicates at the beginning the presence of "Pharisees and teachers of the law who had come from every village of Galilee and Judea and Jerusalem" (Luke 5:17). Before this remarkable gathering Jesus demonstrates his power (δύναμις) to heal (5:17) and his authority (ἐξουσία) to forgive (5:24). There have been previous references to Jesus' δύναμις and ἐξουσία (4:14, 32, 36), but now the readers are shown that Jesus' authority includes the authority to release sins. This point is made in 5:24 in a general assertion about Jesus' authority and continuing activity: "In order that you may know that the Son of Man has authority on earth to release sins (repeatedly).[4] . . ." These words (and the healing to which they point) interpret Jesus' role throughout the gospel. They indicate that the release which Jesus was sent to proclaim according to 4:18 includes the release of sins.

Luke 5:27–32, the call of Levi and the meal in Levi's house, is linked to 5:17–26 by the continuing theme of opposition from scribes and Pharisees to Jesus' behavior toward sinners. This is also true of the Markan parallels to these scenes, but in Luke the thematic connection is supported by a tighter narrative sequence. The reference to Jesus teaching the crowd by the sea, found between the healing of the paralytic and the call of Levi in Mark 2:13, is not present in Luke. Luke's version makes it appear that the call of Levi occurred soon after Jesus left the house where the paralytic was healed. In Luke the continuity between the call of Levi and the meal in the tax collector's house is also strengthened, for it is made clear that

---

[2] However, forgiveness of sins has already been mentioned in connection with the work of John the Baptist. See 1:77; 3:3. In relation to the important theme of repentance and forgiveness, Luke does not contrast Jesus with John the Baptist but presents Jesus as the "stronger" one (3:16) who continues what John began.

[3] The verb ἀφίημι, prominently used in this story, comes from the same root as the noun ἄφεσις. In certain contexts it can be translated "forgive," although it has a broader range of uses than this English word. "Release" covers more of this broad range, but even it cannot be used to translate the Greek word in all contexts. Speaking of the "release of sins" does remind us, however, that this is one of several kinds of release which Jesus was sent to proclaim.

[4] The present infinitive implies repeated or continuous action.

this was a meal given by Levi in his own house, while it is not clear whose house is meant in Mark 2:15.

These connections help Luke 5:27–32 to develop the role of Jesus as forgiver of the sinful, which begins in 5:17–26, and the role of the Pharisees and scribes as opponents of such forgiveness. Now the "tax collectors and sinners" are introduced. This is not the last time that we will hear of Jesus eating with tax collectors and sinners, which produces grumbling from critics (cf. 15:1–2; 19:7; all three passages use γογγύζω or διαγογγύζω to express the grumbling). The narrator is using a technique which Robert Alter has called the "type-scene,"[5] a technique of forming episodes from a set of motifs which can be repeated with variations. This allows a skillful writer to emphasize and enrich the narrative portrait of a leading character by using the motifs again. As in the healing of the paralytic, the story of the meal in Levi's house makes a general point about Jesus' role: "I have not come to call righteous people but sinners to repentance" (5:32). By including such statements the narrator is progressively clarifying Jesus' commission, expanding the initial statement in 4:18–19.

Luke 7:18–50 has a number of points of contact with previous material, including the material which we have just discussed. The question of John the Baptist in 7:19 allows Jesus to summarize his previous activity. Jesus' response to John recalls for the reader previous stories about Jesus' benefits for the lame, the leper, the dead, and his beatitude for the poor (6:20). Jesus' work is described in rhythmic phrases which are reminiscent of the prophecies of Isaiah, and the first and last of these phrases (τυφλοὶ ἀναβλέπουσιν, "blind receive their sight"; πτωχοὶ εὐαγγελίζονται, "poor have good news preached to them") are clearly related to the words of Isaiah quoted by Jesus in 4:18. Thus the reply to John indicates to the reader that the fulfillment of the commission announced in Nazareth is underway.[6]

There is no direct reference in 7:22 to Jesus' commission to proclaim release of sins. However, we are reminded of this aspect of his work soon after, in 7:31–50. Within the context of Luke's Gospel, the words of Jesus in 7:34 ("The Son of Man has come eating and drinking, and you say, 'Behold, a glutton and a drunkard, a friend of tax collectors and sinners.'") clearly relate to 5:29–32, the only previous scene in which Jesus is shown to be eating and drinking with tax collectors and sinners. The phrasing of 7:34 makes the connection especially clear: ἐλήλυθεν ("has come")—the perfect tense as in 5:32, not the aorist as in Matt 11:19; "eating and

---

[5] See *Art of Biblical Narrative*, 47–62.
[6] On 7:18–23 see further pp. 79–81.

drinking"—the accusation in 5:30 has "eat and drink," while the parallel in Mark 2:16 has only "eat" (according to the best texts); "tax collectors and sinners" as in 5:30. So in 7:31–35 Jesus comments on the reaction which he has encountered in fulfilling the role announced in 5:32, where he was replying to the same kind of reaction.

Jesus' reply in 7:31–35 to criticism of his association with sinners leads into 7:36–50, the story of the sinful woman in the Pharisee's house. As in many of the pronouncement stories and parables with three characters, the characters in this scene represent contrasting attitudes. Jesus and Simon the Pharisee have contrasting attitudes toward the sinful woman. This also results in contrasting attitudes toward Jesus by Simon and the woman. The latter contrast is emphasized by the parable of the two debtors and by the words of Jesus in 7:44–46. This scene's concern with responses to Jesus, the bringer of God's forgiveness, relates 7:36–50 closely with 7:31–35. However, the scene does not end, as we might expect, with Jesus' rebuke of the Pharisee. Verses 48–50, which might seem to be a clumsy addendum, tie 7:36–50 to the story of the healing of the paralytic in 5:17–26. In both 5:20–21 and 7:48–50 faith is connected with release of sins, and Jesus' statement, "Your sins have been released," provokes the response, "Who is this who . . . ?" (dif. Matthew, Mark). Thus the story of the sinful woman in the Pharisee's house reminds us of the previous conflict over Jesus' authority to release sins, suggesting that this is a continuing conflict. This reminder may also help readers to recall Jesus' basic claim of authority to release sins in 5:24.[7]

In 15:1–2 the narrator provides a setting for three following parables by the "type-scene" technique: the motifs of 5:29–32 (the meal in Levi's house) are reused, including the reference to the Pharisees and scribes "grumbling" and to Jesus eating with sinners, although no meal is reported at this point. Thus Luke 15 presents another, more extensive reply to the objection already voiced in 5:30. The connection with 5:29–32 extends to the parables in Luke 15, for the contrast between the "righteous (δίκαιοι)" and sinners who repent in 5:32 reappears in 15:7, with an echo in 15:10. Thus the parables of the lost sheep and lost coin provide parabolic comment on the statement of Jesus' commission to call sinners in 5:32. The three parables are united by the image of something "lost": a sheep, a coin, a son (15:4, 6, 8, 9, 24, 32; the last two references form a refrain within the third parable). This image will reappear in a statement about Jesus' mission in 19:10.

The contrast between the "righteous" and the tax collectors-sinners in 5:32 and 15:7 reappears in 18:9–14, with this variation: the parable of the

---

[7] On 7:36–50 see further pp. 116–18, 177–78.

Pharisee and the tax collector is addressed to those who "trust in themselves that they are righteous" (18:9), and the final comment on the parable announces the reversal of their supposed status, for the tax collector, rather than the Pharisee, goes home "justified" (δεδικαιωμένος="righteoused"). There is also variation in the level of narration. Instead of narrating a story about Jesus encountering Pharisees and tax collectors, the narrator has Jesus narrate a story about a Pharisee and a tax collector. This story, like the parables of the great supper, lost sheep, lost coin, lost son, rich man and Lazarus (Luke 14–16), should be understood in the context of the larger Lukan story as comments on the kind of people that Jesus is encountering in his mission. Specifically, the story of the Pharisee and the tax collector is a comment on the Pharisees and tax collectors in previous scenes and provides further support for Jesus' acceptance of sinners.

In the story of Zacchaeus (19:1–10) another individual (besides Levi) emerges from the anonymous crowd of tax collectors and sinners. He has a name, some individual traits, and is allowed to speak. This contributes to the interest of the story. There are clear connections between this story and previous Lukan material. In 19:7, as in 5:30 and 15:2, we have the motif of "grumbling" at Jesus' association with a "sinner," although this time the crowd does the grumbling. This scene of conflict over association with a tax collector ends with a general statement of what Jesus "came to" do (19:10), just as in 5:32. In both of these statements Jesus' association with tax collectors and sinners in the respective scenes is interpreted as illustration of a general mission to these excluded groups. Furthermore, the use of "Son of Man" in 19:10 may relate this statement to the general statement about Jesus' authority to forgive in 5:24, where this title was also used. But the parables of chapter 15 are also influential, for according to 19:10 it is Jesus' mission "to seek and to save the *lost*." This suggests that, in the view of the implied author, the seeking shepherd of 15:4–7 is a figure for Jesus.

The story of Zacchaeus is placed late in the narrative of Jesus' ministry, shortly before his arrival in Jerusalem. This is useful for two reasons. First, there is a link with the story of the rich ruler in 18:18–23 (both he and Zacchaeus are described as "rich [πλούσιος]" in 18:23; 19:1). The story of Zacchaeus provides an answer to the question of whether and how a rich man can be saved (see 18:24–27). Second, 19:10 provides a retrospective summary of Jesus' saving work. The connection between 5:32 and 19:10 suggests that they form an inclusion. That is, we have similar general statements about Jesus' mission early and late in his ministry, statements which serve to interpret the whole ministry which lies between them. Through repetition and significant placement the narrator emphasizes that these are important and comprehensive interpretations of the purpose of Jesus in God's plan.[8]

We have seen that 5:17–32 shows Jesus fulfilling his commission to proclaim "release" (4:18) and relates this commission to the release of sins. We have also noted a whole series of scenes in Luke which show some resemblance to 5:17–32. Indeed, all of the scenes discussed following our consideration of 5:17–32 (except for 7:18–23, which is related to 4:18 but does not refer to the release of sins or Jesus' ministry to sinners) show such resemblance. The narrator is creating thematic unity out of separate scenes, suggesting relationships among scenes through repeated reminiscences of previous episodes.

Some implications of the preceding discussion can be briefly stated:

(1) Jesus' mission to proclaim "release of sins" has thematic importance for the implied author. Its importance is indicated not only by the number of scenes which relate to this theme but also by its appearance in fundamental statements about Jesus' mission and authority. At the beginning of his public ministry Jesus announces that he has been sent and authorized by God to proclaim release (4:18), and in 5:24 he proclaims his authority to release sins. These disclosures are supported by the interpretations of Jesus' mission in 5:32 and 19:10, where Jesus indicates that he has come to call or seek sinners or the lost. This mission and authority belong to Jesus from the beginning of his ministry. This perspective may explain why the implied author felt no need to emphasize that forgiveness comes through an atoning death.[9]

(2) The narrator presents an impressive portrayal of Jesus' work of releasing sins by linking scenes related to this theme. These links contribute to the unity of the narrative. They also suggest that Luke's Gospel is shaped to make its impact through a process of emphasis and enrichment which takes place as readers make significant connections among episodes, recalling previous events and comparing them with new events. In this reading process of recall and comparison, new events in the story call forth enriching harmonies from the previous narrative. The narrator encourages this process.

(3) In most of the scenes discussed in this section, Jesus is responding to criticism. Negative reactions appear not only because Jesus claims the authority to forgive but also because through forgiveness he is calling and accepting people who are outcasts. Forgiveness has social implications. Those whom God forgives must be accepted into the religious community. But the people Jesus accepts remain unacceptable in the eyes of many.

---

[8] On 19:1–10 see further pp. 122–25.
[9] See below, p. 285.

Since Jesus, through forgiveness, redefines the religious community, his work is a challenge to social existence. His call of the outcasts of Israel is the first step in the formation of a community which tears down old walls by including the previously excluded. In a second step the Gentiles will also participate.

(4) Material shared with other gospels may nevertheless have special importance in Luke. Although Luke 5:17–32 has parallels in both Matthew and Mark, the repeated reminders of these episodes later in Luke testify to their special importance.

Sayings and Parables of Reversal

Human society perpetuates structures of injustice and exclusion, but God intervenes on the side of the oppressed. The disruptive effect of this intervention is often presented in Luke as a reversal of the structures of society: those with power, status, and riches are put down and those without them are exalted. This reversal was proclaimed in the Magnificat (1:51–53). A similar overturn of the established order was anticipated in Simeon's prophecy that Jesus "is set for the fall and rising of many in Israel" (2:34).

The disruptive reversal caused by Jesus is announced in short sayings and in parables. It is also depicted in pronouncement stories. I will discuss the sayings and parables briefly and will study pronouncement stories (specifically, quest stories) more extensively.

Jesus proclaims a sharp reversal of situation as he preaches good news to the poor in the beatitudes (6:20–23). Contrasting terms are used (the hungry will be filled, the weeping will laugh), and there is also contrast between the beatitudes and the woes, which declare that the rich will suffer a negative reversal. Not only the possession of riches but also honored status in society is judged negatively (6:24–26). Later Jesus announces in short sayings a reversal in the situation of the wise and the babes (10:21), the last and the first (13:30), those who exalt themselves and those who humble themselves (14:11; 18:14; see also 16:15). Similarly, a desire for positions of honor is an occasion for woe and warning (11:43; 14:7–10; 20:46). The disciples, too, are warned that they must take account of God's reversal, which determines that only the least can be great (9:46–48; 22:24–27).

The reversal takes narrative form in some of the parables. The parable of the great supper is preceded by teaching about whom to invite to dinner, not friends, relatives, and rich neighbors, but the poor, maimed, lame, and blind (14:12–13). The same contrast between people of social standing and wealth, on the one hand, and beggars, on the other, is present in the parable (14:16–24). Those originally invited were people of property. But it is the beggars brought in from the street who partake of the banquet, upsetting normal expectations. Reversal after death takes place in the story of the rich man and poor Lazarus (16:19–31). The parables present not only the reversal of rich and poor but also the reversal of those who think of themselves as righteous and the sinners or tax collectors. The story of the Pharisee and the tax collector praying in the temple is told to those who "trust in themselves that they are righteous," but, contrary to their expectations, the penitent tax collector is declared to be the righteous one (18:14). The parable of the lost son is addressed to the Pharisees and scribes who are critics of Jesus' meals with tax collectors and sinners (15:1–2). In the story the initial situation is reversed: the son who leaves his father and squanders the family wealth finally shares his father's joy and banquet, while the son who faithfully stayed home is estranged from his family. In the parable of the good Samaritan, the Samaritan does not reverse his situation, but he upsets expectations of a Jewish audience. He surprisingly fills the role of the one who knows the meaning of the command to love the neighbor (10:29–37).

Some of the neglected and excluded groups to whom Jesus ministers appear in fictional form in these parables. Thus there are points of correspondence between certain parables and the stories of Jesus' ministry to needy persons. Three of the four names in the list of those to be brought into the banquet in 14:21 are also included in the summary of Jesus' ministry in 7:22, where Jesus, in response to John the Baptist, recalls and clarifies his mission as stated in 4:18.[10] The parable which favors the repentant tax collector (18:9–14) fits with Jesus' defense of calling sinners and tax collectors to repentance in 5:27–32 and 19:1–10. The setting of the parable of the lost son (15:1–2) relates it closely to Jesus' meals with tax collectors and sinners, and a festive meal for the lost son has a central place in the parable. In the parable of the good Samaritan, a Samaritan is contrasted with a Jewish priest and Levite, while the Samaritan leper in 17:12–19 is favorably contrasted with other lepers who fail to show gratitude for healing. The standard opinions of Jesus' society are reversed both in the parables and in the stories of Jesus' ministry, and some of the same groups appear in both.

---

[10] The terms which correspond with 14:21 are placed first, second, and last in the list in 7:22, positions of emphasis. The first and last in 7:22 ("blind" and "poor") also appear in 4:18.

QUEST STORIES

Synoptic pronouncement stories are brief narratives which report how Jesus responded in words (and sometimes also in action) to something said or observed on a particular occasion. In previous study of these stories, I divided them into five types, based on the variety of ways in which Jesus' response relates to the cause of that response.[11] Jesus may respond by correcting what he has seen or heard, or he may commend it. His response may answer an objection against his behavior, or it may simply answer a question. Thus many of the pronouncement stories can be classified as correction, commendation, objection, or inquiry stories.

In addition, there is another type of pronouncement story, the quest story. This type is more common in Luke than in the other gospels. In the synoptic quest story someone approaches Jesus in quest of something very important to human well-being. This quest is a dominant concern of the story; its importance is shown by the fact that the episode does not end until we are told whether the quest is successful or not. While many pronouncement stories simply end with Jesus' pronouncement, with no indication of how the other person responded to this, the quest story indicates how the encounter comes out for the person who approaches Jesus. We are shown that the person was either successful or unsuccessful. This type of story, therefore, shows greater interest in the persons who encounter Jesus than do most pronouncement stories. The limits of the episode are defined by the quest of such persons, for the episode begins by introducing a questing person and ends when we learn that the quest was successful or unsuccessful. The quest holds the episode together as a unity, for the development from beginning to end shows progress toward the goal of the quest or obstacles which block such progress. Jesus remains the person of authority in the scene, and his pronouncement will determine whether the quest is successful. But the quester is also given real importance in the scene. He or she has an important need, and the need tends to elicit sympathy from hearers of the story. The tension arising from this need unifies the story, and it comes to a meaningful conclusion when we learn whether the need has been fulfilled or not.

Suspense is heightened by the presence of some difficulty or conflict which blocks fulfillment of the quest. The conversation in the scene will highlight this difficulty or conflict. Jesus may pose a difficult condition or raise an objection. Or an objection may be expressed by another party. There may also be contrasting characters who represent conflicting ways

---

[11] See Robert C. Tannehill, "The Pronouncement Story and Its Types"; Tannehill, "Varieties of Synoptic Pronouncement Stories"; Tannehill, "Types and Functions of Apophthegms."

of acting or judging. Through these devices the storyteller focuses attention on a particular issue as the crucial issue for the success or failure of the quest. The stories speak to these issues, and indirectly they seek to persuade. Because Jesus in Luke is presented as a person of authority and insight, the narrative tends to persuade us to accept Jesus' definition of the issues and his judgments about them. Placement of Jesus' words in climactic position contributes to this persuasive effect.[12]

Quest stories are especially common in Luke. Of the nine synoptic quest stories, seven are in Luke and four of these are unique to Luke. As a group, these pronouncement stories are comparatively long and vivid. Furthermore, they are a major means of portraying Jesus as one who intercedes for the oppressed and excluded, for in the stories which report a successful quest (six of the seven) Jesus is dealing with such people. In each of the six stories the needy person has some characteristic which, in the eyes of some, would seem to disqualify that person from sharing in God's salvation, for these stories concern a sinful paralytic, a Gentile, a sinful woman, a Samaritan leper, a chief tax collector, and a crucified criminal. In contrast, the one quester who fails is a person of high status (a rich ruler). Thus the quest stories demonstrate the reversal proclaimed in the Magnificat. In these stories Jesus focuses his saving mission on the excluded, despite their negative characteristics, and defends the rightness of doing so. These stories dramatically portray Jesus as the one through whom God reaches out to include the outcasts.

In 5:17–26[13] someone approaches Jesus in need of healing, and the scene ends with the healing and the crowd's amazed response. So the scene has features of a typical healing story. However, it also has features typical of the pronouncement story or apophthegm. Like many of the apophthegms which Bultmann called "controversy dialogues,"[14] there is an objection from scribes and Pharisees to which Jesus responds with a statement (and, in this case, also an action). The combination of quest for wholeness with this objection and response—a response that has a crucial role in the outcome of events—turns the scene into a special type of pronouncement story, the quest story. Bultmann believed that the objection and response involving the scribes and Pharisees is a later addition to this story, which was originally just a healing story.[15] Whether this is so or not, this part of the story has a meaningful function within the whole, resulting in a quest story quite similar in composition to Luke 19:1–10,

---

[12] On the pronouncement story as a form of influence or persuasion, see R. Tannehill, "The Pronouncement Story and Its Types," 3–4.

[13] On this scene see also pp. 104–5 above.

[14] See Rudolf Bultmann, *History of the Synoptic Tradition*, 12–21, 39–54.

[15] *History of the Synoptic Tradition*, 14–15.

the story of Zacchaeus. In both cases there are two obstacles which must be overcome in order to bring the quest to its goal. First, the quester is blocked by the crowd from reaching Jesus and must adopt unusual measures to obtain access. In 5:18–19 the roof is torn apart in order to let the paralytic down from above (cf. 19:3–4). Jesus sees this as a sign of faith and responds favorably. Then a second, more important obstacle appears in the form of an objection to Jesus' behavior (5:21; cf. 19:7). This objection has a clear function within the quest story: it heightens suspense by blocking immediate fulfillment and focuses attention on the issue raised in the objection as the crucial factor in the success of the quest. Jesus must now respond to this objection in order to respond to the need of the questers. Thus Jesus' climactic response, through which the scene comes to resolution, has a double focus: it addresses both the objectors and the questers (5:22–24; cf. 19:9–10).[16] In 5:22–24 Jesus first confronts his critics and indicates that he is about to demonstrate his authority to release sins, then turns to the paralytic with his healing command. The healing both brings the quest to a successful conclusion and answers the critics' objections by demonstrating that "the Son of Man has authority on earth to release sins (repeatedly)." This is a comprehensive claim, as is shown by the use of the present infinitive, suggesting repeated action, and by the scope of this authority, which the Son of Man exercises "on earth."

The importance of this claim to authority for the narrator is shown by the literary links which bind this scene, and the scene which follows in 5:29–32, to subsequent scenes in which Jesus exercises his authority to release sins.[17] These links will show that 5:17–32 functions within the narrative as a basic disclosure of Jesus' mission and authority which remains valid for the rest of his work. The healing of the paralytic both discloses the nature of Jesus' mission and acquaints the readers with the type of person that Jesus helps. The man is not only physically handicapped; he is a sinner. It is assumed that the release of sins is the key to recovery for him. That is why the healing can be viewed as a demonstration of Jesus' authority to release sins (5:24). The crowd blocking the paralytic's access could be read as a literary symbol of the paralytic's exclusion by society as a recognized sinner.[18] In any case, both the healing of the paralytic and the call of Levi prepare for the scene of Jesus eating with tax collectors and sinners in 5:29–32. Levi is an example of the tax collectors and the paralytic is an example of the sinners who respond to Jesus' message and with whom Jesus celebrates the availability of salva-

---

[16] On the double focus of 19:9, see below, p. 124.
[17] See above, pp. 103–9.
[18] Cf. Zacchaeus and the crowd, discussed pp. 122–25.

tion. Thus the narrative provides us with vivid scenes of Jesus' ministry to such people early in the story. It will repeatedly remind us of these scenes as the story develops.

Tax collectors and recognized sinners are not the only excluded groups to whom Jesus ministers, as subsequent quest stories show. Two Lukan quest stories concern a Gentile and a Samaritan (7:2–10; 17:12–19). These persons are members of groups that will be important in the mission of the church (see Acts 8–11). The narrator distinguishes between the scope of Jesus' mission and that of the church. On two occasions Jesus enters foreign territories (Gentile and Samaritan) but in each case is rebuffed (8:37; 9:52–56). Jesus is willing to minister to such people but does not launch a continuing mission in their areas, for the Gentiles and Samaritans are not yet ready to receive him. The quest stories of the centurion and the Samaritan leper balance these rejections with a Gentile and a Samaritan who are helped by Jesus and commended for their faith.

The healing of the centurion's servant (7:2–10) speaks to the issue of whether it is appropriate for Jesus to include Gentiles in his healing ministry. In contrast to some of the other quest stories, the issue is not raised through an objection by a third party (or an objection by Jesus himself, as in Mark 7:27). The conversation is entirely between Jesus and the centurion's representatives, who speak for the centurion and support his cause. Nevertheless, the speakers show awareness of the problem. The Jewish elders insist that the centurion is worthy of help because he has been a patron of local Jews. Such an argument is only necessary because the centurion is not himself a Jew. The speech of the centurion transmitted by the second delegation shows that he is very conscious of the religious barrier between Jews and Gentiles. The centurion maintains his distance out of respect for Jewish sensibilities, and he communicates this in a deferential way. He did not come to Jesus himself because he did not count himself worthy, and he now stops Jesus from approaching his house because he is not worthy to have Jesus enter. The centurion's decision to stop Jesus shows awareness that entry into a Gentile house is considered a source of defilement by Jews concerned with ritual purity.[19] The very careful and courteous way in which Jesus is being treated results from the shared assumption that help for a Gentile requires special social negotiation because of a major social barrier.

While the centurion states that he is unworthy to have direct contact with Jesus, the Jewish elders insisted that he was worthy to be helped. The centurion seems to rate himself lower than others view him, a sign of his willingness to subordinate himself to Jesus for the sake of the sick

---

[19] See J. Fitzmyer, *Luke I–IX*, 652.

slave. Structuring the story with a double delegation of spokesmen (vv. 3–5, 6–8) permits this significant contrast in views of the centurion and helps to fill in the portrait of this quester, who begins to become an interesting individual.

While Jesus makes the final and climactic statement, the centurion, through his representatives, makes a rather long speech for a secondary character in a pronouncement story. Although he says that he is unworthy, he is a man who exercises authority, and he attributes to Jesus a similar ability to act by an authoritative word. Jesus replies, "I say to you, not even in Israel have I found such faith" (7:9), and a report of the healing immediately follows. A commendation of the quester by Jesus is one way in which a quest story can come to a successful conclusion. Such a commendation tends to turn the quester into a model for readers of the gospel to imitate. Furthermore, Jesus' commendation helps to nullify the supposed disqualification of outsiders like this Gentile. When Jesus declares that the centurion is an outstanding example of faith, it becomes difficult for any of his followers to deny this Gentile's share in the salvation which Jesus brings.

The faith which Jesus praises is a willingness to trust Jesus' authoritative word, even at a distance. It is also a faith which trusts that Jesus can and will bring healing in spite of the social and religious barrier which separates Jews and Gentiles, a barrier which the centurion recognizes and respects. This is faith not only in Jesus as healer but also in a saving power that leaps divisive walls. The centurion's willingness to request Jesus' help in spite of a major barrier relates him to other persons in Luke who come to Jesus and are commended for their faith because they go beyond accepted and polite behavior to obtain what Jesus can offer (see 5:19–20; 7:36–50; 8:43–48; 18:35–43).

The request and response take place without any direct contact between the centurion and Jesus. In this respect Luke's story differs from the parallel accounts in Matt 8:5–13 and John 4:46–54. This spatial separation heightens the sense of social separation that constitutes the problem with which the story is working. The barrier which excludes Gentiles is only gradually broken down in Luke-Acts. Jesus is willing to heal the centurion's servant and even willing to come to his house. But the centurion assumes that this is too much to ask and prevents him. In Acts 10 another Gentile centurion appears. Peter does associate with him and stays in his house, behavior which he must defend when he returns to Jerusalem (Acts 10:28–29, 48; 11:3). Both of these Gentiles, however, are already sympathetic to Judaism, and Cornelius is a worshiper of the Jewish God. Only later are Gentiles converted directly from paganism, and the right of Gentiles to be in the church without becoming Jews is officially established only in Acts 15. The development takes place by careful steps.

The rather lengthy episode of the sinful woman in the Pharisee's house (Luke 7:36–50)[20] is linked to the preceding narrative in several ways. It is immediately preceded by a reference to Jesus as "glutton and drunkard, friend of tax collectors and sinners" (7:34), recalling the meal with tax collectors and sinners in 5:29–32. It ends with a declaration and response (7:48–49) which recall the story of the sinful paralytic (5:20–21). The Pharisee's skeptical remark about Jesus as a prophet (7:39) can be understood as a reaction to the crowd's proclamation of Jesus as a "great prophet" in 7:16.

The final verses of the scene (7:48, 50) indicate that it is a quest story. The scene ends when Jesus assures the woman that she has received what she has been seeking, release from her sins. While the woman does not express her quest in words at the beginning of the scene, the narrator tells us that she is a sinner, one in need of forgiveness. Although most of the conversation in the scene is between Jesus and Simon the Pharisee, the inclusion of Jesus' words to the woman at the end shows that the narrator is concerned with the meaning of the encounter for the woman and recognizes her as important in her own right. The additional words to the woman in 7:48, 50 help to restore balance in the story between attention to the woman and to the Pharisee.

At the beginning the woman places herself in a very vulnerable position, for (1) she is a recognized sinner, yet (2) she enters space which the Pharisee controls (his house), and (3) she is a woman who does not behave properly in the presence of men.[21] Conflict first appears in v. 39, where the Pharisee both rejects the woman and makes a negative statement about Jesus, who cannot be a prophet if he does not recognize that a sinful woman is touching him. Jesus comes to the woman's defense. Thus the scene presents two contrasting judgments about the woman and her extravagant behavior. Moreover, in responding to the Pharisee's criticism, Jesus contrasts the ways in which Simon the Pharisee and the sinful woman have responded to him. Thus Jesus and the Pharisee make contrasting judgments about the woman, but the woman and the Pharisee also take contrasting attitudes toward Jesus. The importance of the latter contrast is indicated by a significant detail of plotting. The narrator has withheld relevant information about the Pharisee's attitude toward Jesus until it can be used to contrast the woman and the Pharisee. Only in vv.

---

[20] On this scene see also pp. 95–96, 106.

[21] In 7:39 the Pharisee objects especially to the sinful woman touching Jesus. For a woman to unbind her hair in the presence of men was also regarded as improper. See Joachim Jeremias, *The Parables of Jesus*, 126.

44–46 do we learn that the host did not supply water for washing of feet, nor a kiss, nor oil for anointing when Jesus arrived at the dinner. In her own strange way the woman supplied all of these things. Her actions indicate her great love (and, by contrast, the Pharisee's little love) for Jesus, the one through whom God proclaims the release of sins. Significant plotting also appears in the fact that we are not told about Jesus' reaction to the woman as she wets and anoints his feet. We are told first about the Pharisee's reaction, then Jesus' attitude is presented as a contrast and correction of the Pharisee.

Jesus gets the last word, both with the Pharisee and with the woman. His response is extensive, makes use of a short parable, and contains strong contrast that makes the host's response to Jesus seem very cold compared to the woman's. This speech (and the closing words of Jesus to the woman) controls evaluation of characters in the scene. Jesus, the person of authority in Luke's Gospel and the dominant speaker in this scene, puts the Pharisee in a negative light and the woman in a positive light, reversing the situation which existed before Jesus intervened. Apart from Jesus, the Pharisee was the person of status in the community and was presumably in control of events in his own house. The woman was a despised sinner in the town, who had made herself especially vulnerable by her presence and behavior in the Pharisee's house. Jesus' commendation of the woman's strange behavior turns the initial situation upside down.

It is the woman's demonstrative love for Jesus, the one who brings the release of sins, which is commended. This point is expressed most clearly in v. 47, which also contains a well-known ambiguity. An initial reading seems to indicate that she is being forgiven because of her great love, although love comes from forgiveness according to the parable in vv. 41–42. This shift is strange, for Jesus in v. 47 speaks of those who love much and little, apparently applying the parable to the situation (cf. v. 42). Since communication depends on the presumption that there are meaningful consistencies in texts, which we should seek to understand unless this proves impossible, scholars have rightly proposed another interpretation, namely, that v. 47a speaks of love not as the basis for forgiveness but as the basis for knowing that the woman has been forgiven.[22] Thus "for she loved much" supports not "her sins are forgiven" but the first part of the sentence, "therefore I tell you." Her great love is the sign that she has experienced forgiveness and so the basis on which one may confidently

---

[22] The view adopted by J. Fitzmyer, *Luke I–IX*, 686–87, 692; I. H. Marshall, *The Gospel of Luke*, 306–7, 313; and Ulrich Wilckens, "Vergebung für die Sünderin," 404–11, among others.

assert that forgiveness has taken place. This meaning also provides a fitting antithesis to v. 47b, where little love is said to result from little forgiveness. This is a possible interpretation of v. 47a, and it seems to be required by the connection of this sentence with the preceding parable and with v. 47b.

However, v. 48 complicates the situation. After speaking of the woman's great love, Jesus turns to her and announces that her sins have been released. This seems to suggest that assurance of the release of sins may follow love after all. The simple picture of love caused by forgiveness in the parable becomes more complex. This can be a valuable aspect of the story. The relation between experienced forgiveness and love may move in more than one direction. A willingness to love, and to show that love, may indeed lead to assurance of forgiveness. Love involves a trust in the other which enables us to hear the other speaking forgiveness. The resulting portrait of the woman in the story is not necessarily chaotic. When she anointed Jesus' feet, the woman could have experienced a love for Jesus which included faith in his power to redeem (cf. v. 50) and gratitude for what he had done or would do for her, corresponding to the view in the parable. A person may experience all this and yet not know clearly what one is experiencing. Through Jesus' closing words the woman may have learned something about the nature of her own actions and feelings. Furthermore, Jesus' words of forgiveness in v. 48 could be important as reassurance even if the woman had already begun to believe that she was forgiven. These remarks do not pretend to penetrate the psyche of an actual individual of the distant past. They are merely meant to suggest that the story, with its complex view of forgiveness and love, does not thereby leave the realm of what many people may experience or imagine.

Three quest stories appear early in the narrative of Jesus' ministry, in Luke 5 and 7. Three reappear toward the end of Jesus' journey to Jerusalem, in Luke 17, 18, and 19. Thus they appear early and late in the narrative of Jesus' ministry prior to his arrival in Jerusalem. The tendency to bracket Jesus' ministry with this type of story suggests the importance of these encounters in Jesus' total activity.

In 17:12–19, the cleansing of the ten lepers, the healing takes place early in the scene and is reported without emphasis. The scene focuses on what happens afterwards. Following the healing, a contrast is introduced: one of the healed men returns glorifying God and giving thanks to Jesus; the other nine do not. It is this contrast which provokes Jesus' comment in vv. 17–18. The action of the one leper who returns to give thanks is highlighted by singling him out and contrasting him with the other nine. His behavior would be regarded as appropriate by most Christian readers, and in the scene Jesus responds to him favorably. The readers are

told that he is a Samaritan only after they have received a positive
impression of the leper through strong depiction of his gratitude. This
important information is introduced late in the scene as a surprise. By this
device the scene jars the stereotypes of readers or hearers of Jewish
background. The scene introduces them to a person combining characteristics that they are not accustomed to combine: grateful recipient of
salvation (positive) and Samaritan (negative). Jesus also speaks of him as
"this foreigner" (17:18), which shows that he is being viewed from a
Jewish point of view as an outsider. Only the Samaritan responds appropriately to his healing by Jesus, and at the end of the scene Jesus turns to
him and commends his faith. The marked appropriateness of the response
which the Samaritan alone shows makes it difficult for any to deny that it
is appropriate for Jesus to include him in his saving work.

Thus the quest stories attack stereotypes and prejudices by presenting a
series of remarkable individuals who combine characteristics which seem
incompatible according to the stereotypes: gratitude and Samaritan, great
love and sinful woman (7:36–50), outstanding faith and Gentile (7:2–10).

The Samaritan leper experienced more than a change from sickness to
health. All of the lepers were healed, but the Samaritan is singled out
because he was changed in a deeper way: his life now overflows with
praise of God and thankfulness to Jesus. The context of the story implies
that Jesus' final words to the Samaritan, "Your faith has saved (σέσωκεν)
you," refer to a salvation which includes but goes beyond healing.[23] The
strong contrast with the nine in vv. 17–18 suggests that this statement
applies to the Samaritan leper in a way that it does not apply to the other
nine. The joy of praising God is an integral part of the salvation which the
Samaritan has experienced through faith.

Notice that the Samaritan not only glorifies God but also gives thanks to
Jesus (17:16). The importance of the latter becomes clear when we
recognize that it alone explains the need for the lepers to *return* to Jesus,
which the nine failed to do. God can be glorified elsewhere. A return is
required in order to give thanks to *Jesus*. Jesus underscores the importance of such thankfulness by criticizing those who fail to show it. Thus
the scene is concerned with a transformation which creates a more permanent bond of gratitude between Jesus and those helped by him.
Prejudices against outsiders are undermined by having a foreigner dem-

---

[23] So also C. Talbert, *Reading Luke*, 165. The verb σώζω is used in Luke-Acts both of Jesus'
ministry of healing and of other aspects of his saving work. It appears, for instance, in the
summary of Jesus' ministry in 19:10, following the "salvation" which Jesus brings to
Zacchaeus. Healing is an integral part of the salvation which Jesus brings and can
symbolize this salvation in its fullness, as Peter's comment on the healing of the lame man at
the temple gate shows (see Acts 4:9–12).

onstrate what is needed. The role of the nine who fail to return suggests a somber awareness that many of those whom Jesus helped did not relate to him in a permanent bond of gratitude.

In the quest stories discussed so far, those who seek help from Jesus have some negative characteristic which might seem to disqualify them. Nevertheless, they are successful. This will also be the case with Zacchaeus and the criminal on the cross. On the other hand, the one quester who has a desirable place in society fails to obtain what he is seeking. He is the rich ruler in 18:18–23. Thus the quest stories illustrate the reversal of rich and poor, high and low, righteous and sinners, proclaimed in 1:51–53, 2:34, and 5:32.

In 18:23 there is no indication that the rich man departs (dif. Matthew, Mark) and so no indication that the scene terminates at that point. Although Jesus is no longer speaking to the rich man, he continues in dialogue on the subject of riches. Thus 18:18–30 is a unified scene in Luke, and Jesus makes several major points to different people, which is not typical of a pronouncement story. A more complex dialogue has come into being. Nevertheless, this is built upon a quest story. The scene begins with a statement of the ruler's quest, and v. 23 reports the unsuccessful outcome of the quest. The expected development aborts in the case of the rich ruler, but there are others who have responded to Jesus' challenge in v. 22 and can carry the quest to its completion. In v. 28 Peter, speaking for the disciples, indicates that they have fulfilled the difficult condition which Jesus imposed on the rich ruler. Peter picks up the thought and some of the language of v. 22 and declares that the disciples have fulfilled Jesus' requirement, emphasizing the contrast with the ruler.[24] In response Jesus promises the disciples the "eternal life" which the rich man was seeking (cf. vv. 18, 30), ending the scene on the theme with which it began. Thus there are two sets of questers in this scene, the rich ruler and the disciples. Response to Jesus' challenge in v. 22 marks the difference between them. The rich ruler is unable to face this challenge. The disciples have already faced it successfully and are promised the eternal life which the rich ruler sought.

Tension in the story increases when Jesus poses the difficult condition in v. 22. The difficulty of this condition is underscored both by the rich ruler's failure and by Jesus' comment on the great problem which rich people have in entering God's reign (vv. 24–25). The rich man must sell all that he has and give it away. The reasons for the command to sell all are briefly indicated in the three short sentences that follow: (1) The poor

---

[24] Note ἡμεῖς ("we") in v. 28. This nominative pronoun emphasizes the contrast with the quester who failed.

need what others have. They are unjustly deprived of basic requirements for life. Goods are to be sold so that this need may be fulfilled and this injustice corrected. Unlike the other Lukan quest stories, Jesus in this scene does not speak directly to someone who is oppressed or excluded. Nevertheless, his words arise in part out of concern for the poor. (2) Possessions are a false, temporary treasure which lures people away from the true "treasure in heaven." Dependence on riches conflicts with devotion to God (16:13). The reference to treasure in heaven in 18:22 recalls similarly worded warnings of such conflict in 12:21, 33–34. (3) Disciples must devote themselves to following Jesus. Possessions and family are competing concerns which must be renounced (see 9:57–62; 14:25–33).

In spite of the reaction of the hearers in v. 26 ("Who is able to be saved?"), the story does not suggest that leaving all in order to follow Jesus is impossible. Not only does v. 27 assert that such things are possible with God, but the narrator presents the first followers of Jesus as concrete examples of persons who have renounced their possessions and left their families. Peter states as much in v. 28, and Jesus accepts Peter's statement, promising a reward in vv. 29–30. Peter's claim fits the view of the disciples already developed in Luke, for when the disciples were first called, we were told that they left all and followed Jesus (5:11, 28). The emphasis on leaving "all," which differs from the call stories in Mark 1:16–20 and Matt 4:18–22, corresponds to the command to sell "all" in Luke 18:22, a detail which differs from Mark's and Matthew's stories of the rich man. Peter, Levi, and others have already renounced all their possessions in order to follow Jesus. This is not the achievement of a few outstanding followers, but a requirement of discipleship (at least in the time of Jesus), as Jesus made clear in 14:33. Thus when Jesus tells the rich ruler to sell and give all, he is simply repeating a requirement which applies to all his followers who have possessions.

In contrast to Mark and Matthew, Jesus' words about the difficulty of the rich entering God's reign are not addressed to the disciples in Luke. These words do not apply to the disciples, for they have made themselves poor in becoming disciples.[25] Furthermore, Luke does not poke fun at the disciples' desire of reward for their sacrifices, as does Mark. In Mark 10:30 Jesus' promise of reward is surprising and humorous. In grandiose language Jesus promises that the disciples will get back a hundredfold exactly what they have sacrificed, "houses and brothers and sisters and mothers and children and fields," but with persecutions. This is not the great reward the disciples expected.[26] The hope of reward is also qualified

---

[25] See Luise Schottroff and Wolfgang Stegemann, *Hoffnung der Armen*, 99–100.
[26] On Mark 10:28–30, see R. Tannehill, *Sword of His Mouth*, 147–52.

by a warning in Mark 10:31. In Luke, however, we have a straight-
forward promise of reward, with no critical undertone, for the narrator
wants to affirm the importance of leaving one's possessions in order to
follow Jesus.

Thus the scene in 18:18–30 can be read as an illustration and fulfillment of the beatitudes and woes in 6:20–26.[27] The rich ruler is unable to
"enter God's reign" (18:24–25) or find the eternal life which he seeks,
while the disciples, who have renounced all, are promised eternal life.
Earlier Jesus had pronounced a woe upon the rich and declared the poor
(including the poor disciples; cf. 6:20) to be blessed,[28] because God's reign
belonged to them. The woe falls upon the rich ruler not because he is
inevitably condemned as a member of his economic class but because he is
unable to choose justice for the poor and the dedicated life of discipleship.

The story of Zacchaeus (19:1–10)[29] is also a quest story, although the
goal of the quest is only gradually disclosed. We must understand the
deeper need which guides Zacchaeus' actions from the gift that he receives
at the end of the scene, namely, "salvation" (v. 9). At the beginning,
however, we are only told that Zacchaeus wanted to see who Jesus was (v.
3). Thus Zacchaeus is presented as a seeker, but the deeper need which
motivates his search is at first disguised. The way that the deeper quest is
gradually disclosed suggests that the results progressively overshoot Zacchaeus' limited expectations at the beginning. He not only sees Jesus, but
Jesus chooses to stay at his house. Jesus not only stays at his house, but
Zacchaeus receives salvation through this encounter.

The important role which a quester has within a quest story is especially clear in this scene, for the narrator gives this chief tax collector
individual traits. We are not only told his status in society (information
important for understanding following events); his name and his small
stature are also indicated. Furthermore, he climbs a tree in order to see
Jesus, a striking departure from normal, dignified behavior. This adds
some striking detail to the initial description of Zacchaeus and underscores his eagerness. Such detail encourages interest in this unusual
individual and curiosity about his motives. Readers may become concerned with Zacchaeus and with the outcome of his story, leading to
sympathetic involvement in his quest. Sympathetic involvement may be
necessary to balance negative reaction to the fact that he is a chief tax
collector.

The crowd acts as a blocking force to Zacchaeus' quest. This happens

---

[27] See L. Schottroff and W. Stegemann, *Hoffnung der Armen*, 100–101.
[28] On the addressees of the beatitudes, see pp. 206–8.
[29] On this scene see also pp. 107–8.

in two stages: first, they prevent Zacchaeus from seeing Jesus; second, they object to Jesus staying with Zacchaeus, whom they describe as a "sinner" (v. 7). In both cases the crowd blocks contact between Jesus and Zacchaeus. The negative reaction to Zacchaeus expressed in v. 7 may suggest that the crowd was actively hostile to him even in v. 3; that is, Zacchaeus was unable to see Jesus because people were not willing to make room for him at the front, as they would for honored members of the community. Whether this is so or not, Zacchaeus' isolation from the community is clear in v. 7 and is a major issue in the scene as a whole. The crowd as physical barrier and Zacchaeus' strange position up in a tree can serve as spatial symbols of his isolation from his community.

The objection of the crowd is answered in vv. 8–10. First, it is made clear that a real change has taken place in Zacchaeus. He is no longer the sinner that the crowd disdains; he is now a repentant sinner. The signs of repentance are appropriate for one who is a chief tax collector and rich, one who, it is assumed, would be attached to his money and oppressive in obtaining it.[30] In v. 2 Zacchaeus was introduced as "rich ($\pi\lambda o\acute{u}\sigma\iota o s$)," a word which links him to the story of the rich man in 18:18–23. These two quest stories illustrate contrasting results when rich people encounter Jesus. In reflecting on the failure of the rich ruler, Jesus emphasized the great difficulty of a rich person sharing in God's reign but also stated that "what is impossible with humans is possible with God" (18:27). The story of Zacchaeus indicates how it is possible for the rich to share in God's reign, through a repentance that radically changes their use of possessions. Zacchaeus responds to Jesus in the right way and is promised salvation. The rich ruler failed in his quest because he was unable to meet the challenge of selling all that he had and giving it to the poor.

At first glance there seems to be a difference between Zacchaeus' announcement that he is giving *half* of his goods to the poor and Jesus' requirement that the rich ruler sell *all* his possessions and give them to the poor. However, it is doubtful that Zacchaeus is getting by more cheaply than the rich ruler. As a rich tax collector Zacchaeus has two responsibilities. Repentance for him requires an end to his callous disregard of the poor, but it also requires restitution to those he has defrauded. These are two different groups, for the poor are not likely to be moving goods in trade, which would be subject to Zacchaeus' taxes.[31] Although we might

---

[30] In Luke 5:32 Jesus announced that he came to call sinners "to repentance" (dif. Matthew, Mark). In 3:10–14 John the Baptist declared that repentance involves sharing possessions with others and an end to oppression (dif. Matthew, Mark). The apostles are told by Jesus to proclaim not just forgiveness but "repentance for forgiveness" (24:47). Luke makes clear that Jesus does not offer cheap grace but transforms lives. The change in behavior involved in repentance is a necessary part of that transformation.

[31] In discussing attitudes toward tax collectors, L. Schottroff and W. Stegemann argue that,

like Zacchaeus to give an exact accounting so that we would know
precisely how much he must pay in restitution, the narrator is not
concerned with such details. Zacchaeus has two responsibilities if he is to
free himself from a life of injustice and callous greed, and his property is
simply divided in half to meet these two responsibilities. There is no
reference to anything being left over. Hence it is a mistake to assume that
the story is trying to present a realistic compromise that permits the rich to
retain part of their goods for their own use. Zacchaeus is an example of
radical repentance, not of practical wisdom, and it is assumed that his
response will leave him pretty much in the same financial state required of
the rich ruler.[32]

The final response of Jesus in vv. 9–10 has a double function. This is
indicated by the fact that Jesus addresses two audiences at once. In v. 9 we
are told that Jesus spoke to "him," i.e., Zacchaeus, yet he speaks of
Zacchaeus in the third person because he is also speaking to the crowd.
His words address Zacchaeus, affirming that he has found what he needs,
but also reply to the crowd's objection.[33] Thus the quest comes to a
successful conclusion as the principal obstacle is removed.

Jesus affirms that the salvation sought by Zacchaeus, perhaps uncon-
sciously, has come to him. The story supplies supporting reasons for this
affirmation in response to skeptics, like the people in the crowd. The
radical repentance of Zacchaeus demonstrated in v. 8 can function as one
such supporting reason, but additional support is given in the double
rationale for Jesus' judgment in his final words. First, Jesus recalls
something about Zacchaeus: "He also is a son of Abraham." This will
seem to be an irrelevant remark unless we recognize that the principal
tension in the story is caused by the rejection of Zacchaeus by the Jewish
community. We have noted that the crowd twice acts as a blocking force
and, in the second instance, rejects Zacchaeus as a recognized sinner with
whom one should not associate. Zacchaeus has been ostracized. Nevertheless, Jesus affirms that he is a son of Abraham and therefore an heir to the
promises of salvation given in Scripture to the Jewish people. These
promises "to Abraham and to his offspring" were recalled in 1:54–55 and
1:68–75. Salvation rightly belongs to one who is a son of Abraham. But
the crowd must be reminded of this, for they have defined the people of the

---

    although tax collectors were despised by traders and prominent people, the poor and day
    laborers would hardly be concerned with them. They didn't need to pay duty on goods
    because they had no goods to pay duty on. See *Hoffnung der Armen*, 23–24.
[32] This interpretation differs from that of Walter E. Pilgrim, who believes that 19:1–10
    contrasts with passages which call for total surrender of possessions, since it indicates that
    all of one's possessions need not be surrendered. See *Good News to the Poor*, 98–102, 132–
    34.
[33] Luke 5:24–25 have a similar double function, as indicated above, pp. 112–13.

promise in a way that excluded Zacchaeus and others. In declaring that Zacchaeus shares in the promised salvation, Jesus reinstates him as a Jew.[34]

This story, like many other pronouncement stories, is composed for the purpose of changing attitudes among its hearers.[35] Jesus has the final and decisive word about the situation. He intervenes in a situation of alienation for the sake of the excluded. The story bears a double message, depending on where one stands in relation to such situations. To the excluded it is invitation and reassurance, although repentance may be required. To the religious community which has defined itself in ways that exclude many, it is a challenge to change from rejection to acceptance. This change in attitude is encouraged partly through the portrait of Zacchaeus but primarily through the portrait of Jesus, who defends Zacchaeus' right to share in salvation.

While the first rationale (v. 9c) speaks of Zacchaeus, the second rationale (v. 10) says something about Jesus: "For the Son of Man came to seek and to save the lost." This final statement turns the story of Zacchaeus into a key example of Jesus' mission as a whole, which is concerned with restoring the outcasts of Israel to their rightful place as participants in the salvation promised in Scripture. This summary of Jesus' mission directs our attention backward to all the stories about Jesus' work with the oppressed and excluded, drawing from these stories a general conclusion about the nature of Jesus' mission.[36] This statement also invites us to reread the story of Zacchaeus not as a story of Zacchaeus seeking Jesus but as a story of Jesus seeking Zacchaeus, since this is what "the Son of Man came" to do.

The six Lukan quest stories discussed so far occur near the beginning of Jesus' public ministry and as he approaches Jerusalem on his final journey. One further quest story has been integrated into the passion story. This scene, unique to Luke's Gospel, shows the implied author's continuing interest in Jesus' ministry to the excluded and suggests that it is one of these outcasts who is best able to understand the mystery of Jesus' divinely ordained path.

In 23:39–43 the narrator reports a brief conversation between Jesus and the two criminals crucified with him. The two criminals take con-

---

[34] Several recent interpreters believe that Zacchaeus was meant to be a paradigm for rich Christians in Luke's situation. See L. Schottroff and W. Stegemann, *Hoffnung der Armen*, 137–38; W. Pilgrim, *Good News to the Poor*, 129–34. While we need not deny that Zacchaeus has relevance for rich Christians, this interpretation ignores the fact that the story speaks first of all to the problem of alienation within Judaism.

[35] See Robert C. Tannehill, "Attitudinal Shift in Synoptic Pronouncement Stories," 183–97.

[36] Earlier I suggested that 5:32 and 19:10 bracket and interpret the Lukan narrative of Jesus' ministry to sinners. See pp. 107–8.

trasting attitudes toward Jesus. The first joins the derisive cries of the rulers and the soldiers, who call on Jesus to save himself if he really is God's Messiah, the king of the Jews (23:35, 37, 39). To these people Jesus' helplessness is obvious proof that he is not the Messiah. The second criminal provides an answer to these derisive words. Normally Jesus himself answers the objections and challenges which he encounters. Allowing the second criminal to step into this role gives him unusual prominence. He does most of the speaking in the scene. Jesus speaks only in the last verse (v. 43), indicating his approval of the second criminal's statements.

The second criminal's quest is not disclosed until v. 42, where he asks, "Jesus, remember me when you come into your royal power (βασι-λείαν)." Before this, however, the criminal has already demonstrated remarkable insight, which immediately enables Jesus to respond positively to the criminal's request. This positive response makes clear that, in the judgment of the implied author, the second criminal is a perceptive person who contrasts sharply with the imperceptive people who are calling on Jesus to save himself. The perceptive criminal rebukes the other criminal, thereby showing that he rejects the view that Jesus would save himself if he were the Messiah. The perceptive criminal shows repentance for his crimes by admitting that he is suffering justly. He also recognizes Jesus' innocence. And his request of Jesus shows faith that Jesus will receive royal power as Messiah in spite of the death by crucifixion which they are sharing. The criminal recognizes that Jesus' death is not a refutation of messianic claims but a prelude to messianic power.

Execution as a criminal is an extreme form of exclusion from society. Again in this scene the narrator shows Jesus ministering to one of the socially excluded. The indication of the criminal's repentance fits with the interest in repentance shown in such places as 5:32, 18:13, and 19:8. His faith in Jesus' messianic power is especially striking in the situation, for Jesus has been rejected and is near death. Jesus' positive response to the criminal's request shows that he has correctly understood Jesus. Jesus is also affirming that the criminal's quest will be successful, with, perhaps, a minor element of surprise. The salvation sought by the criminal need not wait until some distant time. He will share in paradise immediately upon death.

The impact of this scene is heightened by its location in the passion story. It is placed just before Jesus' final words and death. In this dramatic situation it provides a perspective on Jesus which balances and corrects the blind rejection which he is experiencing. The dying criminal who speaks of Jesus entering his royal power is the only person who shows

some awareness that Jesus' death is part of a divine plan that will lead to
Jesus' enthronement. Jesus had tried to inform his disciples about his
death and resurrection, but they did not understand (9:44–45; 18:31–34).
This failure is overcome only when the risen Messiah interprets the
Scripture to his blind followers (24:25–32). In Jerusalem Jesus had given
several public indications that he was about to be exalted to messianic
power, though this would take place through rejection and death (20:13–
17, 41–44; 22:69). The repentant criminal, however, is the only one who
understands and believes that the Jesus who is being rejected and killed is
on his way to messianic power. In this scene the repentant criminal is
given the role of the reliable and perceptive interpreter of Jesus, whose
insight contrasts with the blindness of all those who are rejecting Jesus.
The centurion's response to Jesus' death, important in Mark, is reduced
in Luke to a partial echo of the criminal's words (see 23:47). The criminal
is the last person who turns to Jesus for help during Jesus' ministry; he is
also the one person who understands and accepts the path which Jesus
must follow to fulfill God's purpose: through death to enthronement at
God's right hand.

In Luke, Jesus' role as savior of the oppressed and excluded is given
narrative emphasis especially through the quest stories which we have
discussed. These stories show a continuing interest in dramatizing this
aspect of Jesus' work. To them could be added some additional scenes in
which Jesus supports persons who have inferior status in society or
defends them when they are attacked for stepping out of their proper
place. These scenes would include Jesus' commendation of the poor
widow (21:1–4), his defense of the children who are being rejected by the
disciples (18:15–17), and some of the scenes to be discussed in the last two
sections of this chapter. These scenes, together with many of the healing
stories, especially those in which Jesus helps lepers, demoniacs, and a
woman who is unclean through a flow of blood (8:43–48), also contribute
to the rich portrait of Jesus as helper of the oppressed and excluded.

THE POOR AND THE RICH

The poor have an important place among the oppressed groups to whom
Jesus announces God's help. We have already noted the importance of
preaching good news to the poor in the description of Jesus' mission in
4:18, and God's help for the hungry was celebrated by Mary in 1:53.
While the terms "poor" and "hungry" are subject to metaphorical expansion and need not be limited strictly to those who are physically hungry
and economically poor, God's mercy on the physically hungry and eco-

nomically poor is a major theme in Luke. This is true despite the valid point made by Luise Schottroff and Wolfgang Stegemann that, rather than calling Luke the evangelist of the poor, "one could with greater right call Luke the evangelist of the rich . . . in the sense that he is an extraordinarily sharp critic of the rich and is interested in their repentance."[37] It is true that much of the teaching about possessions in Luke is directed to those who have possessions, not the poor. Nevertheless, this teaching is motivated by a concern for the poor, as we will see below. Jesus' announcement in Nazareth that he has been sent "to preach good news to the poor" is not forgotten in the following story of Jesus' ministry.

This good news to the poor rings out in the beatitudes as Jesus says, "Blessed are the poor, for yours is the reign ($\beta\alpha\sigma\iota\lambda\epsilon\iota\alpha$) of God" (6:20). The parallel with the hungry and the contrast with the rich and full in the following verses helps to make clear that these words are primarily addressed to people who are economically deprived. It is appropriate that these words are spoken as Jesus "lifted up his eyes to his disciples." The narrator wants to make clear that the disciples, who have left all to follow Jesus (5:11, 28), will share in this blessing on the poor. However, the fact that Jesus is looking at the disciples does not mean that he is speaking only to them. In fact, he continues without break by addressing woes to the rich. Jesus is announcing the happiness of the disciples who have chosen poverty for his sake, but his words are also addressed to a larger audience, to the rich and to the poor among the crowd.[38] Thus this scene portrays Jesus preaching good news to the poor, in accordance with his commission announced in 4:18.

Furthermore, Jesus' reply to John the Baptist in 7:22 suggests that Jesus' work of healing is part of the good news which he proclaims to the poor. In reciting his activities, Jesus ends with "the poor have good news preached to them," recalling his commission in 4:18. But the preceding rhythmic list focuses on Jesus' ministry to the blind, lame, lepers, deaf, and dead. Ending this list by referring to the poor is less strange when we recognize that in the ancient world most disabled persons would be unable to support themselves and would be poor beggars. The blind beggar in 18:35–43 and the lame beggar in Acts 3:1–10 are concrete examples of such persons. The healing which Jesus brings to handicapped persons is part of his good news to the poor.

The significance of Jesus' ministry for beggars is confirmed by the parable of the great banquet (14:15–24). The parable contrasts people of

---

[37] *Hoffnung der Armen*, 150. On the poor and rich in Luke-Acts see also Luke T. Johnson, *The Literary Function of Possessions*; W. Pilgrim, *Good News to the Poor*; D. Seccombe, *Possessions and the Poor*.

[38] On the addressees of the beatitudes, see further pp. 206–8.

wealth—those who can buy a field and can use five yoke of oxen—with
the street beggars. Again the poor are listed among those with various
disabling conditions: "the poor and crippled and blind and lame" (14:21).
These people need a free meal, and they will be found out on the streets
because they are begging there. The poverty of all these people is clear
from the description of these same groups as persons who "cannot repay
you" in 14:13–14. The parable interprets Jesus' ministry as the occasion
for bringing the poor to the banquet table, where people of property and
position supposedly belong. The parable is introduced with the suggestion
that the banquet represents the reign of God (14:15). Thus its message to
the poor is the same as the beatitude in 6:20, "Blessed are the poor, for
yours is the reign of God." While the poor beggars in the parable may
represent all sorts of needy persons, including the tax collectors and
sinners, the parable highlights first of all the contrast between people of
property and the poor, interpreting Jesus' ministry as good news for the
poor.

The challenge which Jesus directs to the rich is also part of his good
news to the poor. In this challenge Jesus emphasizes the danger of riches.
Riches provide a false security which lures people away from "being rich
toward God" (12:21). Riches are a master that competes with God. It is
impossible to serve both God and mammon (16:13). Riches hold people
back from following Jesus (18:22–23). But Jesus' teaching to the rich is
not only a negative warning of spiritual danger. There is also a positive
reason why the wealthy should let go of their possessions. This reason is
the desperate need of the poor. The coming of God's reign can also be good
news for the poor if it transforms people of property so that they share
with the poor. This is an important goal of Jesus' teaching in Luke.

John the Baptist instructs the crowds to share with the destitute (3:11).
Jesus gives similar instructions in his sermon on the plain. He commands
unlimited generosity to all those who request aid ("Keep giving[39] to
everyone who asks you," 6:30). In Luke (dif. Matthew) the command to
love enemies is applied to loans for people from whom one does not hope
to receive anything (6:34–35). In 6:32–33 we find a development of the
commands to love enemies and do good to them in 6:27, and we would
expect this to continue with a similar development of the commands to
bless and pray for them in 6:28. The series of parallel sentences does
continue in 6:34, but instead Jesus speaks of making loans. This shows
concern for applying love of enemies to the use of possessions. It is not
entirely clear whether the disciple is being asked to renounce hope of
repayment (in which case it becomes a gift, in accordance with the

---

[39] Present imperative of repeated action.

command in 6:30) or whether disciples are being asked to renounce hope of receiving a similar favor in return.[40] Even if the latter is in mind, two sorts of situations would seem to make this command relevant and necessary: situations where one is not likely to receive a favor in return because of the animosity of the other person, and situations where one is not likely to receive a favor in return because of the other person's poverty. In the latter case there is also a good chance that the loan will not be repaid. Disciples are being asked to lend even in situations where they will receive no gain and may suffer considerable loss. Disciples are being asked to join the poor not only by "leaving all" in order to embark on a mission (5:11, 28) but also by offering their resources for the needs of others.

These gifts and loans will be acts of love and mercy which are like the love and mercy of God, making disciples "sons of the Most High" (6:35–36). The approach of God's reign is good news for the poor, for God is acting to rescue them in their need. Those who give and lend to people in need are participating in what God is doing for the poor. They are being "merciful as your Father is merciful" (6:36).

The teaching in this sermon is followed by repeated commands to "give charity (ἐλεημοσύνην)" (literally "mercy" but used of concrete acts of mercy through charitable giving). The Pharisees are urged to give charity in 11:41, and the disciples are told to "sell your possessions and give charity" in 12:33. The command to sell indicates that disposal of major items of property is in mind, not just the use of available cash. The teaching about the ravens and the lilies which precedes this command highlights God's care in order to make possible such radical action. The goal of the command is to detach the disciples from false treasure and guide them into concrete acts of mercy for the poor.

Jesus also teaches such acts of mercy to the "ruler of the Pharisees" who is the host of the dinner party in Luke 14. The host is told not to invite his friends and relatives to his dinner parties but to invite the "poor, crippled, lame, blind," people who "cannot repay you" (14:13–14). The following parable of the banquet refers to the same groups of needy people. If the host follows Jesus' instructions, he will be acting toward the poor in the same way that God is acting toward them in Jesus' ministry, as depicted in the parable. Recall the similar connection between the mercy of God and being merciful through giving and lending in 6:30–36.

The disciples receive further instruction in similar acts of charity in 16:9–13. Following the parable of the steward, "Make friends for yourselves from the mammon of unrighteousness" (16:9) must refer to can-

---

[40] On this problem see I. H. Marshall, *The Gospel of Luke*, 263.

celling debts or making outright gifts to others. While Joachim Jeremias[41] believes that there is a sudden shift from viewing the steward in the parable as a positive example of generosity (v. 9) to using him as a warning against unfaithfulness (vv. 10–12), the emphasis on faithfulness in vv. 10–12 does not mean, at least for the narrator, that the master's money should be conserved and increased but that it should be given away to those in need (as the steward did). The steward who gives is the one who is "faithful in unrighteous mammon." This is supported by v. 13, for the servant who serves God cannot serve mammon by greedily collecting and conserving it. Making friends, being faithful, and serving God rather than mammon are different ways of speaking of the same behavior: not holding onto wealth but giving it to those in need. The instruction to "make friends" with wealth (a lesson derived from the parable) may sound like crass manipulation of others for one's own benefit. Perhaps it should be understood in light of the ideal of true friendship through sharing, borrowed from Greek thought, which seems to lie behind the descriptions of the early church in Acts 2:44 and 4:32.[42]

The concern for the poor which stands behind all these instructions about the sharing of wealth also appears in the parable of the rich man and poor Lazarus in 16:19–31. The parable indicates that God acts for the poor man, who receives the comfort after death which he was denied in life. In 16:25 this is expressed as a reversal of what the two men received in life. The charge against the rich man, however, is not simply that he received good things in life and so must take evil things now to balance things out. The way in which the story is told strongly suggests that the rich man deserves torment because he did not share his wealth with the poor man who was in need. Note how the first scene of the story (16:19–21) is narrated. This scene not only contrasts the luxury of the rich man with the suffering and need of Lazarus but also brings Lazarus into close proximity to the rich man (he is placed "at his gate"), so that he is available as an object of charity. Furthermore, we are told that the poor man was "longing to be fed from what was falling from the rich man's table" (16:21). This clearly indicates the minimum that the rich man might have done, had he been concerned. But he does nothing. Giving Lazarus a name helps to personalize him, and the description of his piteous condition encourages readers to sympathize with him and to condemn the rich man's callousness. It is not simply being wealthy but this callousness toward the suffering poor which is condemned in the parable. That is why "Moses and the prophets" are a relevant warning

---

[41] See *The Parables of Jesus*, 46–47.
[42] See Jacques Dupont, *Salvation of the Gentiles*, 87–91, 95–99. A connection between these Acts passages and Luke 16:9 is asserted by D. Seccombe, *Possessions and the Poor*, 220.

(16:29). There is little tendency to condemn wealth as such in the Old Testament, but the call to share with the needy is clear and strong.[43]

This rich man was so callous that he did not even share the scraps from his table, but other passages in Luke make clear that more is expected of people with property than just sharing their scraps. In 18:22 Jesus tells the rich ruler to "sell all that you have and give to the poor." This command arises not only from a need to be free for discipleship but also out of concern for the poor, as the indication of them as recipients shows. In response to Jesus, Zacchaeus gives half his goods to the poor[44] and so becomes a model of how a rich person may find salvation through repentance. This story portrays the power of Jesus to transform the rich so that they will respond to the needs of the poor.

We see, then, that Jesus preaches good news to the poor not only by announcing that they will share in God's reign and by healing the poor beggars but also by creating disciples who are pledged to share with the poor and by seeking to transform grasping rich people into persons who will give their wealth to the poor. Later the narrator will suggest that Jesus' call has the power to create a community that cares for the poor so that there are no longer needy persons among them (Acts 4:34). Jesus' mission to the poor, claimed by him in the Nazareth synagogue, becomes a major theme in the narrative of Jesus' words and deeds in Luke.

WOMEN

There are also indications in Luke of a desire to enhance the position of women in a male-dominated society.[45] Features of literary design, involving both balanced expression and links between narrative segments, make this desire clear.

We note first a tendency toward doubling, one version referring to a man and the other to a woman, resulting in male-female pairs.[46] This occurs both in Jesus' discourse and in the narrator's stories about Jesus. Doubling not only reinforces the message, since it is presented twice, but

---

[43] See, e.g., Deut 15:1–11; Isa 58:6–7. Both of these passages have influenced Luke-Acts. See Acts 4:34 with Deut 15:4 and Luke 4:18 with Isa 58:6. See further, L. E. Keck, "Poor," 672–73. On the rich man and Lazarus, see also pp. 185–86 below.

[44] On the significance of the reference to "half" in 19:8, see pp. 123–24.

[45] Elisabeth Schüssler Fiorenza links this concern to the concern for the poor just discussed, since a patriarchal system oppresses women economically, as well as in other ways. See *In Memory of Her*, 141.

[46] Luke's tendency to present a woman and a man in sequence, forming a pair, is noted by Henry J. Cadbury, *The Making of Luke-Acts*, 234; Robert Morgenthaler, *Die lukanische Geschichtsschreibung als Zeugnis*, 1:104–5; Helmut Flender, *St. Luke*, 9–10.

also suggests an inclusive application. Women as well as men are encouraged to identify with the characters in miracle stories and parables, applying these stories to themselves.

In some cases there is considerable repetition of words in the same sequence, making clear that the two versions are to be understood as parallel, with the reference to a woman or a man being a primary distinction between them. This occurs most frequently in Jesus' discourse. Thus in Luke 4:25–27 two incidents from the lives of the prophets are recalled. The first establishes a pattern which is followed by the second:

> Many widows there were . . . in Israel . . . and to none of them . . . except to Zarephath of Sidon to a woman who was a widow (πρὸς γυναῖκα χήραν). And many lepers [masculine] there were in Israel . . . and none of them . . . except Naaman the Syrian.

Similarly, the reference to the sign of Jonah is followed by balanced sayings (11:31–32) which refer both to a woman and to men:

> The queen of the south will be raised in the judgment with the men of this generation and will condemn them, for . . . , and behold something greater than Solomon is here. The men (ἄνδρες) of Nineveh will arise in the judgment with this generation and condemn it, for . . . , and behold something greater than Jonah is here.

The pairing of the mustard seed and leaven parables (13:18–21) is also signaled by repeated language:

> It is like a grain of mustard seed which, taking, a man. . . . It is like leaven which, taking, a woman. . . .

Typical situations for a man and a woman are chosen: planting crops and baking. The different social worlds of man and woman in the first century are also reflected in the paired parables of the lost sheep and the lost coin (15:4–10):

> What man of you, having a hundred sheep and losing one of them, does not leave . . . and go . . . until he find it? And finding . . . he calls together friends [masculine] and neighbors, saying to them, "Rejoice with me, for I have found my sheep which was lost." Or what woman having ten drachmas, if she lose one drachma, does not light . . . and seek . . . until she finds? And finding she calls together friends [feminine] and neighbors saying, "Rejoice with me, for I have found the drachma which I lost."

Note also the sayings in 17:34–35:

> On this night there will be two on one bed, the one [masculine] will be taken and the other [masculine] will be left. There will be two grinding

at the same place, the one [feminine] will be taken and the other [feminine] will be left.

The experience of women in both the Old Testament stories and in first century society is deliberately included alongside the experience of men, and the parallel expression emphasizes the similarity and equality of their experience for conveying Jesus' message.

When we move outside Jesus' discourse (some of it unique to Luke—see 4:25-27; 15:8-10) to the frame narrative, there is less repetition of phrases but still suggestions of parallels between women and men, both of whom receive God's messages and share in God's salvation. In the birth narrative Zechariah and Mary have parallel roles as parents in similar annunciation scenes and in scenes with similar canticles.[47] Luke's birth narrative focuses on Mary rather than Joseph (dif. Matthew). She receives a divine message and celebrates God's saving work with powerful, poetic words which recall and resemble Scripture. In the birth story the roles of Simeon and Anna are also parallel (see 2:25-38). Simeon is inspired by the Spirit; Anna is explicitly called a "prophet" (using the feminine form). Both are devout Jews connected with the temple, both are probably old (since Simeon announces that he is now ready to die), and both are "expectantly awaiting ($\pi\rho\sigma\delta\epsilon\chi\acuteo\mu\epsilon\nu\sigma$)" the promised salvation for Israel. Simeon's inspired words, to be sure, are quoted, while we receive only a summary of Anna's (2:38). Nevertheless, the summary suggests that they were similar in content to the joyful words of Mary, Zechariah, and Simeon.

The inclusion of Anna, although she has little new to say, not only shows a concern to balance a man with a woman but is also one of several references in Luke-Acts to female prophets, women who are empowered to speak for God. At Pentecost Peter interprets the church's prophetic ministry with a Scripture text that explicitly includes women as well as men: "Your sons and your daughters shall prophesy . . . ; on my menservants and my maidservants in those days I will pour out from my Spirit, and they shall prophesy" (Acts 2:17-18). While the leading preachers of the word in Acts are all men, this Scripture is not forgotten in Acts. Before the prophet Agabus is introduced in 21:10, the narrator mentions that Philip had "four virgin daughters who were prophesying" (21:9). We hear nothing further about them. Apparently the narrator simply wanted to mention that there were female prophets in the early church. Since the word "daughter ($\theta\nu\gamma\acute\alpha\tau\eta\rho$)" occurs only three times in Acts, this brief statement may be intended to fulfill the Scripture cited in

---

[47] On the parallel structure of the birth narrative, see above, pp. 15-20.

2:17: "Your daughters shall prophesy." In any case, women as well as men can be inspired speakers of God's revelations in Luke-Acts.

Some healing stories also appear to form pairs, with a woman and a man as recipients of Jesus' help. Luke's version of the healing of Peter's mother-in-law is related to the preceding exorcism in the Capernaum synagogue by the statement that Jesus "rebuked (ἐπετίμησεν)" the fever (dif. Matthew, Mark), repeating the word used in the exorcism (4:35, 39). In his first reported miracles Jesus intervenes in the same way for a man and a woman. In 7:1–17 the raising of a widow's son follows the healing of a centurion's servant. In the case of the widow, the narrator suggests that Jesus is acting for her sake, since we are told that "the Lord had compassion on her" (7:13). The healing of the woman with the flow of blood is found in the midst of the account of Jairus and his daughter, a position that encourages comparison (see 8:40–56). Jairus and the woman are contrasting figures. Jairus is a ruler of the synagogue. The woman would be continually unclean from her flow of blood and therefore would be shunned. Her affliction is probably related directly to the fact that she is female; her flow of blood is probably a pathological menstrual flow. Jesus helps the man of social prominence, but on the way the woman whom some would ostracize is also healed. The narrative may also suggest a comparison between Jairus' daughter and the widow's son. In these two resurrection stories the dead or dying persons are described in a similar way: the one is "an only son to his mother (μονογενὴς υἰὸς τῇ μητρὶ αὐτοῦ)," the other "was an only daughter to him [Jairus] (θυγάτηρ μονογενὴς ἦν αὐτῷ)."[48] Not only the reference to a dead or dying child but also the similar wording alerts the reader that a familiar situation has returned, but with a shift in sex of both parent and child.

Finally, the two Sabbath healings in 13:10–17 and 14:1–6 form a pair even though the second does not follow the first immediately. Not only do they (1) share the motif of Sabbath healing, but (2) the characters in need of healing are introduced in a similar way (13:11: "And behold a woman [καὶ ἰδοὺ γυνή]"; 14:2: "And behold a man [καὶ ἰδοὺ ἄνθρωπος]," followed in both cases by a description of the affliction), (3) Jesus makes similar appeals to the way that animals are treated on the Sabbath in defending his healing, and (4) the two scenes close by indicating that the opponents are put to shame or are unable to reply. In the one case Jesus heals a woman, in the other case a man.

It is important that women are placed alongside men in sayings and stories, for this pattern of doubling shows that women share in what Jesus

---

[48] See 7:12; 8:42. "Only (μονογενής)" is rare in Luke (three occurrences) and is never used in Matthew or Mark.

brings and women's experience is an equal means of access to Jesus' message. In addition, there are scenes in Luke which present women as oppressed and degraded persons whose cause should be defended. For instance, widows are frequently mentioned (2:37; 4:25–26; 7:12; 18:3, 5; 20:47; 21:2–3).[49] Most of these passages presuppose the widow's economic helplessness in a male-dominated society and assume that she should receive special support, which is not always forthcoming. Furthermore, the story of the sinful woman in the Pharisee's house (7:36–50) presents Jesus supporting and reassuring a woman. She is in a vulnerable position not only because she is a woman but also because she is a recognized sinner. She is contrasted with a man of religious standing. In 13:10–17 Jesus defends the right of a woman to be healed in spite of Sabbath restrictions. He calls her a "daughter of Abraham" (13:16), thereby affirming her importance and dignity as one who rightly shares in the promises to Israel.[50] The healing of the woman with the flow of blood is not just an ordinary healing story, for the focus of attention is on what follows the healing. The primary issue is not whether the woman will be healed—this happens early in the scene—but how Jesus will respond to an unclean woman who violates religious taboos by touching him without permission.[51] Therefore, the woman tries to hide until she realizes that she cannot; then she comes forward "trembling." Jesus does not rebuke her but praises her faith and tells her to go in peace (8:48).

Even more important are passages which present women as followers of Jesus who are led by him beyond normal social roles and the restrictions which confine them to the family. The story of Mary and Martha (10:38–42) contrasts Martha, who represents the expected role of a woman in serving a dinner, with Mary, who neglects this responsibility in order to listen to Jesus' word. Martha's complaint raises the issue of whether Mary is right in neglecting her woman's duty and leaving her sister to work alone.[52] In spite of the burden this places on Martha, Jesus

---

[49] Only the last two passages have parallels in the other gospels.

[50] Compare the reference to Zacchaeus—a person ostracized by the Jewish crowd—as a "son of Abraham" (19:9). Jacob Jervell asserts that "daughter of Abraham" is a designation "unknown in the literature from this period." See "The Daughters of Abraham," 148.

[51] Lev 15:19–30 makes the impurity of such a woman clear. See further Marla J. Selvidge, "Mark 5:25–34 and Leviticus 15:19–20," 619–23.

[52] Ben Witherington III questions whether Martha was simply doing traditional women's work because "in a Jewish context . . . women were not allowed to serve at meals if men were in attendance, unless there were no servants to perform the task." See *Women in the Ministry of Jesus*, 101. Evidently there were no servants in this household, for Martha complains of being left "alone" to serve. On the same page Witherington comments, "Though . . . women could attend synagogue, learn, and even be learned if their husbands or masters were rabbis, for a rabbi to come into a woman's house and teach her specifically is unheard of. Further, being alone with two women who were not one's relatives was considered questionable behaviour by the rabbis. Thus, not only the role Mary assumes, but

affirms that Mary has chosen rightly and her "good portion" will not be taken from her.

The significance of this scene is enhanced when we recognize that it fits into a repeated discipleship theme of hearing and doing the word, relating that theme to women. Both the indication that Mary had "seated herself beside the Lord's feet"[53] and the statement that she "was hearing his word" (10:39) show her beginning to assume the role of a disciple. She is beginning to respond to Jesus' call to hear his words and do them (6:47). If she continues by not only hearing but doing, she will be included in Jesus' family, for "my mother and brothers are these who hear the word of God and do it" (8:21).[54] This challenge and invitation is reemphasized in 11:27–28, following the story of Mary and Martha, and there is special concern to indicate that this challenge to discipleship applies to women as well as men. To the cry of a woman in the crowd ("Blessed is the womb that bore you and the breasts that you sucked"), Jesus responds, "Blessed rather are those who hear the word of God and keep it." Jesus' statement is generic and inclusive in meaning. In New Testament Greek, generic meanings are often expressed in the masculine, since this is the dominant gender. The masculine was used even in 8:21, where Jesus was speaking not only of his "brothers" but of his "mother." But the setting in 11:27 suggests special concern with the situation of women. A woman speaks to Jesus and her statement implies an understanding of how a woman may be accounted blessed: through being the mother of a great son. While the implied author may not wish to reject such blessedness completely (the woman's statement is, after all, similar to statements about Mary in 1:42, 48), the emphasis in 11:28 falls on a greater blessedness which is open to all, women as well as men: "Blessed are those who hear the word of God and keep it." A woman's happiness and fulfillment are not simply by-products of her role as wife and mother. Therefore, Jesus protects the right of Martha's sister Mary to be free from domestic duties in order to begin the path of discipleship.

Furthermore, in 8:1–3 there is a remarkable statement about women traveling with Jesus during his mission in Galilee. Jesus' choice of the twelve apostles is reported in 6:12–16. When the twelve are next mentioned in 8:1, a group of women is associated with them. Three of them are named, although the narrator indicates that there were "many others."

---

also the task Jesus performs in this story is in contrast to what was expected of a Jewish man and woman."

[53] For this reflexive sense of the verb, see BAGD, 616. This position is typical of the disciple with the teacher. See B. Witherington, *Women in the Ministry of Jesus*, 101 and n. 133.

[54] On the interpretation of 8:19–21, see pp. 212–13.

These women are not simply part of a crowd which shows temporary interest in Jesus, for they have a continuing role in the narrative.

The women "were serving" them from their possessions, which probably refers primarily to supplying and preparing the needed food. This was a traditional female role (at least when no servants were available), so there is no suggestion here that women should avoid traditional roles in order to demonstrate their new freedom. It is a role dignified by the fact that Jesus also performs it, urging the apostles to follow his example (22:26–27). Serving tables for the needy continues to be an important function in the early church (Acts 6:1–6).

On the other hand, traveling around with a religious teacher conflicts strongly with traditional female roles in Jewish society.[55] Such behavior neglects a husband's rights and a wife's responsibilities to her family. It would probably arouse suspicion of illicit sexual relationships. In his later teaching Jesus will repeatedly tell his disciples that his call requires a break with the family (Luke 9:57–62; 12:51–53; 14:26; 18:28–30). The last two of these passages speak of leaving "house" and "children," which could apply to either a man or a woman, but these statements are male-oriented in that they also speak of leaving "wife" but not husband.[56] Nevertheless, 8:2–3 refers to women who have evidently taken the drastic step of leaving home and family in order to share in the wandering ministry of Jesus.[57] The discipleship of women is conceived as radically as for men—perhaps even more radically, since women of that time were very closely bound to the family—involving a sharp break with social expectations and normal responsibilities.

The women followers of Jesus are mentioned in Mark 15:40–41, but they are introduced much earlier in Luke, which shows their importance to the Lukan narrator. Furthermore, only the twelve and the women are mentioned in 8:1–3. These women are not part of a large crowd of disciples but have special importance and deserve special mention. Their special role continues. When the apostles are listed for a second time in Acts 1:13–14, they are in prayer "with the women ($\sigma\grave{\upsilon}\nu$ $\gamma\upsilon\nu\alpha\iota\xi\acute{\iota}\nu$)[58] and

---

[55] B. Witherington comments, "This was conduct which was unheard of and considered scandalous in Jewish circles." See *Women in the Ministry of Jesus*, 117.

[56] However, 12:53 indicates that the division in the family caused by someone becoming a disciple will involve women as well as men.

[57] If they were simply accompanying their husbands, we would expect the husbands to occupy a prominent place in the list of those following Jesus and supporting the mission from their means. We would not expect special reference to the *women's* possessions.

[58] See BDF, no. 255: "The article can be omitted in prepositional phrases." See also no. 257, 3. If the narrator did not have in mind a particular group of women, i.e., those mentioned in Luke, it is difficult to understand why only women, not men, are mentioned, except for Jesus' brothers. The 120 mentioned in Acts 1:15 included men, as Peter's address in 1:16 makes clear.

Mary the mother of Jesus and his brothers." Again this special group of women is mentioned along with the apostles, with Jesus' mother and brothers now added. These women, like the apostles, have the important distinction of being followers and learners during Jesus' ministry in Galilee and on the fateful journey to Jerusalem. This is an important qualification for the apostles (Acts 1:21–22; 13:31). It is also an important distinction of these special women, as shown by the mention of their presence in Galilee at Luke 8:1–3 and the repeated emphasis on their following Jesus from Galilee in 23:49, 55.

While the apostles, and later Paul, are the leading witnesses to Jesus in Acts, these women are Jesus' witnesses at one crucial point in the narrative. At the transition from crucifixion to resurrection, the narrator indicates that the women were present to see the crucifixion (23:49), then saw the burial (23:55), then had "seen a vision of angels" (24:23) and had "announced . . . to the eleven and all the others" what they had seen and heard (24:9). The angels ask the women to "remember" what Jesus had told them about his death and resurrection (24:6–8). This command presupposes that the women were instructed in these important matters along with the male disciples. The women delivered the message to the apostles as they were instructed to do (in contrast to Mark 16:8). They are the first human witnesses to the resurrection. It is not clear whether the women immediately believe what the angels tell them. It is quite clear that the apostles do not believe the women (24:11). It will take some effort to open the blind eyes of Jesus' followers, but the risen Christ will confirm that the women's message is true. Those who will be Jesus' witnesses in Acts are first instructed by the women, whose words prove to be a true witness to the risen Jesus.

We have seen that the narrator of Luke shows active concern and uses literary skill to present Jesus' ministry to the oppressed and excluded in an impressive way. Episodes in which Jesus offers release of sins to outcasts are linked with one another and thereby repeatedly remind readers of this important aspect of Jesus' work. A series of major quest stories highlights the possibility of the excluded finding what they seek through Jesus. Both Jesus' ministry to the poor and his ministry to women are well developed. All of this material demonstrates the fulfillment of the commission which Jesus announced in Nazareth, the commission to preach good news to the poor and proclaim release to the captives and oppressed.

Chapter Five

JESUS AND THE CROWD OR PEOPLE

The narrator of Luke refers frequently both to the "crowd" or "crowds (ὄχλος, ὄχλοι)" and to the "people (λαός)." Use of the latter term is somewhat distinctive, for it occurs only twice in Mark, fourteen times in Matthew, but thirty-six times in Luke. "Crowd" and "people" are basically synonymous terms in Luke. The shift from one to the other does not indicate that a new group has appeared on the scene. Rather, the narrator can shift terms within the same scene and mean the same group.[1] Furthermore, the same functions in the narrative are attributed to the crowd and the people. Jesus teaches the crowds (5:3), who gather to hear and be healed (5:15), but the people also come to hear and be healed (6:17–18). There is emphasis on the large size of both the crowd and the people attracted to Jesus (6:17; 12:1). Both the crowds (11:14; 13:17) and the people (18:43) marvel and give praise when Jesus heals. Both the crowd (22:6) and the people (19:48; 20:19; 22:2) support Jesus in Jerusalem and so prove to be an obstacle to his arrest. The same group is intended.

Nevertheless, the term "people" has a special connotation which should not be ignored. This term is frequently used in the Septuagint to refer to the people of Israel in its distinctiveness.[2] The influence of such usage is clear in Acts, where the "people (λαός)" can be distinguished from the "nations (ἔθνη)" without need to explain that the Jewish people is meant (26:17, 23; cf. 4:27 and Luke 2:32). Furthermore, Peter's speech in the temple and Paul's speech in the synagogue, speeches addressed to the "people" (Acts 3:12; 13:15), address "Israelites," "sons of the prophets and of the covenant," "sons of the family of Abraham," and those for whom the promises have been fulfilled. In these and other passages it is clear that the "people" means the Jewish people, understood in light of the scriptural heritage and promise which give it a special place in God's purpose. This is also clear in some passages in Luke, for instance, when the people is

---

[1] See 3:7, 10, 15, 18, 21; 6:17, 19; 7:24, 29; 8:42, 45, 47; 9:11, 12, 13, 16; 22:2, 6; 23:4, 13; 23:27, 48.

[2] H. Strathmann points out that, by the time of the LXX and NT, λαός had become rare in Greek prose, belonging to "an archaic and poetic mode of speech." But it is very common in the LXX, where it undergoes "a shift of meaning, so that the word is now a specific term for a specific people, namely Israel, and it serves to emphasize the special and privileged religious position of this people as the people of God." *TDNT* 4:29, 32. See also Paul S. Minear, "Jesus' Audiences," 81–84.

described as *God's* people (1:68, 77; 2:32; 7:16). Even when "people" substitutes for "crowd" in describing the large groups which surround Jesus and the early missionaries, some of this special connotation is probably present.[3]

THE BAPTIST AND THE CROWD OR PEOPLE

John the Baptist was sent to "prepare for the Lord a people made ready" (Luke 1:17) as part of his mission to "prepare the Lord's way" (3:4; cf. 1:76; 7:27).[4] The gospel shows him preparing the people when it describes John's ministry in 3:7–18. John is speaking to crowds who have come out to be baptized (3:7). The narrator assumes that there is continuity between these crowds and the crowds who will surround Jesus during his ministry, and John's response to them already gives some hints of what to expect in the future.

On the positive side, the people come to John when he proclaims a baptism of repentance and accept his baptism (3:7, 21). There is remarkable stress on the fact that "all the people" were baptized by John (3:21; 7:29; cf. Acts 13:24). John's influence is comprehensive (except among the religious authorities). Jesus, in speaking to the crowds surrounding him, will later assume that they were among those baptized by John (7:24: he asks the crowd facing him, "What did you go out into the desert to see?"). The people continue to be fervent supporters of John, as 7:29 and 20:6 indicate. Their attitude contrasts with that of the chief priests, scribes, and elders (20:1–5), and with that of the Pharisees and lawyers (7:30).[5] Thus the people addressed by Jesus have already been prepared for his coming by John's baptism of repentance. The repeated mention of John's baptism in the Acts speeches shows the importance of John's preparation of the people of the promise (cf. Acts 1:22; 10:37; 13:24).

On the negative side, John's harsh response to the crowd in Luke 3:7–9 leaves us in doubt about the seriousness of their repentance. In words so strong that Matthew applies them to Pharisees and Sadducees (Matt 3:7), John calls the crowd "offspring of vipers" and warns them against the

---

[3] In Luke, λαός always refers to a group which is Jewish. (Use of the plural is different; cf. 2:31.) H. Strathmann indicates that, when a crowd is mentioned in Acts, λαός always refers to a Jewish crowd. When it is a non-Jewish group, the narrator does not use λαός but ὄχλος or ὄχλοι. *TDNT* 4:53. However, Acts 15:14 and 18:10 seem to extend the special term for God's people to include Gentiles.

[4] See above, pp. 23–24.

[5] The carping "persons of this generation" in 7:31 cannot be the same as the "people" in 7:29, as the conflicting attitudes toward John in 7:29, 33 show. Furthermore, the attitude toward Jesus in 7:31–34 fits the description of the Pharisees and scribes in 5:30.

presumption of a feigned repentance. He insists that they must produce "fruit worthy of repentance" (3:8), backs this with an eschatological threat to trees not bearing good fruit (3:9), and warns against assuming that descent from Abraham will protect an unrepentant people (3:8). These same notes are later sounded in the preaching of Jesus, showing the continuity between the preaching of these two messengers of God. In a variety of ways Jesus speaks of "fruit" as the crucial test for individuals and people (6:43–44; 8:8, 15; 20:10), and he echoes John's warning that the tree which does not bear fruit for its owner will be chopped down (13:6–9).[6] Jesus (6:30, 34–35), like John (3:10–11), requires sharing of goods with others, and Jesus applies John's warning when he describes the fate of one who calls on "Abraham as father" but has not produced "fruit worthy of repentance" through sharing with the poor (16:19–31; cf. 3:8). John's suspicion of the crowds that have come to be baptized appears to be justified in light of later developments, for Jesus must repeat John's eschatological warnings to a people that has become complacent (12:54–13:9), and eventually opposition to Jesus will appear not only from the Pharisees and scribes but also among the people (11:15–16, 29). Nevertheless, at the beginning of Jesus' ministry the acceptance of John's baptism of repentance by the people gives reason to hope that they are ready to respond to Jesus' message.

LUKE 4–8

Apart from the scene in Nazareth, discussed previously,[7] the crowd responds favorably to Jesus in Luke 4–8, although there are indications in chapter 8 that the crowd's response is superficial and inadequate. In 4:15 the positive response is summarized: Jesus is "being glorified by all." The reaction in Capernaum is very favorable, although 4:42 indicates that the people there had a different understanding of Jesus' mission than he did. Reports of Jesus' spreading fame, as he attracts crowds from wide areas, indicate the positive impression that Jesus is making on people. Soon people from the whole Jewish land (and beyond) are hearing about him and coming to him (6:17–18; 7:17). The crowds quite appropriately glorify God when they witness Jesus' mighty acts (5:26; 7:16; cf. 9:43). They are not attracted merely by curiosity and fascination with the spectacular, for the narrator indicates that they come both to hear and to

---

[6] Peter and Paul also continue the preaching of John the Baptist. See Luke 3:3, 5, 8, 10 with Acts 2:37–38, 40; 26:20.

[7] See above, pp. 68–73.

be healed (5:15; 6:17–18). When Jesus returned from the country of the Gerasenes, the crowd "welcomed" him (8:40), and later in 9:11 Jesus "welcomed" the crowds (ἀποδέχομαι in both cases). All of these statements in the narrative indicate that Jesus is highly popular and that the crowds are very attentive to Jesus' words and works.

Before this bright picture of the crowd's response darkens in chapters 10–13, there are indications that the crowd's favorable attitude means less than it seems. While we are not told of incidents in which the crowd shows hostility to Jesus (except for the Nazareth scene), we do encounter statements by Jesus suggesting later negative developments and devaluing the crowd's understanding of his message. Speaking to his disciples in 6:22, 26, Jesus indicates that being hated and excluded by "people (οἱ ἄνθρωποι)" is a sign of blessing, while being honored by them brings woe. This fits poorly with the popularity which Jesus is enjoying at this time but will begin to make sense as the story moves on. At the end of this sermon Jesus declares that coming to him and hearing him, as both the people and the disciples have done (6:17–18), is not enough. The crucial question is whether they will also act according to Jesus' words (6:47–49). The sermon ends with this challenge to the disciples and the people, raising the question of whether they can fulfill this requirement. The difficulty of accepting Jesus and his words is underscored in 7:23, where Jesus declares blessed "whoever does not take offense" at him. Although the crowds are not yet taking offense, Jesus' statement suggests that many people will.[8]

In 8:4–21 the parable of the sower and its interpretation are presented as a basis for evaluating responses to "the word of God," which Jesus is preaching (see 5:1 with 8:11). Only the last of the four listed responses is adequate, since it involves not only hearing the word but holding it fast and bearing fruit (8:8, 15). This is equivalent to "hearing the word of God and doing it" (8:21). Thus Jesus' address in 8:4–18, with the connected episode in 8:19–21, reemphasizes the requirement expressed at the end of the previous sermon (6:46–49). This is a challenge to the disciples, who are warned that initial acceptance of the word does not guarantee that they are good soil (8:13–14). However, this challenge to the disciples is accompanied by clear negative statements about the people who have heard Jesus but have not become disciples.[9] In 8:10 Jesus indicates to the disciples that "to you it has been given to know the mysteries of the reign

---

[8] 7:22–23 is a reminder of Jesus' mission announced in Nazareth and the rejection he encountered there. See pp. 79–81.

[9] Note that by this time there are already a large number of disciples. See 6:17. The disciples are not a select group but consist of all those who have made the decision not only to hear but do the word of God. The crowd has heard but has not accepted the necessity of doing.

of God." This is not true for "the rest." This reference to "the rest" in 8:10 is explained further in 8:12. They are "those who hear, then the devil comes and takes away the word from their heart, in order that they might not believe and be saved." They have had a chance to respond but have not. Jesus is apparently already encountering this lack of response to his word. For such people Jesus' message consists of incomprehensible parables "in order that seeing they might not see and hearing they might not understand." This fateful lack of understanding on the part of those to whom knowledge of the kingdom's mysteries has not been "given" begins to control the narrative from this point on. Here the plot begins to pivot. Even though a reader new to Luke would not yet know how Jesus' statement in 8:10 relates to subsequent events and statements, such as Jesus' statement that the things leading to peace have been hid from Jerusalem's eyes (19:42) and Paul's final statement to the Roman Jews in Acts 28:26–27 (where we have a full quotation of the Isaiah text to which Luke 8:10 alludes),[10] the reader may still be put on the alert for further signs of unresponsiveness and resistance in the following narrative.

The blindness which Jesus notes does not indicate that all hope for the Jewish crowd is past at this early point in the story. The omission of the final line of Mark 4:12, ". . . lest they turn and it be forgiven them," may show a desire to avoid the idea that the possibility of forgiveness is already past, which would not fit with the offer of forgiveness by the apostles in Acts. Also, the sayings about the lamp and about the uncovering of what is hidden in 8:16–17, although open to several interpretations, may speak against the view that the blindness of 8:10 is reason for Jesus and his followers to give up their mission in despair.[11] Even though 8:10, Jesus' statement about the crowd which has not understood his word, suggests a tragic turn to the narrative, the story of Jesus, his followers, and the Jewish people is far from over, and there will be positive as well as negative developments before it ends.

LUKE 9:1–13:21

In Luke 9 we find additional indications of a positive relationship between Jesus and the crowd but also some hints of tension, a tension which will

---

[10] It is true that the statement about seeing and hearing in Luke 8:10 has been simplified compared to the parallel in Mark 4:12, which also reduces the degree of similarity in wording to Isa 6:9–10 LXX. However, Isaiah's paradoxical combination of seeing and not seeing, hearing and not understanding, is retained, and the importance of Isa 6:9–10 in Luke-Acts is shown by the prominent position of the quotation at the end of Acts.

[11] The saying in 8:16 is repeated, with minor variation, in 11:33, right after a harsh condemnation of "this generation." It may have the same function in that setting.

increase in chapters 11–13, where we learn that an important segment of the crowd is rejecting Jesus and Jesus' warnings against failure to respond become more intense.

On the positive side, Jesus' prophetic role is recognized by the crowd. The declaration in 7:16 that Jesus is a "great prophet" is followed by indications that there is continuing, intense speculation among the crowds concerning Jesus as a prophet (9:7–8, 18–19). While this may show less insight than Peter's confession in 9:20, it shows a positive attitude toward Jesus and is appropriate as far as it goes, for even Jesus speaks of himself as a prophet (4:24; 13:33). Furthermore, Jesus welcomes the crowd and feeds it in 9:11–17, and the crowd responds to the healing in 9:37–43 by rightly recognizing it as a manifestation of "the majesty of God."

However, Jesus will announce his coming rejection by the religious authorities in 9:22 and will declare that his followers must now be willing to deny themselves and take up crosses. The twelve and the seventy-two[12] are also prepared by Jesus to face rejection as they preach and heal in the various towns. They are given instructions on what to do when they are not received by a particular city (9:5; 10:10–11). Jesus clearly anticipates opposition to this widening mission, opposition that will be characteristic of towns as wholes. In 10:12 the instructions to the seventy-two are followed by a condemnation of "that city" which refuses to receive them, and in 10:13–15 three towns in Galilee which have not repented in spite of Jesus' mighty acts are condemned. This puts a new perspective on Jesus' previous ministry. While the people of Capernaum were excited by Jesus' healings and tried to prevent him from leaving (4:42), this was evidently not a sufficient response, for Capernaum will be condemned in the judgment, according to 10:15. This makes it doubtful whether the crowd that glorifies God for Jesus' healings and regards him as a prophet is responding adequately. In 10:13–15 it begins to appear that Jesus is demanding repentance from the general population. Prior to this he has spoken only of calling sinners, i.e., the outcasts, to repentance (5:32). Following 10:13–15 there are repeated references to the need for repentance in Jesus' words to the crowd (11:32; 13:3, 5).

Another development adds tension to the relationship between Jesus and the crowd. Jesus begins to speak to the crowd about the harsh demands of discipleship. He has previously insisted on the importance of not only hearing his words but doing them (6:46–49; 8:21). Those who take this demand seriously become part of Jesus' "great crowd of disciples" (6:17). In 9:23–27 Jesus begins to inform the crowd that following him as a disciple means renunciation of the things which seem most

---

[12] On the question of seventy or seventy-two missionaries in 10:1, see below, pp. 232–33.

precious in ordinary life. In 9:23 the narrator makes clear that Jesus' following words are addressed "to all," in contrast to the preceding words to the disciples. Some important teaching on discipleship is addressed to the crowd because it is a potential source of disciples and its members need to know what discipleship implies. In 9:23–27 Jesus is challenging the crowd to become disciples, and he uses strong words which make the full extent of the commitment clear. He speaks of taking up one's cross daily and losing one's life, which make discipleship much more difficult than it had seemed before.

The importance of the challenge in 9:23–27 is indicated by the appearance of two similar passages in the later narrative. In 9:57–62 Jesus responds to three candidates for discipleship in ways that emphasize the conflict between discipleship and desires for a home and normal family relationships. He harshly denies requests to fulfill family duties before following as a disciple. The words addressed to the crowds in 14:25–35 are also related. They summarize previous statements by bringing together three requirements for discipleship. This triad is highlighted by the fact that all three parts end with the refrain ". . . cannot be my disciple." The first (14:26) intensifies the demand for a break with the family in 9:59–62. The second (14:27) repeats the requirement of bearing one's cross in 9:23. The third (14:33) is related to previous scenes in which particular disciples left all when called by Jesus (5:11, 28), but now Jesus announces a general requirement that disciples must abandon their possessions. Family, safety, possessions—discipleship threatens all three. The crowds are told that those who cannot abandon these treasures cannot be Jesus' disciples. Such people are worthless salt, which will be thrown out (14:34–35). The concluding call for hearing by those who have ears recalls 8:8, suggesting that Jesus' words about discipleship clarify what it means for the seed to bear fruit in the parable of the sower.

In 11:14–36 we discover that a segment of the crowd no longer responds favorably to Jesus. Nor are they merely unresponsive. Open opposition to Jesus emerges from the crowd. Following an exorcism, the crowds marvel, a response familiar from earlier healing stories, but "some of them" accuse Jesus of using the power of Beelzebul, while "others" put him to the test and ask for a sign from heaven (11:14–16). Both of these are regarded as negative reactions from segments of the crowd. Jesus responds to the first in 11:17–26 and to the second in 11:29–36, so that 11:14–36 forms a single section of controversy with segments of the crowd. The accusation that Jesus is working by the power of Beelzebul is attributed to the Pharisees in Matt 12:24 (see also 9:34) and to the scribes from Jerusalem in Mark 3:22. Luke alone attributes it to some of the crowd. Again, Matthew and Mark attribute the request for a sign from heaven to the Pharisees (Mark 8:11), the scribes and Pharisees (Matt 12:38), or the Pharisees and Sadducees (Matt 16:1). To have these severe challenges emerge from the crowd presents sections of the crowd in strongly negative roles. To be sure, these challenges are not expressed by the crowd as a whole. The narrator distinguishes attitudes, suggesting that divisions have developed within the crowd.

The narrator previously distinguished between the attitudes of the scribes/Pharisees and the crowd or people (7:29–30). Now the opposition to Jesus characteristic of the former is emerging in the latter.

Jesus' reply shows the same sense of eschatological crisis and critical need for repentance previously expressed in the instructions to the seventy-two (see 10:9–15). The exorcisms show that "God's reign has come upon you," as Jesus declares in 11:20, a statement similar to the proclamation given to the seventy-two: "God's reign has come near to you" (10:9, 11).[13] In his mission instructions Jesus had stated that those towns not receiving his messengers and repenting would be condemned. This note of judgment is repeated and expanded as Jesus warns the crowd in 11:29–32 and 12:54–13:9. These related passages in chapters 10–13 suggest that the fault of Jesus' accusers in 11:15 lies not only in their false accusation but also in their failure to recognize the approach of God's reign and repent. The reply to those who seek a sign in 11:29–32 is especially close to the words of judgment in 10:12–15, for in both passages people of Jesus' time are condemned by an unfavorable comparison with sinful or pagan cities or individuals mentioned in Scripture. The comparison between Jesus and Jonah indicates that "this generation" is doomed apart from repentance.[14] As Jesus speaks of Jonah in Nineveh, he himself is on his way to Jerusalem, and the events there will confirm Jesus' judgment that the men of Nineveh will rightly condemn this generation.

In the midst of his reply to hostile groups in the crowd, Jesus responds to a woman with a beatitude for those who "hear the word of God and keep it" (11:28). This is a reminder of previous statements by Jesus. Jesus previously declared that his hearers must not only hear but do, and identified such persons as the seed which falls in good soil and bears fruit (6:46–49; 8:15, 21). This reminder of Jesus' norm for response to his teaching, found in the midst of a section where active opposition to Jesus is

---

[13] There may also be a connection between the saying about the strong man conquered (11:21–22) and the vision of Satan fallen from heaven (10:18).

[14] The references in 11:29–32 to "this generation" as an evil generation, which will rightly be condemned by people of previous times, generalizes in a way that heightens the negative image of the crowd. Jesus is apparently speaking of a much larger group than those who raised the issue of a sign in 11:16.

appearing, suggests that this opposition is a manifestation of the basic failure to hear and keep the word of God. The opponents in the crowd are examples of seed which failed to grow.[15] Jesus' response to his critics ends with a warning "lest the light which is in you be darkness" (11:35). Evidently there is still hope of avoiding that result.

In spite of the appearance of opposition in the crowd, the narrator indicates that the crowds are increasing (11:29) and reach tremendous size (12:1). Whatever the attitudes of people toward Jesus, they have not lost interest in him.

The narrator indicates some of the inadequacies of the crowd while still allowing variety within it by having a particular member of the crowd approach Jesus with a request or question (12:13; 13:23). Jesus' responses show that these individuals represent larger groups. In 12:13, which leads into Jesus' teaching about the danger of the search for riches, Jesus first rebuffs the individual and then continues with warnings on the same topic addressed "to them" (12:15, 16). Evidently a number of people in the crowd need to be warned not to be like the rich fool. A similar shift to the plural occurs when Jesus answers "someone" in 13:23–24.

The warnings in 12:54–13:9 are directed to the crowds in general. The tone is harsh. Jesus' hearers are called "hypocrites" and are blamed for failing to "examine this time" (12:56). Only repentance can save them from sudden destruction, and this warning applies to "all" (13:3, 5). Only a short time remains for them to act (12:57–59); there is one last chance to bear fruit (13:6–9). John the Baptist had warned the crowds that they must produce "fruit worthy of repentance," for "the ax is laid to the root of the trees" (3:8–9). Now Jesus speaks to the crowds the way John did (13:6 9). "This time" is critical, but the crowds, so alert to the weather, are ignoring this crucial time. Here we do not find open opposition to Jesus, as at 11:15, but there are clear indications of a potentially disastrous failure to respond to Jesus' message, a failure which Jesus tries to correct with urgent words. The reason for the urgency is hidden behind figurative language, but in the context of Luke-Acts the urgency may be caused by other events than an imminent cosmic judgment. In the course of the narrative there are several crucial points of decision which will shape the story of Jesus Messiah and the Jewish people. As Jesus approaches Jerusalem, a representative core of the Jewish people are approaching a decision point which will have heavy consequences for the future. In the context of Luke, "this time" in 12:56 may refer to the decision point which is fast approaching as Jesus journeys to Jerusalem.

---

[15] Note also that the saying about the lamp in 8:16 recurs in variant form at 11:33, providing a further tie between these sections of Jesus' teaching.

Now Jesus is warning people about their blindness to "this time (καιρόν)." When he arrives at Jerusalem, he will lament the bitter fact that "the time (καιρόν) of your visitation" is passing unrecognized, with tragic consequences. The images of imprisonment, Roman slaughter of temple worshipers, and collapse of buildings in 12:57–13:5 are quite appropriate to the results of the Jewish-Roman war, to which 19:42–44 clearly refers. The approach of a fateful decision at Jerusalem makes the urgent tone of 12:54–13:9 appropriate.

LUKE 13:22–19:10

The crowd continues to come to Jesus for healing and rejoices "at all the glorious things being done by him" (13:14, 17). However, at the next shift of scene Jesus responds to "someone" (an anonymous member of the crowd)[16] with a severe warning of exclusion from God's reign (13:22–30). While the question is posed by an individual, Jesus addresses his audience in the plural, indicating that the warning concerns others in the crowd as well, of whom the questioner is a representative. The questioner asks whether few will be saved, and Jesus' answer ("Many will seek to enter and will not be able") suggests that those of the crowd who will be saved are, in fact, few, which is a decidedly pessimistic view of the further progress of Jesus' mission. Those being addressed shared table fellowship with Jesus, perhaps provided him hospitality, and Jesus taught in their streets. Nevertheless, they are rejected as "workers of iniquity." Their appeal to past association with Jesus is of no avail when repentance is lacking. They are warned that they may be excluded from the banquet in God's reign. Past rank and present expectations will be overturned when members of Jesus' audience discover that they are shut out and people of distant lands take their places (vv. 28–30). Simeon's prophetic preview of Jesus' meaning for Israel ("This one is set for the fall and rising of many in Israel": 2:34) fits Jesus' harsh words here, although the reference to people from distant lands may extend the upheaval beyond Israel. The themes of sharing in the banquet of God's reign and reversal of positions prepare for the parable of the great supper in 14:15–24.

Thus in four major statements to the crowd or members of it (11:14–36; 12:13–21; 12:54–13:9; 13:22–30), we find that some of the crowd are opposing Jesus, and that the crowds are accused of being unresponsive and are threatened with judgment and exclusion. In Luke 11–13 it appears that the previous interest of the crowd in Jesus' teaching and

---

[16] Cf. 12:13–14, where Jesus responds to "someone from the crowd."

miracles was in many cases a superficial, inadequate response. Further-more, it is becoming increasingly problematic whether Jesus will be the "glory of your people Israel" and bring the "redemption of Jerusalem," as anticipated in 2:32, 38. Tension is developing in the plot, for the expecta-tions of salvation aroused by the birth stories are being threatened. Not only do many of the religious authorities oppose Jesus, but members of the crowd, which often seemed to favor Jesus, must be warned that they may lose the salvation which Jesus came to bring.

The warning about exclusion in 13:23–30 is linked by the narrator with Jesus' following words about Jerusalem and his own death. The reminder that Jesus is journeying to Jerusalem in 13:22 not only provides a general setting for the warning to the crowd but also anticipates Jesus' words in 13:32–35 (cp. especially vv. 22 and 33). The section begins by reminding us that Jerusalem is the goal of Jesus' journey and ends by clarifying the significance of Jerusalem as goal. The connection is strengthened by the indication in v. 31 that Jesus' following words were spoken at the same time ($\dot{\epsilon}\nu$ $a\dot{v}\tau\hat{\eta}$ $\tau\hat{\eta}$ $\ddot{\omega}\rho\alpha$) as the preceding warning. The narrator's efforts to link these two narrative segments suggests some connection in meaning.[17] This need not indicate that the people who are seeking to enter God's reign but fail are responding to Jesus in the same way that Jerusalem will. Rather, a progression seems to be implied. The inadequate response of the people now will become deadly rejection by the leaders and "people" of Jerusalem later.

Some Pharisees warn Jesus that he should "go ($\pi o\rho\epsilon\acute{v}ov$) from here, for Herod wants to kill ($\dot{a}\pi o\kappa\tau\epsilon\hat{\iota}\nu\alpha\iota$) you." Jesus' reply plays with the ideas of going and being killed, highlighting the Pharisees' ironic misunder-standing of the true situation. Jesus, indeed, "must go ($\delta\epsilon\hat{\iota}$ . . . $\pi o\rho\epsilon\acute{v}\epsilon\sigma\theta\alpha\iota$)" (v. 33), but this is a journey to the place of death, not the escape from death that the Pharisees urge. He is going to Jerusalem, the city that "kills ($\dot{a}\pi o\kappa\tau\epsilon\acute{\iota}\nu ov\sigma a$) the prophets" (v. 34). The persecution and killing of prophets has already been mentioned in 6:22–23 and 11:47–51, but now this motif is given specific application: the prophet is Jesus and the place will be Jerusalem.[18]

Jesus says that he must go "today and tomorrow and on the next day" to reach his destiny in Jerusalem (v. 33). He also says that he is casting out demons and accomplishing healings "today and tomorrow, and on the

---

[17] On the link between 13:22–30 and 31–35 see further A. Denaux, "L'hypocrisie des Pharisiens," 245–49. Denaux notes other cases in which a Lukan introduction serves to draw together isolated pericopes.

[18] The wording of 13:34 is similar to 11:49. The latter speaks of "prophets and apostles ($\dot{a}\pi o\sigma\tau\acute{o}\lambda ov\varsigma$)" (dif. Matthew), while the former speaks of "the prophets . . . and those sent ($\dot{a}\pi\epsilon\sigma\tau a\lambda\mu\acute{\epsilon}\nu ov\varsigma$)." Both speak of the killing of these messengers.

third day I am brought to my goal" or "finished ($\tau\epsilon\lambda\epsilon\iota o\hat{v}\mu a\iota$)" (v. 32).
Verse 32 is often understood as a reference to Jesus' death. However, in v.
33 the sequence of three days refers to the time of travel to Jerusalem. It
would be remarkably awkward and confusing for the narrator to refer to
three day periods twice in adjacent verses, using largely the same wording,
and yet intend to refer to different periods. This problem disappears if we
translate $\tau\epsilon\lambda\epsilon\iota o\hat{v}\mu a\iota$ as "I am brought to my goal" and understand the
goal as Jerusalem.[19] Verse 33 makes clear that Jesus' required goal is
Jerusalem, and v. 32 should be interpreted in light of this verse.[20] Thus
$\tau\epsilon\lambda\epsilon\iota o\hat{v}\mu a\iota$ does not refer directly to Jesus' death. Nevertheless, a secondary reference to Jesus' death need not be excluded, for vv. 33–34 speak
of Jerusalem as the place of death, and Jesus' arrival in Jerusalem may
anticipate what will happen to Jesus there.

This interpretation is supported by three points of connection between
this scene and the Lukan narrative of Jesus' approach to the city.[21] (1) In
13:32 Jesus says, "I am bringing to completion" or "finishing ($\mathring{a}\pi o\tau\epsilon\lambda\hat{\omega}$)
healings today and tomorrow. . . ." Luke alone uses the approach to
Jerusalem as an occasion to recall and celebrate Jesus' mighty acts of
healing (19:37), which at that point are complete.[22] (2) The statement,
"Blessed is the one who comes in the name of the Lord," in 13:35 is
repeated verbatim (with the addition of "the king") in 19:38. (3) Jesus'
lament over Jerusalem's rejection in 13:34 is paralleled by a similar
lament over Jerusalem in 19:41–44 (found only in Luke). Thus Jesus'
words in 13:32–35 specifically anticipate the later scene in which Jesus
approaches Jerusalem and views the city. It is this goal which is in mind
when Jesus says, "And on the third day I am brought to my goal."

The vagueness of the time references in the rest of the Jerusalem
journey makes it difficult to know whether the narrator intends to portray
Jesus arriving at Jerusalem literally on the third day after Jesus' statement in 13:32–33. In any case, the sequence of a few days in Jesus'
statement indicates that the time is now short. Jesus' reply to the Pharisees carries a sense of urgency and imminent crisis as the time of arrival
approaches. Much important teaching of Jesus is crammed into the last

---

[19] Mentioned as a possibility by J. Fitzmyer, *Luke X–XXIV*, 1031. If this verb is passive
rather than middle, as assumed here, it suggests the hidden divine action behind Jesus'
action. This fits with the emphasis on divine necessity in v. 33.

[20] $\pi\lambda\acute{\eta}\nu$ probably has an intensifying sense, such as "moreover." So I. H. Marshall, *The
Gospel of Luke*, 572, and M. Rese, "Lukas XIII, 31–33," 217–18.

[21] See D. Tiede, *Prophecy and History*, 73: "Simply on a literary level . . . it is clear that Luke
13:31–35 has been structured in close correlation to the third gospel's account of Jesus' entry
into Jerusalem."

[22] The healing of the ear of the high priest's servant (22:51) is exceptional. It is required to
compensate for an injury caused by one of the disciples.

few days of Jesus' journey to Jerusalem (13:22–19:27). All of the gospels give a large amount of space to Jesus' last days in Jerusalem. Luke extends this intensified account of Jesus' words and actions back to the final days of the Jerusalem journey. This results in a large amount of Jesus' teaching being given with the final crisis impending.

Jesus speaks with emotion and with a strong sense of the destiny which he must shortly fulfill. Emotional tension was already expressed in 12:49–50: "I came to cast fire on the earth, and how I wish that it were already ignited! I have a baptism to be baptized with, and how distressed I am ($\sigma\upsilon\nu\acute{\epsilon}\chi o\mu\alpha\iota$) until it is accomplished!" To this is added in 13:34–35 Jesus' emotional reaction to Jerusalem's rejection of his mission. Jesus speaks in words of lament directed to the city itself, beginning with a repetition of the city's name. He expresses his unfulfilled yearning to "gather" Jerusalem, contrasting his repeated desire ($\dot{\eta}\theta\acute{\epsilon}\lambda\eta\sigma\alpha$) with their refusal of that desire ($o\dot{\upsilon}\kappa \ \dot{\eta}\theta\epsilon\lambda\acute{\eta}\sigma\alpha\tau\epsilon$). The image of the hen and her chicks adds to the pathos. Jesus is the caring, anguished parent, yearning to gather close the wayward children. Although Jesus addresses Jerusalem as killer of the prophets, his words are primarily words of lament, not of condemnation. But Jerusalem's rejection will have consequences. Jerusalem's "house" is forsaken, and its people will not "see" Jesus until they say, "Blessed is the one who comes in the name of the Lord." As noted above, these words are repeated when Jesus descends the hill to Jerusalem. However, the narrator makes clear that it is not the people of Jerusalem but "all the multitude of the disciples" who greet Jesus in this way (19:37; dif. Matthew, Mark). In contrast, Jerusalem does not recognize the time of its visitation (19:44). The function of 13:35 is not to anticipate what will happen in 19:37–38 but to lament what will not happen. Indeed, 13:35 would make little sense in Luke if it were fulfilled upon Jesus' arrival at Jerusalem, for it is obvious that the people of Jerusalem would not see him until he arrives there. This statement is important and is emphatically expressed ("I say to you, you will certainly not see me") because a much more serious separation is in mind than the remaining miles of Jesus' journey to Jerusalem. Jerusalem does not recognize God's saving visitation when Jesus arrives. It does not "see" and acknowledge its messianic king and therefore cannot share his benefits.

Nevertheless, Jesus holds open the future. When he states, "You will certainly not see me until you say,[23] 'Blessed . . .'," Jesus holds open the possibility that at some future time Jerusalem might welcome its king and share in the messianic salvation. Dale C. Allison, Jr., interprets Luke 13:35b as a conditional prophecy of a salvific coming which is still possible

---

[23] Or "until it shall come when you say."

for Jerusalem, in spite of its rejection of Jesus. He rightly rejects the common view that this sentence refers to the final coming of Jesus as judge, which can only mean condemnation for Jerusalem, pointing out that "bless" and "blessed" are "not words of fear and trembling" but are "usually expressions of joy, and they consistently have a very positive connotation."[24] It would be strange for people facing divine wrath to greet their judge in the same way that people greeted the pilgrims coming to Jerusalem to celebrate the feasts[25] and in the way that Jesus' disciples greeted him when he approached Jerusalem (19:38). There is no indication when or even if Jerusalem will finally accept Jesus as its Messiah. The importance for the narrator of holding open this possibility, in spite of much negative experience, is indicated by Acts 3:19–21, which makes the coming of the Messiah to the people of Jerusalem depend on their repentance. This is also the implication of Luke 13:35. Luke 21:24 provides some further support for this interpretation, for it appears to hold open the possibility of an end to the destruction that will befall Jerusalem.

Luke 13:35 and 21:24 are part of four connected passages (two of them unique to Luke) about Jerusalem's rejection of Jesus and the resulting judgment on the city (see 13:32–35; 19:41–44; 21:20–24; 23:27–31). The implications of the statement in 13:35 that "your house is left" or "forsaken" will become clear in the later passages, which speak of the conquest and destruction of the city, with great suffering for its people. The mood of lament and pathos in 13:34–35 will continue. Jesus will weep over the city and use graphic images of devastation which will fall upon all the inhabitants of the city, even the women and children. The repeated appearance of these laments over Jerusalem, beginning already in chapter 13, makes their importance to the narrator clear. The tragic effect of these passages is all the stronger because of the joyful expectation in the birth narrative, with its prophecy that Jesus would fulfill the hope of those awaiting the "redemption of Jerusalem" (2:38).

In 14:25 we are told that the crowds not only surround Jesus at points along the way but accompany him as he journeys. They are "going with" Jesus, as disciples should. However, their commitment to discipleship is dubious. Jesus must still warn them about the requirements for those who share his journey.[26] He explains how one must "come after" him, namely, bearing a cross (14:27), and indicates that traveling with him means

---

[24] See "A Conditional Prophecy," 75.
[25] A use of Ps 118:26, which is being quoted in Luke.
[26] Jesus' teaching here summarizes and reinforces previous teaching on discipleship, as discussed above, p. 149.

saying farewell to all one's possessions (14:33).[27] These warnings are necessary because the crowd's attraction to Jesus may simply show that they are fools who carelessly begin what they cannot finish (14:28–32). Such people are worthless salt which will be thrown out (14:34–35). Like the people in the parable which immediately precedes this teaching to the crowd, they are invited to a great banquet but at the last minute may foolishly excuse themselves because they are concerned about property and family.[28]

Before and after Jesus' entry into Jerusalem, there are important passages which indicate that the relation of Jesus to the people is coming to a crisis. Before discussing them, we should note a few brief indications of the crowd's failure to understand or respond to Jesus which lead up to these important passages. Jesus' words in 17:26–30 are addressed to the disciples, but they comment on the behavior of the many people who are going about their business oblivious to the impending crisis. They have not been changed by Jesus' warnings in 12:54–13:9. Later Jesus indicates how difficult it is for those having property to enter God's reign, and "those who heard" respond by asking, "Who is able to be saved?" (18:26). These members of the crowd think that Jesus' statements pose impossible conditions for them.[29] The desire for riches, about which Jesus warned the crowd in 12:13–21, is still a problem. In 18:36–39 a blind man hears a crowd passing through and calls out, "Jesus, Son of David, have mercy on me." "Those going ahead" of Jesus, members of the crowd, rebuke the blind man. The reason for the rebuke is not entirely clear, but it may well be that "Son of David," understood as a messianic title, seems inappropriate. To the narrator, however, it is appropriate (see 1:32; Acts 2:29–31, 36), and the crowd's reaction shows a blindness which is similar to that of the Pharisees, who in 19:39 want Jesus to rebuke his disciples for proclaiming him king. In 19:7 "all" grumble at Jesus' association with a sinner, the chief tax collector Zacchaeus. Here the crowd takes the same position as the scribes and Pharisees in 5:30 and 15:2, thus showing a lack of understanding of Jesus' mission to call sinners and save the lost (5:32; 19:10).

While in 4:31–8:40 there seemed to be a clear distinction between the crowd, which was favorable toward Jesus, and the scribes and Pharisees, who were not, Jesus begins to issue harsh warnings to the crowd in Luke

---

[27] Using ἀποτάσσομαι, which, since a journey is clearly in mind, retains the meaning "say farewell," "take leave," as in 9:61.

[28] Helmuth L. Egelkraut, *Jesus' Mission to Jerusalem*, 181, notes that Jesus' statement, "If anyone comes to me . . . ," in 14:26 is connected with the invitation, "Come," in 14:17. The conditions for discipleship in 14:26, 33 are antithetically related to the excuses in 14:18–20.

[29] Members of the crowd, not the disciples, are speaking in 18:26. The disciples have already left their property and do not share the crowd's problem. See 18:28.

11–13, and, as Jesus approaches Jerusalem, the crowd's attitudes are hardly distinguishable from those of the scribes and Pharisees, who reject Jesus' teaching on riches (16:14), think that proclaiming Jesus as king deserves a rebuke, and grumble when Jesus associates with tax collectors and sinners.

LUKE 19:11–21:38

In the period of Jesus' teaching in the temple a contrast between the people and the religious leaders (now described as chief priests, scribes, and "first men of the people": 19:47) reappears. We are not told that the people now recognize the critical time, repent, and become disciples. Nevertheless, they show enthusiastic interest in Jesus' teaching. The popular support of Jesus is so strong that the religious leaders, who are seeking to destroy Jesus, are unable to arrest Jesus in public. The "people" (λαός is frequently used from 19:47–24:19, while ὄχλος ["crowd"] is used only four times in this section)[30] do not plan Jesus' death; indeed, they are the chief obstacles to the leaders' plot (see 19:47–48; 20:6, 19; 22:2, 6). In the temple Jesus continues his ministry of teaching the people and proclaiming good news, and the people are eager to hear him (see 19:47–20:1 and 21:37–38, passages which frame Jesus' temple teaching). However, this impression of strong support from the people is undermined by words of Jesus which indicate that popular support will not determine the course of events and that Jerusalem as a whole will be implicated in Jesus' rejection and will suffer the consequences. These words imply that the popular response is flawed in some respect. It is not sufficient to bring a happy outcome to the plot. Thus there is tension in the narrative between the apparently favorable situation and Jesus' awareness of what is coming.

In portraying the people, Luke, in contrast to Matthew and Mark, specifies that it is the "multitude of the disciples" who rejoice at Jesus' entry into Jerusalem and say, "Blessed is the one who comes in the name of the Lord."[31] This gains in significance when we recall that Jesus had previously said to Jerusalem, "You will certainly not see me until you say, 'Blessed is the one who comes in the name of the Lord'" (13:35). Jerusalem does not join in saying this and so does not "see" Jesus in the crucial sense. The disciples also proclaim Jesus as "the king" in 19:38.

---

[30] See Jerome Kodell, "Luke's Use of *Laos*," 327–43.

[31] Note also that this "multitude of the disciples" praises God for "all the mighty acts which they had seen." This is not a group encountering Jesus for the first time but witnesses of Jesus' previous ministry who have accompanied him for some time.

Jerusalem, whether leaders or people, does not join in this proclamation. It is an appropriate proclamation at this crucial point in the story. When Peter made his messianic confession in 9:20, Jesus "rebuked (ἐπιτιμήσας)" the disciples and commanded them to tell this to no one. In 19:38–40 "some of the Pharisees from the crowd" ask Jesus to do what he had previously done, i.e., "rebuke (ἐπιτίμησον)" his disciples. This time Jesus refuses. Now is the time for public revelation and public acknowledgement of Jesus' messianic kingship. But only the disciples acknowledge Jesus as king.

Furthermore, there are three scenes just before and shortly after the arrival at Jerusalem which provide previews of what will happen there. They indicate that the king will be rejected by his citizens and that this will bring disaster upon the city as a whole, both the leaders and the people. These three scenes are the parable of the pounds (19:11–27), Jesus weeping over Jerusalem (19:41–44), and the parable of the vineyard tenants (20:9–19). I will begin with the second of these, which refers explicitly to the destruction of Jerusalem.

In 19:41–44 Jesus addresses the city of Jerusalem and speaks about its coming destruction. This will befall the city as a whole and its inhabitants ("your children in you"), that is, the people of Jerusalem, not just the religious leaders. The city's destruction will be divine punishment for its blindness (see "because you did not know" in 19:44). This theme of divine retribution for the people of the city reappears in 21:23, where the destruction of Jerusalem is described as "wrath on this people (λαός)." The verb ἔγνως ("you knew") occurs both at the beginning and near the end of Jesus' statement, emphasizing that the city's failure to recognize its opportunity ("the time of your visitation") is the critical factor in sealing its fate. This fits with the fact that it is the disciples accompanying Jesus, not the inhabitants of the city, who proclaim Jesus as king when he arrives at Jerusalem (19:37–38). The disciples proclaim the "peace" which comes with the messianic king, while the city does not recognize "the things that lead to peace" (19:38, 42). In 1:78–79 Zechariah prophesied that "a dawning from on high will visit (ἐπισκέψεται) us . . . to guide our feet into a way of peace." But now Jerusalem fails to recognize the crucial time of "visitation" or the things that lead to "peace."[32] There are further links between Zechariah's Benedictus and Jesus' words over Jerusalem: both refer to Israel's or Jerusalem's "enemies" (1:71, 74; 19:43) and both give importance to knowledge or knowing (1:77; 19:42, 44). Furthermore, the

---

[32] J. Fitzmyer detects a play on the name Jerusalem in the emphasis on peace in 19:42, for in popular etymology the last element of the city's name, i.e., salem, had become identified with the Hebrew or Aramaic word for peace. Thus "the city, whose very name is associated with peace, fails to recognize what makes for its own peace." See *Luke X–XXIV*, 1256.

theme of Jesus as messianic king, which is strong in the birth narrative (see 1:32–33), returns in 19:38 in words that resemble the angels' announcement in 2:14. These links make it highly likely that the narrator intends to connect the arrival in Jerusalem with the birth narrative in order to highlight the tragic turn which the narrative is now taking. The great expectations in the birth narrative for the redemption of Israel and Jerusalem are not being realized in the anticipated way and with the anticipated fullness, because Jerusalem is failing to recognize the time of its visitation. The great expectations aroused at the beginning contribute to the tragic effect of this turn in the plot, for we feel the loss more keenly in contrast to these great hopes.[33]

Later Peter will say that both the people of Jerusalem and their leaders acted in "ignorance" (ἄγνοια, Acts 3:17; cf. 13:27). Jesus is speaking of this same fateful ignorance as the cause of the city's destruction. While there is still a possibility of repentance for the people of Jerusalem following Jesus' death, as Peter's speeches in Acts make clear, there is no suggestion that the destruction of the city can be avoided. Jesus' mood while viewing the city is one of tragic pathos, not of vengeful anger. He is depicted as weeping, a remarkable thing since Luke, when compared with Mark, shows a tendency to avoid descriptions of Jesus' emotions.[34] If it is appropriate for Jesus, it is also appropriate for his followers to weep for Jerusalem: such is the force of Jesus' example. The destruction is pictured as total, but, just as in 13:34, Jesus yearns ("If you knew . . .") for a different response and result. Pathos is increased by Jesus' direct address to the city about its fate. Jesus is emotionally involved in the city and its future and speaks to it directly out of personal concern. This concern is conveyed through repeated use of the second person singular pronoun, often placed at the end of the short, choppy clauses.[35] In this unique Lukan scene we have clear indication that the narrator understands a major aspect of the story in Luke as the tragedy of the Jewish people to whom Jesus preached. The story of Jesus and the Jewish people comes to a climax in Jerusalem. There the religious authorities lead a major portion of this people into the tragic error of refusing the offered peace of the messianic kingdom. This has serious consequences for Israel's history, in the narrator's view. Whether Israel can recover from this tragic error is an important question in the rest of Luke-Acts.

---

[33] See R. Tannehill, "Israel in Luke-Acts," 69–81.

[34] See J. Fitzmyer, *Luke I–IX*, 95.

[35] This pronoun occurs twelve times in just three verses. The first instance (καὶ σύ) is clearly emphatic. David Tiede, in discussing the "sense of crisis and pathos" in this passage, notes the "fractured syntax" (see v. 42a) as well as the "heaping up of phrases." He also asserts that the pathos is intensified through a scriptural coloring which recalls the previous destruction of Jerusalem of which Jeremiah spoke. See *Prophecy and History*, 79, 81–82.

The "ignorance" of the people and their rulers is most clearly displayed in their denial and killing of Jesus (Acts 3:13–15, 17–18; 13:27–28). Jesus' weeping over Jerusalem is followed in Luke 20:9–19 by a parabolic preview of the killing of Jesus (the story of the murderous vineyard tenants), and the narrator makes clear that not only the Jerusalem leaders but also the people will suffer the consequences. In conformity with Mark, the scene ends with the remark that the scribes and chief priests "knew that he spoke this parable to them." However, Jesus is not addressing the leaders alone. Unlike Matthew and Mark, Luke indicates a change of addressee at the beginning of the parable (20:9): Jesus speaks the parable "to the people (λαός)." Therefore, the people must also be the respondents in 20:16 who react to the words of judgment at the end of the parable by saying, "May it not be!" (RSV: "God forbid!"). The people fear that they will share in the prophesied destruction. Jesus' reply does not assuage this fear, for the quotation about the rejected stone is followed by a sentence which emphasizes the destructive power of this stone: it will crush everyone who falls on it and whomever it falls upon. This reinforces the threat of destruction for everyone involved in the death of the vineyard owner's son. In light of 19:41–44, the statement, "He will come and destroy these tenant farmers," in 20:16 probably refers to the destruction of Jerusalem, an event which will affect all of its inhabitants.

The references in 19:14, 27 to the citizens who try to prevent a nobleman from reigning over them as king should be interpreted in a similar way. In Acts 3:13–15 the people of Jerusalem are accused not only of killing Jesus but also of denying him. This repudiation is emphasized in the story of the throne claimant, an addition to the parable of the pounds found only in Luke. Again Jesus anticipates what is about to happen in Jerusalem. The citizens do not want the nobleman to be their king. This mirrors the response of Jerusalem to Jesus. At the entry to Jerusalem only the disciples proclaim Jesus as king. Later he is accused of claiming to be a king (23:2) and is mocked as king (23:37) but is not acknowledged as king by the people of Jerusalem. Nevertheless, he will be enthroned at the right hand of God. The bloody slaughter in 19:27 may reflect well-known experiences in political power struggles. If this verse also suggests the destruction of the rebellious citizens at Jesus' final coming, this would result only from persistent opposition, for the preachers in Acts make clear that the citizens of Jerusalem who rejected Jesus have an opportunity to repent.[36]

---

[36] Jack T. Sanders charges Luke with "anti-Semitism" because of this parable and other Lukan material. See "The Parable of the Pounds," 660–68. My reply is found in "Israel in Luke-Acts," 81–85.

Therefore, as Jesus nears Jerusalem and enters the temple, we find three related scenes which interpret in advance Jesus' rejection and its consequences, making clear that the judgment will fall on the city as a whole, both the leaders and the people. The guilt and the judgment are shared corporately by the first-century inhabitants of Jerusalem.[37] Through the words of Jesus in the three scenes just discussed, which make clear in advance what will happen to him and to Jerusalem, readers have been warned not to regard the people's support of Jesus, which prevents the chief priests and scribes from acting, as permanent and decisive for the plot. The readers have been prepared for the success of the conspiracy against Jesus and for some role of the people in Jesus' death, with tragic consequences for Jerusalem.

In contrast to Matthew and Mark, there is no change in setting for the eschatological discourse in Luke 21. Jesus is still in the temple, not on the Mount of Olives, and his audience has not changed since the remark in 20:45 that Jesus was speaking to his disciples "while all the people were listening." This double audience is appropriate to the eschatological discourse because, while much of it is directly relevant to the disciple, it deals once again with the fate of Jerusalem, a topic of special importance for the people who are listening. In response to admiration for the temple, Jesus repeats his words about stone not being left on stone (see 21:6 with 19:44). When Jesus again speaks of the destruction of Jerusalem in 21:20–24, his words recall what he said when he wept over the city (see "encircled" in 21:20 with 19:43). Luke's text differs from Matthew and Mark in that Luke is not concerned with the "abomination of desolation" as an apocalyptic sign but simply with Jerusalem's desolation. Furthermore, Luke is not concerned with the fate of the "elect" in this crisis but with the fate of the city, which will experience divine judgment (21:23: "wrath for this people"). This will fulfill "all the things written" (21:22), and the connection of this judgment with scriptural prophecy and precedent is underscored by the use of scriptural words and phrases.[38]

Although this section of Luke differs considerably from Matthew and Mark, Luke does include the woe to the pregnant and nursing women (21:23). This woe fits the pathetic mood which characterizes Luke's references to the destruction of Jerusalem. The suffering of defenseless women and children will be reemphasized in 23:28–31, where Jesus

---

[37] Guilt for Jesus' death is not attributed to Jews in general. Note that Paul, in addressing diaspora Jews, does not accuse them of Jesus' death but attributes it to "those dwelling in Jerusalem and their rulers" (Acts 13:27).

[38] See I. H. Marshall, *The Gospel of Luke*, 773; C. H. Dodd, "The Fall of Jerusalem," 69–83.

speaks to women of Jerusalem about the disaster which will strike them and their children. Jesus' words about Jerusalem in 21:20–24 clearly refer to judgment in history by military conquest, not to the final judgment. Judgment in history allows no fine distinctions about degrees of guilt. Indeed, the evil consequences of historical decisions affect many people who are essentially victims rather than responsible participants. The narrator graphically depicts the coming disaster and also suggests sympathy for such victims through pathetic description of women and children caught in the city's destruction. Perhaps the "people" in general are partially victims of the false decisions of mistaken leaders, but at one crucial point, according to the narrator, they are persuaded to actively participate in the rejection of Jesus and God's reign of peace.[39]

At the end of v. 24 a time limit for the judgment on Jerusalem is indicated: "until the times of the Gentiles are fulfilled." This clause could be understood to refer to the whole time between the present and the end of history with the intention of excluding all hope for the restoration of Jerusalem. It is more likely, however, that it, together with 13:35 and Acts 3:19–21, deliberately holds open the future for Jerusalem and Israel.[40] This view fits an important theological concern of the narrator, a concern which would press toward hope for Jerusalem and Israel even when the historical situation does not encourage this. Through prophets and scriptural references the narrator has indicated that it is God's purpose to bring redemption to Jerusalem and to Israel, this being an essential part of the revelation of God's salvation to all flesh (see 1:68; 2:38; 3:6).[41] Admission that all hope for Jerusalem and for a large portion of Israel is lost would represent either loss of faith in the power of God or modification and limitation of the grand vision of God's purpose with which the story begins. I do not find signs of these results in Luke-Acts. Of course, this position requires interpretation of key statements about Jews in Acts, a task which must be postponed until volume 2.[42]

---

[39] See pp. 164–65, 197–98 below on 23:13–25.

[40] Acts 3:19–21, in particular, makes clear that there is hope of salvation for Jerusalem, for the coming of the Messiah will mean times of "relief" and "restoration" for it. However, this depends on repentance. Some would hold that the course of the narrative in Acts indicates that the narrator has given up hope of repentance by Jews who have rejected the gospel. This issue must be discussed later in vol. 2.

[41] See the discussion on pp. 21–22 concerning four types of material which are particularly illuminating in understanding the narrator's view of God's purpose. This material would include the verses noted, which come from inspired prophets of the near past or from Scripture.

[42] For preliminary discussion see R. Tannehill, "Israel in Luke-Acts," 69–85, especially 81–85.

LUKE 22–23

It is the group of Jewish leaders centered in the Sanhedrin and the temple who plot against Jesus and finally take action to get rid of him. But when the Sanhedrin is called "the council of elders of the people" (22:66), the narrator may be suggesting that this official body has authority over the people and the right to act in their behalf. Indeed, the people are directly involved, for when the narrator comes to the crucial scene in which the final decision for Jesus' death is made, the people support their leaders in calling for Jesus' death. This represents a drastic shift from the favor which Jesus previously enjoyed with the people. No effort is made to provide a motivation for this shift of position. We need not assume that all those flocking to hear Jesus in the temple now seek his death, but the narrator makes no effort to distinguish two groups with different attitudes. Both those who supported Jesus and those who call for his death are simply called "the people ($\lambda a \acute{o} s$)," obscuring distinctions which might be made. This fits with features of Luke-Acts that we have already noted: in the speeches in Acts the people of Jerusalem, along with their rulers, are said to share in the guilt of rejecting and killing Jesus, and Jesus' prophecies in Luke indicate that the punishment will fall on the city as a whole.

The narrative in 23:13–25 places strong emphasis on the responsibility of both the leaders and the people for Jesus' death. As the final decision about Jesus approaches, Pilate convokes a comprehensive group of Jerusalemites, including "the chief priests and the rulers and the people" (23:13). Pilate's repeated declarations that Jesus is innocent of the charges and should be released not only underscore Jesus' innocence for the readers but also accent the responsibility for Jesus' death borne by those who oppose Pilate's plan. Apart from their objections, Jesus would have been released. Pilate's role in the trial does not make the Romans look good, for justice that bends to a mob is not justice. But the refusal to accept Pilate's proposal to release Jesus makes the leaders and people look bad. Three times they shout for Jesus' death. The narrator emphasizes that they cry out "all together ($\pi a \mu \pi \lambda \eta \theta \epsilon \acute{\iota}$)," making clear that the people, not just the leaders, are participating. They not only call for Jesus' death but for the release of Barabbas, a man being held for insurrection and murder. The call for Barabbas' release seems gratuitous in Luke, for there is no explanation of why Barabbas should have anything to do with a decision about Jesus. However, Barabbas' role in an uprising suggests the people's support for a course of action that will eventually lead to widespread rebellion and the destruction of the city by the Romans. Thus in part, the scene is a dramatic preview of a fateful political choice that will be made in the following decades as the rebels receive popular support, with the way of Jesus and the way of armed rebellion posed as alternatives.[43] In v. 25 the narrator repeats the description of Barabbas as a rebel and reemphasizes the responsibility of the Jerusalem leaders and people: Barabbas is the man "whom they were asking for," and Jesus is "handed over to their will."

The participation of the people in the rejection and death of Jesus is understood as a tragic error by a group which has, in part, been presented sympathetically. The people make one fateful misjudgment which brings disaster. Although the people did not recognize Jesus as king when he approached Jerusalem, they eagerly listened to him in the temple. Furthermore, as soon as Jesus' fate is sealed by Pilate's decision, the people no longer appear as the supporters of the chief priests and rulers nor as rejectors of Jesus. The narrator is not engaged in polemics against enemies but is working with the emotions of tragedy—pity and fear at blind tragic error.[44] These emotions depend on sympathy with those caught in the tragic situation.

The people are present not only at the trial but also at the crucifixion, according to 23:27, 35, 48. While one may wonder whether the "large multitude of the people" in v. 27 is the same group that was shouting for Jesus' death, the fact that it is described as following Jesus from the place of judgment supports identity. The attitude of the people to Jesus at this point is unclear. Only the women are described as mourning Jesus (in a scene unique to Luke). However, these women who mourn for Jesus are a first indication of a shift of attitude that will affect the people in general in v. 48. The women who mourn for Jesus do not escape the communal punishment of Jerusalem. In fact, their mourning becomes the occasion for Jesus to speak one last time of the coming destruction of the city, emphasizing that this disaster will befall these women and their children. The pathos of the scene is clear. The narrator awakes sympathetic sorrow by the time-tested device of emphasizing the suffering of women and children, the most defenseless and least guilty of Jerusalem's inhabitants, and by depicting a scene of communal mourning, which Jesus redirects toward the mourners themselves. There is added poignancy for readers who know Isaiah well, as the author of Luke evidently did, for the "daughters of Jerusalem" can be understood as individualized spokes-

---

[43] Cf. 19:41–44: Jesus represents "the things that lead to peace," and the alternative is war's destruction. Barabbas is the dramatic embodiment of the rebellion leading to such destruction.

[44] See D. Tiede's discussion of "Luke's tragic narrative of the passion" in *Prophecy and History,* 103–18, and R. Tannehill, "Israel in Luke-Acts," 69–85.

persons for the "daughter of Zion," a personification of the city itself (Isa 52:2; 62:11). Furthermore, Jerusalem or Zion is used in Isaiah as a synonym for God's people (Isa 40:1–2; 51:16; 62:11–12; 65:19). Against this background, the words of Jesus to the mourning women are a tragic reversal of the oracles of salvation to Jerusalem in Isaiah 40–66. While Isa 49:21 and 54:1 joyfully portray salvation as a shift from barrenness to motherhood, Luke 23:29 declares that barren women are more fortunate than those with children.

In 23:35 the narrator simply reports that "the people stood watching." This prepares for 23:48, where the response of these spectators to Jesus' death is made clear. The people do not participate in the scorn, mocking, and reviling by the rulers, soldiers, and one of the criminals (23:35–39), nor is there any Lukan parallel to Mark's statement that Jesus was reviled by passersby (Mark 15:29). Immediately following Jesus' death, attention shifts to a centurion and two groups of onlookers, who are described as "all the crowds who had come together" and Jesus' acquaintances. The narrator reports the responses of the centurion and the crowds to Jesus' death. The centurion recognizes Jesus' innocence. The crowds evidently do the same, for they leave "beating their breasts." In Luke 18:13 this phrase expresses remorse for sin. Remorse is appropriate if these watching crowds include the people previously shouting for Jesus' death, who now belatedly recognize their complicity in the death of God's prophet. This picture of remorse prepares for the next stage in the story of the people of Jerusalem, for in Acts they are cut to the heart by Peter's preaching and repent in large numbers (Acts 2:37–41). Peter's sermons in Jerusalem deal directly and explicitly with the responsibility of the leaders and people of Jerusalem for Jesus' death, for their violent rejection of Jesus constitutes a major problem which must be faced and resolved in order that God's purpose of salvation for Israel might be realized.

Chapter Six

JESUS AND THE AUTHORITIES

Jesus in his ministry encounters persons with authority in Jewish society (the scribes, Pharisees, and synagogue rulers) and several political rulers (Herod and Pilate). In this section we will consider how the narrative of Jesus' ministry is affected by his interaction with these authority figures.

The birth narratives have warned us that Jesus' coming means upheaval within society. Some with power and status will lose their privileges, for God has "put down the mighty from thrones" (1:52) and Jesus is set "for the fall and rising of many in Israel" (2:34). These general statements begin to be realized concretely as Jesus challenges the assumptions of the religious authorities of his people in order to fulfill his mission. This upheaval also affects the rich. However, only the teaching on riches directed to the scribes and Pharisees will be considered in this chapter.[1]

The "scribes ($\gamma\rho\alpha\mu\mu\alpha\tau\epsilon\hat{\iota}\varsigma$)" claim, and are commonly recognized to have, authority to teach concerning the law. This is made clear to the reader by the use of "lawyers ($\nu\omega\mu\iota\kappa\omega\acute{\iota}$)" and "teachers of the law ($\nu\omega\mu\omega\delta\iota$-$\delta\acute{\alpha}\sigma\kappa\alpha\lambda\omega\iota$)" as synonyms for "scribes." The equivalence of "teachers of the law" and "scribes" is indicated in the scene in which this group is introduced: the narrator first speaks of "Pharisees and teachers of the law" (5:17) and then refers to this same group as "scribes and Pharisees" (5:21). Thus at the first appearance of the scribes, the narrator informs the reader that they are persons who claim authority to teach concerning the revelation which is the basis of Jewish life.

It is not so obvious that the Pharisees are persons of authority, for they were a lay brotherhood and could not automatically claim the credentials of the scribes. Nevertheless, within the story they are presented as persons who claim authority in religious matters. The Pharisees are closely associated with the scribes or teachers of the law, the two often acting as one group (5:17, 21, 30; 6:7; 7:30; 11:53; 14:3; 15:2). Even when scribes are not present, Pharisees claim to know what is permitted by the law (6:2) and what persons are sinners to be shunned (7:39). The Pharisees, like the scribes, are accused of seeking positions of preeminence in the synagogues (11:43; 20:46) and are warned against the tendency to exalt themselves

---

[1] For further discussion of the rich and poor in Luke, see pp. 127–32.

(14:11; 16:15; 18:14). Thus the Pharisees are presented as persons who claim status and try to exercise authority within Jewish society.[2]

In addition to the scribes and Pharisees, we will note how Jesus relates to individual Jews who are called either a "ruler (ἄρχων)" or a "synagogue leader (ἀρχισυνάγωγος)." We must also consider the role of the Sanhedrin when Jesus arrives in Jerusalem, as well as the roles of Herod and Pilate.

The story strongly emphasizes the tension between the scribes-Pharisees and Jesus. Study of the references to scribes and Pharisees in Luke up through 19:39–40 (where Pharisees last appear in the gospel, although scribes will continue to play a role) shows that these groups are mentioned almost entirely in pronouncement stories or similar scenes in which they interact with Jesus by objecting, posing a testing inquiry, or taking a position which Jesus corrects.[3] The only exceptions are the statements about Pharisees and scribes in 7:30, 9:22, and 12:1. In the scenes of interaction with scribes and Pharisees, there is considerable tension, often a tension which the scribes and Pharisees initiate (through their objection or testing inquiry) but sometimes a tension which Jesus initiates through correcting their statement or behavior.[4] This persistent tension does not mean that there is irreconcilable conflict from the start. Through much of the gospel the two sides remain in conversation. This is highlighted by the fact that Jesus is repeatedly invited to dinner by Pharisees and accepts these invitations. However, the tension between Jesus' perspective and that of his host always becomes apparent at these dinners.

In presenting Jesus' relation to the scribes and Pharisees, the narrator makes use of four recurrent "type-scenes." A type-scene is a basic situation which recurs several times within a narrative. Each occurrence has a recognizably similar set of characteristics, sometimes highlighted by the repetition of key phrases, but this similarity permits—even requires, if boredom is to be avoided—new variations in the development of the scene.[5] Therefore, comparison of all the instances of the type-scene will

---

[2] In spite of the close connection between Pharisees and scribes, there may be a difference in their reaction to Jesus: Lawyers are accused of killing the prophets (11:47–51) and scribes participate in the plot against Jesus in Jerusalem. Pharisees, on the other hand, share in group action against Jesus (6:11, 11:53–54), but we are not told that they carry this to the point of plotting Jesus' death.

[3] These correspond to types of pronouncement stories that I have called objections, testing inquiries, and corrections. Some scenes begin with a similar type of interaction, but Jesus' response is a fairly long discourse which does not come to a climax in a brief, pointed saying. This distinguishes these scenes from pronouncement stories. For the definition and typology of pronouncement story presupposed here, see Robert C. Tannehill, "The Pronouncement Story and Its Types"; Tannehill, "Types and Functions of Apophthegms."

[4] There is an element of correction even in 13:31–35, although the Pharisees in this scene may be positively concerned about Jesus' welfare. See pp. 153, 178, 196.

[5] On type-scenes in Hebrew Scripture, see Robert Alter, *Art of Biblical Narrative*, 47–62.

present a richer picture of the possibilities of human response within that situation and (if the same character appears in all the instances) of the characteristics and capabilities of the leading character. The repeated use of a basic situation suggests that it held special interest for the narrator.

The four type-scenes in which Jewish leaders participate are as follows:

(1) Jesus eats with tax collectors and sinners; scribes and Pharisees grumble; Jesus replies. See 5:29–32; 15:1–32 (with a parabolic mirroring of the situation in 15:25–32); 19:1–10 (where, however, the crowd grumbles). Repeated key words: "grumble ($\gamma o \gamma \gamma \dot{v} \zeta \omega$, $\delta \iota a \gamma o \gamma \gamma \dot{v} \zeta \omega$)," "tax collector," "sinner." Closely related variants: "eat with" and "lodge with."

(2) Jesus heals on the Sabbath in the presence of Jewish leaders who either verbally or silently oppose his behavior; Jesus defends his action with a question to which his critics do not respond. See 6:6–11; 13:10–17; 14:1–6. Repeated key words: "Sabbath," "heal ($\theta \epsilon \rho a \pi \epsilon \dot{v} \omega$)." Closely related variants: "Is it lawful on the Sabbath . . . ?" (14:3; cf. 6:9) and "Was it not necessary . . . on the day of the Sabbath?" (13:16). Additional connections between two of the three stories: teaching in a synagogue on the Sabbath (6:6; 13:10); Pharisees and scribes "watching closely ($\pi a \rho a \tau \eta \rho \dot{\epsilon} \omega$)" (6:7; 14:1); opponents put to shame or unable to answer (13:17; 14:6).

(3) Jesus eats in a Pharisee's house; a specific point of conflict arises; Jesus criticizes the views and behavior of the Pharisee(s). See 7:36–50; 11:37–54; 14:1–24, and note similarities in wording in the first verse of each. The second and third of these passages resemble each other in that Jesus presents a series of points of criticism of the scribes and Pharisees at the dinner.

(4) A Jewish leader asks Jesus what he must do to inherit eternal life; the law is cited as a preliminary answer, but the outcome of the man's quest is made to depend on an interpretation of the law, or an additional requirement, which goes beyond the Jewish leader's expectation. See 10:25–37; 18:18–23. Again the similarity of these two scenes is called to the reader's attention at the beginning, for the "lawyer" and "ruler" both address Jesus as "teacher" and then ask exactly the same question (literally, "Doing what, I shall inherit eternal life?"). Clear repetition in the opening of the scenes helps readers to note quickly the connection between scenes so that additional similarities and differences may come to mind as the scenes develop.

The scribes and Pharisees tend to collect negative values, thus becoming the representatives of those things which the narrator wants readers to avoid. To some extent, a process of growth in this direction can be traced. In addition to their other negative qualities, the scribes and Pharisees in

Luke are rich and greedy, a characteristic much clearer in Luke than in tradition shared with the other gospels. We should be very cautious about reading Luke's portrait of scribes and Pharisees as a historical record of groups which existed in the time of Jesus.

LUKE 5:17–6:11

Conflict with the religious authorities first appears in the series of related scenes in 5:17–6:11. In these scenes scribes and Pharisees repeatedly object to the behavior of Jesus or his disciples and finally attempt to find grounds for a formal charge against Jesus (6:7). The strong emphasis on Jesus' conflicts with scribes and Pharisees in this section of material will naturally have a strong effect upon the reader's understanding of characters in the story. This remains true even if the material is derived from Mark. Furthermore, similar conflicts will return later, including the specific issues of eating with tax collectors and sinners and healing on the Sabbath. Many scenes at various locations in Luke are tied together because they are related as type-scenes or are more loosely linked by some thematic repetitions. In this way these scenes of interaction with religious leaders are given an important role in the narrative as a whole and function not merely as individual scenes but as part of a complex network which repeats and develops dominant relationships and themes. It will help us to understand the function of an individual scene if we understand how it is linked with other scenes which reinforce, enrich, and modify its implications, so that it becomes part of a larger developing portrait of Jesus and his contemporaries.

At this point in the story, Jesus enters a time of testing of his mission. The authority of Jesus has been emphasized by Jesus' announcement of his divine commission in the Nazareth synagogue and by the amazed recognition of the authority of Jesus' word in the Capernaum synagogue (4:32, 36). But the authority of Jesus' teaching is tested when he encounters those commonly recognized as authoritative teachers and they object to what Jesus is saying and doing. The potential for conflict is immediately suggested in the description of the setting in 5:17, where the narrator indicates that Jesus "was teaching" before "teachers of the law" (dif. Matthew, Mark). This potential for conflict between teachers is quickly realized in the following events. Furthermore, from the beginning this is more than a local affair. The series of conflicts begins with a scene in which Jesus is faced with "Pharisees and teachers of the law who had come from every village of Galilee and Judea and Jerusalem" (5:17). Religious authorities from the whole area of the Jewish homeland note what Jesus is doing, challenge it, and witness what he says and does in reply. This is the beginning of a repeated testing and conflict which will continue through Jesus' final encounter with the authorities in Jerusalem.

As he responds to these challenges, Jesus demonstrates his ability to defend his mission and teachings. He is presented to the readers as one who passes each test. That he can do this in situations of conflict should increase appreciation for his power as a teacher. These scenes also present Jesus' views in their distinctiveness. Jesus is presented as one who introduces change into his society and who courageously and powerfully defends his views before those who are unsettled by them. The major issues which appear in these scenes of conflict become important defining characteristics of Jesus' way. We should pay special attention to aspects of these scenes which are repeated and developed in the narrative as a whole, suggesting that they have special importance in defining Jesus' mission and its significance for those whom Jesus encounters.

We have already explored the relation of the healing of the paralytic and the meal in Levi's house with later Lukan material, noting that Jesus' mission of releasing sins and calling sinners is repeatedly emphasized through later episodes which recall in some way one of these two scenes in chapter 5.[6] This process of recall gives these scenes basic importance and suggests connections among a series of scenes, resulting in a richer overall picture of this aspect of Jesus' mission. We also noted that Jesus' climactic statements indicate that the issues being discussed concern his mission as a whole, not just a local and temporary problem. In 5:32 Jesus discloses in a general statement what he "has come" to do, and in 5:24 he speaks of his fundamental "authority on earth." A basic aspect of Jesus' mission is dramatized in these scenes in which Jesus releases sins and invites sinners to his fellowship.

The "righteous" who are not invited, according to 5:32, will be described later as those who "declare themselves righteous (οἱ δικαιοῦντες ἑαυτούς) before people" (16:15) and who "trust in themselves that they are righteous and despise the others" (18:9). These negative descriptions apply to the Pharisees,[7] who are also being addressed by Jesus in 5:32.

The question about fasting (5:33–35) does not begin with the introduction of new characters or any other indication that the scene has shifted (dif. Matthew, Mark). Thus the meal in Levi's house causes comment not only because Jesus and his disciples are eating with tax collectors and sinners but also because they are feasting instead of fasting, and both

---

[6] See above, pp. 103–9.
[7] On 18:9, see p. 186.

objections probably come from the same group, the Pharisees and scribes.[8] The two objections also appear together in 7:34, where Jesus is accused of being a "friend of tax collectors and sinners" and a "glutton and a drunkard," i.e., one who eats and drinks beyond the normal because he is often at parties. Making 5:33–35 part of the reaction to the meal in Levi's house suggests that this meal was like a wedding feast. It is also described in 5:29 as a "great banquet" (dif. Matthew, Mark). These festive meals with tax collectors and sinners receive further attention not only in 7:34 but also in 15:1–32. Behind these scenes hovers the question of who will share in the banquet of God's reign, as is clear in 14:15–24, where Jesus tells a story about another "great dinner."[9]

In contrast to Matthew and Mark, Luke sets off slightly the sayings about the patch and new wine by a new introduction: "And he was also saying a parable to them" (5:36). It is the narrator's custom to highlight Jesus' parables by introducing them with a new discourse tag (such as the sentence just quoted) even though there is no change of speaker or audience (see 6:39; 11:5; 12:16; 13:6; 15:11; 18:1; 21:29). This separation from the preceding verses may also suggest that Jesus' statements about the difficulty of combining old and new apply not only to the question of fasting but also to the question of eating with tax collectors and sinners. Indeed, they may apply to the whole series of conflicts with the scribes and Pharisees in 5:17–6:11. In each scene Jesus is resisting his critics' attempt to destroy the new garment for the sake of an old one and to store the new wine in old wineskins. These sayings about the garment and the wineskins enable Jesus to make a general comment on his critics' thinking without being restricted to the issues which they pose. This comment highlights the strange and dangerous thinking of the critics, who are willing to ruin the new for the sake of the old. Jesus also recognizes, however, the strong tendency to prefer the old (5:39) which is manifest in the reactions of the scribes and Pharisees.

The last two controversies of the section (6:1–11) concern the Sabbath. In the first of these scenes Jesus cites the biblical precedent of David, who disregarded cultic rules in a situation of need. The high regard in which David is held in Luke-Acts, as one who enjoys God's favor and fulfills God's will, is especially clear in Acts 13:22. David did not allow cultic regulations to stand in the way of fulfilling his divine calling of becoming king of Israel. Jesus has a similar mission which makes him "Lord of the Sabbath," one who is authorized to decide when Sabbath regulations must

---

[8] In spite of the speakers' reference to "the disciples of the Pharisees" instead of "our disciples."

[9] For further comment on the meal scenes and imagery of Luke, see pp. 217–19, 289–92.

be set aside to fulfill a greater divine purpose. His lordship will be further demonstrated in the Sabbath controversies which follow in 6:6–11, 13:10–17, and 14:1–6, where Jesus makes clear that his mission to release the captives from their crippling ailments overrides the Sabbath restrictions.

The Sabbath healing in 6:6–11 begins by indicating that Jesus entered the synagogue and was teaching "on another Sabbath." This remark links this scene to the Sabbath scene in 6:1–5, and these two scenes begin with similar sentences (ἐγένετο δὲ ἐν σαββάτῳ infinitive αὐτόν). However, the reference to entering a synagogue and teaching on the Sabbath also recalls the earlier scene in 4:31–37, in which not only the setting but also the central event is similar: Jesus dramatically helps a man in need in the synagogue. The fact that this was done on the Sabbath provoked no comment in 4:31–37, but the scene did end by indicating that the report of this event spread widely. In 6:7 the narrative presupposes that the scribes and Pharisees have heard about this or similar events. When the man with the crippled hand appears, they are "watching" Jesus to see if he will heal on the Sabbath in order that they might bring an accusation against him. A formal accusation with legal consequences seems to be in mind, something more than the rebukes already voiced in preceding scenes. The scribes and Pharisees have already formed a negative opinion of Jesus and now are seeking a good basis for a legal charge. Thus there is a suggestion that the controversies with the scribes and Pharisees may take a dangerous turn for Jesus. However, here, as later, the scribes and Pharisees are unable to carry through with their threatening plan.

As "lord of the Sabbath" Jesus is authorized to fulfill his mission in spite of Sabbath restrictions. Jesus was sent by God to bring release to the captives. If he failed to help these people, he would "do evil" or "destroy" rather than carrying out his saving mission. Jesus presents this sharp alternative in his rhetorical question to his critics in 6:9. Doing good and saving life are always God's will, even on the Sabbath. Failing to respond to serious need means the opposite of this: doing evil and destroying. The one who was anointed and sent by God must respond to human need by doing good and saving life. These thoughts are packed into a provocative question by which Jesus addresses his critics. Similar argumentative questions will be used by Jesus in later Sabbath healings (see 13:15–16; 14:3, 5). These questions will expand on the question in 6:9, adding the point that the opponents are willing to act on the Sabbath when they have a self-interest in helping the creature in need. The later Sabbath controversies will emphasize that the opponents are put to shame by these questions and are unable to respond (13:17; 14:6). Also in 6:9–11 there is no response to Jesus' question. This shows the helplessness of those who wanted to bring an accusation against Jesus. The final verse of the scene indicates that they have not been won over by Jesus. They are still discussing "what they might do to" him. But they do not follow through on their plan to accuse Jesus if he heals on the Sabbath. Jesus' sharp question in 6:9 has evidently undermined the popular support which his opponents need to act against Jesus. A similar threat is dissolved by Jesus' question in 14:1–6.

In 6:11 we are also told that the scribes and Pharisees "were filled with ἄνοια" ("madness," "folly," "lack of understanding"). It is not clear whether this describes their reaction to this healing or is a general comment on the imperceptiveness which they have shown since 5:17 and continue to show in discussing what they might do to Jesus. In the former case, it probably refers to an extreme anger and frustration which makes them act like they were deranged.[10] Even if this is the implication, the choice of the word ἄνοια (dif. Matthew, Mark), which can refer to foolishness and a general lack of comprehension as well as madness, may prepare readers for a later manifestation of a fateful "ignorance (ἄγνοια)" which will lead to Jesus' death (Acts 3:17; cf. 13:27). This ignorance can be overcome by repentance, but it persists to the end of Acts, where it is emphasized in Paul's closing statement about Israel's ears that do not hear, eyes that do not see, and heart that does not understand (Acts 28:26–27).

LUKE 7:29–10:37

Jesus' words about John the Baptist in 7:24–28 are followed by the narrator's comment on the reaction of "all the people," on the one hand, and "the Pharisees and lawyers," on the other (7:29–30). Here we find explicit negative evaluation of the Pharisees and lawyers by the narrator, who indicates that they "rejected the purpose of God for themselves." This rejection is serious, for the "purpose" or "plan of God (βουλὴ τοῦ θεοῦ)" is an important Lukan phrase used to describe the central divine purpose realized in past events of the biblical story and in the recent events reported in Luke-Acts (see Acts 2:23; 4:28; 5:38–39; 13:36; 20:27). This failure of the scribes and Pharisees is connected with their refusal to share in John's baptism. Thus they did not join the "people prepared" through repentance for "the stronger one" who has come after John. Later the religious authorities in Jerusalem will also be contrasted with the people because of their negative response to John (20:1–6). This is one of several

---

[10] I. H. Marshall, *The Gospel of Luke*, 236, puts it this way: "The impression given is that they are at their wits' end and do not know what to do."

indications that the chief priests, scribes, and elders in the Jerusalem narrative show the same basic attitudes as the scribes and Pharisees earlier in Luke.

In 7:31–35 Jesus speaks of the carping "persons of this generation" who reject both John and himself, for opposite reasons. Since the narrator has just said that "all the people" responded favorably to Jesus' words of praise for John, these same people cannot be the "persons of this genera-tion" who reject John in 7:31–35. Indeed, the statement in 7:35 that "wisdom has been justified by all her children" seems to echo 7:29: "All the people and the tax collectors justified God."[11] This would indicate that the people and tax collectors, in contrast to the scribes and Pharisees, are regarded favorably as wisdom's children. Furthermore, the negative view of Jesus' feasting, and of his association with tax collectors and sinners, has already been expressed by Pharisees and scribes in 5:29–35. In 7:34 Jesus is commenting on this reaction presented earlier in the narrative.

The following scene provides further illustration of the negative atti-tude noted in 7:34 by presenting a Pharisee who reacts negatively when Jesus proves to be a friend of sinners (7:36–50). The two groups to whom Jesus relates in the conflicts which we are discussing, the tax collectors and sinners, on the one hand, and the scribes and Pharisees, on the other, are here personalized in individual representatives, and the issue is dramatized in a longer scene. The focus now is on the contrasting relation of these two persons to Jesus, the one who brings release of sins. Follow-ing his parable, Jesus asks who will love more the one who forgives; then he goes on to emphasize the contrasting ways in which the Pharisee and the sinful woman have treated him. This is a comment on the contrasting ways that Pharisees and sinners have reacted to Jesus to this point in the story. The Pharisee's comment in 7:39 also seems to reflect prior develop-ments in the story. Following Jesus' raising of the widow's son, the crowd declared, "A great prophet has arisen among us" (7:16). The Pharisee appears to be rejecting this view when he says, "If this fellow were a prophet, he would know. . . ." Thus attitudes toward Jesus are beginning to solidify.

However, the scribes' and Pharisees' continuing criticism of Jesus because he is a friend of tax collectors and sinners does not mean that communication has been broken off between these Jewish leaders and Jesus. While statements of sharp censure are made by both parties, up to the point of his arrest and trial (see 22:67–68) Jesus continues to appeal to

---

[11] J. Fitzmyer, *Luke I–IX*, 677–78, notes the connection between "justified" and "all" in 7:29 and 35 ·and describes 7:31–35 as "an interesting reflection on the two preceding Lucan verses."

his opponents with strong words designed to change their view of themselves and of Jesus' mission. Parables have a prominent place in this
appeal (see 7:41–43; 10:30–37; 14:16–24; 15:3–32; 16:19–31; 18:9–14).
These parables provide an imaginative bridge which invites Jesus' opponents to step over and see the situation from Jesus' perspective. They
contain sharply negative comments about the Jewish leaders to whom
they are addressed, but in some cases the possibility of change on their
part is clearly left open (see 10:37 and the ending of the prodigal son
[15:31–32], which stops before the older son's final response to his father
is determined).[12] Furthermore, 7:36–50 is the first of three reported
occasions (see 11:37–54; 14:1–24) on which Jesus is invited to dine at a
Pharisee's house, and each of the three is a comparatively lengthy scene.
This type-scene repetition suggests that this is a characteristic situation
during Jesus' ministry and one of special interest to the narrator. Each of
these scenes is an occasion of conflict. The meal setting may intensify this
conflict by providing a situation of face to face encounter involving social
obligations, a situation which then explodes. Since the issue of who is
qualified to share in a meal has already been raised through rejection of
tax collectors and sinners, the fact that Jesus is invited to dinner by
Pharisees is significant. Some Pharisees are interested in Jesus and are
willing to have him in their homes. Likewise, Jesus is willing to associate
with them, although he does not politely hide his views as the occasion
might seem to demand.[13]

   It is also noteworthy that the impression which seems to be encouraged
by most scenes—that the Jewish leaders form a monolithic party of
opposition to Jesus—is softened by the appearance of individual exceptions. Jairus, a "ruler of the synagogue" (8:41; cf. 8:49), is such an
exception. While in 13:14 a synagogue leader shows an attitude characteristic of the scribes and Pharisees, opposing Jesus' healing on the
Sabbath, Jairus comes to Jesus for help and receives it. In 13:31 "some
Pharisees" are apparently concerned about Jesus' safety, warning him
that Herod wants to kill him.[14] Joseph of Arimathea, a "councillor," i.e., a
member of the Jerusalem Sanhedrin, is another exception to the general
impression that Jewish leaders oppose Jesus (23:50–53). Gamaliel, a
Pharisee, will speak with reason and fairness when his colleagues on the

---

   [12] In 8:10, however, the parables seem to be viewed as an instrument of the dark purpose of
God which is working through human blindness and incomprehension.
   [13] For more detailed discussion of 7:36–50, see pp. 116–18.
   [14] This interpretation (rather than the alternative view that the warning is a deception) is
defended by M. Rese, "Lukas XIII, 31–33." The warning by the Pharisees, even if meant
honestly and with good intent, shows misunderstanding of the divine purpose which controls
Jesus' destiny. See pp. 153, 196.

Sanhedrin are carried away by angry passion and wish to kill the apostles (Acts 5:33–40). There is also reference in Acts to Christian believers from the party of the Pharisees (15:5). Thus the majority of the religious leaders appear as opponents of Jesus, but the narrative presents important exceptions.

In 9:22 Jesus announces that he will be rejected by the "elders and chief priests and scribes." The narrative from this point on repeatedly calls attention to this future rejection in Jerusalem. Meanwhile, Jesus on his journey continues to encounter Jewish leaders who have specific questions and objections. In 10:25–37 Jesus interprets the law to a "lawyer." The lawyer does not begin by objecting to something that Jesus has said or done, as frequently happens with the religious leaders, but comes with an important and valid question ("What shall I do to inherit eternal life?") and addresses Jesus as "teacher." The openness to Jesus which this might suggest is limited, however, by negative comments about the man's motives. The lawyer is "putting Jesus to the test," posing his question as a hostile challenge.[15] When the first exchange with Jesus simply produces agreement, he asks a further question "to justify himself" (10:29). This false concern with his own position is particularly characteristic of the religious leaders, according to Luke. In 16:15 Jesus will say to the Pharisees that "you are those justifying yourselves before humans," and in 18:9 he responds "to some who trusted in themselves that they are just" by telling a story about a Pharisee. These descriptions fit with Jesus' accusation that the scribes and Pharisees want to be "exalted among humans" (16:15) and seek the positions of honor in the synagogues and at banquets (11:43; 14:7–11; 20:46). Conflict arises with the scribes and Pharisees not only because they object to Jesus' association with tax collectors and sinners and accuse Jesus of breaking the Sabbath but also because Jesus exposes the religious leaders' tendency to use their religion to advance their own status in society.

Like the similar story of the rich ruler in 18:18–23, the scene in 10:25–37 first affirms what the Jewish leaders and Jesus have in common—their recognition of the commandments of the law cited in the scene—and then emphasizes what is distinctive of Jesus. Jesus insists that the lawyer must do as the Samaritan did if he is to be a neighbor and fulfill the commandment. This requires an active concern for others which ignores social and religious barriers. Jesus' command to do as the Samaritan did touches a major problem in the lives of the scribes and Pharisees, as depicted in Luke. They have already shown that they wish to preserve the purity of

---

[15] Elsewhere in Luke Jesus is "put to the test" only by the devil (4:2) and by members of the crowd whom Jesus calls "an evil generation" (11:16, 29).

religion (and their own superior position) by excluding the tax collectors and sinners. Jesus is urgently seeking to change this exclusive attitude. The poor beggars are another excluded group for whom Jesus will appeal to the Pharisees. He will urge them to invite the poor and cripples to their parties, instead of their friends and rich neighbors (14:12–14), and warn them of the dire consequences of failing to attend to the needs of the poor (16:19–31).[16] At a number of key points, then, Jesus is urging the religious leaders to move beyond their established limits of concern to include the sinner, the poor, the enemy. Through the parable of the good Samaritan and the following command (10:37), the lawyer is asked to follow an enemy who ignores such limits and thereby becomes a disturbing example.

Luke 11:37–18:27

Luke 11:37–54 begins by repeating the stock situation of Jesus accepting a Pharisee's invitation to dinner (cp. 11:37 with 7:36). Again something happens which provokes the Pharisee's negative reaction, in this case Jesus' failure to ritually wash before eating. Jesus' response, however, is not primarily a defense of his own behavior but a sweeping attack on the Pharisees and lawyers. This attack touches on a number of points which are repeated elsewhere in the gospel. Thus this scene provides a fairly comprehensive summary of the failings of the scribes and Pharisees. Since this attack is sharp in tone, broad in its points of criticism, and general in its application (Jesus is speaking to "you Pharisees" and "you lawyers," not just to a particular Pharisee), it goes beyond anything that Jesus has said so far. The narrator is evidently aware of this and reports an appropriate reaction from the scribes and Pharisees at the end of the scene (11:53–54). They become terribly angry or begin to put fierce pressure on Jesus,[17] "lying in wait for him to catch something from his mouth" (either so that they might immediately contradict it or to use it as a basis of accusations). This indicates a new level of opposition to Jesus, with vigorous counteraction. The narrator's statement in 11:53 suggests that this heightened opposition begins at this point and will continue.[18] We will discuss below whether the narrator follows through with this indica-

---

[16] There is no change of addressee between 16:14 and 16:19. Jesus is still speaking to the Pharisees when he tells the story of the rich man and Lazarus.

[17] The meaning of δεινῶς ἐνέχειν is not entirely clear. The former translation presupposes that χόλον, "anger," is to be supplied.

[18] ἤρξαντο, "they began" (which is not pleonastic in this verse), plus present infinitives of continuous or repeated action.

tion that the scribes and Pharisees are now vigorously opposing Jesus and trying to catch him.[19]

The Pharisees are accused of hypocrisy (their inside does not reflect the concern with cleanliness which they show in externals, 11:39; they are like unseen graves, 11:44), predatory greed ($\dot{\alpha}\rho\pi\alpha\gamma\dot{\eta}$="extortion" in RSV, 11:39), neglecting "justice and the love of God"[20] (11:42), and loving the first seat in the synagogues and respectful greetings in public (11:43). The accusation of hypocrisy will quickly reappear in the next scene, where Jesus warns his disciples against "the leaven of the Pharisees, which is hypocrisy" (12:1). Thus this characteristic is reemphasized and used as a negative example in teaching. The accusation of predatory greed introduces a concern which will be developed later. Greed for money and property is meant, for its opposite and corrective is to "give alms" (11:41).[21] Later the narrator will describe the Pharisees as "lovers of money" who ridicule Jesus' teaching that one must "make friends for yourselves" with unrighteous mammon by giving it away and that one cannot serve God and mammon (16:9–14). They must be warned about the judgment which awaits a rich man who neglects the needs of the poor (16:19–31). The scribes will also be described as people who "devour widows' houses" (20:47). This characterization of the Pharisees and scribes as the greedy rich who prey upon the poor makes them negative examples not only for teaching about such standard synoptic themes as inclusion of the sinners and avoidance of hypocrisy but also for the major Lukan theme of the responsibility of those with possessions for the poor. There may have been some basis in prior tradition for this portrait (see the parallels to Luke 11:39 and 20:47 in Matt 23:25 and Mark 12:40), but it is emphasized in Luke, where the narrator evidently found it useful in giving forceful expression to Jesus' teaching about the rich and the poor.

The Pharisees' concern with social prominence ("You love the first seat," 11:43) mingles with their predatory greed. To be rich is also to be prominent and powerful. These false desires also appear together in 16:14–15, where the Pharisees are first described as lovers of money and then Jesus warns them about their desire to be exalted among humans. Similarly, the scribes who love the positions of prominence also devour widows' houses (20:46–47). The accusation in 11:42 that the Pharisees

---

[19] See below, pp. 182–83.

[20] Or possibly, "the judgment and the love of God."

[21] The phrase $\tau\grave{\alpha}$ $\dot{\epsilon}\nu\acute{o}\nu\tau\alpha$ ("the things within") can be understood either as the contents of utensils and vessels such as those mentioned in v. 39 or as an accusative of respect referring to the predatory greed and wickedness inside people (also mentioned in v. 39). In the latter case, the Pharisees are being told that the way to cleanse the greed inside them is to give alms. In either case, a literal giving of alms to the poor is meant.

neglect the love of God (dif. Matthew)—not an obvious charge for a highly religious group—may also be illuminated by Jesus' exchange with the Pharisees in 16:13-15, for the Pharisees scoff at Jesus' declaration that it is impossible to serve both God and mammon, since one must "hate" the one and "love" the other, nor do they realize that "what is exalted among humans is an abomination before God." The Pharisees who neglect the love of God do have a love: they "love the first seat in the synagogues" (11:42-43). The love of mammon and prominence excludes the love of God. This may be the basis for the charge of neglect in 11:42.

The response of the "lawyer" in 11:45 makes clear that the previous accusations against the Pharisees apply to the scribes as well. In addition, the lawyers have failed to help others as teachers (11:46, 52), and they share responsibility for the persecution and death of God's messengers, the prophets and apostles. The last point is made with great emphasis and is accompanied by a threat of judgment. When we next hear of a prophet being killed, Jesus is talking about his own death in Jerusalem (13:33-34). The accusation of killing the prophets directed against the lawyers anticipates the role which the scribes, as a part of the Sanhedrin, will have in Jesus' death, a role already revealed in 9:22. The vigorous efforts to oppose and trap Jesus, which begin immediately after Jesus' words to the lawyers, may suggest that they are already beginning to play the role of prophet killers that Jesus attributes to them. The persecution of Jesus' witnesses in Acts is a continuation of the persecution of the prophets and apostles mentioned in 11:49. Therefore, it is significant that in the next scene Jesus instructs his followers about persecution (12:4-12).

The type-scene of Sabbath healing returns in 13:10-17 and 14:1-6. Again, Jewish leaders are present who oppose healing on the Sabbath. In 13:10-17 the "synagogue leader" is spokesman for this opposition, but a larger group is involved, for the narrator ends the scene by noting that "all those opposing him were put to shame." The situation is soon repeated at a meal on the Sabbath in the house of "one of the rulers of the Pharisees," with "lawyers and Pharisees" present (14:1-6). While previous invitations to dinner by Pharisees seem to show the Pharisees' interest in Jesus, the motive behind this invitation is suspect, for the narrator says, "They were watching him closely" (14:1). This repeats the statement in 6:7, where the intention was to use Jesus' healing on the Sabbath as the basis for an accusation against him. Other apparent Sabbath violations were reported shortly before 6:6-11 and 14:1-6. These violations could provoke opponents to try to catch Jesus on this issue (see 4:31-37; 6:1-5; 13:10-17). In 14:1, however, it is not only the previous Sabbath healings which might lead the scribes and Pharisees to watch Jesus closely in anticipation of a Sabbath violation. This watching can also be understood as the continuation of the sharpened opposition reported in 11:53–54, where the scribes and Pharisees began to "lie in wait" to trap Jesus. Thus there is some confirmation here that the narrator has not forgotten the statements in 11:53–54 and that throughout the rather lengthy remarks of Jesus to the scribes and Pharisees in 14:1–24, 15:1–32, and 16:14–31 these groups are present because they are lying in wait to catch him.

However, nothing comes of this. The opponents are unable to catch Jesus. The Sabbath healing scenes in 13:10–17 and 14:1–6 make a special point of the failure of the opponents' efforts: "All those opposing him were put to shame" (13:17); the scribes and Pharisees "were unable to answer back to these things" (14:6). Efforts to trap Jesus on the Sabbath issue have proved fruitless. Jesus has reduced his critics to silence.

This permits Jesus to continue speaking to the scribes and Pharisees at the dinner without having to defend himself. First, he seeks to correct two characteristic faults which he could observe at the dinner party itself. The love of Pharisees for the "first seat" (11:43) is demonstrated at the dinner party by the efforts of the guests to get "the first couches" (14:7). Jesus corrects them radically, telling them to act in the opposite way, "for everyone who exalts himself will be humbled, and everyone who humbles himself will be exalted." This antithetical aphorism[22] will be repeated in 18:14, following the story of the Pharisee and the tax collector, and Jesus makes a similar statement to the Pharisees in 16:15. The repeated need for such warnings makes self-exaltation a primary characteristic of the Pharisees in Luke.

The dinner guests are assumed to be people of social standing, people of a rank similar to the "ruler" who invited them. So 14:12–14, which is formally parallel to 14:8–10, is a second correction of what Jesus observes at the party. Rather than inviting these people of wealth and social standing, Jesus instructs the host to invite the poor and crippled, who will not be able to repay him. The scribes and Pharisees whom Jesus meets at dinner parties are understood to be persons of wealth who need instruction in their social responsibility for the poor. Jesus will rebuke and warn them more sharply on these issues in 16:14–31, which includes the story of the rich man and Lazarus. The promise in 14:14, "It will be repaid to you in the resurrection of the just," is the positive counterpart to the warning in the story of the rich man and Lazarus, which indicates the punishment awaiting a rich man who fails to feed the poor. Thus teaching to the rich about their responsibilities to the poor is a repeated theme in Jesus' discussions with scribes and Pharisees.

---

[22] On antithetical aphorisms, see R. Tannehill, *Sword of His Mouth*, 88–101.

In 14:15 a guest says, "Blessed is whoever will eat bread in God's reign," and Jesus responds with the parable of the great banquet. The teaching of Jesus in 14:7–24 is connected by the shared image of a banquet, which is also represented by the setting in which this teaching is placed. This shared image yields multiple meanings, for it is approached in several ways. In 14:7–14 Jesus seems to be giving instructions on social behavior at a party such as he is attending, but the remark about the banquet of God's reign in 14:15 introduces a new dimension into the discussion. The humbling of those who exalt themselves and the invitation to the poor and disabled are now considered in light of this greater banquet. The reversal of the humble and those who exalt themselves in 14:11 is mirrored in the parable by the replacement of people of social position and wealth with beggars off the street. Jesus' instruction to his host to "invite poor, crippled, lame, blind" (14:13) is mirrored by the inclusion of the same groups at the banquet in the parable (14:21). Thus the instruction to the host is a call to reflect in human behavior what is happening in the call to God's reign, as interpreted in the parable. Similarly, the addition of the parable turns 14:7–11 into something more than advice about how to avoid social embarrassment, for the reversal of positions discussed there also applies to invitations to the kingdom banquet. The social behavior of the guests in the Pharisee's house already gives a clue as to whether they are ready to accept God's way of giving a party.

The parable discloses to the scribes and Pharisees what is happening through Jesus' ministry and comments on the course of Luke's story. It reflects the rejection which Jesus is experiencing from people of religious prominence and wealth and the acceptance of his message by sinners and the poor. It recognizes that there has been a lack of response to Jesus' invitation by important people but declares that God will have the party anyway, ignoring human standards and expectations. The final verse (14:24) focuses the message on Jesus' audience in the context: "None of those men given invitations will taste my banquet."[23] This is a sharp warning to the scribes and Pharisees that they may be excluded from the banquet of God's reign unless something changes.

John Dominic Crossan, noting the connection between 14:21 and the injunction in 14:13 to invite the poor and handicapped, accuses Luke of moralizing Jesus' parable.[24] Actually, the complex relation of the parable to its context suggests that the narrator is aware of the polyvalence, i.e.,

---

[23] The perfect passive participle applied to the rejected invitees in 14:24 was previously applied to Jesus' audience in 14:7.

[24] See *In Parables*, 71–72.

the multiplicity of meaning, in a parable.[25] The immediate context applies the parable as a warning to lawyers and Pharisees, viewed as people of wealth and social standing who would expect to be invited to a great banquet. But the context also suggests that the parable shows how God's rule of exalting and humbling (14:11) is working itself out in Jesus' ministry and how human action can imitate divine action by inviting the poor, while relating all of these themes to the banquet of God's reign. The larger context of Luke would also support reading the parable as a gracious word to the poor and the outcasts, who are unexpectedly invited to share in God's reign.[26]

Issues of conflict between Jesus and the religious leaders which have already surfaced in the narrative are addressed in parables in chapters 14–16. This section of Luke has a special character because Jesus' discourses are dominated by major parables which are primarily addressed to the scribes and Pharisees. These parables contain strong contrasts between the rich and the poor, the righteous and the sinner. The scribes and Pharisees to whom Jesus is speaking are among the rich and righteous. Those who turn down the invitation to the party in 14:18–19 are people who have property and give it high priority. They are replaced by poor beggars. Jesus responds to the grumbling of Pharisees and scribes by telling the parables of the lost sheep and coin, applying them to the situation of the repentant sinner, who is contrasted with the righteous (15:7). This contrast is developed in the parable of the two sons which follows.

Without any indication of a change of scene, Jesus gives instruction about wealth, first to the disciples (16:1–13) and then to the Pharisees in response to their ridicule (16:14–31). Although 16:16–18 strays from this topic, Jesus' response is primarily a rebuke of the Pharisees as people who are concerned with their own standing in society as the righteous (they "justify themselves before humans"), are exalted in human eyes, and are lovers of money (16:14–15). Since there is no indication of a change of scene in 16:19, the parable of the rich man and poor Lazarus is addressed to such Pharisees. The parable has a number of details in common with other Lukan passages but is also made to fit the audience being addressed. The conversation in the afterlife is presented from a distinctly Jewish perspective. Abraham is present, and the rich man appeals to him as "father Abraham." In response to the rich man's appeal for his brothers, Abraham says, "They have Moses and the prophets; let them hear them"

---

[25] See John Dominic Crossan, *Cliffs of Fall*.

[26] On this point, see the remarks about the parable of the great banquet on pp. 128–29.

(16:29). The demands of the law and the prophets for compassion on the poor would be a telling point in addressing rich Pharisees. Within the context of Luke-Acts, the story can awaken echoes of earlier passages which reverse the situation of the rich or well-fed and the poor or hungry (1:53; 6:20–21, 24–25),[27] show the futility of the unrepentant appealing to Abraham as father (3:8), and ask the rich to invite the poor to their feasts, with a promise of reward "in the resurrection of the just" (14:12–14). The two parables in chapter 16 begin in the same way ("A certain man was rich [ἄνθρωπός τις ἦν πλούσιος]"), which suggests that they are a pair of comments on the question of wealth, although addressed to different audiences. Furthermore, 16:28 uses the word διαμαρτύρομαι ("warn," "bear witness"), which is repeatedly used in Acts of Christian preaching and is a characteristically Lukan word,[28] and the concluding comment about the inability of one who has risen from the dead to bring some to repentance fits neatly with the actual resistance which the preaching of the risen Christ will encounter in Acts.[29]

In chapter 18 a parable and a narrative episode provide further comment on the religious leaders. The emphasis is again on their self-exaltation, their rejection of sinners, and their attachment to riches. In 18:9–14 Jesus tells a parable about a Pharisee and a tax collector. Since the characters in the parable are identical with familiar characters in the frame narrative, the narrator feels no need to label the addressees in the usual way. Rather, they are described as "some trusting in themselves that they are just (δίκαιοι) and despising the others." The parable makes clear who is meant, as does the previous reference to the Pharisees as "those justifying themselves (οἱ δικαιοῦντες ἑαυτούς) before humans" (16:15; cf. 10:29). In some previous passages in which the "just" or "righteous" are contrasted with sinners, the claim to be just is accepted without challenge (see 5:32; 15:7). When, however, the Pharisees are described as "justifying themselves" or "trusting in themselves that they are just," the claim becomes suspect. The claim is undermined altogether by this parable, for Jesus declares that the tax collector, rather than the Pharisee, "went down to his house justified" (18:14). The saying about those who exalt them-

---

[27] On the connection of the parable with the beatitudes and woes: Lazarus, a poor man who was "longing to be filled (χορτασθῆναι)," can be understood to be an example of the poor and hungry who are promised in the beatitudes, "You shall be filled (χορτασθήσεσθε)." The rich man in the parable would be an example of the rich to whom Jesus addresses the woes. Lazarus "is being comforted" (16:25), while the rich have already received their "comfort" (6:24) or "good things" (16:25).

[28] It is used ten times in Luke-Acts, three times in the Pastorals, twice in the rest of the New Testament. With Luke 16:28 compare especially Acts 20:21: "bearing witness of repentance to God."

[29] On the rich man and Lazarus, see further pp. 131–32.

selves being humbled, already used in 14:11, is added as rationale. Those who exalt themselves and despise others cannot be righteous before God.

The religious leaders have repeatedly been presented as people who exalt themselves (11:43; 14:7–11; 16:15; 18:9–14) and as greedy rich people who neglect the poor (11:39–41; 14:12–14; 16:14, 19–31).[30] However, Jesus has not given up all hope that some of these people will change. This is apparent in the scene in 18:18–27. A "ruler (ἄρχων)" comes to Jesus asking how he can inherit eternal life. He is evidently a Jewish religious leader. The following conversation makes clear that he is a Jew, and elsewhere in Luke the rulers whom Jesus meets are a "ruler of the synagogue" (8:41), "rulers of the Pharisees" (14:1), and members of the Jewish leadership in Jerusalem, associated with the chief priests (23:13, 35; 24:20). Jesus has not yet reached Jerusalem, so the first two references are the best guide to the narrator's meaning. This ruler is an earnest seeker, and Jesus does not challenge his assertion that he has kept the commandments. But when Jesus invites him to become a disciple, which will mean selling all that he has and giving it to the poor, the attachment to wealth, characteristic of the rich and prominent in previous episodes, asserts itself. The man is unable to commit himself to the life of discipleship, which is the "one thing" still needed to gain his goal. He provides a further example of those in the parable of the great supper who turn down the invitation because they are tied to their property. Here the bitter denunciations found in some previous passages are replaced by a sense of tragedy. Without change of scene, Jesus comments on the great difficulty those with possessions have in entering the reign of God. Nevertheless, he has not given up all hope, for "what is impossible with humans is possible with God" (18:27), and in 19:1–10 a rich man will actually be transformed.[31]

LUKE 19:39–23:43

The last reference to the Pharisees in the Gospel of Luke is found in 19:39–40, where "some of the Pharisees from the crowd" ask Jesus to rebuke his disciples for proclaiming that he is "the king who comes in the name of the Lord" and Jesus refuses to do so. The reference to "some of

---

[30] Jack T. Sanders argues that, in depicting the Pharisees, the author of Luke-Acts was portraying traditionally Jewish Christians of his own time. See "The Pharisees in Luke-Acts." While there may be points of contact between the Lukan portrait of the Pharisees and Jewish Christians, the emphasis on greed and self-exaltation makes it unlikely that the former is as fully the mirror image of the latter as Sanders thinks.

[31] On the rich ruler, see further pp. 120–22.

the Pharisees" leaves open the possibility that there are also some Pharisees who do not reject Jesus' kingship or will later come to accept it (see the mention of believers from the Pharisees in Acts 15:5). Nevertheless, the present focus is on a negative response from Pharisees. They are rejecting the claim of the one who comes to Jerusalem to assume his place as king of Israel. Thus as Jesus comes to Jerusalem, a new point of conflict between Jesus and the Pharisees appears, caused by the public proclamation of Jesus' kingship in 19:38. Previously, the primary causes of conflict have been Jesus' association with tax collectors and sinners, his behavior on the Sabbath, the Pharisees' desire for positions of honor, and their predatory greed, which neglects and oppresses the poor. Now the conflict centers on Jesus' role and claims. The rejection of the claim that Jesus is king, first voiced by Pharisees, will be repeated by the chief priests, scribes, and elders, i.e., the Sanhedrin, who become the primary opponents of Jesus in the Jerusalem section of Luke. Jesus is accused before Pilate on the basis of this claim (23:2), and later the rulers and soldiers mock the one who is supposed to be Messiah and king (23:35–38). The rejection of Jesus' kingship surfaces in the Pharisees' objection in 19:39, thereby introducing a major theme of the passion story. The Pharisees who object in 19:39 stand in the same camp as the Sanhedrin in rejecting Jesus as Messiah.

However, the Sanhedrin is not content to oppose Jesus verbally. At the first mention of this group in the Jerusalem section of Luke, we are told that they are seeking to destroy Jesus (19:47). This increases the stakes in the conflict and suggests that it is moving toward its climax. The chief priests, scribes, and elders (="the first of the people" in 19:47) were mentioned once before in Luke, in the first announcement of the passion in 9:22. This group's appearance on the scene in 19:47, with the specific intent of destroying Jesus, makes clear that Jesus' prophecy in 9:22 is nearing fulfillment.

While the cause of the Sanhedrin's desire to kill Jesus is not specified very clearly, it evidently involves more than just Jesus' encroachment on the rights of the temple authorities by driving out the merchants from the temple. The statement that the Sanhedrin wished to destroy Jesus does not follow that event directly. A notice that Jesus "was teaching daily in the temple" intervenes. The confrontation of the Sanhedrin with Jesus in 20:1, which, as we shall see, is a first attempt to carry out the Sanhedrin's death plot, also follows a reference to Jesus' temple teaching. Evidently this teaching is a further cause of the Sanhedrin's opposition. It would be a mistake to suppose that Jesus' teaching to the people was confined to the points mentioned in Luke 20–21. Luke 20 is concerned with Jesus' responses to and comments on his Jerusalem opponents, and 21:5–36 focuses on the future. When Jesus is described as "teaching the people and preaching good news" (20:1), we are to conceive his message as broader, resembling what he has already said elsewhere.[32] Thus the issues of conflict which have already surfaced in Luke have continuing relevance for the climax of conflict in Jerusalem, since they arise from Jesus' teaching, which evidently provokes the same negative reaction from the Sanhedrin as previously from the scribes and Pharisees (see 23:5).

Jesus' prophesied death in Jerusalem seems to be rapidly approaching, since the Sanhedrin is already seeking to destroy him. Its plot, however, is not immediately successful. The Sanhedrin is unable to act because of Jesus' popularity with the people, who all "hung on him listening" (19:48). The success of the plot seems to depend on undermining Jesus' support by the people. The Sanhedrin's need to do this adds suspense to the encounters between the Sanhedrin or its representatives and Jesus that follow 19:47–48. Each of the questions posed to Jesus may cost him the people's support if he fails to give an impressive answer, so his fate hangs in the balance. This purpose behind the questions is made especially clear in 20:26, which reports the failure of one of these attempts to "catch him by a word before the people" (dif. Matthew, Mark).

The persistent efforts of the Sanhedrin to find a way of removing Jesus in spite of the people's support is an important unifying thread in the narrative from 19:47 until Jesus' arrest. Jesus' enemies try several approaches. They begin by confronting him directly about his authority in the presence of the people (20:1–8), but they are unable to answer Jesus' counterquestion, so this attempt to undermine his support fails. Then Jesus responds with a parable in which he portrays Israel's leaders as rebellious and murderous vineyard tenants. The chief priests and scribes know that this is meant to apply to them and want to arrest Jesus at that very time because of this provocation. Again they are restrained by fear of the people (20:19).

They try another tactic. Two questions are presented to Jesus which are designed either to endanger Jesus politically or to make him look foolish. First, there is an effort to entrap Jesus by asking whether it is lawful to pay Caesar tribute. Whether Jesus answers yes or no, it appears that he will lose. Support for payment of this hated tribute, regarded by some Jews as irreconcilable with loyalty to God, would offend some of the people, while rejection of it would provide a specific accusation against Jesus before the Romans (see 23:2). This question is presented as a

---

[32] Note that "preaching good news" in 20:1 is a reappearance of a theme that goes back to Jesus' statement of his commission in 4:18 and is used repeatedly in summary statements of Jesus' or the apostles' preaching (4:43; 7:22; 8:1; 9:6; 16:16).

revival, under new conditions of danger, of the previous efforts of scribes and Pharisees to "catch" Jesus on the basis of some specific statement (see 20:20 with 11:54), "watching closely" while he acts and speaks (see 20:20 with 6:7; 14:1). But Jesus' brilliant answer, which combines, in a brief aphorism, permission to pay the tax with an affirmation of primary loyalty to God,[33] enables him to escape the trap. The opponents, marveling at his answer, are reduced to silence (20:26; cp. 13:17; 14:6).

This is followed by a question from the Sadducees. Once again the intention is to "catch" Jesus, this time by embarrassing him before the people through a trick question. It is obvious that this, rather than an honest desire to learn, is their motive, for the question assumes as true what they deny: that there is a resurrection of the dead. Again Jesus escapes the trap, and "some of the scribes" admit that Jesus has answered well. This admission indicates the defeat of the authorities' attempt to "catch" Jesus on a specific issue, "for they were no longer daring to ask him anything" (20:40). The attempt to undermine Jesus' authority with the people by asking dangerous or difficult questions is doing just the opposite. Now this tactic is also abandoned. From this point Jesus is no longer responding to questions in his temple teaching but takes the initiative, posing a question which the religious authorities evidently cannot answer (20:41–44) and denouncing the scribes (20:45–47). Jesus continues to awaken a high degree of interest among the people (21:38). The authorities have not succeeded in undermining his popular support, and their plan of getting rid of Jesus is no closer to realization.

In 22:2 the narrator reminds us of the Sanhedrin's plan and problem: afraid of the people, it is still seeking some way of doing away with Jesus. Then comes the opportunity: Judas offers to betray Jesus to them "apart from the crowd" (22:6). Now the story begins to move toward its prophesied climax. As it does so, Jesus reminds the Sanhedrin leaders that they were not able to defeat him by open inquiry and fair public debate but could only arrest him secretly and with massive force. This is emphasized when, at his arrest, Jesus responds to "the chief priests and captains of the temple and elders" (who are evidently understood to be personally present) by saying, "Have you come out as against a robber with swords and clubs? While I was with you daily in the temple you did not stretch out hands on me" (22:52–53). Since the opponents have now abandoned all pretense of open inquiry and fair debate, further attempts to communicate with them are useless, as Jesus indicates in his first response at the interrogation after his arrest: "If I tell you, you will certainly not believe, and if I question you, you will certainly not answer" (22:67–68; dif.

---

[33] On the aphorism in 20:25, see R. Tannehill, *Sword of His Mouth*, 173–77.

Matthew, Mark). This is not simply a reflection on the hostility of the Sanhedrin at the moment. Jesus' reproaches are supported by past behavior reported in the narrative. The chief priests, scribes, and elders did not believe John the Baptist, and when Jesus questioned them concerning him, they refused to answer (20:3–7). Jesus indirectly told the Sanhedrin who he is by speaking of the vineyard owner's beloved son, the stone which becomes head of the corner, and the Lord whom God seats at the right hand (20:13, 17, 42). The last two of these references are scriptural quotations which are parts of questions directed to his hearers—questions which receive no answers. The unanswered questions in 20:4, 17, 41–44 help to explain Jesus' statement, "If I question you, you will certainly not answer" (22:68), which otherwise is rather strange in its context. Jesus' questioners at his interrogation have shown that they are not willing or able to respond to Jesus' questions; nor are they willing to believe his statements about himself. Nevertheless, he indicates that his previous riddle about the Son of David who sits at God's right hand as David's Lord is now becoming reality (22:69; see 20:41–44).

From the time that Jesus arrives in the temple, the narrator concentrates attention on the opposition to Jesus from the chief priests, scribes, and elders. Much of the suspense and movement of the plot is based on what this official body of leaders plan and do. The climax of this story is no minor incident with minor characters. It is a confrontation between Jesus and the religious leaders at the highest level. Nevertheless, there is continuity between the opposition which Jesus encounters in Jerusalem and what he encountered before. Not only are scribes mentioned in both contexts, but there is a similar set of attitudes and actions from the two sets of opponents, indicating that the kind of opposition which Jesus met earlier is encountered in a more powerful and dangerous form in Jerusalem. Both before and after the Sanhedrin enters the plot, Jesus' opponents reject his kingship (19:38–39; 23:2, 35–38) and his teaching (6:11; 16:14; 19:47; 23:5), refuse to respond to the Baptist's message (7:30; 20:5), seek first positions and are filled with avarice (11:39–43; 14:7; 16:14; 20:46–47), "watch" Jesus "closely" in order to catch him (6:7; 11:54; 14:1; 20:20, 26), but are put to shame or silenced (13:17; 14:6; 20:26, 40). Thus the Sanhedrin steps into an already well-defined role. To be sure, this group is more powerful than previous opponents, and it is intent on Jesus' destruction from its first appearance in the Jerusalem narrative (19:47), heightening the sense of danger as the story moves toward its climax.

In Jesus' temple teaching there are some places where Jesus takes the initiative, and these include some interesting comments on the deeper meaning of developments at this point in the story. In 20:9–19 Jesus uses a parable to make a comment to the people about the leaders who have just challenged him, revealing the disastrous effect of their plot. Understanding the parable in the context of the gospel brings out several nuances which might otherwise be missed. In 20:2 Jesus is asked, "Who is the one who gave you this authority?" No answer is given to the questioners, since they refuse to answer Jesus' question, but an answer was previously given to the readers in Jesus' baptism, announcement at Nazareth, and transfiguration. The parable reminds readers of this when the vineyard owner speaks of "my beloved son" (20:13), repeating the words used by the heavenly voice at Jesus' baptism. The correspondence is exact, in contrast to Matthew and Mark. Readers would easily identify the tenant farmers in the parable with the chief priests, scribes, and elders with whom Jesus has just been talking, especially when they hear them say of the son, "Let us kill him" (20:14), for the Sanhedrin's desire to kill Jesus has just been stated in 19:47. Following the killing of the son, Jesus predicts that the owner of the vineyard will come and destroy these murderous tenant farmers. Shortly before this scene, Jesus was talking about the destruction of Jerusalem, which suggests that the same event is in mind. The shared image of a stone, associated with destruction, also supports this connection (19:44; 20:18). The religious leaders understand that the parable applies to them (20:19), but the people, when they hear of the coming destruction, wish that it may not happen (20:16). The people are affected by what their leaders do, and the conquest of Jerusalem will mean death and suffering for all its inhabitants.

Thus the parable interprets the events which are unfolding as a story of murderous rebellion which will lead to destruction. The same events, however, lead to Jesus' exaltation. This is brought out through the reference to the rejected stone that becomes head of the corner in 20:17 (a quotation from Ps 118:22). This quotation is inserted in a question, "What is this which is written?" No answer is given either by Jesus or his hearers. To be sure, the context suggests some connection between the builders who reject the stone and the tenant farmers who murder the son, but this still leaves part of the quotation a dark riddle. The larger context of Luke provides additional help. In his first announcement of his passion, Jesus said that he must be "rejected by the elders and chief priests and scribes," using the same verb as in 20:17 ($\dot{\alpha}\pi o\delta o\kappa\iota\mu\dot{\alpha}\zeta\omega$), "and be raised on the third day" (9:22). The scriptural quotation in 20:17 does not speak primarily of resurrection, however, but of becoming head of the corner, i.e., of exaltation to honor and power. It proclaims a reversal of status from dishonor to high honor, which means that the rejection of the stone by the builders will produce the exact opposite of their intention. This ironic reversal is the hidden purpose of God being realized through Jesus' suffering and rejection.

It is the function of Scripture to reveal this hidden purpose of God, but even the disciples will not understand this significance of Scripture until the risen Jesus opens their minds (24:25–27, 32, 45). The necessity that "the Messiah suffer . . . and enter into his glory" (24:26), in fulfillment of the Scriptures, is heavily emphasized in Luke 24. This shows the importance of the quotation in 20:17, which cites in advance a specific Scripture in which this suffering and glory are prophesied. Its special importance is confirmed by the second reference to Ps 118:22 in Acts 4:11.

Later Jesus again asks a question about a Psalm quotation, this time Ps 110:1 (Luke 20:41–44). This is even more clearly a riddle for the participants in the story, for, as Jesus points out, the quotation seems to conflict with the view that the Messiah is Son of David, and the immediate context in Luke does not help to answer Jesus' question. The two Psalm quotations are related, for Ps 110:1, as understood in Luke-Acts, also proclaims the exaltation of Jesus to honor and power. Again, the importance of this quotation is emphasized by the fact that it reappears in Acts, in Peter's Pentecost speech (Acts 2:34–35). Both of these Psalm quotations are found in the same location in Matthew and Mark as in Luke, and all three gospels contain an additional reference to Ps 110:1 in Jesus' statement in response to the Sanhedrin (Matt 26:64; Mark 14:62; Luke 22:69). These Psalm texts have special significance in Luke, however, for they have an important function in the larger narrative. They are recalled in the Acts speeches, which review how God's purpose was realized in the death and resurrection of Jesus. They are also recalled when the risen Jesus insists that it was necessary for the Messiah to suffer and enter into his glory, in fulfillment of Scripture (24:25–27).[34] The specific Scriptures cited in Luke which prepare the reader to understand that Jesus' suffering will lead to glory are Pss 118:22 and 110:1.[35] Luke 24:27 contains a reference to Moses and all the prophets, as well as a general reference to "all the Scriptures." This gives the impression that the scriptural witness to the Messiah who suffers and enters his glory is widespread. The second scene in which Jesus opens the minds of the disciples to understand the Scriptures gives a similar impression, but this passage contains a specific reference to the Psalms (Luke 24:44). This is the only place in the New Testament where the biblical book of Psalms is mentioned, except in other passages in Luke-Acts where a specific Psalm citation is being introduced

---

[34] On the interpretation of this key passage, see pp. 282–89.

[35] Perhaps Isa 53:12 (quoted in Luke 22:37) should be added, although the part of the verse that might be used to show that the suffering leads to glory is omitted in the quote. Only Ps 118:22 clearly refers to both rejection and glory, although the quotation from Ps 110:1 in Luke 20:42–43 refers to the Messiah's "enemies," which could be applied to those who rejected him (see 19:27).

(Luke 20:42; Acts 1:20; 13:33). This unusual reference to the Psalms shows awareness of the importance which the Psalms had in revealing the way which Jesus had to go through suffering to glory. This reference also fits the special importance which the narrative has given to Pss 118:22 and 110:1 in preparing the reader to understand the rejection and exaltation of Jesus as necessary parts of God's saving purpose.

In response to a question of the Sanhedrin, Jesus makes a major announcement, "From now on the Son of Man will be seated at the right hand of the power of God" (22:69). In contrast to the parallels in Matthew and Mark, this contains no reference to a future coming of the Son of Man. Instead, attention is focused on a change to take place in the immediate future, resulting in Jesus' heavenly enthronement, in fulfillment of Ps 110:1. The mention of the "power of God" suggests that Jesus will share this power through his exaltation to God's right hand. Jesus' enthronement will be the basis for a new phase of the mission through which God's universal saving purpose is being realized. Jesus' enthronement and the expanded mission are the hidden goals of Jesus' suffering.

The trial and crucifixion scenes are the climax of the fateful rejection of Israel's Messiah by the Jewish authorities in Jerusalem, whom the people support at a crucial point (23:13–25). The high hopes aroused in the birth narrative, hopes for the Messiah who would "rule over the house of Jacob forever" (1:33), here encounter a tragic reversal, for the leaders in Jerusalem have rejected the Messiah, and the people of Jerusalem are also caught in this tragedy. This tragic reversal includes several layers of irony. On the one hand, the rulers and people of Jerusalem are blindly acting against Israel's true interests, for the realization of the messianic promises is being rejected. On the other hand, the rejection and killing of the Messiah, while it will bring destruction on Jerusalem, does not mean the defeat of God's purpose in Jesus. God's purpose, in contrast to human purposes, has the power to turn defeat into victory. The God of Luke-Acts is a God who works by irony, using human rejection to realize a saving purpose to which humans are blind. God's hand appears in the ironic reversal of human intentions and expectations as people attempt to resist God and God's Messiah.[36]

In its interrogation the Sanhedrin specifically asks Jesus whether he is the Messiah and the Son of God (two closely related if not synonymous titles in Luke-Acts).[37] Jesus' answer is understood by the Sanhedrin as a

---

[36] On the God of irony in Luke-Acts, see further pp. 282–84.

[37] See above, pp. 25–26. J. Fitzmyer (who insists that there is a distinction between Messiah and Son of God in Luke) points out that the Sanhedrin's two questions about these titles correspond to Gabriel's affirmations about Jesus in 1:32, 35. See *Luke X–XXIV*, 1462, 1467–68.

claim to be the Messiah, and on this basis they proceed to accuse him before Pilate (22:70–23:2). Thus the decision to seek Jesus' death from Pilate is specifically a rejection of Jesus as Messiah. However, the accusations made before Pilate are broader and reflect several issues which have previously emerged in the narrative. The charge that he calls himself "Messiah, a king" stems from the immediately preceding scene of interrogation (but see also 19:38–40). The charge that Jesus opposes making tribute payments to Caesar recalls the attempt of Jesus' opponents to catch him on this issue in 20:20–26. The charge that Jesus has been "perverting our nation" calls attention to the effect of Jesus' teaching in general. It is clarified in 23:5, where "perverting our nation" becomes "stirs up the people" through his teaching. This accusation reflects the conflict over Jesus' teaching with the scribes and Pharisees earlier in the gospel and the opposition from the Jerusalem leaders which immediately follows references to Jesus' teaching in 19:47 and 20:1–2. The charge of perverting the people through his teaching is repeated three times in the trial scene (23:2, 5, 14), making it almost as important as the claim to kingship. Matthew and Mark do not specifically mention this charge. Luke alone preserves continuity between the earlier controversies with the scribes and Pharisees and the charges against Jesus at his trial by making the effect of his teaching an important part of those charges. Thus what Jesus taught throughout his ministry ("beginning from Galilee to here," 23:5) is an important cause of the religious leaders' rejection of him in Jerusalem.[38]

The charge of opposing payment of tribute to Caesar is false, as 20:20–26 makes clear. The other accusations show the Jewish leaders' perspective on events, but they are not simply false, for they have a basis in the preceding narrative.[39] The narrator has emphasized the strong attraction of Jesus' teaching for the people, which has made the leaders afraid of the people, of whom they have lost control (19:47–48; 20:19; 21:38; 22:2). From the viewpoint of the leaders, Jesus has been stirring up the people through his teaching. The narrator has also made clear that Jesus is the Messiah and has specifically emphasized the royal aspect of this office (1:32–33; 19:11–27, 38–40). Furthermore, Jesus does not clearly deny that he is a king. His answer, "You say it," parallels his answer to the Sanhedrin in 22:70, which the Sanhedrin took to be a clear enough affirmation to proceed with legal action. But Pilate responds differently.

---

[38] Another indication of the continuing importance of Jesus' teaching is found in Acts 1:21–22, which indicates that an apostolic witness must have accompanied Jesus throughout his ministry and so be acquainted with Jesus' deeds and teachings from the beginning.

[39] Daryl Schmidt challenges the view that the charges in 23:2 are blatantly false. See "Luke's 'Innocent' Jesus."

He immediately declares that he finds no guilt in this man. He seems to decide without really investigating the issue, a lapse which would be serious if the readers were not already convinced that Jesus, though a king, is no competitor with Caesar.

The scene in which Jesus is examined by Herod is unique to Luke. Evil and threatening rulers hold some interest for the narrator, as is shown by the attention given to Herod Antipas (Luke 3:19-20; 9:7-9; 13:31; 23:6-12; Acts 4:27) and to Herod Agrippa I (Acts 12:1-23).[40] Both of these rulers persecute prophets or apostles. The narrator has managed to create a connected story line out of the widely scattered references to Herod Antipas in the gospel. In 3:19-20 Herod is accused by John the Baptist for his evil deeds and responds by putting John in prison. In 9:7-9 Herod is puzzled by the reports concerning Jesus, who is being described as John raised from the dead, Elijah, or some prophet of old. Here we learn that Herod not only imprisoned John but also beheaded him. The scene ends with the indication that Herod "was seeking to see" Jesus. Since Herod has already demonstrated how he treats meddlesome prophets, his interest in this new prophet, whom some even regard as John returned, suggests a threat to Jesus. This threat becomes explicit in 13:31, when some Pharisees warn Jesus, "Get away and go from here, for Herod wants to kill you." Even though the warning comes from Pharisees, the threat should be taken seriously, for Jesus does not reject the Pharisees' words as false. Instead, he minimizes the importance of this threat by telling the Pharisees, and through them Herod, that his prophetic work will end shortly anyway. The Pharisees' warning contains an ironic misunderstanding. They think that he can escape death if he will "go ($\pi o \rho \epsilon \acute{v} o v$) from here" (13:31). He must indeed "go ($\pi o \rho \epsilon \acute{v} \epsilon \sigma \theta a \iota$)," Jesus says, but this is a journey to his death in Jerusalem (13:33). Jesus is threatened with death both here and there. Going will not mean escape, for his journey will lead him to his destined place of death.[41]

Herod does have a role in Jesus' death, not in Galilee but in Jerusalem. He is not the prime mover behind this event, for the Jewish leaders have this role. Nor does he judge Jesus to be guilty. Nevertheless, he is among those who despise and mock Jesus, and among the kings and rulers who "were gathered together against the Lord and against his Messiah" (Acts 4:26-27). The scene of Jesus before Herod is presented as the fulfillment of Herod's longstanding desire to see Jesus because of what he had heard about him. Thus 9:7-9 functions as preparation for this scene (note the

---

[40] Erwin Buck suggests that "Luke intended to draw a conscious connection" between the appearance of Jesus before Herod Antipas "and Peter's arrest by another Herod in Acts 12:1ff." See "Jesus before Herod," 174.

[41] On 13:31-35, see further pp. 153-56.

connection between 9:9 and 23:8). Having heard of "all the things happening" through Jesus (9:7), Herod hopes that he will see Jesus perform a sign. Jesus previously refused to perform a sign on request (11:16, 29). Now Jesus responds neither to Herod's hopes for a sign nor to his questions. Not finding the miracle-working prophet he had sought, Herod "treated him with contempt" and "mocked" him. Here the narrator uses terms used elsewhere in passion prophecies and the passion story to describe those who reject and kill Jesus,[42] showing that Herod shares the same attitude of contemptuous rejection.

Thus not only religious but also political authorities reject Jesus in the passion story. The narrator could not make this so clear in the case of Pilate as he does with Herod, not only because Christians had to continue to live under Roman rule but also because Pilate was needed to play another role: that of the official proclaimer of Jesus' innocence (see 23:4, 14–16, 20, 22). To be sure, Pilate is joined by other witnesses to Jesus' innocence: Herod (according to Pilate in 23:15), a crucified criminal (23:41), and the centurion at the cross (23:47). But Pilate's repeated testimony to Jesus' innocence is especially strong and impressive. Nevertheless, in the important review of the passion story in Acts 4:25–28, Herod and Pilate are both included among the kings and rulers who oppose the Lord's Messiah but ironically work God's preordained purpose. Gentiles and Jews, political and religious authorities, are joined in one massive front of opposition. The reference to Herod and Pilate becoming "friends" in Luke 23:12 may prepare for this interpretation of the death of Jesus as the time when the rulers and peoples were "gathered together" against the Lord's Messiah.[43]

In Luke 23:13–25 the rejection of Jesus by the rulers and people of Jerusalem is powerfully dramatized as the final decision for death is made. Not only the rulers but the "people" are present (23:13) and take part in the demands for Jesus' death. This agrees with the accusations in the Acts speeches that the people of Jerusalem and their rulers denied and killed Jesus (Acts 3:13–15, 17; 13:27–28).[44] The scene begins with Pilate summarizing the results of the preceding examinations. He has examined Jesus on the charges and has found no grounds for legal action against

---

[42] In Acts 4:11 ἐξουθενέω ("treat with contempt") is used as a substitute for ἀποδοκιμάζω ("reject") in Luke 20:17. Both passages apply Ps 118:22 to the rejection of Jesus. ἐμπαίζω ("mock") appears in 18:32 (a passion prophecy) and in 22:63; 23:36.

[43] Some scholars understand Herod and Pilate's new friendship as a sign of the saving effect of Jesus' death, which brings reconciliation. See John Drury, *Tradition and Design in Luke's Gospel*, 16–17, and Robert J. Karris, *Luke: Artist and Theologian*, 85. It seems to me that the explicit reference to Herod and Pilate in Acts 4:27, where they are part of an evil alliance, is a sounder basis for interpreting Luke 23:12.

[44] On the role of the people in the passion story, see further pp. 164–66.

him. Pilate mentions Herod as a second witness for this conclusion and especially emphasizes that Jesus has done nothing worthy of death. This somewhat wordy summary leads up to the reasoned conclusion–which sounds like an official verdict—"Therefore, I will release him" (23:16). But his conclusion provokes immediate protest from the chief priests, rulers, and people. Here the pace of the narrative picks up. Three times the protesters cry out for Jesus' death, while Pilate tries to maintain his decision, reemphasizing that Jesus should be released. Then Pilate suddenly gives in. When he does so, it is made very clear that he is granting "their request," is releasing Barabbas, the prisoner "whom they requested," and is acceding to "their will" (23:24–25). This does not necessarily absolve Pilate of responsibility, for a little reflection makes clear that a ruler who gives into mob pressure and releases a rebel and murderer to them is hardly a model of justice. This is sufficient to qualify Pilate for a place in the evil alliance of Acts 4:25–27. But the focus of attention in Luke 23:13–25 is on the innocence of Jesus, to which Pilate bears repeated witness, and on the determination of the people and their rulers that Jesus die in spite of this.

Barabbas serves as a contrast figure. In contrast to Jesus, he has done something worthy of death; he is a rebel who has committed murder. When the people and their leaders ask for him rather than Jesus, they show the inclination to choose armed revolt against Rome rather than "the things that lead to peace" (19:42). This foreshadows the Jewish revolt of 66 C.E., and the terrible consequences of this are expressed in Jesus' words to the "daughters of Jerusalem" in 23:28–31.

While on the cross, Jesus is ridiculed (23:35), mocked (23:36), and reviled (23:39) by three different participants in the scene. In each case their words contain a challenge to Jesus to save himself. Jesus' refusal to do this, indicated by his silence, reemphasizes his commitment to the dark plan of God which includes Jesus' death, a commitment which was repeatedly expressed prior to the arrest (22:22, 37, 42). The three challenges reveal a strange incongruity. "Others he saved, let him save himself" (23:35). The saving power which he has demonstrated, and which will continue to be available in his name, cannot be used for himself. "If you are the king of the Jews, save yourself" (23:37). Jesus is a king but now is powerless. These mocking words highlight the contrast between the cross in human perception, which sees it as the refutation of Jesus' messianic claims, and the hidden divine purpose which is there being fulfilled, as proclaimed in Acts 2:23 and 4:28.

These mockers contrast with a more perceptive person, the criminal on the cross who asks to be remembered by Jesus. This man's words contain three important affirmations: (1) He recognizes the justice of his own punishment and so is repentant. (2) He recognizes Jesus' innocence. (3) Most important, he recognizes that Jesus' failure to save himself does not contradict the claim that he is the messianic king. Therefore, he appeals to Jesus to "remember me when you come into your royal power (βασιλείαν)" (23:42). Jesus has repeatedly indicated to those plotting his death that he is about to be exalted to share God's power (20:17, 42; 22:69). He also instructed his followers about his rejection and resurrection, but they were unable to understand his words (9:22, 44–45; 18:31–34). The repentant criminal is the only one who recognizes that rejection and death are, for Jesus, the way to royal power at the right hand of God, as Jesus has been saying. These three perceptions call forth Jesus' promise of salvation and strong approval. This unique Lukan scene occupies a place of prominence immediately before Jesus' death. It is important not only because it shows again Jesus' concern for the outcast but also because it points to the goal of Jesus' way, which is hidden from almost all human eyes.[45]

---

[45] On this scene, see further pp. 125–27.

Chapter Seven

JESUS AND THE DISCIPLES

Luke 4:31–9:50

The Beginning

In contrast to the sequence of events in Mark and Matthew, Luke's Gospel indicates that there is contact between Simon Peter and Jesus before Simon is called to follow. In 4:38–39 Jesus heals Simon's mother-in-law in Simon's house, and the narrator probably assumed that Simon was also present for the other healings and exorcisms in Capernaum. When in 5:5 Simon says, "At your word I will let down the nets," agreeing to something that seems foolish to experienced fishermen, he is acting on the basis of previous experience of Jesus' powerful word. Furthermore, the healings in Capernaum, plus the great catch of fish, provide a motivation for leaving all and following Jesus, which is strikingly lacking in the call stories of Matthew and Mark.

Luke 5:1–11 can be divided into three sub-scenes: Jesus preaching from Simon's boat (5:1–3), the great catch of fish (5:4–7), Simon's reaction and Jesus' response (5:8–11). In the first of these, Jesus is engaged in the mission which he described in 4:43. In the third he tells Simon about Simon's role in this same mission. Thus this mission material frames the central part of the scene, which deals with the catch of fish. Furthermore, Jesus' statement to Simon, "From now on you will be catching people alive," applies metaphorically to people the role of the fish in the preceding fishing scene. This is signaled by a wordplay: Simon has just made a great "catch" of fish; from now on he will be "catching" people.[1] This relates the two sub-scenes closely, but with a metaphorical twist which suggests a second sense to the great catch of fish. Through its connection with the "catching" to which Simon is being called, the great catch of fish becomes a symbolic narrative of the amazingly successful mission which Simon and others will conduct.[2] This gives to the narrative greater unity

---

[1] The verb ζωγρέω, "catch alive," is formed from ζωός, "alive," and ἀγρέω, "seize," "catch," and so is related by root to the noun ἄγρα, "catch," in 5:4, 9. See J. Fitzmyer, *Luke I–IX*, 568. The play on words in Mark 1:16–17 is different, but, as in Luke, it fits the description of the situation preceding the call: "They were fishers. . . . become fishers of people."

[2] Jean Delorme remarks that the figurative language of 5:10b, unlike ordinary referential language, draws attention to itself by playing with words and establishes resemblance between the miraculous catch and a later catch. Therefore, "the reader is invited to reread

than was apparent at the beginning. The saying of Jesus about catching people in 5:10 relates 5:1–3 and 4–7 with each other, for now Jesus' preaching and the great catch of fish are not unrelated events which happened to follow one another. Rather, the great catch is a symbolic portrayal of the expanding mission in which Jesus is already engaged in 5:1–3. The double sense of the great catch gives it a double function in the narrative. On the one hand, the great catch precedes and causes Simon's reaction in 5:8. On the other hand, it prefigures what will happen following the call in 5:10.

The interaction between Jesus and Simon dominates the scene, although James and John are mentioned secondarily. Two problems or obstacles appear in the course of this interaction, problems which might block the progress of events toward the destiny which Jesus announces for Simon in 5:10. The first appears in 5:5 as Simon responds to Jesus' command to go out into the deep and let down the nets. Despite their best efforts Simon and his friends have caught nothing. Any further effort now would seem to be useless. But Simon has already learned enough about Jesus to set aside ordinary calculations. He obeys, and one possible problem is overcome. The great catch, however, does not directly cause Simon to follow Jesus. Indeed, Simon reacts by saying, "Depart from me, for I am a sinful man, Lord" (5:8). Instead of binding Simon to Jesus, the amazing catch causes Simon to desire separation, for a sinful man cannot associate with one who wields divine power. This is a further obstacle to the progress of the narrative. Jesus' commanding invitation in 5:10 bridges this separation in order to create a new future for Simon.

Jesus' call of a sinful man to share his life and work is equivalent to a declaration of forgiveness. This becomes clearer when we consider the related story of Levi's call (5:27–28), which comes soon after the call of Simon. This time a tax collector is called to follow, and Jesus justifies his association with such people by declaring, "I have come to call . . . sinners to repentance" (5:32). Both of these call stories are stories of sinners called to a new future as followers of Jesus. So when Simon begins to follow Jesus, he has already encountered him as healer (4:38–39), as one who can bring success where his own efforts failed (5:4–7), and as one who can offer the sinful a new future (5:8–10).

In Luke, both Simon and Levi leave all they have when they follow Jesus (dif. Matthew, Mark). This binds the two stories together and shows that Simon, who will be one of the twelve, and Levi, who will not be, face the same conditions in following Jesus. Not only the twelve but also a larger group of followers, of which Levi may be an example, will

---

the narrative of the catch while thinking of the capture of people." "Luc v. 1–11," 333–34.

later share in Jesus' mission (10:1–24). The repeated indication that possessions were abandoned shows the narrator's concern with this aspect of discipleship and prepares for Jesus' address to the disciples as the poor in 6:20.

Jesus' statement to Simon, "From now on you will be catching people alive," is both a promise and a task for the future. It is an indication to the readers of Peter's role in the following narrative. However, Peter will not begin his task immediately. Further developments must take place and serious problems must be faced before Peter can enter fully into his appointed role.

Although the narrator only tells specifically how Simon, with his partners James and John, and Levi became disciples, these episodes evidently serve as examples of many other callings, for the narrative assumes a rapid increase in the number of disciples. In 5:30 the Pharisees and scribes complain "to his disciples," a group of indeterminate size, but in 6:13 there is a sufficiently large group that Jesus decides to select twelve from them for special responsibility. Indeed, in 6:17 the narrator refers to "a large crowd of his disciples," and in 10:1 Jesus is able to appoint seventy-two for a special mission.[3]

As Jesus begins to encounter criticism from the Pharisees and scribes in 5:17–6:11, the narrator makes clear that the criticism also falls on the disciples. On three occasions the Pharisees and scribes complain about the behavior of Jesus' disciples (5:30, 33; 6:2), and two of these complaints are addressed to the disciples rather than Jesus (5:30; 6:2).[4] Already the disciples find themselves in the midst of controversy. These conflicts provide an initial basis for Jesus' beatitude for persecuted disciples in 6:22–23 and for his words about the time of testing and the need for endurance in 8:13, 15. The conflicts surrounding Jesus directly affect the disciples. From the very beginning they must show toughness under pressure.

Jesus prepares for the selection of the twelve apostles by praying through the night (6:12), an indication of the importance of this choice. Almost all of the numerous references in Luke to Jesus praying occur before important new developments or crises, suggesting that the prayer is Jesus' preparation for what is about to take place (3:21, in preparation for the descent of the Spirit and the beginning of Jesus' ministry; 5:16, before the first conflicts with the Pharisees and scribes; 6:12, before the choice of the twelve; 9:18, before Peter's confession and the first announcement of

---

[3] The number may be seventy or seventy-two. On this textual problem see pp. 232–33.

[4] In both passages Luke uses the second person plural where Matthew and Mark use the third person, which increases the sense of direct confrontation with the disciples.

the passion; 9:28–29, at the transfiguration; 22:40–46, before the passion).[5] While the parallel passage in Mark 3:14–15 provides a summary of the future mission of the twelve, this is absent from Luke. It is too early to think of a mission of the twelve. They must first learn from Jesus through his teaching and by being with him as he engages in his mission (see 8:1). There is only one indication of the future role of the twelve at this point: they are named "apostles," a title which will recur in connection with the mission of the twelve (9:10) and also at the supper before the passion (22:14), where Jesus will grant them a share in his royal power and a place on thrones judging the twelve tribes of Israel (22:29–30). These suggestions of the function of the apostles will be developed further in Acts.

Only in the case of Judas Iscariot is there a clear indication of his future role. He is the one who betrayed Jesus, we are told. While the plot of Jesus' enemies in 6:11 is less definite than its counterpart in Mark 3:6, the healing of the man with a withered hand and the choosing of the twelve are adjacent episodes in Luke (dif. Matthew, Mark), and both end with indications of danger to Jesus.

The Sermon on the Plain

After the selection of the apostles, the instruction of the disciples begins to occupy an important place in the narrative, as shown by Jesus' speech in 6:20–49. Here the life of the disciple is being defined in essential aspects. This does not mean that only disciples are being addressed. While the beatitudes are spoken as Jesus looks at his disciples (6:20), Jesus' reference to his audience in 6:27 seems designed to make clear that he is speaking to everyone, not only the disciples but also the "people" of 6:17–18. In 6:27 Jesus says, "But to you I say, you who are listening." The reference to "you who are listening" should be understood to include the "great multitude of the people . . . , who came to listen to him" (6:17–18). Note also the reference to the audience at the end of the speech: "When he finished all his words in the hearing[6] of the people . . ." (7:1). Elsewhere in Luke, teaching which defines the conditions of discipleship is addressed to the people or crowd, for they are regarded as potential disciples who must make their decisions in light of these conditions (see 9:23–27; 14:25–35). The private instruction of disciples introduced by a disciple's question is frequent in Mark but almost disappears in Luke. Even when Jesus is addressing the disciples, the narrator of Luke sometimes indicates that

---

[5] Perhaps 11:1 is an exception, for here the prayer of Jesus serves as an occasion for teaching about prayer.

[6] Or "ears," using the noun ἀκοή, which is related to the verb ἀκούω, "hear," "listen."

others are present and listening (see 16:14; 20:45).[7] Luke's Gospel shows no interest in esoteric teaching. The sermon in 6:27–49 concerns discipleship but is addressed to all who will hear, both the disciples and the crowd, for it is not only instruction to those who are disciples but invitation and challenge to those who might become disciples.

Nevertheless, the beatitudes are spoken while Jesus is looking at his disciples. This is appropriate for several reasons. While the commands in 6:27ff. are open challenges, applicable to anyone who will respond, the beatitudes and woes are prophetic declarations which apply to particular groups. The fourth beatitude, which speaks of those who are hated and rejected "because of the Son of Man," is obviously most appropriate to disciples, who have already experienced the verbal attacks of the Pharisees and scribes and who will suffer worse in the future. It is also appropriate for Jesus to address the disciples as "the poor." We have already noted references to those called by Jesus "leaving all" (5:11, 28), and in 18:28 this is mentioned again. The disciples are not likely to acquire new wealth in light of Jesus' commands to "give to everyone who asks you" and to loan without hope of return (6:30, 35). Jesus' later teaching about possessions will be equally strict. In their mission Jesus and his disciples are dependent on the hospitality of others, which may or may not be offered as they travel from town to town (see 9:4–5, 57–58; 10:8–11).

Jesus is fulfilling an important part of his commission as he says, "Happy are the poor, for God's reign is yours," for he was sent to "preach good news to the poor" and "preach good news of God's reign" (4:18, 43). Does the indication that Jesus said these words as he looked at his disciples mean that disciples alone can share in this good news? This is not likely. Jesus' glance at his disciples suggests that his words have direct relevance for them, but it does not mean that Jesus is speaking to them alone. The narrator has already indicated that a "great multitude of the people" is present along with the disciples.[8] Jesus is also speaking to individuals in this multitude, for he shifts from beatitudes for the poor to woes for the rich with no indication of a change of audience. These woes do not apply to the disciples, who have left all to follow Jesus, and must be

---

[7] Joachim Gnilka, *Die Verstockung Israels*, 120–21.

[8] Jacques Dupont, in spite of his careful discussion of Jesus' addressees in the Lukan beatitudes and woes, too quickly assumes that the multitude of the people represents the later Christian community for Luke. See *Les Béatitudes*, 3:24. The use of the term "people (λαός)" does not support this, for Lukan usage is influenced by the LXX, where this word frequently refers to the people of Israel with its distinctive calling and promises. Even in Acts "people" always refers to the Jewish people, not the Christian church. The rare exceptions are 15:14 and 18:10, which extend the special term for God's people to include Gentiles. On the "people" in Luke-Acts, see further pp. 143–44.

addressed to the rich and honored in the larger audience.[9] Since the woes
are addressed to the larger audience, it would be a mistake to deny that
members of the crowd are included in the beatitude to the poor. Jesus is
also preaching good news to the poor among the crowd. The beatitude
speaks of happiness for the poor, in which the disciples will share.[10]

The Magnificat, in proclaiming God's purpose and work through the
Messiah, speaks simply of God's intervention for the humble and hungry,
not of the privileges of the special group of poor who follow Jesus (1:52–
53). God's intervention brings a social reversal in which the proud,
mighty, and rich are cast down. The beatitudes and woes proclaim the
same reversal, for they are sharply antithetical and announce a radical
change in the situation of contrasting economic and social groups.[11]
Indeed, the woes in 6:24–25 use some of the same vocabulary as 1:53 in
announcing the same reversal: πλούσιοι/πλουτοῦντες, "rich"; πεινάω,
"hunger"; ἐμπίμπλημι, "fill," "satisfy."[12] The disciples are the vanguard
of a larger group who will experience the upheaval announced in 1:51–
53. They are the poor who know about the good news because Jesus has
proclaimed it to them, and they have responded with initial acceptance.
Through his sermon on the plain more of the poor may hear the good
news and respond.

The instructions in 6:27–38 are directed to all who are listening. They
seek to clarify for the disciples the manner of life expected of them, while

---

[9] W. Pilgrim, *Good News to the Poor*, 107, 163–66, asserts that the material on wealth and
poverty, including the woes, is addressed primarily to rich Christians in Luke's own day.
My question is different: I am asking how the narrator pictures Jesus' first followers, and
we have already noted evidence that they have voluntarily renounced their property in order
to follow Jesus. Therefore, the woes would not apply to Jesus' first followers but must be
addressed to the larger audience.

[10] George A. Kennedy, *New Testament Interpretation*, 40–41, arrives at the same conclusion
through studying the sermon in light of ancient rhetoric: "In Luke 6:20 . . . Jesus first raises
his eyes to the disciples and then begins to speak, employing the second person plural as
early as the first beatitude; again the second person cannot be easily limited to the disciples.
In most rhetorical situations there is a formal addressee, for example a chairman in a
meeting, who is nominally addressed, though practically speaking the speaker is addressing
all those present and sometimes turns directly to them. In classical oratory, apostrophe, or
the turn from the nominal addressee to someone else, is even more common than in modern
public address."

[11] The "poor" here refers to an economic class, as is shown by the parallel between the poor
and the hungry and the contrast with the rich and full. Jacques Dupont expresses the
reason for the reversal clearly: "The privilege of the poor . . . has its theological foundation
in God. If we seek to base it on the moral dispositions of the poor, and in this way force
ourselves to spiritualize their poverty, we are on a false path. The poverty of those to whom
Jesus announces the good news of God's kingdom is seen as a humanly bad situation. . . . It
is an evil. This is precisely why the sufferings and privations of the poor stand out as an
affront to the royal justice of God. God has decided to put an end to it." See "The Poor and
Poverty," 41.

[12] The last of these words is characteristic of Luke-Acts, occurring there in three of its five
New Testament uses.

also seeking to move the larger audience toward this manner of life. The reference to the disciples being hated in 6:22 shows that there is a special reason why disciples need to be instructed on how to act in response to enemies, those who hate and curse them (6:27–28). The commands concerning love of enemies are accompanied by commands concerning possessions: when possessions are taken away by force or when beggars and borrowers ask for them, let them go (6:29–30, 34–35). Here Jesus urges the audience to let loose of possessions, as Simon, Levi, and others have already done. Two commands with comparisons (both using καθώς, "as") provide standards which can increase the ethical sensitivity of the listeners. The first is the standard of our own needs and desires, of which we are usually more sharply aware than of the needs of others (6:31: "as you wish that people do to you"). The second is the standard of God's character (6:36: "as your Father is merciful").[13] Jesus calls his hearers to live in accordance with God's mercy, which means loving enemies, giving, and not judging. While the word οἰκτίρμων ("merciful") is rare in the New Testament, occurring only one other time (James 5:11), we do hear of God's mercy (ἔλεος) elsewhere in Luke. Indeed, this is a theme word in the Magnificat and Benedictus (1:50, 54, 72, 78; see also 1:58), where the saving event, the sending of the Messiah, is understood as a demonstration of God's mercy. This mercy appears later in the forgiveness of sinners and in the parables that Jesus tells to defend this forgiveness. The creditor who forgives his debtors (7:41–42) and the "joy in heaven" at the return of the lost sheep, the lost coin, and the lost son (15:3–32) make God's mercy vivid. This mercy is the standard by which Jesus is calling his hearers to live in 6:36.

Jesus ends the speech with a warning to those who call him Lord yet do not do what he says (6:46), which is developed in a parable contrasting the one who hears and does Jesus' words with the one who hears but does not do (6:47–49). This may lead readers to examine their response to Jesus' extreme commands, but in the context of the narrative it also raises a question about the disciples: will they do as well as hear? The importance of doing what one hears will be reemphasized in the following narrative (8:21; 11:28). The first of these two passages follows the parable of the sower and its interpretation (8:4–15), which pose a similar question: will those who hear the word of God through Jesus bear fruit? Hearing and doing, hearing and bearing fruit—these are aspects of a single concern. Beyond the narrative world this may lead readers to examine their own response to the word, but within the narrative world this concern directs

---

[13] The comparison with God's character and action is important throughout 6:35–38, for the passive verbs in 6:37–38 refer to God's judgment and forgiveness.

our attention to responses to Jesus' message demonstrated by characters in the story, including the disciples.

The Parable of the Sower

In 8:1–3 the narrator associates the twelve with Jesus' mission, although they are not yet authorized to proclaim and heal as Jesus is doing. Being with Jesus while he carries out his mission helps to prepare the twelve for their mission in 9:1–6. In addition, a group of women, three of whom are named, accompany Jesus. These women have a continuing role in the story and are always closely connected to the apostles (see Luke 23:49; 24:9–10; Acts 1:13–14). The distinction of having accompanied Jesus during his traveling ministry and trip to Jerusalem, which is one of the qualifications of the apostles (see Acts 1:21–22), is shared by them with these women (Luke 8:1–2; 23:49).[14]

Since the twelve and the women are with Jesus, they are present for Jesus' speech in 8:4–18, of which the parable of the sower and its interpretation are the main elements. While the presence of the crowd is noted in v. 4, the disciples respond in v. 9, indicating that they also have heard the parable. Jesus' reply in vv. 10–18 is addressed to these disciples and indicates that the parable is relevant to them.

In his interpretation of the parable of the sower Jesus provides a commentary on what is happening or may happen in response to his preaching. This commentary includes a set of norms by which to evaluate the responses of the crowd and the disciples. To be like the seed that fell along the path, on the rock, or in the thorns is to be a failure, for the seed does not produce a harvest, as a farmer would wish. To be like the seed in the good soil is to be a success. The Lukan version of the parable and its interpretation shows no interest in degrees of success, for the Markan reference to bearing thirty, sixty, and a hundred is missing. This may indicate a desire to avoid claims of superiority among the disciples, a desire which would fit with the later warnings to the disciples when they become involved in disputes about greatness (9:46–48; 22:24–27). In Luke the contrast is simply between bearing fruit and the three preceding possibilities of failure. While in the first of these the devil takes away the word to prevent faith, in the second and third cases there is some initial growth of the seed. The second and third cases could apply to the disciples, who have heard Jesus' word and accepted it but now are being warned that this beginning does not guarantee the harvest. So two types of danger are being emphasized in order to prepare the disciples for them. There is the danger that faith will be temporary and will disappear "in a time of

---

[14] On the women in 8:2–3, see further pp. 137–39.

temptation." There is the danger that faith will be choked out "by cares and riches and pleasures of life." These two dangers have already appeared indirectly in the sermon on the plain, where Jesus addressed his disciples as the poor and the persecuted and urged people to love their enemies and let go of their possessions (6:20–35). If possessions are not handled as Jesus directs and if the situation of persecution is not faced steadfastly, the seed will fail to bear fruit, as the parable warns.

Possessions and persecution will be major continuing concerns in Jesus' later instruction of the disciples. While the "time of temptation" need not be restricted to situations of persecution, persecution must be a major part of the meaning of this phrase, as the use of $\pi\epsilon\iota\rho\alpha\sigma\mu\acute{o}s$ ("temptation") in Luke 22:40, 46; Acts 20:19 indicates.[15] Persecution is one of the major problems for disciples, and Jesus will repeatedly seek to prepare his followers for it (see 9:23–26; 12:1–12; 21:12–19). According to 21:19 persecution must be met by "endurance" or "steadfastness" ($\acute{v}\pi o\mu o\nu\acute{\eta}$), and in 8:15 Jesus points to this same quality as characteristic of those who bear fruit (dif. Matthew, Mark).

As we have noted, the second major danger concerns possessions. In 8:14 the "cares ($\mu\acute{\epsilon}\rho\iota\mu\nu\alpha\iota$)" are anxieties for the daily needs of life which money can provide (see 12:22–32; 21:34), and an interest in "pleasures" also leads one to seek the "riches" that can provide them. The conflict between discipleship and the desire for possessions and financial security is also a subject of repeated instruction to the disciples, including several comparatively lengthy speeches (see 12:22–34; 16:1–13; also 14:33; 18:18–30). Thus the two potential problems for disciples briefly indicated in Jesus' interpretation of the parable of the sower become important themes of Jesus' teaching of disciples in later chapters. The interpretation of the parable of the sower prepares for this.

Those in 8:12 do not have faith; those in 8:13 have faith only for a time. These two references to having faith are absent from the parallels to these verses in Matthew and Mark. Those with a temporary faith in v. 13 contrast with those who "hold fast the word" and bear fruit "with stead-fastness" (dif. Matthew, Mark). This emphasis on firmness and persistence marks the difference between true faith and the temporary faith of those who grow on rocky ground. The story of the storm on the lake,

---

[15] In Luke 22:40, 46 the temptation arises from the threatening power of the Sanhedrin, which is plotting Jesus' arrest, trial, and death. In Acts 20:19 Paul refers to the "temptations" or "testings which happened to me by the plots of the Jews." Jesus is probably referring to the powerful and threatening opposition that he has faced when he speaks in Luke 22:28 of his $\pi\epsilon\iota\rho\alpha\sigma\mu o\acute{\iota}$. Schuyler Brown insists that $\pi\epsilon\iota\rho\alpha\sigma\mu\acute{o}s$ for Luke "is inseparably associated with the sin of apostasy." See *Apostasy and Perseverance,* 21. This may fit Luke 8:13 but not Luke 22:28 or Acts 20:19.

which follows the interpretation of the sower more quickly in Luke than in Mark, shows that the disciples do not achieve this steady faith immediately (see 8:25). The Lukan modifications of the interpretation of the parable, and the connections between it and subsequent teaching and events, show that it is being used to suggest norms by which to evaluate the behavior of characters in the story, especially the behavior of the disciples.

The relevance for the disciples of Jesus' discussion of the different responses to the word is emphasized in v. 18: "Therefore, watch out how you hear." The saying which follows and completes Jesus' discussion with the disciples indicates that the disciples who accept and hold fast Jesus' teaching to this point will receive still more later that will benefit them, while everything will be lost among those who do not hold fast to what Jesus has so far taught. This verse calls attention to a developing process in Jesus' teaching and emphasizes the crucial importance of holding fast to Jesus' initial instructions.

Immediately following this discussion with the disciples, Jesus' mother and brothers come to see him (a sequence different from Matthew, Mark). This provides an opportunity for Jesus to make a further comment about those "who hear the word of God and do it." I think that Joseph Fitzmyer is mistaken when he insists that Luke has changed the point of this Markan scene in order to present Jesus' physical mother and brothers as model disciples.[16] The question is whether Jesus in 8:21 is describing Mary and his brothers outside as those "who hear the word of God and do it" or whether he is describing the indefinite group of people "who hear the word of God and do it" as "my mother and my brothers." Fitzmyer translates, "My mother and my brothers, they [οὗτοι] are the ones who listen to the word of God and act on it." This is a possible translation, which can be taken to support either of the interpretations just mentioned. We should note, however, that the lack of articles with "mother" and "brothers" in 8:21 suggests that Jesus is talking about a less definite group than the messenger was when referring to Mary and Jesus' brothers outside (the articles are present in 8:20). Why do Jesus' words begin with "my mother and my brothers," followed by a resumptive "these (οὗτοι)," a construction not found in Matthew and Mark? As we have noted, Luke's version of this scene follows closely the interpretation of the parable of the sower, which, like 8:21, is concerned with response to the word being preached by Jesus. The connection is strengthened by the fact that 8:21 is patterned after the interpretation of this parable. In 8:14–15 Jesus' statements begin with something that needs to be explained ("that which fell into the thorns," etc.), followed by "these are the ones who. . . ."

---

[16] See *Luke I–IX*, 722–25. See also R. Brown, *The Birth of the Messiah*, 317–18.

Jesus is revealing the meaning of the parable by identifying its imagery with particular groups of people. Similarly, in 8:21 "my mother and my brothers" is taken as a phrase requiring explanation. The explanation is given through identifying those who hear and do the word of God as the family in question.

An application to all who hear the word and do it is supported by 11:27–28, a scene in which Jesus' mother is again mentioned and Jesus responds with words which recall 8:21. Jesus' response in 11:28 contrasts with the preceding praise of his mother (see μενοῦν, "rather"). This is not a contrast between Mary as mother and Mary as model disciple, for 11:28 shifts to the plural. Jesus is not thinking specifically of Mary when he praises those who "hear the word of God and keep it." He is challenging the crowd that surrounds him to discipleship.[17] So also in 8:21 Jesus is declaring that those who prove to be both hearers and doers of the word are his family. Jesus' disciples are expected to be his family by meeting this criterion, which repeats the challenge at the end of the sermon on the plain (6:46–49) and develops the message in the interpretation of the sower.

The story of the storm on the lake reveals that the disciples have not yet reached maturity as hearers and doers of the word. While the Lukan version of this episode softens the irreverent and accusing appeal of the disciples in Mark 4:38 and the harshness of Jesus' response in Mark 4:40, the essential point that the disciples have failed to show faith remains. This is expressed in the accusing question, "Where is your faith?" (Luke 8:25). Perhaps this is not meant to imply that the disciples have no faith at all but that they have failed to respond with faith on this particular occasion. This failure is still sufficient to demonstrate that the disciples do not yet have the faith that holds fast and brings forth fruit with stead-fastness or endurance (8:15), even in a time of testing (8:13). The disciples still need to grow in faith, as the apostles recognize in 17:5 and as is demonstrated anew in the passion and resurrection story, where Jesus must intercede for Peter lest his faith give out (22:32) and accuses others of being "slow in heart to have faith" (24:25). The fact that the disciples address Jesus as ἐπιστάτης ("master") in 8:24 may be a further indication of their inadequacy, for, when used by the disciples, this title always appears in situations in which the disciples fail to understand Jesus' power or purpose (see 5:5; 8:45; 9:33, 49).

---

[17] Cf. Raymond E. Brown, Karl P. Donfried, Joseph A. Fitzmyer, and John Reumann, eds., *Mary in the New Testament*, 171–72. This publication wants to maintain a reference to Mary in 11:28.

The Twelve Receive New Authority and Insight

The scene ends with the disciples' question, "Who then is this, that he commands even the winds and the water, and they obey him?" The disciples' inability to answer this question leaves an unresolved tension in the narrative and alerts readers to look for developments in the disciples' understanding. This question is one of a series of unanswered questions about Jesus which help to unite the narrative and build interest in the answers that will be given by Peter in 9:20 and by the heavenly voice in 9:35. According to 8:10 the disciples have been "given to know the mysteries of God's reign," in contrast to the others, but the question which the disciples raise about Jesus in 8:25 shows that they have not yet appropriated vital aspects of this knowledge. Their question places them on the same level as the crowds, the scribes and Pharisees, and Herod, who raise similar questions.[18] This series of unanswered questions about Jesus may stretch as far back as 4:22, where the people in the Nazareth synagogue ask, "Is this not Joseph's son?" Beginning with 4:36, however, the unity of the series of questions is indicated by verbal markers, the repetition of the words τίς ("who" or "what") and οὗτος ("this") at or near the beginning of the question. This formulation in 4:36 should be noted, even though the question there concerns Jesus' word ("What is this word?") rather than Jesus himself, for 8:25 parallels 4:36 in a further respect: through the repetition of the words ὅτι . . . ἐπιτάσσει . . . καί ("for . . . he commands . . . and"; dif. Matthew, Mark). In 5:21 (dif. Matthew, Mark) and 7:49 (in a scene unique to Luke) the scribes and Pharisees, or the guests at the Pharisee's dinner party, ask, "Who is this?" Then the disciples (8:25) and Herod (9:9) raise the same question, and in the latter case the question in Luke parallels a statement by Herod in Mark. The speculations concerning Jesus listed in the Herod pericope (9:7–9) are repeated in 9:18–19, the introduction to Peter's confession. These two episodes are much closer together in Luke than in Mark, which makes the connection between them much more obvious. This connection indicates that Peter's confession in 9:20 provides a new and, in some respects, better response to the questions and speculations about Jesus to this point in the narrative. This confession is a new insight by Peter, a significant development beyond the amazed bewilderment expressed in 8:25.

A change has taken place in Peter's understanding of Jesus. What has caused this change? While the narrative does not answer this question explicitly, there does seem to be emphasis on the involvement of the

---

[18] J. Fitzmyer, *Luke I–IX*, 730, sees in the question in 8:25 "the beginning of a sense of awareness" in the disciples. I would agree, provided this means that the disciples have come to recognize a mystery about Jesus that they have not yet comprehended.

twelve, and of Peter in particular, in the miracles that are related from 8:26 through 9:17. This section is largely composed of miracle stories, and these include the most detailed miracle stories in the gospel. The narrator emphasizes, for most of these events, that the twelve, or Peter, John, and James, are present and sometimes play an active role. In 9:1–6 the twelve exercize the "authority over all demons and to heal diseases" which Jesus has given them, and in the feeding of the five thousand (9:10–17) the twelve have an important role. In 8:51 we are told that Peter, John, and James were present at the raising of Jairus' daughter, even though all others, except the child's parents, were excluded, and in 8:45 a special interest in Peter appears, for Luke assigns to Peter a role in the story of the woman with the flow of blood which Mark assigns to the "disciples." The narrator suggests, but does not state, that Peter comes to his new insight that Jesus is "the Messiah of God" on the basis of witnessing Jesus' mighty acts on these occasions and sharing in Jesus' healing power on his mission. The feeding of the five thousand may be especially important in awakening this new insight.[19]

In Luke 9 the narrator presents a series of important new developments for the twelve and the larger group of disciples. The exorcism and healing stories in 8:26–56 are followed by an episode in which Jesus grants the same power to the twelve. He also sends them "to proclaim God's reign" (9:1–2), and the narrator reports that they fulfill their two-sided mission of "preaching good news" and "healing" (9:6). The twelve are no longer passive observers of Jesus in his mission; they have progressed to the point that they can be active participants. To be sure, they are still apprentices. The later narrative shows that Jesus still has much to teach them, and some of it will be difficult to learn. However, they have come to the point where they can share in Jesus' two basic activities, healing and proclaiming God's reign.

The apostles' mission conforms to Jesus' mission and is an extension of it. As Jesus' commanding word shows "authority and power" (4:36), so the apostles are given "power and authority" (9:1).[20] As Jesus was sent to "preach good news of God's reign" and "proclaim" (4:43–44; see also 4:18; 8:1), so the disciples are sent by Jesus. The view of the mission and message of Jesus developed on the basis of the Isaiah quotation in Luke 4:18–19 and reemphasized in 4:43–44 also determines the narrator's view of the mission of the twelve.

The instructions of Jesus in 9:3–5 again show that poverty and opposition are important realities in the lives of Jesus' followers. We have

---

[19] See below, pp. 218–19.

[20] The double expression is not used by Matthew or Mark in parallels to the two verses.

already noted how Jesus addressed the disciples as the poor and the
persecuted in 6:20-23 and the attention that he gave to the use of possessions and response to opposition in 6:27-36 and 8:13-14. In sending out
the twelve, Jesus makes clear that they will be traveling without any
means of self-support and so will be completely dependent on the hospitality of those to whom they preach. Yet there will be cities that will not
receive them. The reference to rejection in 9:5 will be repeated and
expanded in 10:10-16 (the instructions to the seventy-two) and 11:14-32,
where Jesus is responding to a portion of the crowd which is rejecting his
mission. These passages contribute to a picture of conflict not only with
the scribes and Pharisees but also with a segment of the people. The
instructions that Jesus will give to the disciples in 12:1-12, 22-34 are
especially appropriate for those who must face the insecurities of the
mission on which Jesus sends the twelve and the seventy-two.

In 5:10 Jesus promised Peter that he would be "catching people alive."
Now Peter and the other apostles have actually begun this mission. In
6:13 the twelve were simply called "apostles ($\dot{\alpha}\pi\acute{o}\sigma\tau o\lambda o\iota$)." Now Jesus
has "sent ($\dot{\alpha}\pi\acute{\epsilon}\sigma\tau\epsilon\iota\lambda\epsilon\nu$)" them on a mission, and we begin to discover what
being an apostle means. But there is more to come. The mission instruc-
tions to the twelve parallel those to the seventy-two (10:1-24). Indeed, this
is climactic parallelism, for Jesus' words to the seventy-two are more
extensive and are filled with an eschatological joy lacking in 9:1-6.[21] And
a greater mission will be announced in 24:46-49, which will lead to more
extensive proclamation and healing.

The Feeding of the Five Thousand

The twelve have a prominent role in the feeding of the five thousand.
The narrator focuses on the interaction between Jesus and the twelve in
9:12-15. A request by the "twelve" (dif. Matthew, Mark) sets events in
motion (9:12). Jesus replies, "*You* give them (food) to eat," and the twelve
disclose the inadequacy of their resources.[22] The emphasis on the twelve is
maintained through emphatic use of pronouns referring to them ($\dot{\nu}\mu\epsilon\hat{\iota}s$,
"you"; $\dot{\eta}\mu\hat{\iota}\nu$, "to us"; $\dot{\eta}\mu\epsilon\hat{\iota}s$, "we"). Jesus gives the disciples a subordinate
but important role in preparing the crowd and distributing the food (vv.
14-16), so that through Jesus' power the twelve are, after all, able to feed
the crowd. In the last sentence of the episode, the narrator places the
number twelve in the emphatic final position.[23] This position emphasizes

---

[21] On climactic parallelism in the two missionary charges see Helmut Flender, *St. Luke,* 22-
23.

[22] Cp. 5:1-11, where Peter's inability to succeed on his own is indicated (5:5) before the great
catch of fish.

[23] Retaining the Greek word order, v. 17 ends thus: "of fragments baskets twelve" (dif.
Matthew, Mark).

the fact that the number of baskets of excess food corresponds to the number of the apostles, "the twelve," as they were called at the beginning of the episode (v. 12) in contrast to Matthew's and Mark's "disciples." This correspondence may suggest that the apostles are abundantly supplied for their future mission also, in which they will continue to feed the crowds.

The feeding of the five thousand is linked to the narrative of the sending out of the twelve by 9:10–11, which reports the return of the apostles from their mission and presents Jesus continuing his mission of preaching God's reign and healing which he began to share with the apostles in 9:2. The reference to Jesus' twofold mission of preaching and healing (dif. Matthew, Mark) not only enables the narrator to introduce a reference to God's reign (a point which I will discuss below) but also integrates the feeding scene into the Lukan picture of Jesus' and the apostles' mission. In some sense their mission includes or leads to this abundant meal for a multitude.

To be more specific, we must note some suggestive associations between this feeding story and other parts of Luke's Gospel. First, in 12:41 Peter responds to the preceding parable of the waiting servants by asking, "Lord, are you saying this parable to us or also to all?" (dif. Matthew). Jesus responds with further comment, relating the parable to a steward who has been placed in charge of household servants while the master is away. That is, the parable is applied to leaders who are given responsibility for others. This responsibility is pictured in terms of feeding the servants; the steward is to give to them at the proper time "the allowance of food ($\sigma\iota\tau o\mu\acute{\epsilon}\tau\rho\iota o\nu$)" and will be judged by whether he has done this faithfully. Here Peter, representing the apostles, is informed about his responsibility within the church and that responsibility is presented parabolically in terms of feeding others. In light of this parable, it may be significant that the feeding follows the mission of the twelve in Luke 9. Following their mission, the twelve have the task of nourishing and caring for the people being attracted by the mission.

The interest in similarities between Jesus and Elijah which we have already noted[24] should remind us that Elijah's successor Elisha fed a hundred men with a meager supply of bread. His servant pointed out the inadequacy of the supply, but the prophet declared, "They shall eat and have some left," and so it happened (2 Kgs 4:42–44). The similarity of Jesus' feeding to this Elisha story, and possible associations with Moses' feeding of the people in the wilderness with manna, would provide further grounds for the crowd's judgment that Jesus is one of the old prophets

---

[24] See above, pp. 72, 87–88, 97.

returned (9:19). However, Peter goes beyond this view and declares that Jesus is "the Messiah of God" (9:20). We have noted that this confession represents a distinct development beyond the bewilderment expressed by the disciples in 8:25.[25] While the feeding may not be the only event which led Peter to his new view of Jesus, its position immediately before Peter's confession suggests that it contributed. Furthermore, in Luke (dif. Matthew, Mark) the feeding of the five thousand is framed by material which raises the question of who Jesus is. The question is left open in 9:7–9 but is picked up in 9:18–19, and these passages are linked by repetition of the same speculations. This frame suggests that the feeding speaks to the question of Jesus' identity. However, it is not immediately clear why feeding a crowd with a few loaves of bread and a few fish should lead anyone to regard Jesus as the Messiah.

The repeated references to meals with eschatological associations in Luke may support the view that there is an implicit connection between the feeding episode and Peter's confession. The reference, immediately before the feeding, to Jesus "speaking about God's reign" (9:11; dif. Matthew, Mark) may in part be designed to recall these eschatological associations, while the statement, "They ate and all were filled ($\dot{\epsilon}\chi o\rho\tau\acute{a}\sigma$-$\theta\eta\sigma\alpha\nu$)," at the end of the feeding scene takes on additional meaning when related to the similar statement in Jesus' second beatitude, "Happy are you who hunger now, for you shall be filled ($\chi o\rho\tau\alpha\sigma\theta\acute{\eta}\sigma\epsilon\sigma\theta\epsilon$)" (6:21). The promise in this beatitude stands in parallelism with the promise, "Yours is God's reign" (6:20). Eschatological fulfillment, and specifically sharing in God's reign, is repeatedly pictured in terms of a festive meal in Luke. This association must be considered when interpreting the meal scenes and references to a future meal in the gospel, which have an unusually prominent place in Luke's account of the ministry of Jesus.[26] The connection between eschatological fulfillment and a festive meal appears in 12:37, where the waiting servants are made to recline for a banquet and are served by their master who has returned; in 13:28–29, where the patriarchs, prophets, and gathered faithful recline for a banquet in God's reign; in 14:15–24, where a statement about eating bread in God's reign is followed by a parable about a dinner party; and in 22:16, 18, where Jesus indicates that he will once again eat and drink when God's reign comes. In 5:34 the present situation of fulfillment is pictured as a wedding feast with Jesus as bridegroom. Finally, 22:30 speaks of an eschatological meal which is a *messianic* meal, for Jesus speaks of the table as his table and the kingdom as his kingdom. In the context of this

[25] See above, pp. 213–14.
[26] Cf. Willibald Bösen, *Jesusmahl, Eucharistisches Mahl, Endzeitmahl*, 78–108.

meal symbolism, we can understand how the narrator could present Peter responding to the feeding of the five thousand, as well as other mighty acts of Jesus, by declaring that Jesus is the Messiah of God. The feeding is a preliminary realization of Jesus' promise in 6:21 that in God's reign the hungry will be filled. Peter's response indicates that the feeding is also a preliminary participation in the messianic meal to which other Lukan passages refer, thus revealing Jesus as Messiah.

The sequence of actions described in 9:16 resembles Jesus' actions with the bread at the last meal before his death (22:19). Even more striking are similarities in wording between the feeding scene and the Emmaus meal in 24:28–31.[27] In both cases we hear of the day declining (using a form of κλίνω; 9:12; 24:29), followed by the use of κατακλίνω of reclining in preparation for a meal,[28] and the same series of actions (taking the bread, blessing, breaking, and giving) is reported in 9:16 and 24:30. That Jesus "blessed" the food on both of these occasions is a minor point of contrast with the last supper, where Jesus instead "gave thanks" (22:19). At the Emmaus meal Jesus is disclosed to disciples who previously did not recognize him. As Jesus breaks the bread and distributes it to them, the disciples recognize that the stranger who told them about the Messiah, a Messiah who had to suffer and enter into his glory (24:26), is Jesus. This scene suggests that a meal with Jesus is an especially appropriate place for the revelation and recognition of Jesus as the (risen) Messiah,[29] and that the feeding of the five thousand is understood by the narrator as a first experience of this revelation at a meal, resulting in Peter's recognition of Jesus as the Messiah. To be sure, this is a preliminary and incomplete recognition, for Peter and his companions do not understand the crucial point explained to the travelers to Emmaus, that the Messiah must suffer. Nevertheless, the explanation which I have offered makes sense of the fact that the Lukan narrator has seen fit, in contrast to Matthew and Mark, to raise the question of who Jesus is both directly before and directly after the feeding scene and that after the feeding Peter declares Jesus to be the Messiah.

Jesus Announces His Coming Death

As soon as Peter declares that Jesus is the Messiah, Jesus responds with a rebuke and a command to tell this to no one (9:21). This rebuke indicates that there is something inappropriate or dangerous in Peter's confession. The rebuke may be caused by the disciples' faulty under-

---

[27] These similarities have been noted in detail by R. Dillon, *From Eye-Witnesses*, 149–50.
[28] This word occurs only in Luke in the New Testament.
[29] Cf. Acts 10:40–41: "God . . . gave him to become manifest . . . to us, who ate and drank with him after he rose from the dead." Cf. also Acts 1:4.

standing of Jesus' messianic role, or it may indicate that his messianic role should not be proclaimed openly now. Probably both of these factors are involved. The problem with the disciples is not that they mistakenly attach royal and political connotations to the title Messiah because of their Jewish background. The royal and political function of Jesus has been proclaimed in the birth narrative by a heavenly messenger (1:32–33), and Jesus will be openly proclaimed as king as he enters Jerusalem (19:38). When some of the Pharisees protest this proclamation, Jesus *refuses* to "rebuke" his disciples (19:39–40). The view that this scene is non-political runs counter to the fact that the narrator has introduced a title with clear political implications, followed by a dialogue which indicates Jesus' approval of this title (dif. Matthew, Mark). So a royal and political conception of the Messiah is not the reason for Jesus' rebuke in 9:21. However, the public proclamation of Jesus as messianic king is part of the final confrontation with the authorities in Jerusalem, in which the leadership of Israel is at stake. It is not yet time for this confrontation. Furthermore, the disciples do not have an adequate understanding of what it means for Jesus to be the Messiah. The narrator immediately indicates what is lacking by attaching to the rebuke, as part of the same sentence,[30] the statement that the Son of Man must suffer. This is a surprising new disclosure for the disciples,[31] and it will be incomprehensible to them even when plainly stated (see 9:44–45; 18:31–34). Even though Peter now knows that Jesus is the Messiah, a crucial aspect of Jesus' role is not and will not be understood by the disciples until they encounter the risen Messiah.

For the present, the disciples are blinded by a basic misunderstanding of Jesus' role, for suffering and resurrection are an integral and necessary part of being the Messiah as this role is understood in Luke-Acts. When we hear of Jesus' suffering (using πάσχω or παθητός), Jesus is almost always referred to as Son of Man or Messiah.[32] Jesus is spoken of as the suffering Son of Man only prior to his death and resurrection (Luke 9:22; 17:24–25); after these events we are repeatedly told that the *Messiah* suffered and was raised (Luke 24:26, 46; Acts 3:18; 17:3; 26:23). In Luke 24:26 and Acts 17:3 this is accompanied by a form of the impersonal verb δεῖ ("it is necessary," but often translated "must"), which shows that these verses are revisions of the passion announcement in Luke 9:22, with Messiah substituted for Son of Man. So when Jesus rebukes Peter and

---

[30] The participle εἰπών in 9:22 is dependent on the verb παρήγγειλεν in the preceding verse, and v. 22 explains part of the reason for Jesus' rebuke and command to silence.

[31] In retrospect, readers can see that 5:35 refers to Jesus' death, but for participants in the story, who do not know how things will turn out, this implication would not be clear.

[32] There are two exceptions, Luke 22:15 and Acts 1:3, where no title is used.

announces that the Son of Man must suffer, he is not rejecting the title
Messiah and replacing it with Son of Man but is disclosing an aspect of
his role as the Messiah which the disciples do not yet understand.

Peter's answer to the question of Jesus' identity is not complete and
final. The issue is still alive, and further pieces of the puzzle can be found
in Luke 9, first in Jesus' statements about the suffering Son of Man (9:22,
44) and then in the voice from the cloud which declares, "This is my Son,
the chosen one" (9:35).[33] Nevertheless, Peter's confession is a turning
point in the narrative. Compared to the amazed bewilderment in 8:25, it
represents a significant insight which enables the disciples to enter a
higher stage of preparation for their mission, a stage of instruction which
Jesus begins immediately in 9:22–27 and which he will continue throughout the long section of journeying to Jerusalem. Peter's confession also
provides the occasion to disclose a new aspect of Jesus' commission. We
have seen how the statement of Jesus' commission from God in 4:18–19
interprets the events which follow in the narrative. In 9:22 we learn that
there is something more that Jesus must do in order to fulfill his
commission.[34] This statement, like 4:18–19, is a program for action. It
defines a course which Jesus will obediently follow in the narrative. It is
not only a disclosure to the disciples of what Jesus must do but also to the
readers concerning the future course of the story, and there will be
repeated reminders of this as the story unfolds. But Jesus' statement raises
a question which it does not answer. While the course of the story may be
clarified by 9:22, the reason why Jesus must be rejected and killed
remains a puzzling mystery. The mystery deepens when we recognize that
Jesus' suffering and death represent his violent rejection by the "elders
and chief priests and scribes." Jesus' death is a crisis in the developing plot
because it means that Israel's Messiah is rejected by the leaders of Israel,
putting in doubt the salvation for Israel which Jesus came to bring.

Jesus' announcement that he must be rejected and killed is a new
disclosure to the disciples. Is it also a new insight by Jesus? This is
possible but is not clearly indicated. It is surely significant that Jesus
raises the question of his identity and announces his future destiny after
prayer (9:18). However, this period of prayer can be understood either as
spiritual preparation for a long recognized task or as a time of new insight

---

[33] J. Fitzmyer, *Luke I–IX*, 771, emphasizes that Peter's confession is one of a series of answers given in chap. 9 to Herod's question in 9:9.

[34] Charles H. Cosgrove, "The Divine Δεῖ in Luke-Acts," 168–90, rightly emphasizes that scriptural prophecy functions in Luke-Acts not only as "proof of divine endorsement" but also as "an imperative to be obeyed." Similarly, "The δεῖ of Luke-Acts characteristically carries this two-fold edge of divine attestation and divine summons to obedience" (pp. 174, 176).

into God's will. The narrator allows the readers to imagine either situation.

The challenge in 9:23–27 is addressed "to all." This challenge concerns discipleship, but it is relevant not only to those who are disciples but also to the crowd as potential disciples. Here Jesus clarifies the conditions for following him. His new and sharper demands conform to the way of suffering which he himself faces. Following, he now reveals, means taking up one's cross. While the sayings about taking up one's cross and losing one's life would seem to refer most directly to threats to life from persecution, there are indications that the narrator wants vv. 23–26 to be understood in a broad sense. If so, these verses belong with subsequent teaching not only about faithfulness in persecution but also about renunciation of family and possessions. All three of these subjects are repeated themes in Jesus' discipleship teaching during the journey to Jerusalem, and 9:23–26 serves an introduction to this teaching which links it with Jesus' announcement of his own suffering in 9:22. This broad sense is suggested by the presence of "daily" (dif. Matthew, Mark) in the command to take up one's cross and by the use of the present infinitive of continuous or repeated action (ἔρχεσθαι; dif. Matthew, Mark) to speak of coming after Jesus. Jesus in Luke is talking about a daily renunciation which may come in many forms. In Luke the saying about gaining the whole world but losing oneself is more clearly linked to the preceding saying about saving and losing one's life than in the parallel versions.[35] Gaining the whole world is an extreme form of the normal desire to accumulate possessions, and the close relation of vv. 24 and 25 suggests that this desire to accumulate is one form of the false attempt to save one's life. Furthermore, variant versions of three of the sayings in 9:23–26 are found later in Luke in contexts that concern various forms of risk and renunciation for disciples. Thus 9:26 is restated in 12:8–9 in a context dealing with persecution, a version of 9:23 reappears in 14:27 as part of a series of requirements for disciples that includes leaving family and possessions (14:26, 33), and a variant of 9:24 is found in 17:33, where it seems to support a command to abandon possessions (17:31–32). These doublets give repetitive emphasis to these sayings and link later teaching on the demands of discipleship to 9:23–26, where these demands are introduced in their full rigor. These doublets also help to make clear that this teaching embraces a broad range of concerns, not only the willingness to give one's life but also to renounce family and possessions.

Insofar as these commands concern family and property, they have already been fulfilled by those who left all to follow Jesus (5:11, 28).

---

[35] See the addition of ἀπολέσας in v. 25, repeating one of the main verbs of v. 24.

However, even Peter will be unwilling to lose his life when he first faces a life-threatening situation in the passion story. The disciples must be transformed before they can fully obey commands such as these.

The Transfiguration

The transfiguration of Jesus is dated "about eight days after these words" (dif. Matthew, Mark). This emphasizes the importance of the words just reported in 9:22-27 and suggests that there may be some connection between these words and the transfiguration. A connection is apparent in the reference to Jesus' "departure" in 9:31, which is related to the announcement of Jesus' coming death in 9:22, and in the command to "hear him" in 9:35, which is divine confirmation of the authority of Jesus' words in 9:22-27 and later. The transfiguration may also partially fulfill the promise in 9:27 that some of those present with Jesus will see God's reign.[36] The absence of Mark's "come with power" in Luke 9:27 makes it possible to apply the saying to a revelation prior to the parousia. The transfiguration is an anticipatory vision of Jesus' "glory" (9:32). Elsewhere we learn that Jesus will "enter his glory" following his death (24:26). Then he will be seated at the right hand of God (22:69) and "enter" his "kingdom" (23:42), a "kingdom" conferred on him by his Father (22:29). This series of texts suggests that the vision of Jesus' glory in the transfiguration is a vision of Jesus as he will be when, through resurrection and exaltation, he begins his messianic reign. Since Jesus' reign is closely connected with God's reign, the transfiguration seems to provide a first fulfillment of the promise in 9:27 that some of Jesus' acquaintances will see God's reign.

The account in Luke summarizes the content of the conversation between Jesus, Moses, and Elijah (dif. Matthew, Mark). They were speaking of "his departure, which he was going to fulfill in Jerusalem" (9:31). Here we find an explicit reference to future events which integrates the transfiguration scene into the larger narrative and enables it to serve as preview for the reader and as preparation for Jesus. For the reader, 9:31 reemphasizes the importance of the announcement of Jesus' death in 9:22 and interprets that event as a part of the divine purpose. Jesus is speaking with Moses and Elijah, who, as representatives of Scripture's prophetic witness, know about God's purpose. They speak of Jesus' ἔξοδος, evoking a comparison with a crucial event of past sacred history,[37] and this exodus is something that Jesus will "fulfill," thereby

---

[36] See J. Fitzmyer, *Luke I–IX*, 786.

[37] This word is used as a euphemism for death as a "departure" from life. See BAGD, 276. However, it would also recall the exodus of Israel from Egypt.

fulfilling God's purpose as announced in Scripture (see 4:21; 24:44). Jerusalem is the place of this fulfillment. This notice alerts readers to the importance of the journey to Jerusalem which will begin shortly.

Peter, John, and James were "weighed down with sleep" (9:32), suggesting that they were only partially aware of events and their significance. They did see Jesus' glory and the two men with him, but the disciples' lack of understanding of Jesus' passion announcement in 9:45 indicates that they did not comprehend Jesus' "departure" in Jerusalem, the subject of the conversation between Jesus, Moses, and Elijah. Furthermore, the phrase "not knowing what he is saying" makes clear that Peter's proposal concerning the three booths for Jesus, Moses, and Elijah shows lack of understanding. The voice from the cloud comes as a correction of Peter's inappropriate proposal and a clarification of what the transfiguration reveals about Jesus. Jesus has the climactic place in God's plan, superior to Moses and Elijah. The divine voice declares that he is "my Son, the chosen one."

This disclosure, recalling the statement of the divine voice to Jesus in 3:22, is followed by the command, "Hear him." The revelation of Jesus as God's Son, the chosen one, underscores the authority and importance of his words. Jesus speaks with divine authority and must be obeyed. The apostles particularly need to hear Jesus' teaching about his coming death, for this will prove difficult for them (see 9:45; 18:34). Furthermore, Jesus' teaching now includes hard words that show how discipleship looks in the shadow of the cross (9:23–26). The command, "Hear him," not only points back to such words in 9:22–26 but also points forward to all the teaching on discipleship which will follow, especially on the journey to Jerusalem. Jesus' passion announcement (9:22) and the transfiguration introduce a new stage in the instruction of the disciples. They are no longer groping to understand who Jesus is. Indeed, three of the apostles have been allowed to see Jesus' glory and have received confirmation of Jesus' divine authority. They should now recognize the importance of what Jesus is saying to them and be ready to obey. Jesus speaks to them now as one who accepts the necessity of suffering and rejection and expects his followers to do likewise. However, crucial gaps will appear in the disciples' understanding and response, gaps which will persist until the encounters with the risen Messiah. Jesus will attempt to overcome these failures and prepare mature disciples. The extensive sections of discipleship teaching during the journey to Jerusalem show Jesus working at this task. They also show that the disciples still have a great deal to learn. One kind of suspense that unites the narrative concerns the efforts of Jesus to prepare his disciples, working against resistance in some areas.

These earnest efforts may arouse the readers' interest in the developing story of the disciples. Some problems in their relation to Jesus need to be resolved. When and how will this happen? The command, "Hear him," provides a clear norm for judging the adequacy of the disciples' response, a norm which underscores the normative character of all Jesus' teaching.

While Matthew and Mark indicate that Jesus commands the three witnesses not to reveal what they have seen, Luke 9:36 states that they, on their own initiative, keep silent about it. This may be an indication of continued fear and lack of understanding.

It is doubtful that we should understand the transfiguration as an event simply staged for the three apostles. Probably it has meaning for Jesus as well. Jesus is discussing with Moses and Elijah the future course of his own life. A process of preparation and planning is taking place, a search for God's will disclosed in Scripture, and this process emerges out of prayer (9:28–29). Jesus is seeking and being given the clarity of purpose which will enable him to "set his face to go to Jerusalem" (9:51). The heavenly voice which declares that Jesus is God's Son recalls the scene of Jesus praying after his baptism in 3:22. In that scene Jesus was preparing for his ministry. In the transfiguration scene he is preparing for the crisis in Jerusalem. To prepare him, Jesus is given an anticipatory experience of the goal of his life and death, the heavenly glory which he will enter when exalted to the right hand of God (see Luke 24:26; Acts 7:55–56).

The Disciples' Failures in Luke 9:37–50

We have already noted that the three apostles at the transfiguration were not fully aware of what was happening and responded in an inappropriate way (see 9:32–33). These indications of weakness are reinforced by the series of scenes which follows, for each of the scenes through the rest of chapter 9 presents disciples (or would-be disciples) failing to respond as disciples should. Several of the problems which emerge will persist until the last chapter of the gospel. Thus at the beginning of the new stage of their instruction, the narrator presents the disciples as seriously lacking in understanding and in need of Jesus' correction. In light of this situation, we can understand the reason for the extensive and emphatic teaching to the disciples during Jesus' journey to Jerusalem. We can also understand the urgency, for Jesus is aware that the time for his teaching is now limited.

The exorcism story in 9:37–43a contains the typical features of such stories in Luke, except for the statement in v. 40 that the disciples were not able to cast the demon out and Jesus' response in v. 41. To whom are Jesus' harsh words, "O faithless and perverted generation!" addressed? If lack of faith by the boy's father were the cause of the problem, we would expect some further discussion of this in the narrative, as is actually the case in Mark 9:21–24. However, these verses are absent from Luke's version of the story. Jesus' harsh words are a response (note ἀποκριθείς, "answering") to the report of the disciples' failure. It is evidently the disciples who have shown themselves to be "faithless," just as they failed to demonstrate faith during the storm at sea (8:25). Since the twelve have been given "authority over all the demons" (9:1), the nine who did not accompany Jesus should have been able to deal with the situation, but they could not.[38] Jesus' response is also conditioned by his awareness of his coming "departure," mentioned shortly before (9:31; see also 9:22). Only a limited time remains for Jesus' ministry, and there is pressing need for the disciples to learn to perform the mission on their own. Their failure shows that they are not yet ready.

There is no shift in setting in Luke 9:43, as there is in the parallels in Matt 17:22 and Mark 9:30. While the crowds are still reacting to the exorcism, Jesus turns to the disciples to stress the point which he had made in 9:22. The need for repetition and the emphatic call for attention with which Jesus begins ("Put into your ears these words") suggest that Jesus is aware of the disciples' failure to understand his first announcement of the passion. In any case, the disciples' failure to understand is emphatically stated in 9:45.

When we compare 9:43b–45 with the parallels in Matthew and Mark, we see that the emphasis has shifted from the passion announcement to the statement of the disciples' failure to understand. The passion announcement is shortened to the single sentence which adds something new to 9:22. The disciples (and the readers) should be able to recall the rest from the previous announcement. On the other hand, Luke 9:45 contrasts with Matthew and expands on Mark in emphasizing the failure of the disciples to understand what Jesus is saying about his death. The disciples are supposed to be the ones who have been "given to know the mysteries of God's reign" (8:10). Three leading apostles were told by a heavenly voice to "hear him," and Jesus introduces his statement in v. 44 with a similar command to hear. But on this crucial point they do not hear with understanding. The disciples are failing to learn what they need to know. Furthermore, the problem will persist. The passion announcement in

---

[38] It may seem strange that the disciples should be addressed as a "faithless *generation*." However, γενεά need not mean all those living at a particular time; it can also mean a particular clan, race, or family. Cf. BAGD, 153–54. The phrase "this generation," with negative connotations, is used in Luke in contexts which show that a select group, rather than all people born at a particular time, is meant. See 7:31–33, after 7:29–30, and 11:50–51, part of an accusation addressed to the lawyers.

18:31–33 is followed by a statement that the disciples "understood none of these things" (dif. Matthew, Mark), and this is underscored with three-fold repetition which resembles 9:45. This situation continues into Easter day, as 24:11, 25–26 indicate. In 9:45 the verb ἀγνοέω ("not know," "be ignorant") is used of the disciples. The theme of ignorance will reappear in the speeches in Acts, where Peter and Paul will declare that the people of Jerusalem acted in ignorance in asking for Jesus' death (Acts 3:17; 13:27). They were ignorant of the meaning of the Scriptures and of the plan of God. Until the encounters with the risen Messiah, the disciples will show the same ignorance. This is not Jesus' intention. He tries to enlighten them, to no avail. This builds suspense in the narrative.

Some interpreters understand the statement, "It was hid from them that they might not understand it," as indication that God prevented the disciples from understanding.[39] While the passive formulation may hint at divine involvement, I would caution against the assumption that human resistance is not an important factor at this point in the narrative. If a divine purpose is involved, it is a purpose which works in and through human resistance, for which humans remain responsible. Such a view would fit the Lukan conception of God's work in the passion events, a topic which must be discussed later.[40] For the present, note that the narrator's remark about the disciples parallels Jesus' statement about Jerusalem: the things leading to peace "were hid from your eyes" (19:42).[41] In spite of this statement, Jerusalem will suffer punishment for its blindness. If we assume that 9:45 does not tarnish the image of the disciples, since God did not intend them to understand at this point, we depart from the viewpoint of Jesus, for he clearly wants and expects the disciples to understand now ("Put into your ears these words"). The tension between Jesus and the disciples at this point highlights the reality and seriousness of the disciples' blindness, which dominate the scene even if there is a hint that God can use human blindness for a divine purpose.

There was no shift of setting in 9:43. Again there is no shift of setting as the narrator introduces the dispute about greatness (9:46–48). Does this suggest that there is some connection between the disciples' failure to understand the Son of Man's way of suffering and their fascination with greatness? Jesus' response when the same dispute reappears at the meal before his death supports this supposition, for with his death impending he makes clear that he is taking the role of servant, which is the opposite of the greatness that the disciples seek (22:24–27). It is those who do not

[39] See, e.g., R. Dillon, "Previewing Luke's Project," 216, who lists other commentators.
[40] See below, pp. 282–89.
[41] The same verb is used in 19:42 as in the narrator's statement about the disciples in 18:34.

understand Jesus' degrading role of servant, most strikingly revealed in his suffering, who would engage in disputes about greatness. Jesus attempts to correct them. However, the problem will persist as long as the disciples fail to understand the suffering Messiah. Just after Jesus proclaims that "everyone who exalts himself will be humbled, and the one who humbles himself will be exalted" (18:14), the disciples will refuse to receive the children being brought to Jesus (18:15–17), and on the eve of Jesus' death they are again arguing about who is the greatest. So in 9:44–48 two major and continuing problems surface, problems which show that the disciples are not yet ready for the role which they must assume in the future.[42] In part, the teaching of Jesus in the rest of Luke is a struggle against these stubborn problems.

John's statement about the exorcist who is not part of their group (9:49) is a response (ἀποκριθείς, "answering") to what Jesus has just been saying about receiving the child and the least being great. Just as with the children in 18:15–17, the disciples want to "hinder" or "forbid" (κωλύω) the exorcist. These observations suggest that the exorcist is an example of the kind of person discussed in 9:48, the "least" or the child who must be received. Although he is not part of the itinerant mission, his work is validated. For this exorcist, just as for the missionaries in 10:16, receiving him means receiving Jesus (9:48). Here we have another indication that John and his fellows have not understood Jesus. They are concerned with their own power and control, while Jesus defends the importance of the "least" who work in his name.

The relation between Jesus and his disciples is strained as Jesus begins his journey to Jerusalem. We will continue to follow developments in the complex relationship between Jesus and his disciples in the next part of this chapter.

Luke 9:51–12:53
and Related Instruction of the Disciples

The Beginning of the Jerusalem Journey

The disciples or would-be disciples are prominent in 9:51 to 10:24. In this section, Jesus' journey to Jerusalem shapes the role of the disciples, for they are presented as either sent before Jesus to prepare his way as he journeys or as called to follow him on his journey. Journeying with Jesus is an important experience which the narrator emphasizes by taking note of the special group of "those who came up" with Jesus "from Galilee to

---

[42] On these two problems, see further pp. 254–57, 277–78, 282–89.

Jerusalem" (Luke 23:49, 55; Acts 13:31; see also Acts 1:21). Those who journey with Jesus not only receive his teaching but receive power to heal and share Jesus' experience of rejection. The common tasks and trials contribute to a pattern of mission experience that first characterizes Jesus and then his witnesses, resulting in parallels between them. Later this pattern of mission experience will pass from those who accompanied Jesus to Stephen and Paul, extending the series of parallels.[43]

Readers of Luke have been carefully prepared for the statement in 9:51 that Jesus "set his face to go to Jerusalem" (see 9:22, 31, 44). This is a turning point in the narrative only in the sense that action is initiated to fulfill a destined role that has already been revealed. Beginning with 9:51, there are repeated references to journeying, sometimes with a reminder that Jerusalem is the goal (9:53; 13:22, 33; 17:11; 18:31; 19:11, 28), and repeated references to the rejection, death, and resurrection that will happen there (12:49–50; 13:33–34; 16:31; 17:25; 18:31–33; 19:14), giving a sense of narrative movement and tension to a long section of Luke's Gospel that otherwise would become a static collection of teachings. The phrase "when the days of his ascension were coming to fulfillment" suggests the fulfillment of divine purpose through the climactic events in Jerusalem.[44] The reference to "the days of his ascension" both indicates the importance of Jesus' heavenly exaltation and encompasses the whole of the last phase of Jesus' story by indicating in advance the event that will bring it to a close.

When Jesus begins his journey to Jerusalem, the disciples receive a new task, as 9:52 indicates: "He sent messengers before his face," who enter a village "in order to prepare for him." While 9:52 might refer to a single occasion, in 10:1 this task is enlarged and generalized. A large group of disciples is involved, and they are sent "before his face to every city and place where he was going to come." I will comment further on the implications of this for the role of the disciples when I discuss the mission discourse in Luke 10. In preparation for that, it is important to note that language borrowed from 7:27 (a scriptural quotation applied to John the Baptist) is applied to disciples in 9:52. Particularly striking is the application of ἀγγέλους ("messengers" but elsewhere "angels") to human beings, which is rare in Luke-Acts (only 9:52, 7:27, and 7:24, which introduces Jesus' discourse about John). This is followed in 9:52 by "before his face," which also reminds us of 7:27. Being sent "to prepare" for another is also characteristic of John the Baptist (1:17, 76; 3:4; 7:27). The narrator, by the adoption of this language, is suggesting a significant

---

[43] See further in vol. 2.
[44] Cf. Acts 2:1, which introduces the fulfillment of the promise of the Spirit.

similarity between the role of the disciples in this new phase of Jesus' journeys and the role of John the Baptist.

Jesus' journey to Jerusalem begins with a report of his rejection in a Samaritan village, just as the narrative of his public ministry began with his rejection in Nazareth (4:16–30). The placement of rejection scenes at such key points puts special emphasis upon them. The Samaritans reject the one who has "set his face to go to Jerusalem" (see 9:53 with 9:51); thus they reject him because of a basic lack of understanding of the divinely determined destiny which Jesus must fulfill in Jerusalem.[45] Other passages suggest that this rejection may have serious consequences. The Samaritans do "not receive" him just as other cities will "not receive" Jesus' messengers (10:10), which brings them under the condemnation expressed in 10:12, apart from the possibility of a later repentance. Jesus' messengers also experience this rejection, and this experience becomes a test for the disciples. The proposal of James and John to use their new miraculous power to destroy these opponents is rebuked by Jesus. So the indications of the disciples' failures which we noted in 9:32–50 continue into the beginning of the Jerusalem journey. As in 9:46–48, 49–50, Jesus must correct an abuse of the power that he has granted to the twelve.

In making their suggestion, James and John use language which recalls what Elijah did in destroying the king's troops (2 Kgs 1:10, 12, 14). Since the deeds of Elijah have provided a positive precedent for the work of Jesus (see 4:25–26; 7:11–17), resulting in the crowd's recognition that Jesus, too, is a "great prophet" (7:16), the disciples' proposal might seem to have scriptural support. However, there are a series of incidents in Luke 9 which distinguish both Jesus and the behavior required of his followers from Elijah. While the crowds identify Jesus with Elijah, Peter's confession is better (9:19–20). The disciples are mistaken when they think that Moses, Elijah, and Jesus are to be equally honored (9:33–36). And Jesus not only rebukes the disciples when they want to destroy their enemies as Elijah did but also denies the request of a would-be disciple to do what Elijah permitted Elisha to do: say farewell to his household before following his new master (see 9:61–62 with 1 Kgs 19:19–21). Thus the Elijah stories are being used critically. Elijah is not only prototype but also antitype, and the contrast receives strong accent in Luke 9. However, if the sending of "messengers before his face" in 9:52 and 10:1 relates to Mal 3:1, a prophecy which is linked at the end of Malachi to the return of Elijah,[46] then not only John the Baptist but also

---

[45] D. Tiede, *Prophecy and History*, 61, comments, "Jesus is rejected on precisely the terms in which his firm resolve has been expressed."

[46] On the relation of Luke 7:27 (which is recalled by both 9:52 and 10:1) to Mal 3:1, see J. Fitzmyer, *Luke I–IX*, 674.

Jesus' disciples share the role of the eschatological Elijah who will restore the people before the day of the Lord comes.[47]

In 9:57–62 three brief encounters between Jesus and candidates for discipleship provide opportunity for clarification of the requirements of discipleship. In each case Jesus corrects the candidate by heightening the requirement beyond normal expectations, using forceful and imaginative language.[48] These encounters fit the journey setting in which they are placed. They take place "while they were going on the way" and the theme word "follow" is repeated in each of them. Jesus' responses indicate the necessary conditions for traveling missionaries whose mission is urgent. The Son of Man and his disciples have no place to lay their heads because they have been refused hospitality in the Samaritan village, but Jesus also speaks of this as an experience that is likely to be repeated for those who follow him on his journey, which suggests that the previous story of rejection discloses a characteristic situation. Following does not mean remaining constantly with Jesus, for in 9:60 Jesus commands the candidate to "go away and proclaim God's reign" (dif. Matthew). The missionary task is in mind, just as in the sending of the twelve and the seventy-two. This section reveals some of the severe demands that the task imposes.

This section is related to 9:23 through the theme word "follow" and the emphasis on the severe conditions for following. It also presents dramatic instances revealing the implications of leaving all in order to follow Jesus, as in 5:11, 28. While 9:23–24 highlights the threat to life which results from following, 9:57–62 focuses on the required sundering of the relation with home and family. Both of these difficult requirements will be the subject of further teaching in the Jerusalem travel narrative, along with parting from possessions. The special importance of these three demands on Jesus' followers appears from the fact that they are enumerated in three parallel sayings in 14:26–27, 33, which provides emphasis through summary and review. What will happen at the end of the journey—being "rejected" in Jerusalem (9:22)—is anticipated at the beginning of the journey when Jesus is "not received" (9:53), and Jesus' messengers will have the same experience as they carry out their mission (10:10). The suffering and rejection at the end of the journey, clearly announced since 9:22, cast their shadow over the journey as a whole and darken the picture

---

[47] The "ascension" or "assumption (ἀνάλημψις)" of Jesus in 9:51 is probably also related to the final story of the Elijah cycle, in which Elijah is "taken up (ἀνελήμφθη)" into heaven (4 Kgdms 2:11). The same word is applied to Elijah is Sir 48:9 and 1 Macc 2:58, as noted by Michi Miyoshi, *Der Anfang des Reiseberichts*, 9.

[48] On forceful and imaginative language in 9:57–62, see R. Tannehill, *Sword of His Mouth*, 157–65.

of following Jesus. The severe demands in 9:23–26, 9:57–62, and 14:25–35, sections of teaching that are related to each other, give emphatic expression to the requirements of discipleship now that Jesus has "set his face to go to Jerusalem." In connecting discipleship with Jesus' journey to rejection and death, the narrator is not merely depicting a unique situation of Jesus' time. The clear suggestions of parallels between Jesus and Paul as they journey to suffering in Jerusalem[49] indicate that dedication to the mission may require similar suffering and renunciation from Jesus' later witnesses.

The Mission of the Seventy-Two

Through placing 10:1 before 10:2–16, the narrator has combined the theme of mission with that of journey to Jerusalem. The statement, "He sent them . . . before his face," is a clear recall of 9:51–53, the beginning of the Jerusalem journey. The mission of the seventy-two takes place under the conditions of the journey to suffering and rejection. The narrator is also presenting a picture of expanding mission. In 9:1–6 twelve were sent out "to proclaim God's reign and to heal." Now seventy-two are sent on a similar mission and receive similar instructions. The type of mission in which the twelve have already engaged will now be carried out more extensively. This second mission by disciples in Luke also shows the narrator's interest in missionaries other than the twelve. The mission of the twelve has priority in time, but the mission of the seventy-two is the occasion for a more extensive discourse, including very strong statements of joy, fulfillment, authority, and revelation in 10:17–24 which make the return of the seventy-two a high point in the experience of the disciples.

The story of Jesus and his disciples journeying to Jerusalem will not depict gradual progress toward religious fulfillment and adequacy as disciples. Instead, the passion story will emphasize the inadequacy of Jesus' followers, followed by a dramatic change in their situation and abilities. It is at the beginning of the journey to Jerusalem, in connection with the mission of the seventy-two, that the narrator emphasizes the powerful gifts that Jesus' messengers have received and speaks of the mission in ways that foreshadow the mission in Acts.

The choice between the textual variants "seventy" and "seventy-two" in 10:1 and 17 is notoriously difficult and has confused the question as to the possible symbolic implications of the number of the missionaries. It is clear that twelve is a significant, not an arbitrary, number in Luke-Acts,

---

[49] See Acts 19:21 with Luke 9:51 and Acts 21:11 with Luke 9:44, 18:32. On the extensive parallels in depicting Jesus' and Paul's journeys, arrests, and trials, see Walter Radl, *Paulus und Jesus im lukanischen Doppelwerk.*

for the twelve apostles correspond to the twelve tribes of Israel (22:30). Seventy or seventy-two may also be significant and foreshadow the mission which moves beyond Israel. To be sure, a reference to the seventy elders who were appointed to share the burden of Moses' work and receive some of his spirit (Num 11:10–17) makes good sense in Luke's context, since Jesus is sharing his own mission with his disciples. However, the reading "seventy-two" seems preferable, since it is an unusual number while seventy is common in the Old Testament,[50] and this makes a reference to the seventy elders less likely.[51] Seventy-two agrees with the number of the nations of the world according to the LXX of Genesis 10, the number of the elders who prepared the LXX according to the Epistle of Aristeas 46–50, and the number of the princes and languages in the world according to 3 Enoch 17:8, 18:2f., and 30:2.[52] If seventy-two is the original reading, it seems likely that a hint of the future universal mission is intended. The technique used here would resemble Acts 2:9–11, where a long list of nations foreshadows the universal mission within the context of the mission to Jews in Jerusalem. This significance of seventy-two would also fit the fact that there are points of contact between the mission depicted here and the mission in Acts, especially the mission of Paul. Uncertainty remains, for the number seventy-two, even though the rarer of the two numbers, could have entered the manuscript tradition secondarily from the desire to relate Luke 10 to the view that there are seventy-two nations of the world.

As previously noted, the statement that Jesus "sent messengers before his face" in 9:52 is related to 10:1 and also to the scriptural description of John the Baptist in 7:27, suggesting some connection between the role of Jesus' messengers and the role of John the Baptist.[53] The significance of this becomes clearer when we note that (1) the narrator also suggests similarities between the work of John the Baptist and the work of the missionaries in Acts, especially Peter and Paul, and (2) these similarities are one aspect of a group of similarities between Luke 10:1–24 and the mission as described in Acts. I will discuss these two points in the order listed. Together they will show that aspects of Luke 10:1–24 provide a model for the mission of the church in Acts.

The disciples in 9:52 and the seventy-two in 10:1 are, like John,

---

[50] See Kurt Aland in Bruce M. Metzger, *A Textual Commentary*, 151.

[51] M. Miyoshi, *Der Anfang des Reiseberichts*, 61, 79, points out that the story in Numbers 11 continues by reporting that Eldad and Medad also received the spirit in the camp. Thus it is possible to arrive at seventy-two by inference. However, the story itself speaks of seventy elders.

[52] Noted by I. H. Marshall, *The Gospel of Luke*, 415.

[53] See above, pp. 229–31.

messengers who prepare for Jesus' coming and are "sent . . . before his face." This relates to a major aspect of John's role, for he is repeatedly described as the one who will "go before" the Lord and "prepare" his "way" (1:17, 76; 3:4). The wording in 9:52 and 10:1 indicates that, following John's death (see 9:9), the disciples take over John's function. In the situation of Jesus' ministry, this function can be depicted as physical movement, with the disciples literally going before Jesus on his journey to prepare for his coming. Their task goes beyond securing lodging for the night, for the seventy-two are missionaries who proclaim God's reign. The theme of going before Jesus disappears in Acts, but other themes associated with John the Baptist, themes which express the religious significance of John's task of going before and preparing, take its place. For instance, John was described as "proclaiming a baptism of repentance for release of sins" in 3:3. The exact phrase "repentance for release of sins" ($\mu\epsilon\tau\acute{a}\nu\omega\iota\alpha$ $\epsilon\dot{\iota}s$ $\ddot{a}\phi\epsilon\sigma\iota\nu$ $\dot{a}\mu\alpha\rho\tau\iota\hat{\omega}\nu$) reappears, again with the verb $\kappa\eta\rho\acute{\upsilon}\sigma\sigma\omega$ ("proclaim"), in the commission of the disciples by the risen Messiah at the end of Luke (24:47).[54] In Acts 2:38 baptism is also associated with repentance and release of sins, as in Luke 3:3. The question, "What should we do?" introduces Peter's response in Acts 2:38. The same question is asked of John in Luke 3:10, 12, 14. Peter goes on to urge his hearers, "Be saved from this crooked generation" (Acts 2:40), applying to his audience the words in Luke 3:5-6 (a quotation from Isaiah) about the "crooked" ($\sigma\kappa o\lambda\iota\acute{o}s$ in both Luke and Acts) and the "salvation of God." Thus Peter's call to repentance at Pentecost is a reawakening of the message of Jesus' forerunner.

Furthermore, reminiscences of John and his mission reappear in connection with Paul. In Acts 13:10 Paul accuses the Jewish false prophet of "twisting the straight ways ($\tau\grave{a}s$ $\acute{o}\delta o\grave{v}s$ . . . $\tau\grave{a}s$ $\epsilon\dot{\upsilon}\theta\epsilon\acute{\iota}as$) of the Lord," another use of the Isaiah quotation in Luke 3:4-5. Even more striking is the fact that Paul, in the climactic trial scene before King Agrippa, summarizes his own mission in language that recalls the mission of John. Like Peter, Paul was sent to call people to repentance so that they might receive the release of sins. In describing this mission, Paul uses a further phrase that recalls the message of John ("doing deeds worthy of repentance," Acts 26:20; cp. Luke 3:8), and the phrase "to turn from darkness to light" in Acts 26:18 combines themes that first appeared in connection with John ($\dot{\epsilon}\pi\iota\sigma\tau\rho\acute{\epsilon}\phi\omega$, "turn," Luke 1:16-17; light in place of darkness, Luke 1:78-79).[55] Finally, the references to a "way of salvation" and "the

---

[54] The variant reading which substitutes $\kappa a\acute{\iota}$ for $\epsilon\dot{\iota}s$ is widely attested, but $\epsilon\dot{\iota}s$ is supported by manuscripts of high quality (P75, Sinaiticus, Vaticanus).

[55] See also Luke 2:30-32, a statement that is related both to Acts 26:18, 23 and to the descriptions of John that I have mentioned. Note "salvation," "prepared," "light."

way of the Lord" in Acts 16:17, 18:25 show the continuing influence of the Isaiah quotation used to introduce the work of John. While John the Baptist passes from the scene after Luke 7:18–35, his role continues. The followers of Jesus continue central aspects of the mission and message of John, a mission and message which are not obsolete. The recall of Luke 7:27 in 9:52 and 10:1 provides a first hint of this.[56]

The missionaries in Acts not only continue the work of John but also the work of the seventy-two, for there are points of similarity between Luke 10:1–24 and descriptions of the mission in Acts which have nothing to do with John the Baptist. Not only does the mission of healing and proclaiming God's reign in Luke 10:9 continue in Acts,[57] but also the two possibilities of acceptance and rejection discussed in the instructions of Jesus (Luke 10:8–12) are repeatedly realized in the mission of Paul. The narrator was aware of this connection and wished the readers also to be aware of it, as is shown by the report of Paul and Barnabas "shaking off the dust of the feet" in response to rejection (Acts 13:51; see also 18:6), which follows instructions given in Luke to both the twelve and the seventy-two (9:5; 10:11). Jesus' instructions to the seventy-two concern two possibilities: either a city will "receive" the messengers (using δέχομαι), or it will not "receive" them (Luke 10:8, 10; see also 9:5). No distinction is made between receiving their message and receiving them as persons, i.e., offering hospitality, for it is assumed that the two will go together.[58] The same language is applied to Jesus in Luke, for he also must endure the insecure life of the traveling missionary. The Samaritan village did not "receive" him (using δέχομαι, 9:53); neither did Nazareth, where Jesus was not δεκτός ("acceptable," 4:24). However, Martha (10:38) and Zacchaeus (19:6) did receive (ὑποδέχομαι) Jesus. In Acts, similar language is applied both to receiving the word or witness (δέχομαι, 8:14; 11:1; 17:11; ἀποδέχομαι in 2:41; παραδέχομαι in 22:18) and to receiving a missionary as a guest (ὑποδέχομαι in 17:7; ἀποδέχομαι in 18:27; 21:17; ἀναδέχομαι in 28:7; παραδέχομαι in 15:4). This vocabulary set is used more frequently in Luke-Acts than in the rest of the New Testament combined. The importance attached to hosts and hostesses who receive missionaries in their houses is indicated by the fact that they are frequently named, although they rarely have any further part in the

---

[56] It is possible that the word ἀναδείκνυμι ("commission," "appoint") in 10:1 is a further point of contact with John, for 1:80 speaks of John's ἀνάδειξις ("commissioning" or "manifestation") to Israel. Both words are rare in the New Testament, the former being used only twice, the latter appearing only in Luke 1:80.

[57] Philip and Paul also proclaim God's reign. See Acts 8:12; 19:8; 20:25; 28:23, 31.

[58] The contrast between receiving or not receiving Jesus' messenger in 10:8, 10, reappears in 10:16, but now Jesus speaks of "the one who hears you," i.e., responds to the message. In 8:13 Jesus speaks of those who "receive the word."

narrative.[59] Thus the concern with whether persons or places do or do not "receive" missionaries and their message, expressed in Luke 10:8, 10, is also characteristic of the rest of Luke-Acts.

Furthermore, the dialogue in 10:17–19 also has points of contact with the mission in Acts. The seventy-two rejoice that "the demons are subject to us in your name" (10:17), and in Acts the "name" of Jesus Messiah continues to be associated with healing and exorcism (3:6; 4:10, 30; 16:18; 19:13). Jesus responds by announcing that Satan has fallen and that he has given his messengers "authority . . . over all the power of the enemy" (Luke 10:18–19). Paul will continue the attack on Satan's power, for he was sent to turn people "from the authority of Satan to God" (Acts 26:18, one of only two references to Satan in Acts) and subdues a false prophet who is described as "son of the devil, enemy of all righteousness," i.e., a representative of the devil's power (Acts 13:10). In Luke 10:19 Jesus also promises that "nothing will harm you," and later the apostles confirm that, although they were sent out without provisions or means of protection, they lacked nothing (Luke 22:35). In Acts the divine protection of the missionaries is presented dramatically through stories of rescue from prison and shipwreck (5:17–26; 12:6–11; 16:25–40; 27:9–44). Paul sums up his own experience by reporting the Lord's promise of rescue and confirming that he has received "help from God until this day" (Acts 26:17, 22).[60] There is not sufficient similarity of language to prove that the Acts passages mentioned in this paragraph are specifically recalling Luke 10:17–19. Perhaps we should say that the passage in Luke and those in Acts share certain mission themes which the narrator liked to emphasize. The passages in Acts also suggest how the narrator may have translated statements like Luke 10:17–19 to fit the continuing mission of the church.

The narrator describes John the Baptist, the "messengers" that Jesus sent "before his face," and the missionaries in Acts in ways that suggest a continuing, shared function and a continuing set of attendant experiences. In Acts indications of this continuity are especially strong in key scenes, for the most striking clusters of reminiscences of John's mission are found at the end of Peter's Pentecost speech (Acts 2:37–40) and in Paul's final summary of his call and mission (26:16–23).

First Jesus proclaimed God's reign and healed while his disciples accompanied him. Then he sent the twelve to proclaim and heal. Now seventy-two are given this task. This sequence depicts an expanding

---

[59] See Henry J. Cadbury, *The Making of Luke-Acts*, 252–53. On hospitality for missionaries in Luke-Acts see also R. Dillon, *From Eye-Witnesses*, 238–40.

[60] The narrator calls attention to the correspondence between Jesus' promise of protection and actual events in Acts by repeating the language of Luke 21:18 in Acts 27:34.

mission. The seventy-two not only share Jesus' work of proclaiming God's reign and healing but also are representatives of Jesus, the bringer of peace. In Acts 10:36 Peter declares that God was "preaching good news of peace through Jesus Messiah," and the birth stories affirm that the coming of Jesus the Messiah means peace (Luke 1:79; 2:14). While the way of peace will not be recognized by Jerusalem (19:42), the narrator notes instances in which Jesus is the conveyor of peace to individuals and to the disciples as a group (7:50; 8:48; 24:36). The instructions to the seventy-two concerning the peace greeting in 10:5–6 should probably be understood in light of the other passages in Luke-Acts in which peace represents salvation. The seventy-two are Jesus' instruments in bringing this peace to homes and towns, where it will either be accepted or rejected.

In spite of the words of threat and condemnation in 10:12–15, which emphasize the rejection that Jesus and his messengers are encountering, the return of the seventy-two is a scene of joy and triumph (10:17–24). There are no indications of failure or inadequacy on the part of the messengers. Even the minor correction in v. 20 does not break the mood, for it points to a greater reason for rejoicing. This is a high point in the disciples' story, a scene in which Jesus' messengers appear with much of the power and insight that they demonstrate in Acts. Their gifts probably include a clear recognition of Jesus as God's Son, for v. 22, which refers to the secret of the Father and the Son, is surrounded by statements which emphasize what has been "revealed" to Jesus' followers and what they "see." They see the coming of God's kingdom and with it also the presence of the promised king and Son of God, the one whom the prophets and the "kings" (dif. Matthew) of the Davidic line longed to see. Thus the Sonship of Jesus, confirmed to Jesus at his baptism and revealed to three apostles at the transfiguration, has also been revealed to the seventy-two.[61] To them, the "babes," this has been revealed, while it is hidden from the wise, an indication that Simeon's words about "falling and rising" (2:34) and Mary's words about the reversal of the proud and the lowly (1:51–53) are being realized. Nevertheless, the weaknesses of the disciples which appeared in chapter 9 have not yet been overcome, for signs of weakness will soon reappear. Despite the power and insight that the seventy-two have demonstrated, the disciples are not yet ready for the mission in Acts.

Instruction in Prayer

The disciples are partially aware of their needs, as their requests for

---

[61] Jesus' status as Son of God and Davidic Messiah are closely related in Luke-Acts. See above, pp. 25–26, 55. The phrase "who is the Son" in 10:22 (dif. Matthew) indicates that the revelation concerns Jesus' special identity. M. Miyoshi also recognizes a Christological aspect to the revelation in this passage. See *Der Anfang des Reiseberichts*, 140–41.

instruction in prayer (Luke 11:1) and for increased faith (17:5) show. Jesus has repeatedly been presented in prayer before decisive moments in the story (see 3:21; 5:16; 6:12; 9:18, 28). In 11:1 observing Jesus at prayer prompts one of the disciples to ask him to instruct them in prayer, so that they can share in what was obviously an important aspect of Jesus' life.[62] The instruction that follows in 11:2–13 takes this recognized need as a sign of a whole range of needs, for Jesus speaks of the prayer of supplication, in which the needy must repeatedly approach God and ask for what they lack. The disciples in prayer will be like impudent people asking for bread in the middle of the night, or like a boy asking his father for food (11:5–13), petitioners for basic needs.

The instruction on prayer looks back to what the disciples have already received and forward to what they will receive after Jesus' exaltation. On the one hand, it presupposes that the disciples, like Jesus, can address God as Father. That God is Father for the disciples is emphasized at both the beginning and end of Jesus' prayer instruction (11:2, 13). On the other hand, Jesus encourages the disciples to pray for a gift which they will only receive at a later time, the Holy Spirit (11:13). There is an unusual concentration of references to God as Father and to the Holy Spirit in 10:21–12:32. Neither is frequently mentioned between Jesus' Nazareth sermon and the passion-resurrection account, except in this section. Repeated reference to these two key terms suggests that the narrator understands 10:21–22 as a fundamental announcement of matters with lasting importance, involving not only Jesus' special relation as Son with the Father but also the special relation of the disciples to God as Father through Jesus. Because Jesus the Son chose to reveal it to them, the disciples now know "who the Father is" (10:22). In 11:1–13 Jesus begins to teach them to relate to God as Father in prayer, explaining that the Father can be trusted to give the children what they need. After further instruction of the disciples, Jesus reminds them of their special relation to the Father in 12:30–32, using words which echo passages which we have just noted: "Your Father knows that you need ($\chi\rho\acute{\eta}\zeta\epsilon\tau\epsilon$ [cf. 11:8]) these things. But seek ($\zeta\eta\tau\epsilon\hat{\iota}\tau\epsilon$ [cf. 11:9–10]) his reign, and these things will be added to you. Fear not, little flock, for your Father has decided with pleasure ($\epsilon\mathring{v}\delta\acute{o}\kappa\eta\sigma\epsilon\nu$ [cf. 10:21]) to give you [cf. 11:13] the reign."[63] The Father to whom the disciples are told to pray for bread and that God's

---

[62] Wilhelm Ott, *Gebet und Heil,* 94–99, emphasizes that Luke presents Jesus in prayer as an example for others.

[63] According to James D. G. Dunn, there is a close connection between 11:13 and 12:32, for "the Kingdom and the Spirit are alternative ways of speaking about the disciples' highest good" and "the presence of the Spirit is the 'already' of the Kingdom." "Spirit and Kingdom," 38. See also Stephen S. Smalley, "Spirit, Kingdom and Prayer in Luke-Acts," 59–71; C. Talbert, *Reading Luke,* 130–31.

reign might come (11:2–3) is the Father who knows their needs and who has already graciously decided that they will receive a place in God's reign.

When Jesus the Son thanked the Father for the revelation to the disciples, he "rejoiced in the Holy Spirit" (10:21). The disciples have not yet received the Holy Spirit, but in his instruction on prayer Jesus makes clear that this is a gift which the Father can be trusted to give to the children who ask for it (11:13; dif. Matthew). This sudden reference to the Holy Spirit as the Father's special gift is striking. The disciples begin to receive this gift at Pentecost, and Luke 11:13 is an anticipation of this event. Indeed, the language used to describe the Spirit in Luke 24 and in Acts serves to remind the reader of the promise in Luke 11:13 that "the Father . . . will give Holy Spirit." For Acts refers repeatedly to the "gift ($\delta\omega\rho\epsilon\acute{a}$)" of the Holy Spirit (2:38; 8:20; 10:45; 11:17), and, as Pentecost approaches, Jesus repeatedly refers to the Holy Spirit as the "promise of the Father" (Luke 24:49; Acts 1:4; cf. 2:33). It is in Luke 11:13 that we are first told that the *Father* will give the Holy Spirit. This is not the first anticipation of the granting of the Holy Spirit to the disciples (see Luke 3:16 with the reminders in Acts 1:5; 11:16; 19:1–7), but it is an important anticipation which relates the gift of the Holy Spirit to God's loving concern for the disciples as God's children.

At the proper time the disciples will receive the gift of the Spirit by asking their Father for it, that is, by asking God in prayer. Acts 1:14, 2:1–4, 4:23–31, 8:14–17, and 9:11–17 indicate that the Spirit comes to the believers following prayer. The Spirit is also the disciples' guide and strength when facing opposition. Jesus makes this clear in the next section of disciple instruction in Luke (see 12:11–12), thereby explaining further the significance of the Spirit for which the disciples should pray. Because of the Spirit the disciples will not need to "be anxious" when they face hostile authorities, and Jesus goes on to tell the disciples that they need not be anxious about food and clothing either (12:22–29), closing with words in 12:30–32 which recall 11:5–13. These potential anxieties are anticipated in the prayer which Jesus teaches the disciples in 11:2–4. The disciples are to ask the Father that bread be given them day by day and that they not be led "into temptation ($\epsilon\grave{\iota}\varsigma\ \pi\epsilon\iota\rho\alpha\sigma\mu\acute{o}\nu$)." Among the "trials" or "temptations" with which the author is concerned are situations in which Jesus and his followers must face opposition, resulting in suffering. Both the way of Jesus and his followers are filled with such situations, for, in summary statements about their past ministries, Jesus speaks of his "trials ($\pi\epsilon\iota\rho\alpha\sigma\mu o\acute{\iota}$)" which the apostles have shared (Luke 22:28), and Paul speaks of the "trials ($\pi\epsilon\iota\rho\alpha\sigma\mu o\acute{\iota}$)" which he has suffered "by the plots of the Jews" (Acts 20:19). Jesus prepares his disciples for such trials in

Luke 12:4–12, which ends with the promise of the Spirit's assistance. Thus a major part of the answer to the petition concerning temptation or testing may be the Father's gift of the Holy Spirit, promised in 11:13 and 12:11–12. In a later situation of danger, Jesus will instruct his disciples to "pray not to enter into temptation" (22:40; dif. Matthew, Mark; see 22:46). Jesus has already prepared for this by his instruction on prayer in 11:4.[64]

The petition for the coming of God's reign (11:2) prepares for the eschatological instruction in 12:35–48, which also concerns a crucial future coming, that of the Son of Man (12:40). Thus the petitions for the coming of God's reign, for bread, and for escape from temptation lead into instruction about eschatological watchfulness, anxiety for food, and faithfulness in persecution when Jesus next returns to teaching his disciples (12:1–12, 22–53). The petition for forgiveness, of course, also relates to a Lukan theme,[65] but this is not a central concern of Luke 12. Jesus' instruction on prayer, therefore, indicates some of the disciples' primary needs, which they are to bring to God in prayer, and prepares for further instruction concerning those needs in later sections of the Jerusalem travel narrative. Luke 12:1–12, 22–53 is an unusually comprehensive attempt to increase the disciples' deficient understanding concerning key areas of need, most of which are mentioned in the Lord's Prayer, while developing and applying the image of God as the Father who can be trusted to meet the needs of the children and give them the Holy Spirit, themes introduced in 11:5–13.

Jesus' Instructions to Disciples in Luke 12

Luke 12:1–13:9 is a single discourse, given at a single time and place but including material directed to two different audiences (the disciples and the crowd) and covering three or four topics. The word "first" in 12:1 is a signal to the reader that more than one topic (or audience) will be included in the discourse. This long discourse, segmented by shifts in topic and audience, is similar in structure to other long discourses during Jesus' journey to Jerusalem. Thus all of 15:1–17:10 is apparently spoken on a single occasion, as the narrator presents it, for there are no indications of change of time or place, nor of events which would require Jesus to conclude his speech and leave.[66] A large proportion of the material in the Jerusalem journey section of Luke is discourse by Jesus, and Jesus'

---

[64] Note that the instructions concerning prayer urge Jesus' followers to pray to escape πειρασμός (11:4; 22:40, 46), while retrospective passages acknowledge that it has been part of the experience of Jesus and his followers (4:13; 22:28; Acts 20:19).

[65] See pp. 103–9.

[66] Luke 8:4–21 is, perhaps, a less fully developed example in the earlier section of Luke. Luke 6:20–49 also contains some indications of segmentation.

addressee is almost always indicated. The discourse segments sometimes begin with only a brief indication of the audience to whom Jesus is speaking, as in 12:22, 54. Frequently, however, a segment begins by indicating a specific provoking cause, which may be the attitude or behavior of some group, or a statement, request, or question from someone. In other words, these discourse segments begin like pronouncement stories, which have two basic parts: the provoking occasion and the response that results.[67] Indeed, some of them are pronouncement stories with additional material attached, expanding Jesus' response into a longer discourse. The Jerusalem journey section of Luke contains a number of pronouncement stories of the typical short length, but it also contains a number of these pronouncement story settings with extensive responses. As Gerhard Sellin has noted,[68] these brief narrative frames are the way in which Luke has turned speech material into narrative. Jesus' discourse is broken up into sections, and variety is introduced by the inclusion of brief dialogues and shifts of audience. A sense of narrative setting is preserved, for Jesus is repeatedly interacting with surrounding individuals and groups. There is a rough rotation among sections addressed to the disciples, the crowd or individuals from it, and the scribes or Pharisees. The shift of addressee may be the occasion for a shift of topic, but Jesus sometimes continues to speak on the same topic while relating it to the new audience (see 12:22–34 after 12:13–21; 16:14–15, 19–31 after 16:1–13), or he may begin to speak on a new topic to the same audience (note the shift at 12:35). Jesus speaks *extempore*, according to the impression given by the narrator, for he is responding to those around him. His words have the sharpness of speech directed to a target rather than aimlessly into a vacuum. Rather lengthy sections are divided only by these minimal indications of a new addressee or a new stimulus to Jesus' speech.

When a specific cause of Jesus' discourse is suggested (something more than the indication that Jesus is speaking to a new group), the types of interaction that take place correspond to types of pronouncement stories. Jesus may respond to a request or inquiry (including some testing inquiries) by giving an answer, he may respond to an objection, or he may correct someone's action, statement, or the assumption behind a question or request.[69] Thus Luke 11, which is not a continuous discourse like 12:1–

---

[67] See R. Tannehill, "The Pronouncement Story and Its Types," 1–6; Tannehill, "Types and Functions of Apophthegms," 1792–96.

[68] Gerhard Sellin, "Komposition, Quellen und Funktion," 112.

[69] These correspond to types of pronouncement stories which I have labeled inquiry stories, objection stories, and correction stories. See my articles just mentioned. There are also commendation and quest stories in the synoptic gospels. The important group of Lukan quest stories is discussed on pp. 111–27.

13:9, is divided into three major sections in which Jesus speaks to three different groups: the disciples (vv. 2–13), sections of the crowd (vv. 17–26, 28, 29–36), Pharisees and scribes (vv. 39–44, 46–52). The first section is introduced by a request from a disciple; the second by both an objection (v. 15) and a testing inquiry (v. 16), to which Jesus responds in turn; the third section is introduced by an objection from a Pharisee and is divided by a further objection from a scribe (v. 45). In Luke 12, vv. 13–21 begin with a request from one of the crowd, which is corrected by Jesus, while vv. 41–53 begin with an inquiry from Peter. A report from the crowd of a specific event begins 13:1–9, and Jesus responds by correcting a possible false impression. An inquiry by "someone" introduces 13:23–30, while 15:1–32 begins with an objection by Pharisees and scribes. An objection by the Pharisees also initiates Jesus' words in 16:14–31. In 17:20–21 Jesus gives a corrective response to the Pharisees' question about the coming of God's reign and then continues with a discourse to the disciples about the coming of the Son of Man. It is also worth noting that many of Jesus' discourses contain parables, which relate to the topic of the discourse but are slightly set off from the rest by a new discourse tag such as "and he said" (καὶ εἶπεν, εἶπεν δέ, ἔλεγεν δέ; cf. 11:5; 12:16; 13:6; 15:11; 18:1). Jesus is interacting with three principal groups: the disciples, the Pharisees and scribes, and the crowd or representatives of it. He shifts from one group to the other as he speaks and is spoken to.

In his discourse in 12:1–13:9, Jesus warns the disciples concerning hypocrisy (12:1–3), admonishes them about the opposition they must face (12:4–12, separated from the preceding by a new statement of address, "And I say to you my friends"), quiets their anxiety about basic material needs and asks them to give away their property (12:22–34), urges them to be faithful in light of the coming of the Son of Man (12:35–48), and warns them of the coming crisis, which will involve division in families (12:49–53). Jesus introduces the teaching about material needs and property by a warning to the crowd about the desire to accumulate property (12:13–21) and continues the eschatological warnings to the disciples with eschatological warnings to the crowd (12:54–13:9). Thus the words addressed to the crowd are related in topic to the instruction of the disciples, which predominates in this discourse.

Jesus' instruction in this discourse is unusually comprehensive, embracing four topics (persecution, loss of possessions, the judgment of the returning Lord, conflict with family) which are repeated subjects of disciple instruction in Luke. All four are difficult challenges which the disciple must face now or in the future. Although these topics are not usually discussed in a single discourse and given such extensive develop-

ment, admonitions concerning two or three of these topics do tend to
cluster in Luke, indicating relations among them. Thus the challenge to
discipleship in 14:25–35 refers to conflict with family (14:26), threat to
life through persecution (14:27; see 9:23–26), and loss of possessions
(14:33) in parallel statements. The warning to the disciples concerning
the unexpected coming of the Son of Man in 17:26–30 points to concern
with family and business as an indication of unpreparedness. This is
followed by a warning not to be concerned about one's "things ($\sigma\kappa\epsilon\acute{\upsilon}\eta$),"
i.e. possessions, in the eschatological crisis (17:31–32).[70] Furthermore,
Jesus' eschatological teaching in Luke 21, with which Luke 12 has some
close links (see below), includes warnings concerning persecution and
conflict in families (21:12–19) and admonitions not to be weighed down
"with cares of daily life ($\mu\epsilon\rho\acute{\iota}\mu\nu\alpha\iota\varsigma\ \beta\iota\omega\tau\iota\kappa\alpha\hat{\iota}\varsigma$)" but instead to "keep awake
at every time" (21:34–36). The future will bring persecution and conflict
with family, while faithfulness in persecution and detachment from
family and possessions are part of the watchfulness which the sudden
return of the Son of Man requires, and so these topics easily mix with
eschatological teaching in Luke 12 and 21. The repeated return to these
topics, often in combination, in the Jerusalem travel narrative involves
both clarification and reinforcement. The narrator prefers returning to
major topics of teaching repeatedly, rather than grouping related teaching
in a single discourse, thus reinforcing through recurrence and suggesting
that Jesus was repeatedly engaged in this type of teaching. When Jesus
keeps returning to the same topics, we realize that he is not dealing with
momentary concerns but with weighty matters of lasting importance.

The disciples (and the readers) have already been introduced to some of
the themes of disciple teaching developed in Luke 12, for Jesus has
already demanded that disciples be willing to give their lives (9:23–26)
and make a clean break with home and family (9:57–62). The narrator
also carefully noted that some disciples left all to follow Jesus (5:11, 28),
while Jesus described both the failure to stand firm in a time of testing and
"cares and riches and pleasures of life" as dangerous causes of the seed
failing to produce a harvest (8:13–14). The development of these themes
in Luke 12, however, will begin to prepare for the story of the post-
Pentecost witnesses in Acts by using language at some points which fits
the narrative there.

I will not be able to discuss in detail all of Jesus' instruction to the

---

[70] I. H. Marshall notes that "precipitate flight will be out of the question when the Son of man
appears, and so the saying must here be taken metaphorically: attachment to earthly things
will lead to disaster." *The Gospel of Luke*, 664.

disciples on the way to Jerusalem and in Luke 21. Instead I will use 12:1–53 as a base and, in discussing it, will note similar material in the later portions of Luke (and Acts). This approach should clarify the ways in which some important themes persist and develop in Jesus' teaching.

Hypocrisy and Persecution (Luke 12:1–12). Although 12:1–12 begins a new scene, Jesus' initial themes are related to events just narrated. These events cause Jesus to warn his disciples. First they are warned against the hypocrisy of the Pharisees (12:1). Jesus had exposed the Pharisees' hypocrisy in 11:39–41, 44, and now this attack on hypocrisy is applied to the disciples. The Pharisees' hypocrisy shows the disciples what to avoid. The teaching in 12:4–12 is also appropriate in light of preceding events, for 11:14–54 shows Jesus in sharp conflict with some members of the crowd and then with Pharisees and lawyers. The scene with the Pharisees and lawyers ends with these groups showing aggressive hostility toward Jesus and looking for an opportunity to catch him.[71]

As this hostility is developing, the crowds have become immense (literally, "tens of thousands," 12:1). Jesus, however, is not fooled by this popularity. The hostility of opponents will control events in the future, and Jesus seeks to prepare his disciples by warning them against fear of "those who kill the body" (12:4). Shortly before, Jesus had spoken of the sending of prophets and apostles (dif. Matthew), some of whom "they will kill and persecute" (11:49), and he accused the lawyers of complicity in this. The disciples must be prepared to take their place among these persecuted prophets and apostles. Hence the teaching in 12:4–12.

Luke 12:4–34 is tied together by word links which highlight central themes. In addressing the disciples, Jesus is trying to counter two kinds of fear (note $\phi o\beta \acute{e}o\mu a\iota$ in 12:4, 5, 7, 32) or anxiety ($\mu\epsilon\rho\iota\mu\nu\acute{a}\omega$ in 12:11, 22, 25, 26). Threatening opposition may cause fear (12:4, 7) and anxiety (12:11). Lack of provision for food and clothing may cause anxiety (12:22, 25, 26) and fear (12:32). Jesus responds to these fears by pointing twice to God's care of birds and flowers, asserting that "you are of more value ($\delta\iota a\phi\acute{e}\rho\epsilon\tau\epsilon$)" than they are (12:7, 24). In addition, the teachings on possessions to the crowd and to the disciples both end by referring to "treasure" or "laying up treasure" (12:21, 33–34). These observations indicate that 12:4–34 is an integrated discourse and that the central problem being addressed in the disciple teaching of this section is the fear

---

[71] The $\grave{e}\nu$ $o\grave{i}s$ ("at which things" or "during which things") at the beginning of 12:1 connects what follows with the threatening situation at the end of Luke 11. As J. Fitzmyer, *Luke X-XXIV*, 954, explains, $\grave{e}\nu$ $o\grave{i}s$ means "in the situation created by what precedes, in the context of the plotting against him."

and anxiety which arise both from hostility of outsiders and from lack of security concerning basic provisions for life.

Luke 12:4–12 reinforces the teaching in 9:23–26 which Jesus gave immediately after the first passion announcement. This is especially clear because the saying about confessing or denying Jesus in 12:8–9 recalls the similar saying in 9:26. These doublets serve a literary function within the narrative: they remind the reader of previous teaching and tie together related sections of teaching which are separated by intervals. Luke 12:8–9 also anticipates events in the narrative, providing a basis for recognizing their importance and a norm for evaluating the actions of characters. These words underline the seriousness of Peter's denial, which, apart from Jesus' special intervention (22:32), would mean loss of salvation for Peter. The connection is suggested by the fact that after 12:9 the two words for "deny" (ἀρνέομαι and ἀπαρνέομαι) recur in Luke only in connection with Peter's denial (22:34, 57, 61). On the other hand, the trial scenes in Acts, in which Peter, Stephen, and Paul confess their faith in Jesus, contrast with Peter's denial, and Stephen's vision of the Son of Man in Acts 7:55–56 has a specific link with Luke 12:8.[72] The very rare use of the title Son of Man outside the gospels connects Stephen's vision with the promise in Luke 12:8 that the Son of Man will confess those who confess Jesus and with Jesus' words in Luke 22:69 concerning the Son of Man's position at God's right hand. The vision of Stephen is assurance that Jesus is able and willing to keep his promise that he will confess before God the one who confesses him at great cost.

Two other promises of Jesus in Luke 12:4–12 play a role in the following narrative. According to 12:7, "Even the hairs of your head are all numbered." Therefore, the disciples need not fear. Twice more "hair" is mentioned in statements about God's protective care. In 21:18, after a statement which recalls 12:11–12, Jesus declares, "Not a hair of your head will perish." Since this follows a statement that "they will put some of you to death," it evidently refers metaphorically to a preservation beyond death. In Acts 27:34 Paul repeats this promise of protected hair to his shipmates, referring to rescue from physical harm. The escape from the storm which follows is witness to the trustworthiness of this promise. Thus the hyperbole of the protected hair appears in various contexts where divine protection and rescue are important, a sign, perhaps, that this figure caught the author's imagination.[73]

---

[72] Josef Zmijewski, *Die Eschatologiereden des Lukas-Evangeliums*, 166–68, discusses this connection.

[73] Henry J. Cadbury lists the two sayings about hair in Luke 21:18 and Acts 27:34 as examples of Lukan style, which favors "repetition (with variation) at widely separate and unrelated passages." See "Four Features of Lucan Style," 95–97.

Even more significant for the following narrative are Jesus' words in Luke 12:11–12. The disciples are not to be anxious about making their defense before authorities, for the Holy Spirit will help them. A similar command and promise are found in 21:12–15, and the two passages find their fulfillment in the arrest and trial scenes in Acts. The verb ἀπολογέομαι ("speak in defense") occurs in both passages in Luke, and in both the disciples are promised that, if they allow it, their defense will come from a higher power than themselves. Apart from two occurrences in the Pauline letters, this verb is found exclusively in Luke-Acts in the New Testament. In Acts this verb, and its related noun, are primarily used in connection with the trials and speeches of Paul following his arrest in Jerusalem. However, Jesus' promises are being fulfilled even earlier in Acts as Peter and Stephen speak before the authorities. When Peter addresses the Sanhedrin in Acts 4:8, he is "filled with the Holy Spirit," in fulfillment of Luke 12:11–12. According to Acts 4:14, the authorities are unable to "speak in reply (ἀντειπεῖν)," in fulfillment of Luke 21:15. Faced with opposition, the whole church is filled with the Holy Spirit and speaks God's word with boldness (Acts 4:31). The description of Stephen in Acts 6:10 ("They were not able to resist the wisdom and the Spirit with which he was speaking") combines features of Luke 12:12 and 21:15, and in Acts 7:55 we are again told that Stephen was "full of the Holy Spirit." The narrator is concerned with showing the fulfillment of Jesus' promises in the life of his witnesses and repeats key words and phrases in order to indicate the connection between promise and fulfillment.

Possessions (Luke 12:13–34). In 12:13 Jesus is interrupted by "someone from the crowd," which permits a shift of topic to instruction on possessions. Jesus first replies to the individual and then addresses the crowd in general. The disciples, however, have not been forgotten, for Jesus turns to them in 12:22, still speaking on the subject of possessions. The teaching in 12:22–32 reflects the special situation of the disciples, who have left home and livelihood to follow Jesus, have been sent out without provisions (9:3; 10:4), and are now traveling with Jesus, dependent on the hospitality of strangers. This hospitality is sometimes refused (9:52–56) and may seem even more difficult to find after the hostility which Jesus produced in the home of his last host (11:37–54). So Jesus speaks to the insecurity of those who do not know where their next meal is coming from (12:22–32). The preceding words to the crowd in 12:13–21 may also have some relevance to the disciples, for in 12:33–34 Jesus addresses to the disciples a fundamental command that would apply to the rich farmer but also to all disciples who still have disposable property: "Sell your possessions and give charity." "Treasure in the heavens" will result, but this requires rejection of the rich fool's attempt to "lay up treasure" for himself (12:21). Thus the rich fool provides a warning for disciples as well as the crowd. This warning is also supported by the contrast between the foolish farmer planning to build bigger "barns (ἀποθήκας)" and Jesus' words to the disciples about the ravens, who "do not sow nor reap, who do not have storeroom nor barn" (12:24). If the disciples learn from the ravens, they will not fall back into the greed of the rich fool. Furthermore, Jesus will later instruct his disciples about possessions with a parable about a steward, who, like the rich fool, asks, "What shall I do? (τί ποιήσω)" (16:3; cf. 12:17), but, in contrast to the "fool (ἄφρων)" (12:20), acts "wisely (φρονίμως)" (16:8) by giving away property in his control. The disciples must be faithful and wise stewards (see 12:42 with 16:8, 10–12), not fools.

There are three major sections of teaching about possessions in the Jerusalem travel narrative (12:13–34; 16:1–31; 18:18–30). Each of these sections includes teaching both to outsiders and to the disciples. Repeated points in these three sections bring out central emphases in Jesus' teaching on this subject, and there is a connection between these emphases and the portrait of the early Jerusalem church in Acts, which had "all things in common" (2:44). Both Luke 12:31–32 and 33–34 are related to this later teaching. The command to the disciples in 12:33 ("Sell [πωλήσατε] your possessions and give charity"; dif. Matthew) is basically equivalent to Jesus' command to the rich man in 18:22: "Sell (πώλησον) all that you have and give to the poor." Thus the command to the rich man is a specific case of a general requirement for Jesus' followers during his ministry.[74] When Jesus instructs the disciples to "make friends by means of unrighteous mammon" in 16:9, he is making a similar point—possessions are to be given in charity to others—and being received "into the eternal habitations" corresponds to the "treasure inexhaustible in the heavens" in 12:33.

The command to "sell" and "give" (or "distribute") is not obsolete after Jesus' ascension, for the narrator portrays the life of the Jerusalem church in such a way as to indicate a particular kind of fulfillment of Jesus' command. The statement that the Jerusalem community was "having all things in common" does not mean that a new legal system was established, involving collective ownership, which would end the right of individuals to sell property. Rather, the narrator is depicting a regularized system of charity in which those with salable assets would liquidate their property in order to care for the needs of the poor (Acts 2:45; 4:34–37). The

---

[74] To be sure, Jesus specifies "all" when he speaks to the rich man, but this should not obscure the fact that in 12:33 and 18:22 we have a sequence of three shared elements: a command to sell possessions, distribute the proceeds in charity, resulting in "treasure in the heavens." Furthermore, 14:33 makes clear that saying farewell to "all" one's possessions is required of everyone who wants to follow Jesus as a disciple.

descriptions of this arrangement feature the words "sell" and "distribute" (using πιπράσκω and διαμερίζω in Acts 2:45, πωλέω and διαδίδωμι in 4:34–35), which correspond to the commands of Jesus in Luke 12:33 (πωλέω and δίδωμι) and 18:22 (πωλέω and διαδίδωμι).[75] Even though the situation of Jesus' followers has changed with the existence of a settled community, the early Jerusalem church found a way to obey Jesus' teaching about possessions in its new context. The repeated command of Jesus and this portrait of the earliest church show that the story places considerable emphasis on Jesus' radical teaching concerning possessions. We are repeatedly told that those with valuable assets are to sell them and distribute the proceeds to the poor, and this is further encouraged by making this an important feature in the portrait of an ideal community.[76]

Furthermore, the words of Jesus in 12:31 ("But seek his reign, and these things will be added to you") are probably related to Jesus' promise to the disciples which follows his words to the rich ruler. After a dialogue about those who have riches, Peter reminds Jesus in 18:28 that they have left τὰ ἴδια, which can mean both "home" and "possessions."[77] Jesus promises that those who have left house and family "for the sake of God's reign" will "receive manifold in this time and in the coming age eternal life." Although the promise for a reward "in this time" is vaguer than in the Markan parallel, the author may well have seen a realization of this promise, and of the promise that "these things will be added to you," in the vital community of the early church and the sharing of possessions which was part of it. The close connection of both Jesus' commands and promises with their fulfillment in the life of the earliest church, as Acts presents it, shows that it is a mistake to interpret Luke 22:36 as a permanent revoking of Jesus' radical teaching about possessions, which is no longer applicable to the life of the church.[78] To be sure, adaptations take place, for it is not assumed in Acts that all believers will abandon home and possessions in order to proclaim God's reign. Nevertheless, Acts portrays several possible ways in which believers may serve God rather than mammon under new conditions.[79]

Servants of the Returning Lord (Luke 12:35–48). At 12:35 Jesus moves into eschatological exhortation without indication of a break. This

---

[75] The reading διάδος differs from Matthew and Mark. The reading δός also has significant manuscript support but is to be explained as a secondary reading which conforms with the other gospels.

[76] On the relation of this portrait to ideals of the ancient Mediterranean world, see Jacques Dupont, *Salvation of the Gentiles*, 85–102.

[77] See BAGD, 370.

[78] On 22:36 see pp. 265–68.

[79] See further in vol. 2, and note the preliminary comments on Paul's attitude toward possessions in vol. 1, p. 250. On the rich and poor in Luke, see above, pp. 127–32.

is understandable in light of indications elsewhere that detachment from possessions and from cares of daily life is an important part of the readiness for the coming of the Son of Man which Jesus wishes to see in his disciples. Thus the closing exhortation of the eschatological discourse in Luke 21 contains these words: "Watch out for yourselves lest your hearts be weighed down with . . . cares of daily life" (21:34; compare 8:14: "cares and riches and pleasures of daily life"). Jesus also warns against these "cares" or "anxieties (μέριμναι)" when he tells the disciples in 12:22, "Do not be anxious (μὴ μεριμνᾶτε)." The eschatological instruction to the disciples in 17:26–30 warns that those destroyed at the times of Noah and Lot were occupied with business and family and so were caught by the sudden destruction. So not being anxious about food and clothing, as well as seeking heavenly treasure instead of earthly, is part of having one's "loins girded" in preparation for the master's return.

The eschatological instruction in 12:35–48 is not concerned with signs of the end. It is concerned solely with the meaning of the Lord's return for his servants who are charged with responsibilities. Since the Lord will come at the very time when he is not expected (12:40, 46), those who are not constantly ready and faithful will be caught in their misbehavior. A delay in the Lord's return is assumed (12:38, 45), but there is no sign that being surprised and caught by the returning Lord has become a remote possibility. The coming of the Lord still functions strongly in exhortation, perhaps partly because the expectation of the coming of the Son of Man in cosmic judgment is supplemented in Luke-Acts by an eschatology for the individual at each person's death.[80] Thus the unexpected encounter with one's master may occur either at the end of the age or after the individual's death, for Jesus will be "judge of the living and the dead" (Acts 10:42).

The promised reward for the watchful in 12:37 is striking. The statement that the servants will be those who recline as guests and the Lord will be the one who serves them is matched only by 22:27. Luke 22:27, however, is placed in the setting of the crucifixion. To picture the *returning* Lord as still serving gives this aspect of his work unexpected prominence. It suggests that service is a permanent characteristic of the Lord, even when he is exalted. Imagery which points to the eschatological banquet appears repeatedly in Luke 12–15 (see 12:37; 13:28–30; 14:15–24; 15:22–32). Here we have another basic image which stimulates the interest and imagination of our author, as well as the collective imagination of the community, as the repeated and varied uses indicate.

In contrast to Matthew's parallel, Jesus' discourse in Luke is broken by

---

[80] See Jacques Dupont, "Die individuelle Eschatologie," 37–47.

a question from Peter concerning the application of "this parable" (12:41). Jesus does not answer Peter's question directly, but he does go on to speak of a "steward" (dif. Matthew) who is charged with care of the master's servants, indicating that at least the words about the "master of the house" and the "steward" in 12:39–48 are directed to the leaders of the church. This concern to admonish the leaders of the church also appears in Jesus' farewell discourse the night before his death (22:24–38) and in Paul's farewell address to the Ephesian elders (Acts 20:18–35). These passages mention various abuses of position by church leaders. The reference to eating, drinking, and getting drunk in Luke 12:45 is similar to the warning to the disciples in general in 21:34, but 12:45 also warns against striking the servants, which may relate to the admonition to the apostles in 22:24–27 to be servants in their leadership, rather than like the kings of the Gentiles.

Although it is largely independent in wording, Paul's farewell to the Ephesian elders is remarkably close to Jesus' admonitions to church leaders in basic themes, an indication that Paul is being presented as the ideal church leader who fulfills Jesus' commands and therefore is an example to others. Rather than disputing with others about his own greatness (see Luke 22:24), Paul has been "serving the Lord with all humility" (Acts 20:19). His devotion to his task on behalf of the church is repeatedly emphasized, and the Ephesian elders are admonished to take their responsibility with equal seriousness. Paul also refers to his past (20:19) and future (20:22–24) sufferings, and he ends the speech by speaking of his attitude toward wealth (20:33–35). These major themes of faithful fulfillment of leadership responsibility, willingness to suffer, and a right attitude toward wealth are also the major themes of Jesus' discourse to the disciples in Luke 12:1–53. To be sure, Paul, in discussing wealth, does not speak of selling his possessions but of not desiring the possessions of others and of working to support himself and his fellow missionaries, while contributing to the needs of others. This can be understood as a flexible, but basically faithful, application of Jesus' teaching about wealth to a changed situation. Where there are established communities, impoverished church leaders might claim support from the church and thus become a burden on the community rather than contributors to the needs of others. Paul makes clear that this is not the path to follow. The Ephesian elders are also admonished to "keep awake ($\gamma\rho\eta\gamma o\rho\epsilon\hat{\iota}\tau\epsilon$)," using a word commonly found in eschatological exhortation in Matthew and Mark, but in Luke-Acts found only in this speech (Acts 20:31) and in Luke 12:37 (and perhaps 12:39). In Acts the eschatological context of this word is not apparent. Note also the similarity between Paul's commitment to "complete ($\tau\epsilon\lambda\epsilon\iota\hat{\omega}\sigma\alpha\iota$) my course" (Acts

20:24) and Jesus' eagerness that his baptism "be accomplished ($\tau\epsilon\lambda\epsilon$-$\sigma\theta\hat{\eta}$)" (Luke 12:50). In both discourses these elements point to the future destiny of the speaker, which involves suffering.

The type of exhortation which we find in 12:35–48 reappears in Jesus' later teaching to the disciples. Luke 19:12–27 is another parable that tells of servants entrusted with a responsibility of which they must give account on their master's return. If we include 12:35–48, there are three major sections of eschatological teaching in Luke. These three sections contain related themes. Luke 21 ends with exhortation similar to 12:35–48, for 21:34–36 warns that "that day" may appear "suddenly," so you must "keep awake." This exhortation can be brief because its key themes have already been developed more extensively in previous sections of the gospel. The unexpected coming of the Son of Man is also emphasized in 17:22–30, and, as we have seen, 17:26–32 contains a warning against attachment to things and involvement in business and family, thus combining ideas found in 12:22–34, 35–48, 51–53.

The Coming Crisis (Luke 12:49–53).   Toward the end of a rather long discourse, 12:49–50 instills a renewed sense of movement to the story as Jesus speaks passionately ("How I wish. . . . How I am distressed. . . .") and dramatically ("fire . . . baptism," both in first position in the Greek sentences) of a task which he must still accomplish. Jesus expresses the tension which he feels, giving the whole narrative a new sense of straining forward. This will be reinforced by Jesus' words about his divinely determined fate, soon to be accomplished, in 13:32–33. The "fire" in 12:49, although it may refer to the coming of the Spirit (see Acts 2:3), seems in this context to be a destructive force (note the reference to Jesus creating division in Luke 12:51). Thus it probably refers to the fire of judgment (3:9, 17; 9:54; 17:29), though not necessarily the final judgment. The parallel statement speaks of Jesus' "baptism," which is probably a metaphorical reference to death, as in Mark 10:38, since to be baptized or immersed can mean to be overwhelmed by some catastrophe.[81] The parallelism between vv. 49 and 50 suggests that they are describing two aspects of the same event; what is "baptism" for Jesus is "fire" for the rest of the world, which will be consumed by signs of God's judgment. If we remove the phrase "Do you think that . . ." from 12:51, we see that it also is formulated so as to parallel 12:49 and 50. Division in families is one of the signs of destruction and judgment that Jesus will cause. Such divisions are part of the crisis which Jesus, as the one "set for the fall and rising of many in Israel" (2:34), is bringing, a crisis which will come to a climax in the passion story but will also continue into Acts.

---

[81] See BAGD, 132 (*s.v.* 3c); I. H. Marshall, *The Gospel of Luke*, 547.

Fire, a baptism to be suffered, division in place of peace—Jesus speaks of them not as the unfortunate result of human blindness but as part of the commission which he came to fulfill. This extreme language emphasizes the inescapability of these experiences if God's plan is to be realized. Jesus asks the disciples, "Do you think that I have come to give peace on earth?" This question is significant, for Luke's portrait of the disciples suggests that they would think this. We have been shown that the disciples do not recognize that the Son of Man must suffer and be rejected (9:44–45), and their failure to grasp this essential aspect of God's plan will be reemphasized in 18:31–34. This is accompanied by premature eschatological hopes, as we will see. The disciples are presented as persons who desire and expect an immediate realization of the promises of salvation without suffering and rejection.

Among these promises is the promise of peace. The previews of God's purpose in the birth narratives would lead the reader to join the disciples in answering yes to the question, "Do you think that I have come to give peace on earth?" We were told that, through John and Jesus, God would "guide our feet into a way of peace" (1:79), and the angels at Jesus' birth proclaimed "on earth peace" (ἐπὶ γῆς εἰρήνη; cp. 12:51: εἰρήνην . . . ἐν τῇ γῇ). This promise of peace is not confined to the birth narrative, for in Acts 10:36 God's message to Israel is summarized in the phrase "preaching good news of peace through Jesus Messiah." Furthermore, Jesus' entry into Jerusalem is accompanied by two significant references to peace. However, these two references show an important modification of the hope expressed elsewhere. Instead of "on earth peace," we find "in heaven peace" (19:38), and Jesus weeps over Jerusalem because it will not find peace (19:42). A number of points of similarity in wording show that the scene of Jesus weeping over Jerusalem represents the tragic disappointment of the hopes expressed in Zechariah's Benedictus (1:68–79), including the hope for peace with which it ends.[82] The tragedy of Israel affects the disciples, too, as Jesus informs them in 12:51–53. Because of human resistance to God's purpose in Jesus, the promised peace does not come immediately. Therefore, the disciples must endure division and conflict. But God can use even division, conflict, and rejection for a saving purpose. This is something that the disciples must learn.

Since detachment from family is another repeated theme in Jesus' teaching about discipleship (see 9:57–62; 11:27–28; 14:26; 18:28–30), the inclusion of 12:51–53 helps to make Luke 12 a comprehensive discourse on central themes of Jesus' teaching to his disciples. However, in 21:16–17 conflict in families is part of the situation of persecution, and the

---

[82] See pp. 36–37, 159–60.

warning concerning this is preceded by words parallel to 12:11–12, so one might argue that Jesus ends his teaching to disciples in Luke 12 by returning to a theme of the beginning, the conflict and persecution which disciples must face. This conflict is forcefully presented with imaginative language in 12:51–53.[83] Such language shows that the disciples are not merely being given information about the future but are being challenged to realign basic goals and expectations in light of a reality which will affect them deeply. Jesus' words require difficult decisions, for they conflict with deep loyalties both for the disciples in the story and for its readers.

Evaluation of characters in a story is a constant and largely unconscious process in reading. The narrator is guiding us to evaluate characters and their actions according to norms established by the teachings of Jesus. We have already noted some specific evidence of this relation between teaching and story events. The warning about denying Jesus before people (12:9) requires a strongly negative evaluation of Peter's denial. On the other hand, when Peter, filled with the Holy Spirit, speaks boldly before the Sanhedrin in Acts 4:8–12, this fits Jesus' promise in Luke 12:11–12, which inspires confidence both in Peter and in the promise. The portrait of Paul in his farewell address in Acts 20:18–35, which corresponds to major themes in Jesus' teaching to the disciples in Luke 12:4–53, suggests a highly favorable view of Paul, which in turn indicates that Paul's life story is a faithful interpretation of God's purpose in Jesus. Jesus' teaching provides norms for evaluating events in the story, while events and characters in the story suggest ways in which Jesus' teaching can be interpreted and applied. This interaction of teaching and events needs to be kept in mind as we read the story.

THE DISCIPLES' DEFECTS
AND THEIR ROLE IN THE PASSION

Jesus' teaching and the disciples reaction to it highlight a cluster of interrelated problems in the preparation of the disciples for their future mission. We have already noted the great emphasis—even stronger than in the parallel passages in Mark—that Luke places on the disciples' inability to understand Jesus' announcements of his coming rejection and death (9:43–45; 18:31–34).[84] Overcoming this failure to understand will be a major concern of the messengers at the tomb and the risen Messiah on

---

[83] See R. Tannehill, *Sword of His Mouth*, 144–47.
[84] See above, pp. 226–27.

Easter day (24:6–7, 25–27, 44–46). This problem is connected with a cluster of problems which appear in the story of the disciples' preparation in Luke 9–23. These problems will be overcome together through the risen Messiah's revelation and the gift of the Spirit. The failure of the disciples to understand the necessity of Jesus' suffering and rejection involves the following interrelated defects: (1) a failure to understand God's plan as announced in Scripture, including God's way of working by using human opposition to fulfill the divine purpose; (2) a failure to accept rejection and suffering as a necessary part of discipleship; (3) a failure to reckon with the rejection of Jesus, resulting in premature, overly optimistic expectations for the immediate enjoyment of the messianic salvation; (4) rivalry over rank because of a failure to recognize that only those who devote their lives as servants can be great as Jesus is great. The first item will be discussed in the final chapter of this volume. The other three items will be discussed in this chapter.

Rivalry over Rank

I will begin by discussing the last of these points, which involves Luke's version of a theme that is also prominent in Mark, the disciples' disputes over greatness. The announcement of the passion in 9:44–45, in which Jesus' announcement is shorter than in Mark but the comment about the disciples' failure to understand is longer and stronger, is followed immediately by the disciples' first dispute about greatness. The two sections are tied more closely together in Luke than in Mark, for in Luke there is no indication of change of location or time as the topic shifts in 9:46. According to Luke, the dispute apparently arose immediately after Jesus announced his coming suffering. This narrative link suggests a connection between the failure to understand the Son of Man's suffering and the rivalry over position among the disciples. This suggestion will be confirmed by 22:24–27, for this second dispute about greatness occurs in the shadow of Jesus' death as part of the farewell discourse at the Last Supper (dif. Matthew, Mark). As Jesus goes to his death, it is fully clear that he is "the one who serves" (22:27), and Jesus' self-giving service of others and of God in his death is a powerful corrective example for the disciples' false ideas of greatness. In both scenes Jesus uses paradoxical words which link greatness to its opposite (9:48: least/great; 22:26: greater/younger; leader/servant), and, unlike Matthew and Mark, the two disputes in Luke begin in similar ways (verb . . . διαλογισμὸς [or φιλονεικία] ἐν αὐτοῖς τὸ τίς . . . μείζων), another literary indication of the link between the scenes.

Luke 9:46–48, then, is not an isolated unit but begins a narrative line. In it a problem surfaces, a persistent problem which will only be resolved when Jesus, through his death, demonstrates that he is the one who serves and, as the risen Messiah, opens the disciples' minds to God's ways. The problem introduces tension into the narrative, for the emphasis on this problem leads us to look for some way in which it will be resolved so that the disciples can fulfill their commission. The longer the problem persists, the stronger the tension becomes, especially when Jesus repeatedly corrects the disciples but the message is not heard. Even on the night before Jesus' death, the dispute about greatness reappears, as we have noted.

The disciples' rebuke of the children in 18:15–17 is also part of this portrait of defective discipleship, for in 9:48 Jesus made receiving a child the test of whether the disciples have understood that "the one who is least among you all, this one is great." Receiving the child in Jesus' name is equivalent to receiving Jesus and the one who sent him (9:48), which makes the child just as important as the missionary who speaks in Jesus' name (see 10:16). However, in 18:15–17, which follows Jesus' statement (dif. Matthew, Mark) that "everyone who exalts himself will be humbled, but the one who humbles himself will be exalted," the disciples rebuke the children, indicating that they do not recognize that the humble will be exalted nor that God's reign belongs to children. Again Jesus must correct the disciples, showing that his teaching about the child in 9:48 is not being heeded.

Jesus also tries to correct the disciples by warning them not to adopt the attitude and behavior of the scribes and Pharisees, who want to have the positions of honor. Jesus' rebukes of the scribes and Pharisees are applied to the disciples as warnings in 12:1 and 20:45–47. After the woes against the Pharisees and lawyers in 11:39–52, Jesus warns the disciples, "Take heed to yourselves because of the leaven of the Pharisees, which is hypocrisy" (12:1). Among the signs of hypocrisy for which Jesus excoriates the Pharisees is their love of "the first seat in the synagogues and the greetings in the market places" (11:43). This desire for a position of prominence also appears at dinner parties.[85] In 14:7–11, while eating in a "home of one of the rulers of the Pharisees" (14:1), Jesus corrects the guests' practice of choosing the "first couches" at the dinner. He concludes with an aphorism, "Everyone who exalts himself will be humbled, and the one who humbles himself will be exalted," which will be repeated at 18:14 after a parable about a Pharisee. Similarly, in 16:15 Jesus accuses the Pharisees of justifying themselves and warns that "what is exalted among humans is abomination before God."

---

[85] E. Springs Steele, "A Modified Hellenistic Symposium?" 384, notes as a parallel the dispute about positions at a symposium in Plutarch, *Dinner of the Seven Wise Men*, 148E–149B.

Luke 20:45–47 recalls previous criticisms of the scribes and Pharisees and utilizes them as a warning to the disciples. Luke makes clear that Jesus' warning is addressed to the disciples (dif. Mark), although Jesus is speaking in the hearing of the people. They are to "take heed" or "watch out" because of the scribes. It is their ways of acting that make them dangerous; the disciples must avoid acting in the same way. Jesus' warning functions as a summary and application to the disciples of the criticisms of the scribes and Pharisees previously noted. As in 11:43 we hear of "loving greetings in the market places and first seats in the synagogues." As in 14:7–11 we hear of loving "first couches at the dinners." The warning is expressed in the same way as the warning against the hypocrisy of the Pharisees in 12:1 ($\pi\rho o\sigma\acute{\epsilon}\chi\epsilon\tau\epsilon$ $\mathring{a}\pi\acute{o}$; dif. Mark), which applied 11:43 and other rebukes of the Pharisees to the disciples. Thus in addition to the other scenes in which Jesus tries to correct the disciples' desire for preeminence, these words against the scribes and Pharisees are brought to bear on this problem, serving as warnings not to act as these people do. In spite of this, the disciples at the Last Supper again argue over who is greatest.

In 17:7–10 Jesus also warns the "apostles" (specified as the audience in 17:5) that they should not expect special reward or honor for their services. When they return from plowing or shepherding, they will simply be asked to serve the meal, and none of this is anything more than they, as "unworthy servants," are obliged to do.[86]

The disciples' rivalry over preeminence also appears in Mark. But this theme is more extensively developed in Luke, where the accusations against the scribes and Pharisees, who enjoy positions of prominence, are turned toward the disciples as warnings about their own behavior. A special stamp is also placed on this theme by relating it to the meals which are featured in Luke. The dinner party in 14:1–24 becomes the occasion for corrective teaching about seeking positions of honor, and the final dispute about greatness takes place in the setting of a meal. At this meal, Jesus uses social roles at a dinner party to make his point, for, in contrast to $\mathring{o}$ $\mathring{a}\nu\alpha\kappa\epsilon\acute{\iota}\mu\epsilon\nu os$, the dinner guest who is served, Jesus describes himself as $\mathring{o}$ $\delta\iota\alpha\kappa o\nu\hat{\omega}\nu$, the servant who functions as waiter at the dinner (22:27). Jesus claims the role of the "one who serves" in relation to the apostles. In Luke this verb $\delta\iota\alpha\kappa o\nu\acute{\epsilon}\omega$ is always used of serving meals (with the possible exception of 8:3) and refers to the role which a woman or slave normally fills (4:39; 8:3; 10:40; 17:8). Jesus steps out of the position which he could

---

[86] Paul S. Minear, "A Note on Luke 17:7–10," 84–85, argues that the three activities ascribed to the servant in this passage correspond to duties commonly assigned to apostles in the early church and that the distinction between duties in the field and those in the house correspond to the distinction between the duties of traveling evangelists and sedentary deacons.

claim and assumes the lowly role of servant of others. In providing food, a servant is working at the behest of a master and is responsible to this master, as Jesus pointed out to the disciples in 12:35–48 and 17:7–10. In Acts διακονία ("service," "ministry") can refer to the commission which an apostle or Paul has received and must perform (see Acts 1:17, 25; 20:24; 21:19). Jesus also has a commission to fulfill, which includes going to his death "according to what has been determined" by God (Luke 22:22). Thus the role of Jesus as the "one who serves" may bring to mind not only his lowly service of others but also his devoted service of God. The context of Jesus' approaching death makes clear that it is especially in his death that both aspects of his serving are completed.

At the Last Supper Jesus speaks to the "apostles" (22:14) as those who are about to assume positions of leadership in the church. He does not speak of those who wish to become great, as in Matthew and Mark, but simply of those who are greater and are leaders (22:26), for the issue is not the general tendency toward ambitious striving but the standard of behavior for recognized leaders of the church. Even at this late hour, they show themselves impervious to Jesus' appeals to renounce the concerns of worldly kings and the desires of scribes and Pharisees. Nevertheless, Jesus proceeds to confer ruling power upon them (22:29–30), for he acts out of an awareness of the great change which is about to take place in the apostles through Jesus' death, resurrection, and sending of the Spirit.

Premature Expectations of Messianic Salvation

The disciples' failure to understand Jesus' announcement that he must suffer and be rejected is associated with another defect in their readiness for mission. Because they do not recognize the necessity of suffering and rejection, they falsely expect the final manifestation of God's reign in the near future. The failure to reckon with suffering and rejection leads them to be overly optimistic. The disciples hope and expect that the promises of salvation for Israel will be immediately fulfilled. Some of the passages which speak most clearly of an eschatological delay, suggesting to many scholars that this is a major concern of the author,[87] relate to this failure of the disciples to recognize that God's way of working in the world requires suffering from God's servants because they are exposed to rejection and that hopes which ignore this necessity are premature.

According to 17:22, the disciples will long to see "one of the days of the Son of Man" and will be disappointed. This verse must refer to disappointment of eschatological expectation, for the coming of God's reign and the Son of Man are the subjects of the whole of 17:20–37, and the

---

[87] See especially H. Conzelmann, *The Theology of St. Luke*, 95–136.

announcements associated with this disappointment in 17:23 ("Behold there; behold here") are announcements of eschatological fulfillment or of eschatological signs (see 17:21). Jesus may be speaking about the disciples' disappointment in the period after the departure of the risen Messiah.[88] However, the narrative indicates that false eschatological expectation will appear even before Jesus' departure. Indeed, the clearest indications of disciples actually expressing an imminent hope that is doomed to disappointment, as Jesus predicts in 17:22, are found in 19:11 and Acts 1:6, while Jesus is still present with the disciples. So the false expectations of which Jesus speaks already begin to show themselves as Jesus draws near to Jerusalem.

Jesus seeks to warn the disciples against such false expectations by declaring that the Son of Man's coming will be sudden and unmistakable, like lightning (17:24), and by adding, "But first he must suffer many things and be rejected by this generation" (17:25). This repetition of the passion announcements (see 9:22, 44) may seem out of place, but the narrator evidently regarded it as appropriate and important in connection with the disciples' false expectation. If the narrator were thinking directly of the problem of the parousia's delay in the time of the church, this statement would not speak to the problem. Since Jesus' suffering and rejection are already past for the church, they would provide no reason for delay. Jesus' passion announcement does, however, have a function within the narrator's developing portrait of the disciples. It suggests a connection between their failure to understand Jesus' passion announcements (9:44–45; 18:31–34) and their premature hopes, doomed to disappointment. Because they do not recognize that suffering and rejection are necessary parts of the realization of God's plan, they expect an immediate fulfillment of God's eschatological promises. Jesus is warning his disciples that approaching Jerusalem does not mean that God's reign is going to appear "immediately" (19:11); it means that Jesus is approaching rejection and death. Furthermore, rejection and persecution will be continuing parts of the developing mission in Acts. But disciples who expect God's reign to appear immediately upon Jesus' arrival in Jerusalem have no room in their minds for that kind of mission.

The false expectation that Jesus must correct is clearly indicated in 19:11, but the group which holds this expectation is not so clear. The unclear "they" who hold the mistaken opinion could refer to the disciples, the crowds, or both. However, only those who associate God's reign with

---

[88] "Days will come" is used in Luke in prophecies of events within future history. It is associated three times with the destruction of Jerusalem (19:43; 21:6; 23:29 [="days are coming"]). In 5:35 it is associated with the period after Jesus' departure, which might be similar to 17:22.

Jesus would expect it to come upon Jesus' arrival in Jerusalem. The narrator refers elsewhere to the disciples' eschatological longings and premature hopes (17:22; 24:21; Acts 1:6), and when Jesus does arrive in Jerusalem, the disciples (not the crowd) proclaim him as messianic king (Luke 19:37-38). Furthermore, parables which speak of servants entrusted with responsibility are applied to disciples in 12:35-48. Such servants reappear in the parable in 19:12-27. This evidence shows that the disciples are among those addressed in 19:11-27, and they are probably the primary source of the false opinion expressed in 19:11.[89]

Shortly before this scene Jesus had repeated his passion announcement to the twelve and had explicitly mentioned Jerusalem as the site of his rejection and death. But "they understood none of these things" (18:31-34). It is this lack of understanding which makes it possible for the disciples to attach a false expectation to Jesus' arrival in Jerusalem. They expect God's reign to appear when Jesus enters Jerusalem because they are thinking of Jesus as the Messiah who comes to his capital to establish the messianic kingdom for Israel. That is why the disciples are disappointed in 24:21 that the expectation for the redemption of Israel, first expressed by Zechariah (1:68), has failed, and that is why Jesus' resurrection awakes new hope of a kingdom for Israel (Acts 1:6). Important indications of God's purpose in Luke-Acts show that this hope is legitimate. A messianic kingdom for Israel with Jesus as king is part of God's purpose, not only as interpreted by Gabriel and Zechariah at the beginning of Luke (1:32-33, 68-71) but also as interpreted by Peter and Paul in Acts (2:30-36; 3:20-21; 13:22-23, 32-34). But the disciples who expect this messianic kingdom to appear immediately are overlooking the crucial role which rejection will play in the working out of God's purpose in history. So Jesus tells a story about a nobleman who went away to receive a kingdom, but his citizens hated him and tried to prevent him from becoming their king (19:14). This, of course, anticipates the passion story, where Jesus' prophecies of rejection are fulfilled while he is both proclaimed and condemned as king (19:38; 23:2-3, 37-38, 42). As in the passion announcements, Jesus in 19:11-27 is trying to get the disciples to face the reality of coming rejection.

---

[89] Luke Timothy Johnson believes that the parable in 19:12-27 is intended to confirm the expectation that the kingdom will appear immediately, for at his entry Jesus is proclaimed as king (19:38), and in the passion story there are further references to Jesus' kingdom (22:29-30; 23:42-43). See "The Lukan Kingship Parable," 139-59. While it is true that Luke associates the events at Jerusalem with Jesus' entry into royal power, the expectation expressed in 19:11 involves something more and (since it does not take account of rejection) something different. The disciples expect the redemption of Israel (24:21), i.e., the restoration of the kingdom to Israel (Acts 1:6). Because Jesus is rejected, this does not happen when Jesus is proclaimed king in Jerusalem.

What in the parable indicates that the kingdom for Israel is not going to appear immediately? The nobleman journeys "to a far country" (19:12), but otherwise the length of his absence is not emphasized. Is the opposition of the citizens a cause of delay in the coming of the messianic kingdom? While the parable does not distinctly indicate this, other passages support this view. In 19:41–44 Jesus weeps over Jerusalem because of its blindness, which will result in Jerusalem's destruction. Jerusalem fails to recognize "the time of [its] visitation" and "the things that make for peace." These are ways of speaking of the messianic salvation which Zechariah described in similar language (1:68, 79).[90] Jesus weeps for Jerusalem not only because of its coming destruction but also because this destruction replaces what rightfully belongs to Jerusalem and Israel by promise, the messianic kingdom. In 19:11 the disciples are pictured as expecting something that should have been and could have been apart from the rejection of Jesus. But because of this rejection, the messianic kingdom for Israel does not come immediately, as the disciples mistakenly hoped. We see that in Luke-Acts the problem of eschatological delay is intertwined with the problem of Jewish rejection.

Acts 3:19–21 supports this interpretation. There Peter makes clear that, even after the crucifixion, repentance by the Jerusalem Jews would result in the promised messianic kingdom. But repentance is the necessary precondition. Therefore, the call to repent is followed by a purpose clause: "Repent . . . in order that times of relief might come from the face of the Lord, and that he might send the Messiah chosen for you, Jesus, whom heaven must receive until the times of the restoration of all that God spoke through the mouth of his holy prophets from of old." The reference to "times of relief" and "restoration" make clear that this coming of the Messiah means Israel's salvation, not judgment, and the connection of the "times of restoration" to Acts 1:6 ("Lord, will you at this time restore the kingdom to Israel?") shows that the messianic kingdom is in mind.[91] Since this cannot happen apart from repentance, continued rejection of Jesus and his witnesses means delay.[92]

Luke 21:8, like 17:23, contains a warning against false eschatological teachers. Among their false teachings is the announcement, "The time has

---

[90] On the connection between Zechariah's Benedictus and Jesus' words over Jerusalem, see pp. 36–37, 159–60. The Benedictus makes clear that Israel's "peace" and "visitation" are aspects of the promised messianic kingdom, which involves the "house of David" and includes "salvation from our enemies."

[91] Acts 1:6–7 and 3:20–21 are linked not only by the unusual words "restore" and "restoration" but also by references to "times" and "seasons." While Jesus in 1:7 rebukes the disciples' concern about the time, he does not reject their hope for a messianic kingdom.

[92] See Ernst Haenchen, *The Acts of the Apostles*, 208: "Thus the conversion will . . . hasten the Parousia."

drawn near" (21:8). The disciples[93] are not corrected by insisting that Jesus must suffer and be rejected "first," as in 17:25, but they are warned that "before all these things" they must face rejection and persecution (21:12–19). Here, too, there is a warning against premature eschatological expectation which points to the prior reality of rejection, in this case rejection of the disciples themselves.

Why would the narrator want to highlight the disciples' hope for immediate fulfillment at Jerusalem, a hope which the readers would know to be false? Several concerns are probably at work here. First, the disciples' false hope plays a role in Luke's story of the tragedy of Israel. Through the disciples is expressed what could have been and should have been, apart from Jewish rejection, which heightens the sense of tragic loss. The fact that the disciples are sympathetic toward Israel, are eager to have its hopes fulfilled, encourages readers to a similar sympathy and thus to feelings of tragic loss.[94] Second, by tracing a change in Jesus' followers from deficient to powerful discipleship, the narrator is able to use them as models of what the church and its leaders should be and also as warnings of what to avoid. By presenting disciples with defects, the narrator is able to gently address later believers with similar failings. By showing the change that will take place in the first disciples, the narrator shows how later believers should change. Some of the points of failure in the disciples before the resurrection reappear in new forms in the church. This evidently includes false eschatological expectations (Luke 17:23; 21:8). Third, the narrative repeatedly emphasizes that God works by reversing human plans. History in Luke-Acts is not a monologue by God; it is a dialogue between God and humans. But in this dialogue the human contribution repeatedly turns out to mean something different than the human actors anticipated. This is the case with rejection, which does not halt God's purpose but simply moves it in a new direction. The disciples have great difficulty in understanding how rejection and the realization of God's purpose can fit together. Their difficulty was no doubt shared by later members of the small and threatened community. Through the disciples' difficulty and through their later insight and courage, the narrator gradually reveals a vision of God's working in the world and shows how this vision inspires faithful and effective mission in spite of continuing rejection.[95]

---

[93] Fridolin Keck rightly argues that the discourse in Luke 21 is primarily addressed to the disciples, although it is given in public with the people listening. The addressees are indicated in 20:45, and they do not change in Luke 21. See *Die öffentliche Abschiedsrede Jesu,* 22, 29–35, 56–57, 67–69.

[94] On the tragedy of Israel in Luke-Acts, see further pp. 34–37, 153–56, 159–63, 280–81.

[95] On this vision of God's working in the world, see further pp. 282–89.

Unwillingness to Face Death

We have discussed the disciples' continuing problems with rivalry over rank and with premature eschatological hopes, and we have noted that these problems are associated with their inability to understand the necessity of Jesus' suffering. There is a third major defect in the disciples' readiness for mission at this point in the story, and this is also associated with their blindness to the place of rejection and death in Jesus' mission. This defect concerns their own willingness to accept rejection and death in Jesus' name. Those who cannot understand the divine purpose behind Jesus' rejection and death cannot understand rejection and death as part of God's purpose in their own lives. Their failure at this point appears in the passion story, and it is highlighted by the words of Jesus at the Last Supper, which expose several kinds of unfaithfulness in the apostles.

Comparison of Luke with Mark's very negative portrait of the disciples in the passion story has led some scholars to assert that Luke is protecting the disciples by weakening material that puts them in a bad light.[96] It is true that Luke makes clearer than Mark that the disciples' failure is temporary, and the negative portrait is softened in some details. Nevertheless, the portrait of the apostles in the passion narrative remains essentially negative, and Luke even has additional material which emphasizes the apostles' failure.

Schuyler Brown argues at some length for a contrary view.[97] According to Brown, Luke's Gospel depicts the apostles' "unbroken faith during the Age of Jesus," which includes "the perseverance of the apostles during the passion."[98] Brown admits that Luke's portrayal of the apostles "is by no means always complimentary"[99] but argues that they maintain a Christological faith, i.e., a basic belief in the fact of Jesus' Messiahship, and that this is crucial for Luke's view of the apostles. While it is true that Jesus prays that Peter's faith "may not give out ($\mu\grave{\eta}$ $\grave{\epsilon}\kappa\lambda\acute{\iota}\pi\eta$)" (22:32),[100] isolating a Christological belief which can exist apart from faithful discipleship imposes a distinction that has little basis in the text. It is better to say that Peter's denial and Jesus' crucifixion are not the end of Peter's faith because the risen Messiah revives it. Brown's thesis results in some strained interpretations of passages, including his assertion that

---

[96] E.g., Günter Klein feels safe in arguing that Luke 22:31–32 is not a Lukan formation because it stands in tension with Luke's presentation of the disciples elsewhere, "which is notoriously aimed at a weakening of the disciples' denial." See "Die Verleugnung des Petrus," 303.

[97] See *Apostasy and Perseverance*, 53–81.

[98] *Apostasy and Perseverance*, 56, 62.

[99] *Apostasy and Perseverance*, 72.

[100] On the meaning of $\grave{\epsilon}\kappa\lambda\epsilon\acute{\iota}\pi\omega$ in this verse see Wolfgang Dietrich, *Das Petrusbild*, 130–33.

24:11 does not show a failure of the apostles' faith, for there they only disbelieve the women.[101] If they disbelieve the women, they also disbelieve their message, the message of the resurrection and the reminder of the necessity of Jesus' death. Indeed, after Jesus' death it is only possible for the apostles to believe that Jesus is the Messiah if they can accept a Messiah who dies in fulfillment of God's purpose, something impossible for them until their minds are opened by the risen Messiah.

Luke 22:21–62 depicts a broad ranging crisis in the relation between Jesus and the apostles due to a series of interrelated failures in following Jesus. Much of Jesus' farewell discourse at the table—a major feature of Luke's account which distinguishes it from Matthew and Mark—is devoted to exposing the faithlessness of the apostles, which in part is already manifest in their behavior and in part is predicted by Jesus and soon realized. Jesus moves directly from his words over the meal to the announcement of the betrayal (22:21–23). While in Matthew and Mark this announcement produces grief and self-examination (Matt 26:22; Mark 14:19), in Luke it causes a dispute in which the apostles are searching for the villain. This leads directly to the dispute about greatness in 22:24, for self-defense against a charge leads easily to claims of superiority. This dispute highlights the apostles' persistent failure, even in the last hours before Jesus' death, to heed Jesus' previous teaching about the least being great.

The farewell discourse also marks an important transition in the lives of the apostles. Whether or not 22:14–38 technically belongs to a recognized genre which can be called "farewell discourse" or "farewell address,"[102] Jesus' words are uttered in light of his impending death and with awareness of the new situation which the apostles are entering, as appears in the command to "do this for my remembrance,"[103] the effort to prepare the apostles for their new role as leaders in 22:24–27, and the gift of a share in Jesus' royal power in 22:28–30.

The End of the Farewell Discourse (Luke 22:31–38). Jesus' words in 22:31–38 expose the apostles' faithlessness in facing the possibility of their own deaths. In 22:31 Jesus speaks of Satan's plan to "sift" the apostles "like wheat." Earlier the narrator reported that Satan had entered into Judas (22:3). Now Satan is at work in all the apostles. The apostles still have a chance to escape Satan's temptation,[104] for at the Mount of Olives

---

[101] S. Brown, *Apostasy and Perseverance,* 74–75.

[102] William S. Kurz believes that it does. See "Greco-Roman and Biblical Farewell Addresses," 251–68. See also Jerome Neyrey, *The Passion According to Luke,* 5–48.

[103] According to the longer text of 22:19–20. On the textual problem see B. M. Metzger, *A Textual Commentary,* 173–77. J. Fitzmyer, impressed by the external witnesses which support the longer text, has joined those who adopt it. See *Luke X–XXIV,* 1387–88.

[104] On the devil as tempter see 4:2, 13.

Jesus commands them, "Pray not to enter into temptation" (22:40; see 22:46). Instead they fall asleep and lose their chance. They are trapped by Satan's temptation, as their behavior shows. So when Jesus says to the arresting crowd, "This is your hour and the power (ἐξουσία) of darkness" (22:53), it is not only Satan's work in Judas which demonstrates the power of darkness but also Satan's power to "sift" the other apostles and expose their faithlessness.

Jesus' response to Satan's plot is to pray for Peter (22:32: "you" in v. 32 is singular, whereas it is plural in v. 31). This indicates that Peter will have a key role in the restoration of Jesus' followers to faithful discipleship following Jesus' death. The focus of Jesus' prayer on Peter also indirectly indicates that the other apostles are temporarily left to Satan's power. Even Peter is not protected from critical failure by Jesus' prayer. Jesus simply prays that this failure will not be the final end of his faith. Later the risen Messiah will help to fulfill this prayer by appearing to Peter. That Peter, too, is involved in faithless behavior is made clear, first, by Jesus' reference to Peter "turning back," and, second, by the connection with 22:33–34, the prophecy of Peter's denial. Peter's denial is an especially dramatic example of broken loyalty to escape danger. The verb ἐπιστρέφω ("turn," "turn back") is repeatedly used in Luke-Acts of a major change in religious orientation, a conversion, which is closely associated with repentance.[105] Thus this verb suggests the seriousness of Peter's fall. While Peter's denial provides an especially striking example of failure in faithfulness, he is not alone in this. When Peter experiences his reformation, he is to strengthen his brothers, including the other apostles, who evidently will be in great need of help.[106] The prediction of Peter's denial is preceded by Peter's assertion that he is ready to go with Jesus to prison and death. This proves to be a false pledge. It makes Peter's denial all the worse. Peter not only rejects Jesus' command to fear God rather than those who kill the body (12:4–5) and ignores his threat to those who "deny me before humans" (12:9), but he lies to outsiders and fails to make good on his pledge to Jesus. It is unlikely that the narrator is trying to distinguish between the denial mentioned in 12:9 and Jesus'

---

[105] Luke 1:16; Acts 3:19; 9:35; 11:21; 14:15; 15:19; 26:18, 20; 28:27. The references to Satan and the power of darkness in Luke 22:31, 53 make Acts 26:18 an especially striking parallel: "to turn (ἐπιστρέψαι) from darkness to light and from the power of Satan to God."

[106] S. Brown, *Apostasy and Perseverance*, 72, understands "your brothers" to refer to Christian disciples, who are to be strengthened by Peter and the other apostles. It is true that "brothers" in Acts often refers to the Christian community as a whole, and in 11:1 the apostles are named alongside them. However, "brothers" can also refer to a group which includes the apostles. See Acts 1:15, 16; 15:7, 13, 23. Since Luke 22:31 refers to Satan's sifting of the apostles, it is probable that they are also the brothers who need to be strengthened in 22:32.

prediction that Peter will "deny to know me," as if this were a lesser offense. In the recall of Jesus' words in 22:61, we simply find "deny me," and the unique placement in Luke of 12:10, with its promise of forgiveness to the one who speaks against the Son of Man, probably indicates that the narrator is aware that 12:9 applies to a case like Peter's.

The narrator presents Peter's denial in detail and with dramatic impact. While Luke does not contain Mark's reference to Peter swearing (Mark 14:71), the emphatic, threefold structure of the episode appears in both, and the final moment is powerfully portrayed. Luke emphasizes this moment with dramatic description which exceeds what we find in Matthew and Mark: the cock crows "while [Peter] is still speaking," and the Lord turns to look at Peter at the same moment. This not only adds to the dramatic impact of the moment of recognition but also heightens the sense of personal betrayal. The scene is narrated in a way calculated to make a strong impression, an indication of the importance of this scene within the narrative. The preparation for this scene by Jesus' prediction in 22:34 also shows the importance of Peter's denial, for this prediction calls the readers' attention to the event before it happens. The fact that Peter, the leader among the apostles, is denying Jesus also adds to the scene's impact.

The dramatic emphasis on Peter's denial will later enable the narrator to highlight the power that brings conversion. The stories of Peter and Paul, the main heroes of Acts, illustrate this power of conversion. When called by Jesus, Peter responded by saying, "Depart from me, for I am a sinful man" (5:8). When the cock crows, Peter again recognizes that he is a sinful man, and he weeps bitterly.[107] It is the contrast between the weak, sinful man and the man who speaks boldly in Jesus' name which seems to interest the narrator. The strong emphasis on Peter's failure contributes to this contrast. The other half of the contrast will appear in Acts, where we will find phrases and settings which recall Peter's denial but show Peter and his companions acting in the opposite way. The Peter who turns away from following Jesus to trial before the Sanhedrin in Luke speaks boldly in Jesus' name before the Sanhedrin in Acts 4–5. His willingness to go to prison and his boldness in witnessing to Jesus before threatening authorities contrast sharply with his previous denial.[108]

The conversation with the apostles at the table ends with Jesus' words about buying a sword and being reckoned with the lawless, to which the apostles respond by showing that they already have swords (22:35–38). The interpretation of these puzzling words should take account of the

---

[107] W. Dietrich notes this connection. See *Das Petrusbild*, 155.
[108] See further in vol. 2.

narrative continuity between this scene and the arrest in 22:47–53, where one of the swords is used to cut off the ear of the high priest's slave. The attack with the sword is more than a rash act of one disciple. The narrator reports that a group of "those around" Jesus (clearly disciples, for they address Jesus as "Lord") ask whether they should strike with a sword (dif. Matthew, Mark). The disciple who actually cuts off the ear of the high priest's slave puts into action the thoughts of a whole group. But Jesus rebukes this use of the sword. This is clear despite the difficulty in translating Jesus' words in 22:51, which have been variously interpreted,[109] for Jesus' actions make his meaning clear. He first undoes the damage caused by the disciple, and then he submits to arrest without calling his disciples to resist, as they are ready to do. Jesus rejects the disciples' proposal of resistance. Therefore, his command to buy a sword in 22:36 is not intended to prepare the disciples to fight for Jesus against his enemies (for which two swords would scarcely be sufficient, in any case).

In 22:37 a reason for the command to purchase a sword is given: "For I say to you that this which is written must be fulfilled in me, 'And he was reckoned with the lawless'." This is commonly understood as a reference to Jesus' crucifixion with two criminals (23:32–33). This connection need not be denied, but we should consider the function of these words in the dialogue between Jesus and the apostles, where they indicate the reason for buying a sword. Jesus may be saying that, since he will now be regarded as a criminal, his followers are also in danger and must protect themselves at all costs. Such an instruction would conflict with Jesus' previous instructions to his followers, and 22:35–36 highlights the conflict by recalling Jesus' previous command not to take purse, bag, or sandals[110] and by reminding the apostles that their needs were supplied despite this, in accordance with the promise in 12:22–32. On this interpretation Jesus would seem to be saying that the apostles can no longer rely on divine protection; now it is every man for himself, even to the extent of selling one's cloak to buy a sword (which, even if meant metaphorically, surely refers to extreme measures). This fits neither the promises to the disciples in Luke (see 12:6–7; 21:18–19) nor the narrative of Acts, which is full of stories of divine rescue. These instructions also conflict with Jesus' own actions and attitude as his death approaches. The narrator takes pains to

---

[109] See I. H. Marshall, *The Gospel of Luke*, 837, for the main options.

[110] It is often noted that the reference to purse, bag, and sandals fits better the mission instructions to the seventy-two than those to the twelve. However, the command in 9:3 to take "nothing for the way," not even "money," can be understood to include the missing references to purse and sandals. In any case, 22:35 indicates that instructions about purse and sandals applied to the apostles.

show that Jesus does not lose hope in divine protection, does not try to rescue himself, but trusts in God to the very end (23:46).

An alternative view is to understand the scriptural quotation in 22:37 as applying to the disciples. They are lawless people with whom Jesus is counted. Jesus' command to buy swords serves to fulfill this Scripture. As it turns out, of course, the apostles already have two swords. So, in the context of the narrative, Jesus' command does not cause something to happen but reveals what the disciples have already done out of fear.[111] Responding to authority with armed resistance can very well qualify people as "lawless," both in the eyes of the authorities and in the eyes of Jesus, who will rebuke and correct the use of a sword at the arrest. To be counted among such lawless people is part of the prophesied suffering of the Son of Man.

It may seem strange, however, that Jesus would command the apostles to take purse and bag (contrary to his previous instructions) and to show themselves to be lawless by buying a sword. Consideration of the Lukan context helps us to understand what is happening. Jesus' words in 22:36 arise out of his foreknowledge of Satan's sifting of the apostles and of the fall from faithfulness which that will involve. Jesus was discussing this fall in the immediately preceding verses (22:31–34), which provide the introduction to 22:35–38. When the disciples were faithful, they did not need purse or bag. But now, under Satan's influence, they are choosing a different path which logically requires not only purse and bag but even a sword—all the means of self-protection which humans can provide. These things are needed because the apostles are no longer following the true path of discipleship, which stands under the promise of God's care. The contrast which Jesus makes between the past (22:35) and "now" (22:36) is a contrast between the apostles' previous freedom and what is required by their present fear. The fact that they already have two swords shows that this fear is controlling their actions. The actual use of one of the swords will demonstrate its full control and, along with it, the fact that Jesus' followers, in contrast to Jesus himself, have become the "lawless."

Luke 22:35–36 is not a permanent change in the regulations for missionary work, distinguishing the situation before and after Easter.[112] If the instructions about purse and bag are literal instructions for the church's mission, it is not clear why the instruction about the sword should be interpreted metaphorically. But there is no evidence in Acts that the missionaries carry swords.[113] The issue of how Jesus' mission instruc-

---

[111] See Paul S. Minear, "A Note on Luke xxii 36," 132–33.

[112] For the contrary view see H. Conzelmann, *The Theology of St. Luke*, 187, 232–33.

[113] Nor is there any reference to "purse (βαλλάντιον)" or "bag (πήρα)" in Acts.

tions apply to the life of the church is not being addressed here. The use of the sword at the arrest and the scriptural reference in 22:37 show that Jesus' words do not refer to the distant situation of the church's mission but to the immediate situation of the passion.

The lawlessness of the apostles in the passion story fulfills Scripture, and so it, too, has a place within God's purpose, which is able to make use of human failure and rejection. Nevertheless, it is part of a sharply negative view of Jesus' followers during the passion story. Indeed, the conversation with the apostles in 22:35–38 discloses their failure whether they are to be identified with the "lawless" or not. As noted above, Jesus' command to buy a sword cannot be a command to prepare for successful armed resistance, for Jesus himself corrects the use of the sword and mends its damage in 22:51. One can, however, understand Jesus' command metaphorically. In that case, the apostles misunderstand Jesus when they produce the swords, and they act on their misunderstanding at the arrest. This, too, shows how far they are from comprehending their Master and following him faithfully. This failing is connected with their failure to understand that Jesus must be rejected and killed, for the use of the sword is an attempt to prevent this from happening. The table conversation ends with the apostles holding their two swords, a dramatic sign of their blindness to Jesus' way at this point in the story.

The Promise of a Share in Jesus' Royal Power (Luke 22:28–30). In the midst of Jesus' words at the table which focus on the apostles' failure (22:21–38), we find 22:28–30, which expresses a covenant promise by Jesus granting a share of his royal power (βασιλεία) to the apostles. The tension between these words and the surrounding material should be noted. Apostles who are blind and faithless are being given a share in Jesus' reign, a place at his royal table, and responsibility as rulers of the twelve tribes of Israel. This tension raises the question: how can such faithless followers share in Jesus' royal power? The answer will come in the course of the narrative, as a dramatic change takes place in the apostles.

The apostles' faithless behavior in the passion story contrasts with their past faithfulness in situations of trial (22:28). This comment on their faithfulness does not refer to the apostles' behavior in the passion story. That would conflict with what we have already discovered. The phrase οἱ διαμεμενηκότες μετ' ἐμοῦ ἐν τοῖς πειρασμοῖς μου ("those who have remained with me" or "have stood by me in my trials"), using a perfect participle, refers to the present significance that the apostles have for Jesus because of their past behavior. It does not refer to their behavior in the near future, which will not measure up to their past faithfulness. Especially in the prayer scene in 22:39–46, it is clear that the apostles do not support Jesus in his most severe trial, in spite of Jesus' command that they pray as he is praying. However, Jesus looks at their past faithfulness rather than their present weakness and entrusts them with central positions in his kingdom.

Luke 22:29-30 contains an important preview of the apostles' future role. Does it interpret their role in Acts or is Jesus' promise purely eschatological? Clear indications of time are lacking, perhaps due to a desire to apply these words both to the apostles' role in the church and to their eschatological status.[114] There is some evidence that these words are meant to apply, in part, to the apostles' role in Acts.[115] In his statement in 22:29, Jesus' conferral of royal power on the apostles is associated with God's conferral of royal power on Jesus.[116] Luke associates Jesus' royal power especially with his coming to Jerusalem and with the events which take place there (see 19:38; 23:38, 42-43), including Jesus' exaltation to the right hand of God (20:17, 42-43; 22:69), which fulfills the promise to David to seat a descendant on David's throne (Acts 2:30-36). Jesus has already been exalted to God's right hand by the time that the apostles begin their mission in Acts. At that point, it is already possible for the apostles to share in Jesus' new power. Furthermore, Luke 22:28-30 is part of Jesus' farewell address to the apostles before his death, and this address contains other indications of an imminent transition in which the apostles will assume positions of leadership.[117] We have already noted that in 22:26 Jesus speaks to the apostles about how "the greater" and "the leader" must behave. These words apply to those who have recognized positions of leadership in the church rather than to one who "wants to become great" (Mark 10:43-44; Matt 20:26-27). Furthermore, the narrator introduces Jesus' table companions as "the apostles" (22:14; dif. Matthew, Mark), a preview of their special role in Acts, and in 22:32 Jesus speaks to Peter about his future leading role among the brethren. Jesus' conferral of ruling power in 22:29-30 fits with these other indications of the new position of leadership which the apostles are about to assume. The reference in Luke 22:30 to the apostles eating and drinking "at my table" also has its correspondence in Acts, for special importance is

---

[114] The phrases in Matthew's parallel (Matt 19:28) which make clear that it applies to the eschatological consummation (especially the reference to the "regeneration" and to the Son of Man in glory) are absent in Luke.

[115] See S. Brown, *Apostasy and Perseverance,* 64; L. T. Johnson, *The Literary Function of Possessions,* 120-21; J. Neyrey, *The Passion according to Luke,* 23-28.

[116] The noun βασιλείαν serves as object of both verbs in 22:29, which accents the similarity being expressed by the καθώς clause. On 22:29-30 see Robert F. O'Toole, "Acts 2:30," 253. He connects these verses with God's promise of a throne and kingdom to Jesus at 1:32-33.

[117] According to J. Neyrey, "A persistent element in most farewell speeches is the concern of the dying leader for his successor." He believes that 22:28-30 shows this same concern. See *The Passion according to Luke,* 25-26.

attached to the fact that the apostles "ate and drank" with the risen Messiah (Acts 10:41).[118] If διατίθεμαι in Luke 22:29 means "confer by a will"—a meaning which is appropriate to the context since this is a farewell discourse in which Jesus consciously speaks in light of his coming death[119]—this may also support the realization of this promise already in the time of the church, for a will takes effect upon death.

However, the promise that the apostles will judge the twelve tribes of *Israel* may refer to the eschatological future, for it is not realized in Acts. It would be easy to take a different view if we could equate Israel with the church or with Jewish Christians, but this would be contrary to usage in Luke, where Israel remains a designation for the Jewish people. In addition, the reference to the twelve tribes calls to mind a particular ethnic group with its particular history. Mention of the twelve tribes also suggests Israel in its restored wholeness. While the apostles in Acts address "the whole house of Israel" and "all the people of Israel" (2:36; 4:10), only a part of this people accepts their message and acknowledges their leadership. The repeated references to Jewish rejection in Acts, culminating in Paul's final statement on the blindness of the Roman Jews (28:25–28), show that the narrator is keenly aware that Israel has not yet been restored to wholeness under its Messiah Jesus and his governors, the apostles.[120]

Jesus grants to the apostles a share in the "royal power (βασιλεία)" that the Father has granted to him. This is an important step in the realization of the promise in 12:32 that the Father will "give to you the kingdom (βασιλεία)." It is an important step beyond the first sending of the apostles to preach and heal (9:1–6) and the revelation of the Father to Jesus' followers celebrated in 10:21–22, for Jesus will soon be seated "at the right hand of the power of God" (22:69), and his apostles will soon be sharing in his ruling power as they address Israel and guide the growing church.

Failures at Prayer; Distant Observers of the Cross (Luke 22:39–46; 23:49). Luke's prayer scene (22:39–46) is simpler in structure than Mark's or Matthew's. Instead of a threefold prayer by Jesus, separated by three encounters with the sleeping disciples, Jesus simply instructs the disciples to pray, prays himself, returns to find the disciples sleeping, and again commands them to pray. As J. Warren Holleran notes, Luke's

---

[118] In Acts 1:4 συναλιζόμενος may also refer to a shared meal. A shared meal is probably meant also in Luke 24:41–43. See pp. 291–92.

[119] See Robert C. Tannehill, "The Theology of Luke-Acts," 201–2.

[120] The word "judging (κρίνοντες)" probably has the broad sense of "governing." See Jacques Dupont, "Le logion des douze trônes," 381. This sense is supported by passages in the LXX. See Ps 2:10; 4 Kgdms 15:5; 1 Macc 9:73; Pss Sol 17:29.

account "is centered on the theme of prayer under trial."[121] Jesus tells the disciples that they must "pray not to enter into temptation" (22:40), for fervent prayer is the way to find the strength to remain faithful in this crisis. Both Jesus' command and Jesus' example should show the disciples what to do. But the disciples fall asleep. Jesus rebukes them and repeats his command to pray to escape temptation, but by that time the disciples' chance is lost. The arresting party approaches as Jesus speaks, and the disciples are unprepared. They react with fear and grab their swords. Their behavior shows that they do not recognize God's will and have not prepared themselves to accept it. They are trapped by Satan's temptation. Luke does not focus on the three leading disciples, as Mark and Matthew do. All the disciples are told to pray not to enter into temptation. They all fall asleep and are caught unprepared.

The narrator says that the disciples were sleeping "from grief ($\lambda \acute{v}\pi\eta$)." It is doubtful that this is intended to excuse the disciples' disobedience. On the contrary, it connects their sleep with depression and exhaustion of moral strength. Jerome H. Neyrey discusses the negative connotations of $\lambda \acute{v}\pi\eta$ in Stoic philosophy and Hellenistic Judaism. In summary, he says that "$\lambda \acute{v}\pi\eta$ is (1) one of the four cardinal passions [which are to be avoided as vices], (2) a typical punishment for sin, and (3) an indication of guilt."[122] The negative sense of the term may be indicated by the different portrait of Jesus in Luke's prayer scene compared to Mark and Matthew. In Mark 14:34 and Matt 26:38 Jesus describes himself as "deeply grieved ($\pi\epsilon\rho\acute{\iota}\lambda\upsilon\pi os$)," but this description of Jesus is not found in Luke. The emotion which Mark and Matthew attribute to Jesus is attributed to the disciples in Luke, which suggests that it is viewed as a sign of spiritual weakness. According to Neyrey, $\lambda \acute{v}\pi\eta$ is the opposite of manly courage, and Luke has omitted "Markan details which might suggest Jesus as distraught or lacking in moral control."[123] But Luke is willing to attribute these emotions to the disciples. Jesus' $\dot{a}\gamma\omega\nu\acute{\iota}a$ ("agony," "struggle") in 22:44 (if this is part of the original text) does not contradict these findings, for this can be interpreted as virtuous struggle.[124]

Following Jesus' arrest, there is no mention of the flight of the disciples, as in Mark 14:50. This difference is significant, for in Luke Jesus' male "acquaintances," as well as the women who accompanied him from Galilee, are distant observers of the crucifixion (23:49).[125] The disciples

---

[121] See *The Synoptic Gethsemane*, 214.
[122] See "The Absence of Jesus' Emotions," 157.
[123] "The Absence of Jesus' Emotions," 158.
[124] See "The Absence of Jesus' Emotions," 159–65. On 22:39–46 see also J. Neyrey, *The Passion according to Luke*, 49–68.
[125] K. H. Rengstorf, *TDNT* 4:446–47, notes that Luke stops speaking of the disciples after the

do not leave Jerusalem but follow the course of events to its end. The purpose behind these unique Lukan touches is not to portray the disciples as faithful, for the material we have examined provides abundant evidence of their unfaithfulness. This is indicated even in 23:49, for Jesus' acquaintances stand "at a distance." This indicates a weakened discipleship that is unwilling to pay the price of discipleship. They are like Peter, who followed Jesus "at a distance" (22:54) but denied him when his own life was threatened. Nevertheless, it is important that they are present at the crucifixion "to see these things," for from this group of disciples will come Jesus' witnesses to the people. They must experience these events not only because they are key events for understanding Jesus and his mission, about which the witnesses must later speak, but also because they have direct relevance for the future experience of the witnesses themselves. The way in which Jesus faces rejection and death provides the pattern for his witnesses, as the description of the death of Stephen (see Acts 7:55–60 with Luke 22:69; 23:34, 46) and the echoes of the passion story in Paul's final journey to Jerusalem (see Acts 21:13–14 with Luke 22:33, 42) show. Jesus' words from the cross in Luke (dif. Matthew, Mark), which show his forgiveness for adversaries (23:34)[126] and his trust in God at the point

---

prayer scene and instead paraphrases with formulations such as "those around him" (22:49) and "his acquaintances" (23:49). According to Rengstorf, "The only possible explanation is that the behaviour of the disciples of Jesus during the passion is equivalent to a breach of the relationship by them, and that it is the task of Jesus to gather disciples afresh after His resurrection."

[126] The absence of these words of forgiveness in early manuscripts representing diverse manuscript traditions prevents certainty as to whether they are an original part of Luke. Nevertheless, arguments for originality are substantial. Not only the witnesses for omission but also those for inclusion represent diverse traditions, and Codex Sinaiticus in the original hand supports inclusion. Anti-Judaism in the early church provides a possible motive for omission. Luke 23:28–31, if understood as an indication of God's final rejection of the Jews, would seem to conflict with 23:34. Matthew may also have been an influence, for there is a conflict between Luke 23:34 and Matt 27:25 which could cause manuscript changes. Eldon Jay Epp, in his study of Codex D, one of the witnesses for omission, detects an anti-Judaic bias and comments on Luke 23:34 and Acts 3:17 as follows: "For the D-text, the Jews could not so easily be excused on the basis of ignorance." See *The Theological Tendency*, 45–46. The thought of the disputed words is Lukan, as is shown by Acts 3:17, 7:60, and the offer of forgiveness to the people of Jerusalem and their rulers in the Acts sermons. Furthermore, Jesus' two prayers to his Father at the moment of crucifixion and at the moment of death can be understood to balance and supplement each other, the first expressing Jesus' attitude toward his crucifiers and the second his relation to God in death. Wolfgang Schenk has argued that the parallels in Acts can equally well be used as evidence against the originality of these words, since the interpolater may have based the words on the Acts parallels. See *Der Passionsbericht nach Markus*, 96. However, the thought in Acts 3:17, 7:60 is similar, but the wording is quite different. Luke 23:34 is not the work of an imitator trying to sound Lukan but shows the variation which is common in the author's own style. (See H. J. Cadbury, "Four Features of Lucan Style," 92: "Variety, then, almost studied variation of phrase and exchange of synonyms, is a distinct feature of the style of this author.") Uncertainty remains, but the arguments for the originality of Luke 23:34a are strong.

of death (23:46), help to give the passion story its exemplary significance.[127]

But Jesus' followers have not yet learned how to face death as Jesus does. Their failure to understand that Jesus will suffer and die, and that these events have a place in God's purpose, a failure emphasized in 9:45 and 18:34, grows into a complex picture of failure as Jesus approaches his death. The disciples have premature hopes for the appearance of God's reign upon their arrival in Jerusalem. The contentious apostles do not follow the lead of the Messiah who serves, but argue over who is greatest. They are unprepared for Satan's sifting and lose their last chance to escape his temptation when they sleep instead of following Jesus' command to pray. Peter claims that he is ready to go with Jesus to prison and death but actually denies Jesus in order to escape these threats. The restoration of Peter requires Jesus' prayer and Peter's repentance. The apostles are no longer able to live without purse, bag, and other means of provision and protection. Indeed, they have already provided for armed self-defense, and they begin to use their swords before Jesus stops them. The failure to understand that it is God's will for Jesus to suffer and die shows its consequences in the disciples' behavior. They resist Jesus' arrest, are not prepared to follow him in suffering, and are concerned about their own status instead of following Jesus' path of lowly service. Such disciples can only become Jesus' witnesses through a great transformation.

Although that transformation has not yet taken place, the passion story gives reason for hope. While Jesus' followers are not yet ready to face death, Jesus' command to them to take the cross and come after him (9:23; 14:27) finds fulfillment in Simon of Cyrene (23:26), who thereby provides a model of what Jesus' witnesses will do.[128] Jesus' saving and transforming power continues as he is crucified. The dialogue with the crucified criminal, in which Jesus grants him a place in paradise, demonstrates this. Jesus' death has a powerful effect on those who witness it, changing their assumptions about what has just transpired. The death of Jesus, in which he demonstrates exemplary trust in God his Father, immediately causes the centurion to make a repentant confession concerning Jesus and causes the crowd to return in repentant mourning (23:47–48). There are

---

[127] On Luke's portrait of Jesus as an exemplary martyr, see C. Talbert, *Reading Luke*, 212–18; Talbert, "Martyrdom in Luke-Acts," 99–110; Brian E. Beck, "Imitatio Christi," 28–47. On the significance of the emphasis on Jesus' faith in God in 23:46 and elsewhere, see J. Neyrey, *The Passion according to Luke*, 146–54.

[128] On Simon of Cyrene as a model of discipleship, see Anton Büchele, *Der Tod Jesu im Lukasevangelium*, 97; Franz Georg Untergassmair, *Kreuzweg und Kreuzigung Jesu*, 160, 173.

no similar signs of repentance among Jesus' followers watching the crucifixion, but we have already been told that Peter wept bitterly following his denials (22:62), and Jesus spoke to Peter about his repentance and future responsibility for his brothers (22:32). The crucifixion of Jesus is not an ending, for the narrator has given us hints of the story's future. However, it is deeply disturbing for many who witness it, for previous assumptions about Jesus have been shattered, and the various groups in the passion story—the disciples, the people, the religious and political authorities—share in various ways in the guilty responsibility for the chain of events leading to Jesus' death.

Chapter Eight

THE RISEN LORD'S REVELATION
TO HIS FOLLOWERS

REVIEW AND PREVIEW

Luke 24 and Acts 1, which partly overlap, bridge the important transition from the story of Jesus to the story of his witnesses. The narrator's concern to build a strong bridge, unifying the story rather than permitting it to disintegrate into two stories, is shown by the amount of material in these chapters which either reviews what has already happened or previews what is going to happen. These reviews and previews also provide opportunity for the interpretation of these events in the way that the narrator finds most illuminating.

Luke 24 is composed of four major scenes, the empty tomb, the journey to Emmaus, the appearance in Jerusalem, and the departure of Jesus. In each of the first three scenes, which make up the bulk of the chapter, there is reference back to earlier parts of the story, especially to Jesus' recent death and to his prophecies of his death and resurrection (24:6–7, 18–27, 44–46). This material links the three scenes with each other, presenting a continuous, developing discussion of Jesus' death and resurrection.[1] By their instruction the messengers at the tomb and Jesus are attempting to overcome a serious deficiency in the preparation of Jesus' witnesses.[2] This instruction also turns Luke's resurrection chapter into a major commentary on the significance of Jesus' death and resurrection. In the third scene this commentary on the past story continues with a preview of major events to come, as Jesus gives a new commission to his followers (24:47–49).

The commentary on Jesus' death and resurrection in these three scenes emphatically repeats themes which have already been expressed in the passion prophecies of Jesus from 9:22 on (see 24:7, 25–26, 44, 46). The statements in Luke 24 are introduced by clear indications that they are repetitions of what Jesus' followers have already heard (24:6, 44). Thus the narrator is placing very strong emphasis on the prophecies of Jesus' suffering and resurrection, carrying them over into the resurrection

---

[1] Paul Schubert was making the same observation when he noted that "Luke pulls the three major items of his materials together by furnishing each of them with the same climax." See "The Structure and Significance of Luke 24," 173.

[2] See P. Minear, *To Heal and to Reveal*, 131–32.

stories, where variations on them appear three different times. Jesus must hammer away on this theme because his followers were unable to understand his words when he earlier announced that he must suffer, die, and be raised (a failure strongly stressed in 9:45 and 18:34), and they are still unable to understand when they first encounter the message of the resurrection. The problem is not easily solved even on Easter. The solution requires more than the appearance of the risen Jesus. Changing the disciples' perceptions involves a rather lengthy process which covers the whole of Luke 24. Only an issue of urgency and importance deserves the amount of attention given in Luke 24 to the revelation to the disciples of the necessity of Jesus' suffering and resurrection.

In 24:5 the angels at the tomb address the women with sharp words of correction which highlight human ignorance: "Why do you seek the living one with the dead?" They then remind the women of something Jesus' followers should not have forgotten; Jesus had told them that "the Son of Man must be delivered into the hands of people who are sinners and be crucified and on the third day arise" (24:7; dif. Matthew, Mark). This had been said while Jesus was "still in Galilee." These words closely resemble Jesus' announcement to his disciples in 9:44, an announcement which is followed by the first strong indication of the disciples' failure to understand. However, 9:44 does not refer explicitly either to Jesus' death or to his resurrection on the third day. These elements are present in Jesus' previous announcement in 9:22, which also supplies the "must ($\delta\epsilon\hat{\iota}$)" that is repeated in 24:7. Thus the angels paraphrase by combining Jesus' first two passion announcements.[3] Since Jesus' words have now been fulfilled, they should be believed, but the empty tomb and the angels' announcement do not bring insight and faith. The women remember Jesus' words and report what they have seen and heard to the eleven and the others, but their report has no effect. It is regarded as "nonsense," for the apostles do not believe the women.

If 24:12 belongs to the original text of Luke,[4] the narrator focuses our attention for a moment on Peter, who checks the women's story by going to the tomb himself. He finds the tomb empty and leaves "astonished"

---

[3] Luke 24:7 differs from both 9:22 and 9:44 in the addition of "sinners" (see Mark 14:41), the substitution of "be crucified" for "be killed," and the use of "arise" instead of "be raised."

[4] It is omitted by manuscripts of the Western text type. Richard Dillon presents a careful argument for inclusion of v. 12. See *From Eye-Witnesses*, 57–67. However, the agreement, even in wording, with John 20:3–10 should continue to cause suspicion. Dillon explains the omission of v. 12 in the Western text as an attempt to avoid conflict with v. 24, which refers to a group of disciples, not just Peter, going to check the women's report (*From Eye-Witnesses*, 60, n. 173). This explanation is not fully convincing. The belated indication that Peter did not act alone may impress us as awkward, but it is not the kind of contradiction that would necessarily disturb a copyist.

(RSV: "wondering"). This astonishment is not to be confused with faith. The word θαυμάζω is frequently used of persons who are amazed by what is happening but do not understand Jesus and may even oppose him and his mission.[5] Peter is in the same state as the travelers to Emmaus, who report in v. 22 that the women "astounded us" but do not understand the significance of recent events. However, v. 12 would suggest that Peter's response is a matter of continuing interest, which might remind readers that Jesus had prayed for Peter and anticipated that he would "turn" and "strengthen his brothers" (22:32). This special role of Peter is not confined to Luke 24, but it begins to be fulfilled in 24:34, where we are told that acceptance of the resurrection message in Jerusalem first arises through an appearance to "Simon." The reference to Peter in 24:12, if it is original, would help to bridge the gap between Jesus' promise of Peter's special role in 22:32 and the first sign of his new leadership in proclaiming the risen Messiah.

The Conversation on the Road

The empty tomb and the message of the angels produce only amazement and unbelief. The story could proceed directly to an appearance of the risen Jesus which overcomes this unbelief, since such appearance stories were available. The narrator does not choose this option but introduces the lengthy scene of the journey to Emmaus. A large part of this scene is devoted to a conversation on the road which climaxes in the revelation that Scripture anticipates a Messiah who suffers and is glorified. This revelation is not forgotten when the risen Jesus is recognized. The summary of the Emmaus scene in v. 35 gives the conversation on the road equal importance with the recognition at the meal (note also the reminder of the conversation at the end of the meal scene in v. 32). Evidently an appearance of the risen Jesus, by itself, does not adequately deal with the disciples' problem. They also need to understand how Jesus' death and resurrection fit into God's purpose and plan. This is disclosed through a new understanding of Scripture. The journey to Emmaus provides an opportunity to begin the needed instruction, which will be continued when Jesus appears later in Jerusalem (24:44–49).

In the conversation on the road the disciples retell the story of Jesus from their point of view. In this way the narrator suggests to the readers

---

[5] It is applied to the unenlightened disciples in Luke 8:25. It is applied to antagonists (Luke 11:38; 20:26; Acts 4:13; 13:41) as well as the crowds. The corrective teaching which sometimes follows shows that the amazement of the crowds does not involve real understanding (Luke 4:22; 9:43; Acts 3:12).

what the story of Jesus means to the disciples at their present level of understanding. Their views are exposed by Jesus' leading questions so that these views can be evaluated and corrected in vv. 25–27. By first presenting the disciples' perceptions and then Jesus' corrective teaching, the story conveys a sense of the revolutionary impact of the new revelation which comes through Jesus' teaching and appearance.

Up to a point the disciples' understanding of Jesus is accurate, from the perspective of the implied author, for it agrees with the way in which Jesus is presented in the rest of Luke-Acts. The description of Jesus in v. 19 as a "prophet powerful in work and word before God and all the people" is not an indication of ignorance but reflects a view of Jesus characteristic of Luke-Acts, being expressed both by authoritative characters and by the narrator. Jesus describes himself as a prophet in Luke 4:24 and 13:33, and the preachers in Acts, who have come to new and deeper understanding of Jesus, present him as the prophet like Moses (3:22; 7:37). The description of Jesus as "powerful in work and word" agrees with the narrator's statement that Jesus began his ministry "in the power of the Spirit" (Luke 4:14) and Peter's declaration that "God anointed him with Holy Spirit and power," resulting in a ministry of "doing good and healing" (Acts 10:38). The statement that "Jesus the Nazarene" was "a man ($\dot{a}\nu\dot{\eta}\rho$) . . . powerful . . . before . . . all the people" resembles Acts 2:22. Note also the description of Moses as "powerful in his words and works" in Acts 7:22.[6] The combination of "work and word" in Luke 24:19 agrees with the narrator's summary of the first volume as covering "all the things that Jesus began to do and to teach" (Acts 1:1).

The disciples continue in Luke 24:20 by summarizing the passion story in words which closely resemble the words of the angels at the tomb and Jesus' passion prophecies on which the angels' words were based (24:7: "must be delivered . . . and crucified"; 24:20: "delivered . . . and crucified"). Inadvertently they are confirming that this aspect of Jesus' prophecies has come true. Those responsible for Jesus' death were "our chief priests and rulers." The term "rulers ($\check{a}\rho\chi o\nu\tau\epsilon s$)" is used of the Jewish leaders in Jerusalem in Luke-Acts but not in Matthew or Mark. The combination "chief priests and rulers" appeared in Luke 23:13. The statement in 24:20 anticipates the accusation of responsibility for the death of Jesus made against the Jewish leaders in Jerusalem in the Acts speeches. However, according to these speeches the people of Jerusalem also participated in Jesus' death (Acts 3:13–15, 17; 13:27–29).

In 24:21 the disciples speak of their hope that Jesus was "going to

---

[6] Joachim Wanke comments that 24:19 "stands in striking parallel" to the Moses typology employed by Luke in Acts 3:22f. and 7:35, 37. See *Die Emmauserzählung*, 64.

redeem Israel." It is, of course, clear that the salvation which Jesus and his witnesses bring, according to Luke-Acts, is open to the Gentiles, and these disciples do not yet understand this. Their past hope, however, is not to be dismissed as an indication of theological narrowness that must be overcome, for it reflects a hope which is emphasized within Luke-Acts as a whole. Specifically, the words of the disciples pick up the joyful proclamation of redemption for Israel in the birth narrative (1:68; 2:38) and express disappointment at the failure of this promise. The noun "redemption ($\lambda\acute{v}\tau\rho\omega\sigma\iota\varsigma$)" and its verb are not used in Luke-Acts except in these three passages, and in each case it is the Jewish people who are the object of redemption. In 1:68–70 this redemption is associated with the promised kingdom of the Davidic Messiah. The preachers in Acts will continue to proclaim that this promise can be fulfilled for the Jewish people through Jesus (Acts 2:30–36; 13:22–23, 32–34), although enjoyment of the benefits of the messianic kingdom requires repentance and faith (2:38–39; 3:19–21; 13:38–39). The principal problem which appears in Luke 24:21 is not a narrow and restrictive hope—this hope for Israel will continue to be expressed at least to the end of Acts—but a failure of hope. The disciples express their hope in the past tense, for it has come to a dead end at the crucifixion.

Perhaps we should add that the pathos of the disciples' statement will reappear in Acts because of continued Jewish resistance to Jesus and his witnesses. The realization of the hope that Jesus will redeem Israel remains a problem throughout Acts, for the narrator can report only partial realization of this hope and is keenly aware of this fact.[7] Although the resurrection will awaken new hope, it will not make the problem disappear, for the preaching of the risen Messiah will lead to renewed conflict over Jesus.

The disciples continue their story in vv. 21–24, repeating what the narrator just told us about the discovery of the empty tomb and stopping short with the negative statement, "But him they did not see" (24:24). This suggests that seeing the risen Jesus would make a crucial difference. Jesus knows, however, that seeing must be accompanied by understanding God's way of working through a rejected and exalted Messiah, as attested in Scripture. The report of the empty tomb and the vision of angels still leaves the disciples sad and with broken hope (24:17, 21). The risen Messiah must not only show himself but also reveal the mystery of God's working in order to change this situation.

Luke 24 relates a development from blindness to sight, from minds without understanding to opened minds. This development concerns both

---

[7] See R. Tannehill, "Israel in Luke-Acts," 69–85.

recognition of the risen Messiah and understanding of God's purpose realized in his suffering and resurrection, a purpose attested in Scripture. In v. 16 we are told that the disciples' eyes "were being held so as not to recognize him," but at the meal in v. 31 "their eyes were opened." The failure to recognize Jesus is part of a larger spiritual blindness which must be cured. When the disciples' eyes are opened, they immediately emphasize how Jesus "opened to us the Scriptures," using the same verb and thereby linking these two events (24:31–32).[8] The later parallel in v. 45 clarifies this, stating that Jesus "opened their mind to understand the Scriptures." The failure of the Emmaus disciples to recognize the risen Messiah is accompanied and probably caused by a lack of insight into God's purpose attested in Scripture and now realized in the death and resurrection of Jesus.

Some scholars interpret the reference to eyes "being held" as a "divine passive," i.e., an indirect way of referring to the action of God through use of the passive voice.[9] If so, the narrator probably was referring to the action of God when stating earlier that Jesus' announcement of his passion "was hidden" from the disciples (9:45; 18:34).[10] The narrator does not intend to suggest, however, that an arbitrary God is whimsically playing with human beings. Rather, there is something inherently difficult in understanding God's way of working through the death of Jesus. God holds human eyes in the sense that God's ways necessarily appear meaningless to humans who understand events in terms of their own purposes and ways of achieving them. A new vision of how God works salvation in the world must be granted to the disciples before a crucified and risen Messiah can be meaningful for them.

The Emmaus narrative serves to highlight the contrast between human understanding, represented by the disciples, and God's way of working in Jesus. It dramatizes human blindness by presenting an ironic situation. The disciples do not recognize that they are trying to inform Jesus about Jesus. Irony is strong as they rebuke Jesus for ignorance (v. 18), when they themselves are the ones who do not understand. They try to explain to Jesus at some length what he knows better than they. We as readers know that the stranger is Jesus. We watch the disciples making their mistake and are thereby given an impression of the way that human

---

[8] The significance of the repeated word increases when we note that διανοίγω, although a characteristically Lukan word, is not common even in Luke-Acts. The occurrences of the word in Luke 24 constitute three of the seven uses of the word in Luke-Acts.

[9] For instance, I. H. Marshall, *The Gospel of Luke*, 893; J. Wanke, *Die Emmauserzählung*, 35.

[10] On these verses see pp. 226–27.

blindness appears, viewed from beyond it.[11] This blindness is pointedly expressed in the charge with which Jesus responds: "O imperceptive people (ἀνόητοι) and slow in heart to believe in all that the prophets spoke!" (v. 25).

This ironic scene is not isolated in Luke-Acts. The interpretation of Jesus' death and resurrection in Acts emphasizes the ironic twist in these events, and there are other ironies after the resurrection as blind humans are surprised by the outcome of events. The interpretation of the death of Jesus in Acts is characterized by two motifs that may appear to conflict. On the one hand, the death of Jesus represents the rejection of him by the people of Jerusalem and their rulers. It expresses their opposition to God's purpose, and for this they must repent. On the other hand, the death of Jesus is the fulfillment of God's purpose. It fulfills a predetermined divine plan, attested in Scripture, and results not in rejection but in God's affirmation of Jesus as Messiah (see especially Acts 2:23–36; 4:25–28). This is a situation of irony. Humans act blindly (note the emphasis on "ignorance" in Acts 3:17; 13:27), and the outcome is the opposite of what they intend. For behind their purpose is a stronger, hidden purpose which uses human blindness to thwart human plans.

The course of the story suggests that the implied author is fascinated by the ironies that arise from the interaction of divine and human purposes. Acts not only presents an ironic interpretation of Jesus' death and resurrection but continues to highlight ironic twists in the plot. In 5:17–26 the actual release of the apostles from prison is narrated briefly while the narrator dwells on the ironic result: the Sanhedrin struggles to make sense of the fact that people who were put in prison are not in prison. In 8:1–4 the great persecution in Jerusalem ironically results in the spread of the gospel. The church, too, is caught in situations of irony. At first Ananias protests against the Lord's command to find and heal the persecuter Saul (9:13–14). Ironically this representative of the church tries to oppose the Lord's work in the church's behalf. This irony is exceeded in Acts 12. Peter is led out of prison but thinks that he is only dreaming (12:6–11), and the church prays for Peter but refuses to believe that its prayer has been answered (12:5, 12–16). God's action is perceived especially in those situations and experiences where God's saving purpose surprises, because it is quite contrary to human plans and expectations.[12] These experiences

---

[11] See Geoffrey Nuttall, *The Moment of Recognition*, 9: In the Emmaus story "a fine irony is added, as the reader (like the reader of a Greek drama) knows already . . . who the stranger is. We watch the two friends tripping as they charge *him* with unbelievable ignorance." Emphasis by Nuttall.

[12] Charles Cosgrove writes of "the Lukan theme of divine reversal, whereby events are turned upside down in what might be described as divine surprise and cunning." He also suggests

emphasize the continuing tension between divine action and human expectation. These experiences are sufficiently important in the plot to describe the God of Luke-Acts as the God who works by irony. The disciples on the road to Emmaus are about to discover that they are the happy "victims" of the God of irony.

The key thing which the disciples have not understood but must now recognize is expressed in v. 26: "Was it not necessary that the Messiah suffer these things and enter into his glory?" Again this reminds us of Jesus' previous passion prophecies (see 9:22; 17:25), with the title Messiah substituted for Son of Man. Jesus attempted to keep his Messiahship secret during his ministry (4:41; 9:20-21), although it became a basis for accusation in the passion story (22:67; 23:2, 35, 39). It will soon become a matter of public proclamation (Acts 2:36). There is another significant change, for Jesus does not speak of being raised on the third day but of entering into his glory. This way of expressing the result of Jesus' suffering is less closely related to Jesus' passion prophecies before and during his journey to Jerusalem than to the scriptural prophecies of his exaltation to which he refers while in Jerusalem (see 20:17, 42-43; 22:69). The interest is not just in resurrection but in Jesus' entry into a new status, which involves becoming "head of the corner" or "sitting at the right hand" of God, thereby sharing in God's power and glory as messianic king. Peter will proclaim that this has happened in Acts 2:30-36. Thus Luke 24:26 combines Jesus' prophecies of the suffering and resurrection of the Son of Man with prophecies of Jesus' exaltation.[13]

Jesus is implying that not only entry into glory but the suffering of the Messiah was a divine necessity. It was necessary to God's purpose that the Messiah enter into the glory of his reign in this particular way. Jesus goes on to explain this necessity through interpretation of Scripture (24:27). Later he will repeat this revelation for the apostles in Jerusalem, first stating that "it is necessary that all the things written in the law of Moses and the prophets and psalms concerning me be fulfilled," then opening

---

that "Luke-Acts functions as a doxology to the God of surprise reversal." See "The Divine Δεῖ in Luke-Acts," 182, 190.

[13] Richard Dillon maintains that "enter into his glory" must refer to the resurrection, since the infinitive "enter" still depends on the past tense verb ἔδει and Jesus in v. 26 is interpreting what the disciples have been discussing, namely, the crucifixion and the discovery of the empty tomb. He then asserts that this phrase is "a resurrection statement, but more." See From Eye-Witnesses, 141-43. I would agree but would not interpret the "more" in quite the same way as Dillon. The disciples must be enlightened by the risen Messiah; therefore, the narrator provides a period in which this can happen, distinguishing between resurrection and ascension. But when the narrator describes the way of Jesus, we find a tendency to present the death, resurrection, and ascension as a single process, leading to Jesus' new position at the right hand of God. This process can be called Jesus' "exodus" (9:31) or the "taking up" of Jesus (9:51). Similarly, "enter into his glory" seems to embrace both resurrection and exaltation, with the emphasis on the new status of Jesus which results.

their minds to understand the Scripture while explaining that the suffering and resurrection of the Messiah are key parts of what is "written"
(24:44–46). Thus the answer to the question of why it was necessary for
the Messiah to suffer is to be found in Scripture, understood as the
revelation of God's purpose in Jesus.

Luke 24 makes this point in summary fashion in preparation for the
mission of the apostles. The mission sermons in Acts refer again to God's
scriptural plan, and we might expect further explanation there. We do
find strong assertions that Jesus' death fulfilled the plan of God (Acts
2:23; see 4:28) or fulfilled Scripture (3:18; 13:27–29). But the significance
of Jesus' death is not explained in the way that other parts of the New
Testament would lead us to expect, namely, as an atonement for sins. The
death of Jesus is never interpreted as atonement for sins in the mission
speeches of Acts,[14] nor is the death of Jesus ever singled out as the basis for
the release of sins or the salvation in Jesus' name which the missionaries
are proclaiming.[15] Since the importance of Jesus' death in God's plan,
though emphasized in the mission speeches of Acts, is not explained in
terms of atonement for sins, we must find other ways to understand the
necessity of Jesus' death in God's saving purpose. But a solution is not
easy to find. We seem to be confronted with an enigma, the same enigma
that the disciples could not understand during the journey to Jerusalem.
Why is the death of Jesus an integral and necessary part of God's saving
purpose?

The general statements in Luke 24 that the death of Jesus fulfills
Scripture are supported by references to specific scriptural passages in
other parts of Luke-Acts. In Acts the death of Jesus is interpreted by
appeal to Ps 118:22 (Acts 4:11), Ps 2:1–2 (Acts 4:25–26), and Isa 53:7–8
(Acts 8:32–33). Ps 16:8–11 (Acts 2:25–28; 13:35), although primarily
applied to the resurrection, clearly presupposes the death of the Messiah,
as this psalm is interpreted in Acts. To these texts we may add references
in Luke to Ps 118:22 (Luke 20:17), Isa 53:12 (Luke 22:37), Ps 31:5 (Luke
23:46), and perhaps to Ps 22:7, 18, and Ps 69:21 (Luke 23:34–36).
Although no saving significance is attributed to Jesus' death by these texts

---

[14] On Acts 20:28, which is not part of a *mission* speech, see the next note.

[15] For discussion of the significance of Jesus' death in Luke-Acts see A. George, *Études sur l'oeuvre de Luc*, 185–212, and Richard Zehnle, "The Salvific Character of Jesus' Death," 420–44. There are only two passages in Luke-Acts which attach some sort of benefit for others to Jesus' death, Luke 22:19–20 (in which the key statements are textually uncertain) and Acts 20:28. These passages regard the death of Jesus as a community-founding event and do not directly address the issue of how individuals find salvation through Jesus. George and Zehnle disagree as to whether these two passages express Luke's own thought or simply the traditions of the community. They agree that Luke-Acts shows remarkable independence from the widespread theme of Jesus' death for sins and that Luke has other ways of expressing Jesus' saving significance.

(even in the portions of Isaiah 53 quoted in Luke-Acts), the simple fact that Jesus' death is believed to be prophesied in Scripture may seem to be sufficient explanation for Jesus' assertion that the Messiah must suffer. Perhaps for the narrator and the intended readers Scripture is a collection of oracles about the future which are simply to be accepted as such. Whether they disclose a divine purpose which makes sense to humans is irrelevant. Although Jesus uses mental concepts, upbraiding the disciples for being "senseless" or "imperceptive (ἀνόητοι)" and then opening "their mind (νοῦν) to understand (συνιέναι) the Scriptures" (Luke 24:25, 45), he was, according to this view, simply concerned that the disciples recognize the predictive significance of particular scriptural passages. He was not concerned with presenting an understanding of the purpose of God that makes sense to humans, nor was the implied author concerned with discovering a deeper theological sense in Jesus' death. The fact that it is predicted in Scripture makes it necessary, whether it makes sense or not.

Before we settle for this interpretation, we should consider some indications that there is a sense to God's way of working in the world, which includes the death and resurrection of the Messiah. The references to Scripture in 24:27, 44 are sweeping in their scope ("Moses and all the prophets," "all the things written in the law of Moses and the prophets and psalms"). This sweeping language seems to point beyond a limited number of scriptural predictions to something that is central to Scripture as such. In Acts 7:51–52 Stephen gives an interpretation of biblical history which is equally sweeping in scope: "You always resist the Holy Spirit, as your fathers, so you too. Whom of the prophets did not your fathers persecute?" This applies to Moses also, for Stephen has just narrated in some detail how Moses was rejected by the people of Israel, who did not understand his saving mission (7:23–41). When Jesus speaks of "Moses and all the prophets" in Luke 24:27, he may be referring not only to parts of Scripture but to figures of biblical history and their stories. Stephen clearly links the stories of Moses and the prophets, who suffer rejection and persecution, to the story of Jesus, who suffers a similar fate (Acts 7:35–39, 52).[16] That Jesus' fate would follow the pattern of previous prophets, who were repeatedly rejected and killed, was also emphasized in Luke.[17] In a unique Lukan passion prophecy (13:33–34), "it is necessary (δεῖ)" reappears but the title applied to Jesus is not (as elsewhere) "Son of Man" or "Messiah" but "prophet." Recall also that the Emmaus disciples refer to Jesus as a prophet in 24:19. Prophet and Messiah are not

---

[16] See further in vol. 2 on the parallels between Moses and Jesus in Stephen's speech.

[17] See the references to Jesus as rejected prophet in 4:24–30 and 13:33 in light of the general references to the rejection and killing of prophets in 6:22–23; 11:47–51; 13:34. See also the discussion pp. 96–99.

competing titles in Luke-Acts. Jesus is both the Messiah and the expected
Mosaic prophet. Perhaps as a result of this merger, the destiny of the
Messiah is understood in light of the destiny of the prophets, who speak
God's word, are rejected and persecuted by their hearers, yet are affirmed
by God. In the cases of Moses and Elijah (who have an important place in
Luke-Acts) this affirmation includes being taken up to heaven.[18] The
Lukan story of Jesus will end in a similar way. Thus it is appropriate
that, in Luke's account of the transfiguration, Moses and Elijah prepare
Jesus for his "exodus" (Luke 9:31).

In interpreting Jesus' death, the narrative emphasizes what Jesus
shares with other messengers of God. The pattern of prophetic destiny
which we have noted links Jesus both with those who preceded him and
those who follow him. Jesus' witnesses in Acts will fit the pattern established by Jesus and the biblical figures before him. In volume 2 we will
note that the account of the mission and destiny of the apostles, Stephen,
and Paul contain many echoes of the mission and destiny of Jesus, echoes
of the passion story being especially clear.[19] Some of these echoes cluster
into groups and reinforce each other. The statements concerning Jesus'
followers which are closest in wording to Jesus' description of himself in
Luke 24:26 are found in Acts 9:16, which speaks of what "it is necessary
($\delta\epsilon\hat{\imath}$) that he [Paul] suffer ($\pi\alpha\theta\epsilon\hat{\imath}\nu$) for my name," and Acts 14:22, which
says of believers in general, "Through many tribulations it is necessary
($\delta\epsilon\hat{\imath}$) that we enter into ($\epsilon\hat{\imath}\sigma\epsilon\lambda\theta\epsilon\hat{\imath}\nu$ $\epsilon\hat{\imath}s$) the reign of God." Following his
first passion prophecy, Jesus made clear that disciples must accept the
pattern of his suffering as valid for their own lives (Luke 9:22–27). In
Acts, Jesus' call to follow him in suffering is dramatized in narrative.

A number of scholars have helped me to recognize this pattern of
prophetic destiny in Luke-Acts. Paul Minear, in discussing "the prophetic
vocation" in Luke-Acts, detected a succession of prophets, including
"John as prophet like Elijah," "Jesus as prophet like Moses," and "the
apostles as prophets like Jesus."[20] Luke Timothy Johnson pointed out
that leading figures in Acts are described according to a common model,
which he called "Men of the Spirit." Johnson summarized by saying,

---

[18] See 2 Kgs 2:11–12; Sir 48:9 for Elijah. The case with Moses is less clear. We have an
incomplete document which is either identical with or became secondarily attached to a
work called in patristic sources ᾿Ανάληψις Μωυσέως ("Assumption of Moses"). See George
Nickelsburg, Jr., *Studies on the Testament of Moses*, 5. While the document breaks off
before reporting an assumption, the title seems to indicate that some sort of ascension or
"taking up" was part of the account. J. Jeremias, to be sure, believes that the text must have
reported an ascension of the soul rather than a bodily assumption. See *TDNT* 4:855. Philo,
in *De Vita Mosis* 2.291, refers to Moses "being taken up" at the end of his life.

[19] For a preliminary discussion see Robert C. Tannehill, "The Composition of Acts 3–5," 229–
40.

[20] See *To Heal and to Reveal*, 81–147.

"The figures in this category shared a certain stereotyped description, which included being filled with the Holy Spirit, speaking God's Word, performing signs and wonders, and stimulating a response of acceptance/rejection. They were, we concluded, described as Prophets." Jesus provides the model for these "Men of the Spirit," and Moses is presented as a biblical type for Jesus.[21] Richard J. Dillon brought related ideas to bear on the interpretation of Luke 24. In discussing 24:26 he said, "The passion's 'necessity' derived from a perennial *law of prophetic endeavour* binding on every spokesman of God's word, 'beginning from Moses.' That law is understood as a destined course which must be followed also by the witnesses who proclaim the messiah."[22] Dillon also asserted that the Lukan tendency to depict Jesus' death as martyrdom connects his death with prophecy and mission and provides a model for understanding the passion which creates continuity between Jesus and his followers.[23]

A pattern of experience rooted in Scripture and applying to both Jesus and his witnesses helps to make sense of their stories. A sacred pattern assures those who accept it that events are not meaningless and chaotic, for they reflect the rhythm of God's work in the world. Events manifest a sacred pattern which hallows and reassures even when it cannot be rationally explained. A sacred pattern can be effective in sustaining faith and guiding life even when it does not lead to theological explanation. The narrator may have been content with this sacred pattern. It translates easily into narrative, while theological abstractions do not. Thus the narrative as a whole seems to suggest that the risen Christ illumines his blind disciples by conveying to them something like this pattern of prophetic destiny as a key to Scripture and his own story.

It is possible to go one step further in the direction of theological abstraction than the narrator seems willing to do. Recall the preceding discussion of Jesus' death as irony. Jesus' death is seen from two perspectives at the same time: it is the rejection of Jesus and of God's purpose in him; it is also the means by which God's purpose is achieved. This achievement surprises. God overrules human purposes and expectations in an ironic reversal of results. The place of Jesus' death in the hidden, divine purpose is expressed by saying that "it is necessary" that Jesus suffer. This necessity derives from the fact that God's purpose must be realized in a blind and recalcitrant world. By not annihilating this world or robbing it of its power of decision and action, God lays upon God's servants the harsh destiny of suffering. For the world will not yield easily

---

[21] See *The Literary Function of Possessions*, 38–78. Quotation from p. 77.
[22] See *From Eye-Witnesses*, 139. Emphasis by Dillon.
[23] *From Eye-Witnesses*, 279–80.

to God's purposes. From this situation the pattern of prophetic suffering arises, a pattern to which Jesus and his followers must submit. But God retains the power of irony, for this suffering does not lead to the defeat which humans expect. Acceptance of Jesus' teaching that suffering was for him the necessary path to glory involves a struggle with evil and meaninglessness on the part of people who are tempted again and again to believe that good has been defeated. The narrator's picture of the dejected disciples can help us to recognize how difficult this struggle is.

THE MEALS WITH THE RISEN LORD

The stranger does not reveal himself immediately or spectacularly. The travelers to Emmaus come to insight through a gradual process which includes rehearsing what has happened and listening as the stranger explains the necessity of the Messiah's way by interpreting the Scripture. Recognition of Jesus is prepared by the strong impression which this interpretation of Scripture made upon them, as 24:32 indicates. The "burning heart" to which the disciples refer was already the beginning of recognition. Scripture—understood in a particular way—is the interpretive key to grasping God's purpose in Jesus and therefore also the key to understanding the narrator's story.

The moment of full recognition comes at a meal, as Jesus takes the bread, blesses it, breaks and distributes it (24:30). Evidently recognition comes at this point because Jesus is assuming a role familiar to the disciples from meal fellowships previously shared. The narrator described Jesus performing similar actions at a meal twice before, at the Last Supper and at the feeding of the multitude in 9:10–17. The description of the Emmaus meal is closer to the feeding of the multitude than to the Last Supper in some details. According to 24:30 and 9:16 Jesus "blessed" the bread. At the corresponding location in the Last Supper scene (22:19), Jesus gives thanks. In describing both the feeding of the multitude and the Emmaus meal, the day is said to "decline," using the verb κλίνω (9:12; 24:29; the only uses of this verb to express time of day in Luke-Acts). The same verb for reclining to eat (κατακλίνω) is used in these two passages, although the narrator knows synonyms such as ἀναπίπτω (used in 22:14).[24] However, the most striking point of contact between 9:10–17 and the Emmaus meal is in the description of Jesus' initiation of the meal through a series of four actions, and at this point the Last Supper closely resembles the other two meals. Jesus takes bread, blesses (22:19: gives

---

[24] See R. Dillon, *From Eye-Witnesses*, 149.

thanks), breaks it, and gives it to his companions. The careful repetition of this sequence of actions would not be necessary if it were not significant. It suggests an intention to recall previous occasions on which this occurred. The repetition may function less as a reminder of the two specific occasions just discussed than as an indication that this was Jesus' habitual practice in his meal fellowships, a practice now repeated at Emmaus. The memory of Jesus presiding at the meal and breaking the bread turns such meals into symbols of continuity in fellowship with Jesus.[25] In particular, the Emmaus meal becomes a symbol of restoration of a fellowship broken by death. It also anticipates the fellowship meals of believers in Acts. In 24:35 the meal scene is summarized by the phrase "the breaking of the bread." Breaking of bread is a repeated phrase in Acts used to designate the believer's fellowship meals (Acts 2:42, 46; 20:7, 11). It is clear that these meals have some religious significance; they are not just a way of satisfying hunger.[26] However, their significance is never explained. The Emmaus meal, described as "the breaking of the bread," provides the link between the meals of Jesus with his followers in Luke and the meals of the believers in Acts. The presence of the risen Christ at Emmaus may also suggest that the meals in Acts go beyond fellowship among the believers to include communion with the risen Lord.

Richard Dillon points out that in both Luke and Acts the "breaking of the bread" is associated with instruction concerning Jesus' person and mission.[27] The combination of meal and instruction-discussion is characteristic of Luke-Acts. We find this combination in the passages we have discussed. The feeding of the multitude is preceded by Jesus' instruction of the crowd "concerning the reign of God" (9:11) and, in an order of events unique to Luke, is quickly followed by instruction about the need to follow Jesus by taking up one's cross (in words directed "to all," according to 9:23). Luke's Last Supper differs from Matthew's and Mark's because it includes extensive instruction and discussion while the group is still sharing the meal (see 22:21–38). In Acts the breaking of bread is mentioned in close connection with the teaching of the apostles and Paul (2:42; 20:7, 11). In Luke 24:13–32 the discussion and instruction takes place on the road rather than at the meal, but these are two closely connected parts of a single sequence of events. The importance of both parts is emphasized by the summary in 24:35. Thus the story of the journey to Emmaus maintains the combination of instruction and meal fellowship which we have noted in other sections of Luke-Acts. The instruction which Jesus

---

[25] See Willibald Bösen, *Jesusmahl, Eucharistisches Mahl, Endzeitmahl*, 78. He speaks of the meal in Luke-Acts as a "continuity-creating symbol."

[26] See Jacques Dupont, "The Meal at Emmaus," 117–19.

[27] See *From Eye-Witnesses*, 105.

gives in conjunction with this meal becomes an occasion for revealing the purpose of God being realized in his own destiny, a destiny which will also shape the lives of his followers.[28]

In Acts 10:41 Peter will declare that the chosen witnesses, including Peter himself, "ate and drank with" Jesus after his resurrection. Therefore, the meal with Cleopas and his companion was not the only meal that the risen Jesus shared with his followers. The clear statement in Acts 10:41 should control the interpretation of Acts 1:4, where the meaning of συναλιζόμενος is debated. Acts 10:41 shows that the meaning "eat salt with," understood as metonymy for sharing a meal with others, is to be preferred. If so, we find in Acts 1:4–8 a scene in which a shared meal is the setting for Jesus' final instructions to his witnesses. Acts 1:3–8 repeats a number of the key points in Jesus' words to his followers at the end of Luke (Luke 24:46–49). These passages are, in fact, simply variant formulations of the same basic commission by Jesus to his followers. The period of forty days during which Jesus appeared and was "speaking of the things which concern God's reign" (Acts 1:3) has no content in the narrative except what is given to it by Luke 24 and Acts 1:1–11. We are left to assume that Jesus kept appearing in the way described and kept teaching concerning the points mentioned in these passages. The content and setting of that teaching is defined by the two similar scenes in Acts 1:3–8 and Luke 24:36–49.

It is probable that the similarity includes not only the content of the teaching but also its setting in the context of a shared meal. To be sure, Luke 24:41–43 does not specifically speak of the disciples eating with Jesus, and Jesus' request for food can be understood as part of his refutation of the disciples' supposition that they were seeing a "spirit" and not a person of flesh and bone. However, it is doubtful that this refutation is the sole purpose of the reference to Jesus eating. References to eating "before (ἐνώπιον)" someone (24:43) occur elsewhere in contexts which clearly imply a meal shared with those "before" whom one eats. This is the case in Luke 13:26, where the point of saying "we ate and drank before you" is not that they rudely ate while Jesus simply watched but that they shared meals with Jesus. We find the same usage in the LXX (see 2 Kgdms 11:13; 3 Kgdms 1:25), which has probably influenced Luke-

---

[28] See R. Dillon, *From Eye-Witnesses*, 105–8. Dillon concludes that "in Lk's mind, *the Master breaking bread with his followers is the Master sharing his mission and destiny with them!*" (p. 107; emphasis by Dillon). W. Bösen, *Jesusmahl, Eucharistisches Mahl, Endzeitmahl*, 87, makes the more general point that Luke uses the schema of the symposium, in which table conversation is an important feature of a dinner party (see Luke 5:27ff.; 7:36ff.; 11:37ff.; 14:1ff.; 22:15–38).

Acts in this as in other respects.[29] In Acts 1:4 and 10:41 emphasis is placed on sharing the meal through repeated use of $\sigma\upsilon\nu$-. The close relation of Peter's account in 10:41–42 with the commissioning scenes in Luke 24:41–49 and Acts 1:4–8 appears when we note that Peter, after stating that "we ate and drank with him," continues, "And he commanded us to preach ($\kappa\eta\rho\acute{\upsilon}\xi\alpha\iota$) . . . and bear witness ($\delta\iota\alpha\mu\alpha\rho\tau\acute{\upsilon}\rho\alpha\sigma\theta\alpha\iota$)" (see Luke 24:47; Acts 1:8). Peter is summarizing the main features of the scenes which are presented more fully at the end of Luke and the beginning of Acts, when Jesus appeared to the apostles. This summary includes eating and drinking with Jesus. So the narrator emphasizes by repetition the combined experiences of appearance of Jesus, shared meal, and commissioning. This combination seems to carry special significance for the implied author.

If the preceding argument is convincing, we can also conclude that the appearance scenes in Luke 24 follow a chiastic pattern. The two scenes in which Jesus is recognized by his followers and shares a meal with them are introduced and followed by periods of instruction in which Jesus opens the Scriptures and explains the necessity of his death. This pattern emphasizes important concerns through repetition. At the same time, there is development toward a climax. Through the return to Jerusalem, the appearance to the Emmaus disciples leads into the appearance to the apostles, which is given climactic position in the sequence of appearance scenes. The instruction to the apostles in Jerusalem also extends beyond the instruction to the Emmaus disciples by disclosing the mission that will follow and thereby providing a preview of Acts.

The Emmaus disciples immediately return to Jerusalem to report their encounter with the risen Jesus. But when they arrive, the eleven and those with them first report that the Lord has appeared to Simon. Even so, the narrator specifically adds that the Emmaus disciples related their own encounter with Jesus to those in Jerusalem (24:35). Thus there are two confirming reports of encounters with the risen Jesus by parties separated from each other. Although the appearance to Simon receives no attention beyond the summary statement in 24:34, it has an additional function within the larger narrative. Through Simon's experience the others begin to be convinced that the women's message about Jesus' resurrection is really true.[30] In this way Simon is beginning to fulfill Jesus' command to "strengthen your brothers" after he has "turned" (22:32). The connection

---

[29] $\grave{\epsilon}\nu\acute{\omega}\pi\iota\upsilon\nu$ is common in the LXX and in Luke-Acts, but in the other gospels it occurs only once, in John 20:30.

[30] "Really" (RSV, "indeed") in v. 34 is an affirmation of the women's message, which was previously rejected. Thus there is an indirect reference to a third source of testimony to the resurrection of Jesus.

between these two passages is reinforced by the fact that they are the only places in Luke where Peter is called Simon after the formal indication in 6:14 that Jesus gave Simon a new name. Simon is warned and charged with responsibility in 22:31–32, and he begins to fulfill that responsibility by bearing witness to the risen Jesus before Jesus' other followers.

THE REVELATION IN JERUSALEM

In spite of the indication in v. 34 that the eleven and those with them are now willing to accept the witness to the resurrection, the following appearance of Jesus at first produces fear, with continuing disbelief. Jesus must convince them that it is really he and not some spirit. Even when he has shown them his hands and feet and has invited them to feel him, the problem is not fully resolved. The narrator indicates that "they were still disbelieving from joy" (24:41). This statement is evidently intended to describe an ambiguous response. They are joyful, but the resurrection of Jesus still seems too much to hope for, and this feeling is viewed as continuing disbelief. This disbelief is expressed with the same word used to describe the rejection of the women's message in 24:11, indicating that the previous blindness to God's power and ways of working is not fully overcome even when people witness the physical presence of the risen Lord with their own eyes. Just at the point where we would expect to be told that the disciples are fully convinced by Jesus' demonstrations of his physical presence,[31] we find instead Jesus' instruction concerning the divine plan in Scripture which is being realized through Jesus. A fully adequate response is narrated only in 24:52. The "great joy" mentioned there exceeds the "joy" of v. 41, especially because it is no longer accompanied by disbelief. Additional steps beyond a physical appearance were necessary to reach full faith. These include the meal with the risen Jesus and especially his instruction about how the events they have experienced fit God's purpose.[32]

The disciples in Jerusalem must understand what the Emmaus disciples were previously told, that the story of Jesus is unfolding according to the scriptural witness to God's purpose and that this applies, in particular, to Jesus' suffering and resurrection. They, too, must have their minds opened to understand the Scriptures. But in 24:47–49 Jesus goes

---

[31] Cf. John 20:20, 27–28, where the showing of hands and side by Jesus is immediately followed by joyful recognition and confession of faith.

[32] See R. Dillon, *From Eye-Witnesses*, 198–99: "The risen Lord persuaded his followers he was 'alive' by his *appearance* and by his *instruction*. The two steps were necessary *together* to show that this was truly he." Emphasis by Dillon.

beyond what he had previously said. When the disciples have finally understood and accepted the necessity of the Messiah's death and resurrection, Jesus can go on to instruct them about their mission. Thus 24:44–49 forms the climax of the risen Lord's revelation to his disciples and also prepares for the transition to Acts.

We have seen that the narrator helps readers to recognize and interpret major developments within the plot through key scenes which reveal the nature of God's purpose that is being realized in the story. I previously suggested that we are likely to find such keys to the plot in scenes which provide a preview or review of central events in the story, state the commission which important characters must fulfill, appeal to Scripture to interpret events of the story, and give weight to an interpretation of major developments by placing it in the mouth of an authoritative character.[33] Luke 24:44–49 fulfills all of these criteria. Jesus both reviews the past and previews the future. In speaking of the future, he is giving his followers a commission which will guide their actions. The appeal to Scripture is strong, even though specific passages are not cited here, and it is obvious that the risen Messiah speaks with authority in Luke-Acts. The function of 24:44–49 as a disclosure and interpretation of central elements of the plot is confirmed by the fact that the story in Acts will unfold as described in Jesus' preview in vv. 47–49.

The Lukan narrative does not stop where Matthew and John stop, with the resurrection of Jesus and his commission to his disciples. Our story is still incomplete at this point. In a sense this is true of the other gospels also, for they contain previews of the time of the church and the return of the Son of Man. However, the preaching to all nations in Jesus' name takes on greater importance in Luke-Acts because the narrative not only provides previews of this preaching but shows it taking place in scenic detail. The result is a story which is not just the story of Jesus. It is the story of a purpose of God that is being realized both through Jesus and his witnesses. "Thus it is written" is followed in 24:46–47 by three coordinate infinitives (in the Greek) which refer to suffering, resurrection, and preaching in Jesus' name as important steps in the realization of God's purpose attested in Scripture. The story of God's purpose in the world is not complete with Jesus' resurrection. It includes the preaching to all nations,[34] and this preaching is important enough to be narrated, not just previewed.

There are further reasons why the story does not stop with the resur-

---

[33] See above, pp. 21–22.

[34] Jacques Dupont makes this point well. See "La portée christologique de l'évangélisation," 125–43. Dupont also argues that the preaching to all nations is part of the work of Christ himself.

rection of Jesus. Among them is the implied author's great concern with the Jewish people's reaction to Jesus and the gospel. The risen Messiah has been recognized by his disciples, but the people of Jerusalem have rejected him. Jesus' resurrection does not resolve this problem. Indeed, the resurrection increases the tension, for by it God has affirmed as Messiah the one who was denied in Jerusalem. A resolution of this divine-human conflict is still possible. This unresolved situation is important enough to the implied author that it must be worked through in the continuing narrative.

The narrator carefully unifies the narrative by an interlacing of elements at major transition points.[35] This interlacing is clearest where the transition is clearest, at the juncture of Books 1 and 2. Jesus' final words in Luke provide a detailed introduction to Acts, where the themes in Luke 24:47–49 will immediately be important. At the beginning of Acts Jesus' "name" becomes a major theme (see especially 2:21, 38; 3:6, 16; 4:7, 10, 12). The apostles' preaching is highlighted, and it is a preaching of "repentance for release of sins" (2:38; 3:19; 5:31). The mission "to all nations" is reemphasized in 1:8, although this mission is only gradually implemented. In Acts 1:4 Jesus again indicates that Jerusalem should be the beginning point of the mission, and the following narrative fits this. The role of the apostles as witnesses is emphasized in the early chapters of Acts (1:8, 22; 2:32; 3:15; 4:33; 5:32). The coming of the Spirit is highlighted in the Pentecost scene, and the descriptions of the Spirit as "the promise of my Father" and "power" in Luke 24:49 are repeated in Acts 1:4, 8; 2:33. Even the indication that this is "power from on high ($\dot{\epsilon}\xi$ $\ddot{v}\psi ovs$)" corresponds to the fact that Jesus pours out the Spirit after he has been "exalted ($\dot{v}\psi\omega\theta\epsilon\acute{\iota}s$)," according to Acts 2:33.

Something further should be noted. Not only does Luke 24:47–49 correspond in detail to the beginning chapters of Acts; this passage is also closely connected with a number of basic statements which describe the missions of leading characters of Luke-Acts. These connections indicate that there is a basic continuity of mission uniting those called by God and unifying the whole of Luke-Acts. The proclaiming of repentance for the release of sins is related to Jesus' own mission "to proclaim release ($\kappa\eta\rho\acute{v}\xi\alpha\iota \ldots \ddot{\alpha}\phi\epsilon\sigma\iota\nu$)" announced in 4:18,[36] and the "power from on high" which Jesus promises his witnesses is the same "power of the Spirit" which was active in Jesus' ministry (4:14). The description of the apostles' message in 24:47 is even closer to the message of John the Baptist

---

[35] Jacques Dupont points out that this corresponds to the advice of Lucian on how to write history. See "La question du plan des Actes," 220–31.

[36] On the significance of "release" in this passage, see above, pp. 65–66.

as summarized in 3:3. Jesus tells the apostles to proclaim repentance for release of sins. John came "proclaiming a baptism of repentance for release of sins." The words are the same, except for the reference to baptism.[37] The term "release ($\H{\alpha}\phi\epsilon\sigma\iota s$)" is not used in Luke after its application to the missions of John and Jesus in 3:3 and 4:18 until it recurs in the description of the apostles' mission in 24:47. The close similarity of 3:3 and 24:47 is not merely the result of unreflective habits of language, for there are other connections between the work of John and the work of Jesus' witnesses. John's promise in 3:16 that another would "baptize in Holy Spirit" is recalled in Acts 1:5, with Jesus' followers as the recipients of this baptism. Moreover, when the apostles begin to proclaim repentance for release of sins, the narrator introduces language reminiscent of John's work. In Acts 2:38 Peter proclaims, "Repent and be baptized, each of you, . . . for release of your sins." This is preceded by the question, "What should we do? ($\tau\acute{\iota}\ \pi o\iota\acute{\eta}\sigma\omega\mu\epsilon\nu$)," which repeats the questions addressed to John in Luke 3:10, 12, 14. Peter's cry, "Be saved from this crooked ($\sigma\kappa o\lambda\iota\hat{\alpha}s$) generation" (Acts 2:40), picks up the language of the Isaiah text used to introduce John's ministry, a text which proclaims that "the crooked ($\tau\grave{\alpha}\ \sigma\kappa o\lambda\iota\acute{\alpha}$)" will become straight and relates this to the experience of "the salvation of God" (Luke 3:5–6).[38] So the basic message of the apostles according to 24:47 is not new. The apostles stand in the tradition of the prophet John, whose message was continued by Jesus. Nevertheless, there are some significant new developments: the proclamation of repentance for release of sins is to take place in Jesus' name and is to be carried to all nations.

It is evidently important for readers to have Jesus' commission to his disciples clearly in mind as the story continues in Acts, for this commission is repeated in Acts 1:8. The shared cluster of themes in Luke 24:47–49 and Acts 1:4–5, 8 indicates that the latter passage is largely repetitive. In both passages we find reference to Jerusalem as starting point, the apostles as witnesses, and the Spirit as promise and power. The mission of preaching to all nations in Luke 24:47 is expressed in Acts 1:8 as a command to be Jesus' witnesses "in Jerusalem and in all Judea and Samaria and to the end of the earth." Here the mission to all nations is developed as a geographical sequence which partly anticipates the course

---

[37] It is uncertain whether we should read "repentance for" or "repentance and" in 24:47, but the former reading is supported by manuscripts of high quality. This detail does not greatly affect my main point.

[38] We previously noted other evidence of a similarity between the mission of John and of Jesus' disciples. The scriptural text, "Behold, I send my messenger before your face," is applied first to John the Baptist and then to Jesus' followers (Luke 7:27; 9:52; 10:1). See above, pp. 229–30, 233–35.

of the story which follows. Repentance for release of sins is not mentioned in 1:8, but Peter's first sermon ends with an appeal to "repent and be baptized . . . in the name of Jesus Christ for release of your sins" (2:38), as we have already noted.

The similarities among the summary descriptions of the mission and message of John, Jesus, and the apostles suggest that these persons share in a common mission which is now expanding to embrace the world. It is not surprising that the description of Paul's mission and message also fits what we have found. In describing his mission in Acts 13:47, Paul quotes Isa 49:6: "I have placed you for a light of nations, so that you may be for salvation to the end of the earth." The last four words of the Greek ($\overset{\text{\'{}}}{\epsilon}\omega\varsigma$ $\overset{\text{\'{}}}{\epsilon}\sigma\chi\acute{\alpha}\tau o\upsilon$ $\tau\hat{\eta}\varsigma$ $\gamma\hat{\eta}\varsigma$) repeat the last four words of 1:8. There, too, they were evidently derived from Isa 49:6. The mission of world-wide scope emphasized in Acts 1:8 and 13:47 also appears in Luke 24:47, and the references to "light of nations" and "salvation" in Acts 13:47 remind us of similar language borrowed from Isaiah in Luke 2:30–32 and 3:6.

The importance of this complex of themes and the concern to highlight the continuity between the message of Paul and the message of his predecessors are especially clear in Acts 26:16–23, a retrospective summary of Paul's mission. In 26:20 Paul describes his past mission in terms of a geographical sequence partly the same as the sequence in 1:8. Then he says, "I was proclaiming that they repent ($\dot{\alpha}\pi\acute{\eta}\gamma\gamma\epsilon\lambda\lambda o\nu$ $\mu\epsilon\tau\alpha$-$\nu o\epsilon\hat{\iota}\nu$) . . . , doing deeds worthy of repentance" (compare the words of John the Baptist in Luke 3:8). Paul had already mentioned in Acts 26:18 that he was sent so that others might "receive release of sins ($\overset{\text{\'{}}}{\alpha}\phi\epsilon\sigma\iota\nu$ $\dot{\alpha}\mu\alpha\rho\tau\iota\hat{\omega}\nu$)." Paul is "bearing witness ($\mu\alpha\rho\tau\upsilon\rho\acute{o}\mu\epsilon\nu o\varsigma$)," and he climaxes that witness with a three step summary of the Christ event which describes the Christ as one who suffers, arises from the dead, and proclaims "light both to the people and to the nations" (26:23). The last part of this is being realized as people "turn from darkness to light" through Paul's preaching (26:18). The three step summary of the Christ event parallels the words of the risen Christ in Luke 24:46–47,[39] where (emphasizing the fulfillment of Scripture, as in Acts 26:22) Jesus spoke of the Christ suffering, arising from the dead, and repentance for release of sins being proclaimed to all the nations. Paul speaks of proclaiming "light," but he has already made clear that the saving message includes repentance and release of sins. Proclaiming light is an alternate image for the saving message, an image borrowed from Isaiah and previously used in Luke 2:32 and Acts 13:47. Thus in Acts 26 Paul repeats the inter-

---

[39] See J. Dupont, "La portée christologique de l'évangélisation," 140. Dupont stresses that the universal proclamation is directly attributed to Christ himself in Acts 26:23.

pretation of the Christ event found in Luke 24:46–47 and presents his own mission as a continuation of the saving mission announced much earlier in Luke-Acts.[40]

Therefore, Jesus' words in Luke 24:46–49 not only provide a bridge to the early part of Acts but fit with a series of statements describing the missions of key characters, from the summary of John the Baptist's mission early in Luke to the summary of Paul's mission late in Acts. Our understanding of this shared mission is enriched when we compare these statements, noting the similarities that appear even when the language varies. The similarities among these mission statements also suggest a common purpose behind this series of preachers. Those sent to proclaim are co-workers in a common task, and a continuous purpose of God is being realized through them all. To be sure, Luke 24:47 is an important turning point in the story of this shared mission. Jesus will no longer directly offer release of sins to the outcasts. He will be exalted to God's right hand, and his witnesses will offer release of sins in his name. Furthermore, Jesus here declares to the apostles that repentance for release of sins must be proclaimed "to all the nations." The mission should begin in Jerusalem but must become universal in scope. Both this beginning and this goal are important, for Luke-Acts represents a faith which remains rooted in Jewish Scripture and is concerned about the fate of the Jews but wants the world to share in God's salvation.

CLOSURE AND OPENNESS

Jesus' instructions to his witnesses hold the story open. There are future events which are important to the plot, and the purpose of God in Jesus will not be fully realized apart from this future in which the apostles must play a central role. Jesus' words in 24:47–49 anticipate specific details of the continuing story (the mission will begin in Jerusalem; it will be related to a powerful manifestation of the Spirit). In partial tension with these instructions that give the story a sense of incompleteness, holding it open toward the future, the final verses of the gospel (24:50–53) provide a point of closure. This tension between openness and closure is not the kind of tension which results from an editor patching together materials which do not fit well together. Rather it is a significant tension which suggests that the Gospel of Luke can be read in two ways: as the story of Jesus, which is now over; as the story of the saving purpose of God, which is not over, for it has far to go to reach its goal.

---

[40] See Jacques Dupont, "La Mission de Paul d'après Actes 26.16–23."

In order to bring the plot of the gospel to a close, Luke 24:50–53 contains features appropriate to a final departure scene. Jesus has given the instructions which his witnesses need in order to carry out their mission when he is gone. The parting that follows is an event of unusual solemnity, for Jesus lifts his hands and blesses his disciples.[41] The final verse summarizes the continuing activity of the disciples over some length of time without any hint of Jesus' return. If the words, "And he was being taken up into heaven" (24:51), are an original part of Luke, it is quite clear that this scene refers to Jesus' final departure from earthly life. Unfortunately, it is uncertain whether this clear reference to Jesus' ascension is original. While the manuscript evidence for these words and for the words "worshiping him" in 24:52 is very strong, there is continuing reason for uncertainty at both points.[42] If the longer reading which clearly refers to the ascension was not part of the original text, the narrator depicts a solemn departure, bringing the gospel to appropriate closure, but the relation of this departure to Jesus' ascension remains unclear. Where to end a story is a literary decision. It need not coincide with the last encounter between the main characters. Nevertheless, the ending must have an air of finality if reader expectations are to be satisfied. The Lukan narrative gains in intensity through rushing to a conclusion within a single day of tremendous change. What lies beyond the ending must be suppressed in order to achieve literary closure.

Nevertheless, what has been closed can be reopened. Our narrator

---

[41] R. Dillon notes that "blessings are hallmarks of final-departure scenes in Jewish literature." He cites Gen 27:4; 48:15ff.; Deut 33; Tob 12:16ff.; Jub 22:10ff.; 45:14; 2 Enoch 57:2. See *From Eye-Witnesses*, 181, n. 76.

[42] In favor of the longer readings: P75, an early papyrus, has joined the many manuscripts that support inclusion, indicating that these readings are not only widespread but also quite early. There are at least two possible explanations for later omission: (1) accidental omission through a skip of the eye of the copyist between the repeated letter combinations NKAIA; (2) deliberate omission in order to avoid two reports of the ascension (here and in Acts 1) which seem to conflict in date, since Luke 24 moves directly from Easter appearance to ascension, with no mention of a forty-day interval. Furthermore, the brief summary of the gospel in Acts 1:1–2 indicates that it ended with the ascension. These and other points supporting the longer reading are presented in B. Metzger, *A Textual Commentary*, 189–90. On the other hand, Mikeal Carl Parsons has recently renewed the argument that in the seven passages in Luke 24 where representatives of the Western Text have shorter readings (24:3, 6, 12, 36, 40, 51, 52) these shorter readings should be followed. See *The Ascension Narratives in Luke-Acts*, 20–61. Despite the early date and wide distribution of these readings, Parsons believes that they reflect theological tendencies which fit the historical context of P75 and include borrowings from the Gospel of John. The theological tendencies include a heightening of Luke's Christology and stress on the corporeality of Jesus' resurrection and ascension in refutation of Egyptian gnosticism. It should be noted that the shorter reading in 24:51 is supported by Sinaiticus as well as by Western witnesses. Furthermore, the reference in 24:52 to people "worshiping ($\pi\rho o\sigma\kappa\upsilon\nu\acute{\eta}\sigma\alpha\nu\tau\epsilon\varsigma$)" Jesus is unusual in Luke-Acts but not in Matthew. When this verb is used elsewhere in Luke-Acts to refer to worship of someone other than God, this worship is always viewed negatively (see Luke 4:7–8; Acts 7:43; 10:25).

wants to have it both ways: to bring the gospel to an appropriate end and
yet tell what lies beyond this end because it is important to the larger
story, continuing in Acts, of which the story of Jesus is part. It is easy for
this narrator to end without telling everything because this ending will
prove not to be the real ending.

Whether we follow the longer or shorter readings, the departure of
Jesus from his followers serves to bring Luke's story of Jesus to a close.
Mikeal Parsons, as part of an extensive discussion of literary methods and
functions of endings and beginnings, notes the relevance of "framing," as
studied by Uspensky.[43] The framing of a narrative assists the readers to
enter it at the beginning and to leave it at the end. This often involves
taking a position more or less external to the narrative at these points of
transition. Uspensky himself, although he was not studying biblical
literature, cited the prologue of the Gospel of Luke as an example of
beginning from a position external to the narrative. Parsons proceeds to
study the ending of Luke in the light of Uspensky's discussion. A closing
scene may be depicted with a broad horizon, as if it were being viewed
from a distance. A "silent scene" (one lacking in dialogue) may result.[44]
Parsons notes the contrast between the preceding narrative in Luke 24,
which is full of dialogue, and the silent scene with which Luke ends. We
are close enough to see gestures but not close enough to hear what is being
said.[45] The narrator has withdrawn to a distance, taking the readers
along. This contributes to a sense of closure. The brevity and vagueness of
the departure scene (the blessing and departure are reported in two verses,
with two verses devoted to the disciples' response) may also contribute to
the sense of distance appropriate to an ending.

The sense of closure is supported by reminders of the birth stories with
which the gospel began, for a return to initial themes is a way of rounding
off a story.[46] Jesus' disciples "returned to Jerusalem with great joy, and
they were continually in the temple blessing God" (24:52–53). The angel
announced to the shepherds a "great joy," and when they had seen the
baby, the shepherds "returned glorifying and praising God" (2:10, 20).[47]
In the birth narratives, joy and praise are expressed through "blessing

---

[43] M. Parsons, *The Ascension Narratives in Luke-Acts*, 151–60; Boris Uspensky, *A Poetics of Composition*, 137–51.

[44] B. Uspensky, *A Poetics of Composition*, 149.

[45] M. Parsons, *The Ascension Narratives in Luke-Acts*, 156–57.

[46] On similarities between the ending of Luke and the birth stories, see P. A. van Stempvoort, "The Interpretation of the Ascension," 35; Gerhard Lohfink, *Die Himmelfahrt Jesu*, 253. See M. Parsons, *The Ascension Narratives in Luke-Acts*, 139–48, for further discussion of the common narrative technique of "circularity," with application to the end of Luke.

[47] The phrase "great joy" does not occur elsewhere in Luke, and "joy (χαρά)" is used only four times in Luke 3–23.

God," just as in 24:53 (see 1:64; 2:28). Indeed, both Zechariah's and Simeon's hymns are ways of blessing God (1:68; 2:28).[48] Action in the gospel story begins in the Jerusalem temple. That is where Zechariah hears of "joy" (1:14) and where Simeon blesses God (2:28). At the end the gospel returns to the same mood in the same location. When we are told that the disciples were "continually in the temple," we may also be reminded of Anna, who "did not leave the temple, serving [God] night and day" (2:37). The return at the end of Luke to the mood of joyful praise of God that filled the birth stories rounds off the story of Jesus; it also affirms that the joy felt by the devoted Jews who greeted the infant Jesus has been justified by later events, bringing the story to a happy resolution. The joy and praise filling the disciples following Jesus' appearance and departure will continue in the life of the early church, as Acts 2:46–47 indicates.

I stated earlier that 24:50–53 is the ending only of the story of Jesus, not of the larger story of God's saving purpose for all flesh. Furthermore, it is a happy ending only in a partial sense. The tension caused by the failure of the disciples to understand Jesus' destined way has been resolved, bringing great joy to them. But the people of Jerusalem, misled by their leaders, have rejected and denied Jesus. This rejection is a continuing obstacle to God's saving work, an obstacle with which the apostles must deal as they call the people to repentance in the mission speeches of Acts. The importance of this unresolved problem appears in the repeated references to Jewish rejection of Jesus and his witnesses from Peter's Pentecost speech (Acts 2:23, 36) to Paul's final statement in Rome (Acts 28:25–28).

---

[48] Apart from 1:64, 2:28, and 24:53, the verb "bless (εὐλογέω)" is not used in Luke-Acts with God as object.

Achtemeier, Paul. "The Lukan Perspective on the Miracles of Jesus: A Preliminary Sketch." *Journal of Biblical Literature* 94 (1975): 547–62.

Allison, Dale C., Jr. "Matt. 23:39=Luke 13:35b as a Conditional Prophecy." *Journal for the Study of the New Testament* 18 (1983): 75–84.

Alter, Robert. *The Art of Biblical Narrative.* New York: Basic Books, Inc., 1981.

Anderson, Hugh. "Broadening Horizons: The Rejection at Nazareth Pericope of Luke 4:16–30 in Light of Recent Critical Trends." *Interpretation* 18 (1964): 259–75.

Auffret, Pierre. "Note sur la structure littéraire de Lc 1.68–79." *New Testament Studies* 24 (1977–78): 248–58.

Baarlink, Heinrich. "Ein gnädiges Jahr des Herrn–und Tage der Vergeltung." *Zeitschrift für die neutestamentliche Wissenschaft* 73 (1982): 204–20.

Bailey, Kenneth Ewing. *Poet and Peasant: A Literary Cultural Approach to the Parables in Luke.* Grand Rapids: Wm. B. Eerdmans, 1976.

Barrett, C. K. *Luke the Historian in Recent Study.* London: Epworth Press, 1961.

Bauer, Walter. *A Greek-English Lexicon of the New Testament and Other Early Christian Literature.* 2d ed. Translated, revised, and augmented by William F. Arndt, F. Wilbur Gingrich, and Frederick W. Danker. Chicago: University of Chicago Press, 1979.

Beck, Brian E. "'Imitatio Christi' and the Lucan Passion Narrative." Pp. 28–47 in *Suffering and Martyrdom in the New Testament,* edited by William Horbury and Brian McNeil. Cambridge: Cambridge University Press, 1981.

Bertram, Georg. "Εὐεργετέω, εὐεργέτης, εὐεργεσία." Pp. 654–55 in *Theological Dictionary of the New Testament,* edited by Gerhard Kittel, vol. 2. Translated by Geoffrey W. Bromiley. Grand Rapids: Wm. B. Eerdmans, 1964.

Betz, Hans Dieter. "The Origin and Nature of Christian Faith According to the Emmaus Legend." *Interpretation* 23 (1969): 32–46.

Blass, F., and A. Debrunner. *A Greek Grammar of the New Testament and Other Early Christian Literature.* Translated and revised by Robert W. Funk. Chicago: University of Chicago Press, 1961.

Blinzler, Joseph. "Die literarische Eigenart des sogenannten Reiseberichts im Lukasevangelium." Pp. 20–52 in *Synoptische Studien: Alfred Wikenhauser zum siebzigsten Geburtstag am 22. Februar 1953 dargebracht von Freunden, Kollegen und Schülern.* Munich: Karl Zink, 1953.

Blomberg, Craig L. "The Law in Luke-Acts." *Journal for the Study of the New Testament* 22 (1984): 53–80.

————. "Midrash, Chiasmus, and the Outline of Luke's Central Section." Pp. 217–61 in *Gospel Perspectives,* vol. 3, edited by R. T. France and David Wenham. Sheffield: JSOT Press, 1983.

Bösen, Willibald. *Jesusmahl, Eucharistisches Mahl, Endzeitmahl: Ein Beitrag zur Theologie des Lukas.* Stuttgarter Bibelstudien 97. Stuttgart: Katholisches Bibelwerk, 1980.

Booth, Wayne C. *The Rhetoric of Fiction.* 2d ed. Chicago: University of Chicago Press, 1983.

Bovon, François. "Le Dieu de Luc." *Recherches de science religieuse* 69 (1981): 279–300.

_____. "L'importance des médiations dans le projet théologique de Luc." *New Testament Studies* 21 (1974–75): 23–39.

Braumann, Georg. "Das Mittel der Zeit." *Zeitschrift für die neutestamentliche Wissenschaft* 54 (1963): 117–45.

Brawley, Robert L. *The Pharisees in Luke-Acts: Luke's Address to Jews and His Irenic Purpose.* Ph.D. diss., Princeton Theological Seminary, 1978.

Brodie, Thomas Louis. "Greco-Roman Imitation of Texts as a Partial Guide to Luke's Use of Sources." Pp. 17–46 in *Luke-Acts: New Perspectives from the Society of Biblical Literature Seminar,* edited by Charles H. Talbert. New York: The Crossroad Publishing Co., 1984.

Broer, Ingo. "Das Gleichnis vom verlorenen Sohn und die Theologie des Lukas." *New Testament Studies* 20 (1973–74): 453–62.

Brown, E. K. *Rhythm in the Novel.* Toronto: University of Toronto Press, 1950.

Brown, Raymond E. *The Birth of the Messiah: A Commentary on the Infancy Narratives in Matthew and Luke.* Garden City, NY: Doubleday & Co., 1979.

Brown, Raymond E., Karl P. Donfried, Joseph A. Fitzmyer, and John Reumann, eds. *Mary in the New Testament: A Collaborative Assessment by Protestant and Roman Catholic Scholars.* Philadelphia: Fortress Press; New York: Paulist Press, 1978.

Brown, Schuyler. *Apostasy and Perseverance in the Theology of Luke.* Analecta Biblica 36. Rome: Pontifical Biblical Institute, 1969.

Buck, Erwin. "The Function of the Pericope 'Jesus before Herod' in the Passion Narrative of Luke." Pp. 165–78 in *Wort in der Zeit: Neutestamentliche Studien,* edited by Wilfrid Haubeck and Michael Bachmann. Leiden: E. J. Brill, 1980.

Büchele, Anton. *Der Tod Jesu im Lukasevangelium: Eine redaktionsgeschichtliche Untersuchung zu Lk 23.* Frankfurter theologische Studien 26. Frankfurt: Verlag Josef Knecht, 1978.

Bultmann, Rudolf. *The History of the Synoptic Tradition.* Rev. ed. Translated by John Marsh. New York: Harper & Row, 1963.

Burger, Christoph. *Jesus als Davidssohn: Eine traditionsgeschichtliche Untersuchung.* Forschungen zur Religion und Literatur des Alten und Neuen Testaments 98. Göttingen: Vandenhoeck & Ruprecht, 1970.

Busse, Ulrich. *Das Nazareth-Manifest Jesu: Eine Einführung in das lukanische Jesusbild nach Lk 4,16–30.* Stuttgarter Bibelstudien 91. Stuttgart: Katholisches Bibelwerk, 1977.

_____. *Die Wunder des Propheten Jesus: Die Rezeption, Komposition und Interpretation der Wundertradition im Evangelium des Lukas.* 2d ed. Forschung zur Bibel 24. Stuttgart: Katholisches Bibelwerk, 1979.

Cadbury, Henry J. "Commentary on the Preface of Luke." Pp. 489–510 in *The Beginnings of Christianity,* part 1, vol. 2, edited by F. J. Foakes Jackson and Kirsopp Lake. London: Macmillan, 1922.

_____. "Four Features of Lucan Style." Pp. 87–102 in *Studies in Luke-Acts,* edited by Leander E. Keck and J. Louis Martyn. Nashville: Abingdon Press, 1966.

_____. *The Making of Luke-Acts.* 2d ed. London: SPCK, 1958.

_____. *The Style and Literary Method of Luke.* 2 vols. Harvard Theological Studies 6. Cambridge: Harvard University Press, 1919–20.

Caird, G. B. *Saint Luke.* Pelican New Testament Commentaries. Harmondsworth: Penguin Books, 1963.

Calloud, Jean. *Structural Analysis of Narrative.* Translated by Daniel Patte. Semeia Supplements 4. Philadelphia: Fortress Press; Missoula, MT: Scholars Press, 1976.

Cambe, M. "La χάρις chez Saint Luc." *Revue Biblique* 70 (1963): 193–207.

Cassidy, Richard J. *Jesus, Politics, and Society: A Study of Luke's Gospel.* Maryknoll, NY: Orbis Books, 1978.

_____. "Luke's Audience, the Chief Priests, and the Motive for Jesus' Death." Pp. 146–67 in *Political Issues in Luke-Acts,* edited by Richard J. Cassidy and Philip J. Scharper. Maryknoll, NY: Orbis Books, 1983.

Chatman, Seymour. *Story and Discourse: Narrative Structure in Fiction and Film.* Ithaca, NY: Cornell University Press, 1978.

Chilton, Bruce. "Announcement in Nazara: An Analysis of Luke 4:16–21." Pp. 147–72 in *Gospel Perspectives,* vol. 2, edited by R. T. France and David Wenham. Sheffield: JSOT Press, 1981.

Combrink, H. J. B. "The Structure and Significance of Luke 4:16–30." *Neotestamentica* 7 (1973): 27–47.

Conzelmann, Hans. *The Theology of St. Luke.* Translated by Geoffrey Buswell. London: Faber and Faber, Ltd., 1960.

Corbin, Michel. "Jésus devant Hérode: Lecture de Luc 23, 6–12." *Christus* 25 (1978): 190–97.

Cosgrove, Charles H. "The Divine Δεî in Luke-Acts." *Novum Testamentum* 26 (1984): 168–90.

Creed, John Martin. *The Gospel according to St. Luke.* London: Macmillan, 1930.

Crockett, Larrimore C. "Luke 4:25–27 and Jewish-Gentile Relations in Luke-Acts." *Journal of Biblical Literature* 88 (1969): 177–83.

———. *The Old Testament in the Gospel of Luke, with Emphasis on the Interpretation of Isaiah 61.1–2.* Ph.D. diss., Brown University, 1966.

Crossan, John Dominic. *Cliffs of Fall: Paradox and Polyvalence in the Parables of Jesus.* New York: Seabury Press, 1980.

———. *In Parables: The Challenge of the Historical Jesus.* New York: Harper & Row, 1973.

Dahl, Nils A. "The Story of Abraham in Luke-Acts." Pp. 139–58 in *Studies in Luke-Acts,* edited by Leander E. Keck and J. Louis Martyn. Nashville: Abingdon Press, 1966.

Danker, Frederick W. *Benefactor: Epigraphic Study of a Graeco-Roman and New Testament Semantic Field.* St. Louis: Clayton, 1982.

———. "The Endangered Benefactor in Luke-Acts." Pp. 39–48 in *Society of Biblical Literature 1981 Seminar Papers,* edited by Kent Harold Richards. Chico, CA: Scholars Press, 1981.

———. "Graeco-Roman Cultural Accommodation in the Christology of Luke-Acts." Pp. 391–414 in *Society of Biblical Literature 1983 Seminar Papers,* edited by Kent Harold Richards. Chico, CA: Scholars Press, 1983.

———. *Jesus and the New Age according to St. Luke: A Commentary on the Third Gospel.* St. Louis: Clayton, 1972.

———. *Luke.* Proclamation Commentaries. Philadelphia: Fortress Press, 1976.

Davies, J. G. "The Prefigurement of the Ascension in the Third Gospel." *Journal of Theological Studies* 6 (1955): 229–33.

Dawsey, James Marshall. *The Literary Function of Point of View in Controlling Confusion and Irony in the Gospel of Luke.* Ph.D. diss., Emory University, 1983.

de Jonge, Henk J. "Sonship, Wisdom, Infancy: Luke II.41–51a." *New Testament Studies* 24 (1977–78): 317–54.

Delorme, Jean. "Luc v. 1–11: Analyse Structurale et Histoire de la Rédaction." *New Testament Studies* 18 (1972): 331–50.

Denaux, A. "L'hypocrisie des Pharisiens et le dessein de Dieu: Analyse de Lc. XIII, 31–33." Pp. 245–85 in *L'Évangile de Luc: Problèmes littéraires et théologiques,* edited by F. Neirynck. Bibliotheca ephemeridum theologicarum Lovaniensium 32. Gembloux: J. Duculot, 1973.

Dietrich, Wolfgang. *Das Petrusbild der lukanischen Schriften.* Beiträge zur Wissenschaft vom Alten und Neuen Testament 94. Stuttgart: W. Kohlhammer, 1972.

Dillon, Richard J. *From Eye-Witnesses to Ministers of the Word: Tradition and Composition in Luke 24.* Analecta Biblica 82. Rome: Biblical Institute Press, 1978.

———. "Previewing Luke's Project from His Prologue (Luke 1:1–4)." *Catholic Biblical Quarterly* 43 (1981): 205–27.

Dodd, C. H. "The Fall of Jerusalem and the 'Abomination of Desolation'." Pp. 69–83 in *More New Testament Studies*. Grand Rapids: Wm. B. Eerdmans, 1968.

Dömer, Michael. *Das Heil Gottes: Studien zur Theologie des lukanischen Doppelwerkes*. Bonner biblische Beiträge 51. Cologne: Peter Hanstein, 1978.

Drury, John. *Tradition and Design in Luke's Gospel*. London: Darton, Longman & Todd, 1976.

Dunn, James D. G. "Spirit and Kingdom." *Expository Times* 82 (1970–71): 36–40.

Dupont, Jacques. *Les Béatitudes*. Vol. 3: *Les Évangélistes*. New ed. Études bibliques. Paris: J. Gabalda, 1973.

_____. "La conclusion des Actes et son rapport à l'ensemble de l'ouvrage de Luc." Pp. 359–404 in *Les Actes des Apôtres: Traditions, rédaction, théologie*, edited by J. Kremer. Bibliotheca ephemeridum theologicarum Lovaniensium 48. Gembloux: J. Duculot, 1979.

_____. "Les discours de Pierre dans les Actes et le chapitre XXIV de l'évangile de Luc." Pp. 329–74 in *L'Évangile de Luc: Problèmes littéraires et théologiques*, edited by F. Neirynck. Bibliotheca ephemeridum theologicarum Lovaniensium 32. Gembloux: J. Duculot, 1973.

_____. "Die individuelle Eschatologie im Lukasevangelium und in der Apostelgeschichte." Pp. 37–47 in *Orientierung an Jesus: Zur Theologie der Synoptiker*, edited by Paul Hoffmann. Freiburg: Herder, 1973.

_____. "ΛΑΟΣ ΕΞ ΕΘΝΩΝ (Ac 15,14)." *New Testament Studies* 3 (1956–57): 47–50.

_____. "Le logion des douze trônes (Mt 19,28; Lc 22,28–30)." *Biblica* 45 (1964): 355–92.

_____. "Le Magnificat comme discours sur Dieu." *Nouvelle Revue Théologique* 102 (1980): 321–43.

_____. "The Meal at Emmaus." Pp. 105–21 in *The Eucharist in the New Testament*, J. Delorme, et al. Baltimore: Helicon, 1964.

_____. "La Mission de Paul d'après Actes 26.16–23 et la Mission des Apôtres d'après Luc 24.44–49 et Actes 1.8." Pp. 290–99 in *Paul and Paulinism*, edited by M. D. Hooker and S. G. Wilson. London: SPCK, 1982.

_____. "The Poor and Poverty in the Gospels and Acts." Pp. 25–52 in *Gospel Poverty: Essays in Biblical Theology*. Chicago: Franciscan Herald Press, 1977.

_____. "La portée christologique de l'évangélisation des nations d'après Luc 24,47." Pp. 125–43 in *Neues Testament und Kirche: Für Rudolf Schnackenburg*, edited by Joachim Gnilka. Freiburg: Herder, 1974.

_____. "La question du plan des Actes des Apôtres à la lumière d'un texte de Lucien de Samosate." *Novum Testamentum* 21 (1979): 220–31.

_____. *The Salvation of the Gentiles: Essays on the Acts of the Apostles*. Translated by John R. Keating. New York: Paulist Press, 1979.

Edwards, O. C., Jr. *Luke's Story of Jesus*. Philadelphia: Fortress Press, 1981.

Egelkraut, Helmuth L. *Jesus' Mission to Jerusalem: A Redaction Critical Study of the Travel Narrative in the Gospel of Luke, Lk 9:51–19:48*. Europäische Hochschulschriften. Frankfurt: Peter Lang, 1976.

Ellis, E. Earle. *Eschatology in Luke*. Facet Books. Philadelphia: Fortress Press, 1972.

_____. *The Gospel of Luke*. Rev. ed. New Century Bible Commentary. Grand Rapids: Wm. B. Eerdmans, 1981.

Eltester, Walther. "Israel im lukanischen Werk und die Nazarethperikope." Pp. 76–147 in *Jesus in Nazareth*, edited by Walther Eltester. Beiheft zur Zeitschrift für die neutestamentliche Wissenschaft 40. Berlin: Walter de Gruyter, 1972.

Epp, Eldon Jay. "The Ascension in the Textual Tradition of Luke-Acts." Pp. 131–45 in *New Testament Textual Criticism: Its Significance for Exegesis*, edited by Eldon Jay Epp and Gordon D. Fee. Oxford: Oxford University Press, 1981.

_____. *The Theological Tendency of Codex Bezae Cantabrigiensis in Acts*. Society for New Testament Studies Monograph Series 3. Cambridge: Cambridge University Press, 1966.

Evans, C. F. "The Central Section of St. Luke's Gospel." Pp. 37–53 in *Studies in the Gospels,* edited by D. E. Nineham. Oxford: Basil Blackwell, 1957.

Filson, Floyd V. "The Journey Motif in Luke-Acts." Pp. 68–77 in *Apostolic History and the Gospel: Biblical and Historical Essays,* edited by W. Ward Gasque and Ralph P. Martin. Grand Rapids: Wm. B. Eerdmans, 1970.

Fiorenza, Elisabeth Schüssler. *In Memory of Her: A Feminist Theological Reconstruction of Christian Origins.* New York: The Crossroad Publishing Co., 1983.

Fitzmyer, Joseph A. *The Gospel according to Luke I–IX.* Anchor Bible. Garden City, NY: Doubleday & Co., 1981.

_____. *The Gospel according to Luke X–XXIV.* Anchor Bible. Garden City, NY: Doubleday & Co., 1985.

Flender, Helmut. *St. Luke: Theologian of Redemptive History.* Translated by Reginald H. and Ilse Fuller. Philadelphia: Fortress Press, 1967.

Ford, J. Massyngbaerde. *My Enemy is My Guest: Jesus and Violence in Luke.* Maryknoll, NY: Orbis Books, 1984.

Francis, Fred O. "Eschatology and History in Luke-Acts." *Journal of the American Academy of Religion* 37 (1969): 49–63.

Franklin, Eric. *Christ the Lord: A Study in the Purpose and Theology of Luke-Acts.* Philadelphia: The Westminster Press, 1975.

Fuller, Reginald H. *The Formation of the Resurrection Narratives.* New York: Macmillan, 1971.

Funk, Robert W. "The Form of the New Testament Healing Miracle Story." *Semeia* 12 (1978): 57–96.

Genette, Gérard. *Narrative Discourse: An Essay in Method.* Translated by Jane E. Lewin. Ithaca, NY: Cornell University Press, 1980.

George, Augustin. "La construction du troisième évangile." Pp. 15–41 in *Études sur l'oeuvre de Luc.* Sources bibliques. Paris: J. Gabalda, 1978.

_____. "Israel." Pp. 87–125 in *Études sur l'oeuvre de Luc.* Sources bibliques. Paris: J. Gabalda, 1978.

_____. "Jésus Fils de Dieu." Pp. 215–36 in *Études sur l'oeuvre de Luc.* Sources bibliques. Paris: J. Gabalda, 1978.

_____. "Le miracle." Pp. 133–48 in *Études sur l'oeuvre de Luc.* Sources bibliques. Paris: J. Gabalda, 1978.

_____. "Par le doigt de Dieu." Pp. 127–32 in *Études sur l'oeuvre de Luc.* Sources bibliques. Paris: J. Gabalda, 1978.

_____. "Le parallèle entre Jean-Baptiste et Jésus en Lc 1–2." Pp. 43–64 in *Études sur l'oeuvre de Luc.* Sources bibliques. Paris: J. Gabalda, 1978.

_____. "La prédication inaugurale de Jésus dans la synagogue de Nazareth. Luc 4,16–30." *Bible et Vie Chrétienne* 59 (1964): 17–29.

_____. "Les récits de miracles. Caractéristiques lucaniennes." Pp. 67–84 in *Études sur l'oeuvre de Luc.* Sources bibliques. Paris: J. Gabalda, 1978.

_____. "La royauté de Jésus." Pp. 257–82 in *Études sur l'oeuvre de Luc.* Sources bibliques. Paris: J. Gabalda, 1978.

_____. "Le sens de la mort de Jésus." Pp. 185–212 in *Études sur l'oeuvre de Luc.* Sources bibliques. Paris: J. Gabalda, 1978.

Gill, David. "Observations on the Lukan Travel Narrative and Some Related Passages." *Harvard Theological Review* 63 (1970): 199–221.

Gnilka, Joachim. *Die Verstockung Israels: Isaias 6,9–10 in der Theologie der Synoptiker.* Studien zum Alten und Neuen Testament 3. Munich: Kösel-Verlag, 1961.

Gryglewicz, Feliks. "Die Herkunft der Hymnen des Kindheitsevangeliums des Lucas." *New Testament Studies* 21 (1974–75): 265–73.

Güttgemanns, Erhardt. "In welchem Sinne ist Lukas 'Historiker'? Die Beziehungen von Luk 1,1–4 und Papias zur antiken Rhetorik." *Linguistica Biblica* 54 (1983): 9–26.

Gunkel, Hermann. "Die Lieder in der Kindheitsgeschichte Jesu bei Lukas." Pp. 43–60 in

Festgabe von Fachgenossen und Freunden A. von Harnack zum siebzigsten Geburtstag dargebracht. Tübingen: J. C. B. Mohr (Paul Siebeck), 1921.

Haenchen, Ernst. *The Acts of the Apostles.* Philadelphia: The Westminster Press, 1971.

Hamel, Edouard. "Le Magnificat et le renversement des situations." *Gregorianum* 60 (1979): 55–84.

Hare, Douglas R. A. "The Rejection of the Jews in the Synoptic Gospels and Acts." Pp. 27–47 in *Anti Semitism and the Foundations of Christianity,* edited by Alan T. Davies. New York: Paulist Press, 1979.

Holleran, J. Warren. *The Synoptic Gethsemane: A Critical Study.* Analecta Gregoriana 191. Rome: Università Gregoriana, 1973.

Houlden, J. L. "The Purpose of Luke." *Journal for the Study of the New Testament* 21 (1984): 53–65.

Jakobson, Roman. "Closing Statement: Linguistics and Poetics." Pp. 350–77 in *Style in Language,* edited by Thomas A. Sebeok. Cambridge, MA: Technology Press of M. I. T., 1960.

Jeremias, Joachim. *Jesus' Promise to the Nations.* Translated by S. H. Hooke. Studies in Biblical Theology 24. Naperville, IL: Alec R. Allenson, 1958.

_____. "Μωυσῆς" Pp. 848–73 in *Theological Dictionary of the New Testament,* edited by Gerhard Kittel, vol. 4. Translated by Geoffrey W. Bromiley. Grand Rapids: Wm. B. Eerdmans, 1967.

_____. *The Parables of Jesus.* Rev. ed. Translated by S. H. Hooke. New York: Charles Scribner's, 1963.

Jervell, Jacob. "The Center of Scripture in Luke." Pp. 122–37, 179–83 in *The Unknown Paul: Essays on Luke-Acts and Early Christian History.* Minneapolis: Augsburg Publishing House, 1984.

_____. "The Daughters of Abraham: Women in Acts." Pp. 146–57, 186–90 in *The Unknown Paul: Essays on Luke-Acts and Early Christian History.* Minneapolis: Augsburg Publishing House, 1984.

_____. *Luke and the People of God.* Minneapolis: Augsburg Publishing House, 1972.

Johnson, Luke T. *The Literary Function of Possessions in Luke-Acts.* Society of Biblical Literature Dissertation Series 39. Missoula, MT: Scholars Press, 1977.

_____. "The Lukan Kingship Parable (Lk. 19.11–27)." *Novum Testamentum* 24 (1982): 139–59.

_____. "On Finding the Lukan Community: A Cautious Cautionary Essay." Pp. 87–100 in *Society of Biblical Literature 1979 Seminar Papers,* edited by Paul J. Achtemeier, vol. 1. Missoula, MT: Scholars Press, 1979.

Jones, Douglas. "The Background and Character of the Lukan Psalms." *Journal of Theological Studies* 19 (1968): 19–50.

Juel, Donald. *Luke-Acts: The Promise of History.* Atlanta: John Knox Press, 1983.

Karris, Robert J. *Luke: Artist and Theologian; Luke's Passion Account as Literature.* Theological Inquiries. New York: Paulist Press, 1985.

_____. "Missionary Communities: A New Paradigm for the Study of Luke-Acts." *Catholic Biblical Quarterly* 41 (1979): 80–97.

_____. *What Are They Saying about Luke and Acts? A Theology of the Faithful God.* New York: Paulist Press, 1979.

_____. "Windows and Mirrors: Literary Criticism and Luke's Sitz im Leben." Pp. 47–58 in *Society of Biblical Literature 1979 Seminar Papers,* edited by Paul J. Achtemeier, vol. 1. Missoula, MT: Scholars Press, 1979.

Kee, Howard Clark. "The Terminology of Mark's Exorcism Stories." *New Testament Studies* 14 (1967–68): 232–46.

Keck, Fridolin. *Die öffentliche Abschiedsrede Jesu in Lk 20,45–21,36: Eine redaktions- und motivgeschichtliche Untersuchung.* Forschung zur Bibel 25. Stuttgart: Katholisches Bibelwerk, 1976.

Keck, Leander E. "Poor." Pp. 672–75 in *Interpreter's Dictionary of the Bible,* edited by Keith Crim, supp. vol. Nashville: Abingdon Press, 1976.

Kennedy, George A. *New Testament Interpretation through Rhetorical Criticism.* Studies in Religion. Chapel Hill: University of North Carolina Press, 1984.

Klein, Günter. "Lukas 1.1–4 als theologisches Programm." Pp. 193–216 in *Zeit und Geschichte: Dankesgabe an R. Bultmann zum 80. Geburtstag,* edited by Erich Dinkler. Tübingen: J. C. B. Mohr (Paul Siebeck), 1964.

_____. "Die Verleugnung des Petrus." *Zeitschrift für Theologie und Kirche* 58 (1961): 285–328.

Kodell, Jerome. "Luke's Use of *Laos,* 'People,' Especially in the Jerusalem Narrative (Lk 19,28–24,53)." *Catholic Biblical Quarterly* 31 (1969): 327–43.

Koenig, John. *Jews and Christians in Dialogue: New Testament Foundations.* Philadelphia: The Westminster Press, 1979.

Koester, Helmut. "Συνέχω." Pp. 877–85 in *Theological Dictionary of the New Testament,* edited by Gerhard Kittel and Gerhard Friedrich, vol. 7. Translated by Geoffrey W. Bromiley. Grand Rapids: Wm. B. Eerdmans, 1971.

Kraybill, Donald B., and Dennis M. Sweetland. "Possessions in Luke-Acts: A Sociological Perspective." *Perspectives in Religious Studies* 10 (1983): 215–39.

Kurz, William S. "Luke 22:14–38 and Greco-Roman and Biblical Farewell Addresses." *Journal of Biblical Literature* 104 (1985): 251–68.

Lampe, G. W. H. "The Holy Spirit in the Writings of St. Luke." Pp. 159–200 in *Studies in the Gospels: Essays in Memory of R. H. Lightfoot,* edited by D. E. Nineham. Oxford: Basil Blackwell, 1955.

Lohfink, Gerhard. *Die Himmelfahrt Jesu. Untersuchungen zu den Himmelfahrts- und Erhöhungstexten bei Lukas.* Studien zum Alten und Neuen Testament 26. Munich: Kösel-Verlag, 1971.

_____. *Die Sammlung Israels: Eine Untersuchung zur lukanischen Ekklesiologie.* Studien zum Alten und Neuen Testament 39. Munich: Kösel-Verlag, 1975.

Lohse, Eduard. "Missionarisches Handeln Jesu nach dem Evangelium des Lukas." *Theologische Zeitschrift* 10 (1954): 1–13.

Maddox, Robert L. *The Purpose of Luke-Acts.* Forschungen zur Religion und Literatur des Alten und Neuen Testaments 126. Göttingen: Vandenhoeck & Ruprecht, 1982.

Marshall, I. Howard. *The Gospel of Luke: A Commentary on the Greek Text.* New International Greek Testament Commentary. Grand Rapids: Wm. B. Eerdmans, 1978.

Masson, Charles. "Jésus à Nazareth." Pp. 38–69 in *Vers les sources d'eau vive.* Lausanne: Librairie Payot, 1961.

Merk, Otto. "Das Reich Gottes in den lukanischen Schriften." Pp. 201–20 in *Jesus und Paulus: Festschrift für Werner Georg Kümmel zum 70. Geburtstag,* edited by E. Earle Ellis and Erich Grässer. Göttingen: Vandenhoeck & Ruprecht, 1975.

Metzger, Bruce M. *A Textual Commentary on the Greek New Testament.* London: United Bible Societies, 1971.

Miesner, Donald R. "The Circumferential Speeches in Luke-Acts: Patterns and Purpose." Pp. 223–37 in *Society of Biblical Literature 1978 Seminar Papers,* edited by Paul J. Achtemeier, vol. 2. Missoula, MT: Scholars Press, 1978.

Minear, Paul S. "Jesus' Audiences, According to Luke." *Novum Testamentum* 16 (1974): 81–109.

_____. "Luke's Use of the Birth Stories." Pp. 111–30 in *Studies in Luke-Acts,* edited by Leander E. Keck and J. Louis Martyn. Nashville: Abingdon Press, 1966.

_____. "A Note on Luke 17:7–10." *Journal of Biblical Literature* 93 (1974): 82–87.

_____. "A Note on Luke xxii 36." *Novum Testamentum* 7 (1964–65): 128–34.

_____. *To Heal and to Reveal: The Prophetic Vocation according to Luke.* New York: Seabury Press, 1976.

Miyoshi, Michi. *Der Anfang des Reiseberichts, Lk 9,51–10,24: Eine redaktionsgeschichtliche Untersuchung.* Analecta Biblica 60. Rome: Biblical Institute Press, 1974.

Moessner, David P. "Jesus and the 'Wilderness Generation': The Death of the Prophet like Moses according to Luke." Pp. 319–40 in *Society of Biblical Literature 1982 Seminar Papers,* edited by Kent Harold Richards. Chico, CA: Scholars Press, 1982.

_____. "Luke 9:1–50: Luke's Preview of the Journey of the Prophet Like Moses of Deuteronomy." *Journal of Biblical Literature* 102 (1983): 575–605.

Morgenthaler, Robert. *Die lukanische Geschichtsschreibung als Zeugnis: Gestalt und Gehalt der Kunst des Lukas.* 2 vols. Abhandlungen zur Theologie des Alten und Neuen Testaments 14–15. Zürich: Zwingli Verlag, 1949.

Nellessen, Ernst. "Gesalbt und gesandt: Ein Beitrag zur Grundlegung der christlichen Spiritualität in der Botschaft des Neuen Testaments." *Bibel und Leben* 8 (1967): 186–95.

_____. *Zeugnis für Jesus und das Wort: Exegetische Untersuchungen zum lukanischen Zeugnisbegriff.* Bonner biblische Beiträge 43. Cologne: Peter Hanstein, 1976.

Neyrey, Jerome. "The Absence of Jesus' Emotions–the Lucan Redaction of Lk 22,39–46." *Biblica* 61 (1980): 153–71.

_____. "Jesus' Address to the Women of Jerusalem (Lk. 23.27–31)—A Prophetic Judgment Oracle." *New Testament Studies* 29 (1983): 74–86.

_____. *The Passion according to Luke: A Redaction Study of Luke's Soteriology.* Theological Inquiries. New York: Paulist Press, 1985.

Nickelsburg, George W. E. "Riches, the Rich, and God's Judgment in I Enoch 92–105 and the Gospel according to Luke." *New Testament Studies* 25 (1978–79): 324–44.

_____, ed. *Studies on the Testament of Moses.* Septuagint and Cognate Studies 4. Cambridge, MA: Society of Biblical Literature, 1973.

Nuttall, Geoffrey F. *The Moment of Recognition: Luke as Story-Teller.* London: The University of London Athlone Press, 1978.

Ó Fearghail, Fearghus. "Rejection in Nazareth: Lk 4:22." *Zeitschrift für die neutestamentliche Wissenschaft* 75 (1984): 60–72.

O'Hanlon, John. "The Story of Zacchaeus and the Lukan Ethic." *Journal for the Study of the New Testament* 12 (1981): 2–26.

Oliver, H. H. "The Lucan Birth Stories and the Purpose of Luke-Acts." *New Testament Studies* 10 (1963–64): 202–26.

O'Toole, Robert F. "Acts 2:30 and the Davidic Covenant of Pentecost." *Journal of Biblical Literature* 102 (1983): 245–58.

_____. *The Unity of Luke's Theology: An Analysis of Luke-Acts.* Good News Studies 9. Wilmington: Michael Glazier, 1984.

Ott, Wilhelm. *Gebet und Heil: Die Bedeutung der Gebetsparänese in der lukanischen Theologie.* Studien zum Alten und Neuen Testament 12. Munich: Kösel-Verlag, 1965.

Parsons, Mikeal Carl. *The Ascension Narratives in Luke-Acts.* Ph.D. diss., Southern Baptist Theological Seminary, 1985.

Patte, Daniel. *What Is Structural Exegesis?* Guides to Biblical Scholarship. Philadelphia: Fortress Press, 1976.

Petersen, Norman. *Literary Criticism for New Testament Critics.* Guides to Biblical Scholarship. Philadelphia: Fortress Press, 1978.

Pilgrim, Walter E. *Good News to the Poor: Wealth and Poverty in Luke-Acts.* Minneapolis: Augsburg Publishing House, 1981.

Plümacher, Eckhard. "Lukas als griechischer Historiker." Col. 235–64 in *Paulys Realencyclopädie der classischen Altertumswissenschaft,* Supplementband 14. Munich: Alfred Druckenmüller, 1974.

Praeder, Susan Marie. "Jesus-Paul, Peter-Paul, and Jesus-Peter Parallelisms in Luke-Acts: A History of Reader Response." Pp. 23–39 in *Society of Biblical Literature 1984 Seminar Papers,* edited by Kent Harold Richards. Chico, CA: Scholars Press, 1984.

_____. "Luke-Acts and the Ancient Novel." Pp. 269–92 in *Society of Biblical Literature*

1981 Seminar Papers, edited by Kent Harold Richards. Chico, CA: Scholars Press, 1981.

Propp, Vladimir. *Morphology of the Folktale.* 2d ed. Translated by Laurence Scott. Publications of the American Folklore Society. Austin: University of Texas Press, 1968.

Radl, Walter. *Paulus und Jesus im lukanischen Doppelwerk: Untersuchungen zu Parallelmotiven im Lukasevangelium und in der Apostelgeschichte.* Europäische Hochschulschriften. Bern: Herbert Lang; Frankfurt: Peter Lang, 1975.

Ramaroson, Léonard. "Le coeur du Troisième Évangile: Lc 15." *Biblica* 60 (1979): 348–60.

Reicke, B. "Instruction and Discussion in the Travel Narrative." Pp. 206–16 in *Studia Evangelica: Papers Presented to the International Congress on the Four Gospels in 1957 Held at Christ Church, Oxford,* edited by Kurt Aland et al. Texte und Untersuchungen zur Geschichte der altchristlichen Literatur 73. Berlin: Akademie-Verlag, 1959.

Rengstorf, K. H. "Μαθητής." Pp. 415–60 in *Theological Dictionary of the New Testament,* edited by Gerhard Kittel, vol. 4. Translated by Geoffrey W. Bromiley. Grand Rapids: Wm. B. Eerdmans, 1967.

Rese, Martin. *Alttestamentliche Motive in der Christologie des Lukas.* Studien zum Neuen Testament 1. Gütersloh: Gütersloher Verlagshaus Gerd Mohn, 1969.

_____. "Einige Überlegungen zu Lukas XIII, 31–33." Pp. 201–25 in *Jésus aux origines de la christologie,* edited by J. Dupont. Bibliotheca ephemeridum theologicarum Lovaniensium 40. Gembloux: J. Duculot, 1975.

Resseguie, James L. "Point of View in the Central Section of Luke (9:51–19:44)." *Journal of the Evangelical Theological Society* 25 (1982): 41–47.

_____. "Reader-Response Criticism and the Synoptic Gospels." *Journal of the American Academy of Religion* 52 (1984): 307–24.

Rice, George E. "Luke 4:31–44: Release for the Captives." *Andrews University Seminary Studies* 20 (1982): 23–28.

_____. "Luke 5:33–6:11: Release from Cultic Tradition." *Andrews University Seminary Studies* 20 (1982): 127–32.

_____. "Luke's Thematic Use of the Call to Discipleship." *Andrews University Seminary Studies* 19 (1981): 51–58.

Ringe, Sharon H. *Jesus, Liberation, and the Biblical Jubilee.* Overtures to Biblical Theology 19. Philadelphia: Fortress Press, 1985.

_____. *The Jubilee Proclamation in the Ministry and Teaching of Jesus: A Tradition-Critical Study in the Synoptic Gospels and Acts.* Ph.D. diss., Union Theological Seminary, New York, 1981.

Robbins, Vernon K. "Prefaces in Greco-Roman Biography and Luke-Acts." *Perspectives in Religious Studies* 6 (1979): 94–108.

Robinson, William C., Jr. "On Preaching the Word of God (Luke 8:4–21)." Pp. 131–38 in *Studies in Luke-Acts,* edited by Leander E. Keck and J. Louis Martyn. Nashville: Abingdon Press, 1966.

_____. *Der Weg des Herrn: Studien zur Geschichte und Eschatologie im Lukas-Evangelium.* Theologische Forschung 36. Hamburg-Bergstedt: Herbert Reich, 1964.

Ryan, Rosalie. "The Women from Galilee and Discipleship in Luke." *Biblical Theology Bulletin* 15 (1985): 56–59.

Sanders, Jack T. "The Parable of the Pounds and Lucan Anti-Semitism." *Theological Studies* 42 (1981): 660–68.

_____. "The Pharisees in Luke-Acts." Pp. 141–88 in *The Living Text: Essays in Honor of Ernest W. Saunders,* edited by Dennis Groh and Robert Jewett. Lanham, MD: University Press of America, 1985.

_____. "The Salvation of the Jews in Luke-Acts." Pp. 104–28 in *Luke-Acts: New Perspectives from the Society of Biblical Literature Seminar,* edited by Charles H. Talbert. New York: The Crossroad Publishing Co., 1984.

Sanders, James A. "The Ethic of Election in Luke's Great Banquet Parable." Pp. 245–71 in *Essays in Old Testament Ethics,* edited by James L. Crenshaw and John T. Willis. New York: Ktav Publishing House, Inc., 1974.

_____. "From Isaiah 61 to Luke 4." Pp. 75–106 in *Christianity, Judaism and Other Greco-Roman Cults,* edited by Jacob Neusner, vol. 1. Leiden: E. J. Brill, 1975.

_____. "Isaiah in Luke." *Interpretation* 36 (1982): 144–55.

Schenk, Wolfgang. *Der Passionsbericht nach Markus: Untersuchungen zur Überlieferungsgeschichte der Passionstraditionen.* Gütersloh: Gütersloher Verlagshaus Gerd Mohn, 1974.

Schmidt, Daryl. "Luke's 'Innocent' Jesus: A Scriptural Apologetic." Pp. 111–21 in *Political Issues in Luke-Acts,* edited by Richard Cassidy and Philip Scharper. Maryknoll, NY: Orbis Books, 1983.

Schnackenburg, Rudolf. "Das Magnificat, seine Spiritualität und Theologie." Pp. 201–19 in *Schriften zum Neuen Testament: Exegese in Fortschritt und Wandel.* Munich: Kösel-Verlag, 1971.

Schneider, Gerhard. *Parusiegleichnisse im Lukas-Evangelium.* Stuttgarter Bibelstudien 74. Stuttgart: Katholisches Bibelwerk, 1975.

_____. "Zur Bedeutung von καθεξῆς im lukanischen Doppelwerk." *Zeitschrift für die neutestamentliche Wissenschaft* 68 (1977): 128–31.

_____. "Der Zweck des lukanischen Doppelwerks." *Biblische Zeitschrift* 21 (1977): 45–66.

Schottroff, Luise, and Wolfgang Stegemann. *Jesus von Nazareth: Hoffnung der Armen.* 2d ed. Urban Taschenbücher 639. Stuttgart: W. Kohlhammer, 1981.

Schubert, Paul. "The Structure and Significance of Luke 24." Pp. 165–86 in *Neutestamentliche Studien für Rudolf Bultmann,* edited by W. Eltester. Beihefte zur Zeitschrift für die neutestamentliche Wissenschaft 21. Berlin: A. Töpelmann, 1954.

Schürmann, Heinz. "Der Abendmahlsbericht Lk 22,7–38 als Gottesdienstordnung, Gemeindeordnung, Lebensordnung." Pp. 108–50 in *Ursprung und Gestalt: Erörterungen und Besinnungen zum Neuen Testament.* Kommentare und Beiträge zum Alten und Neuen Testament. Düsseldorf: Patmos-Verlag, 1970.

_____. *Das Lukasevangelium, Erster Teil, Kommentar zu Kap. 1,1–9,50.* Herders theologischer Kommentar zum Neuen Testament 3. Freiburg: Herder, 1969.

Schütz, Frieder. *Der leidende Christus: Die angefochtene Gemeinde und das Christuskerygma der lukanischen Schriften.* Beiträge zur Wissenschaft vom Alten und Neuen Testament 89. Stuttgart: W. Kohlhammer, 1969.

Schulz, Siegfried. "Gottes Vorsehung bei Lukas." *Zeitschrift für die neutestamentliche Wissenschaft* 54 (1963): 104–16.

Schweizer, Eduard. *The Good News according to Luke.* Translated by David E. Green. Atlanta: John Knox Press, 1984.

_____. "Zum Aufbau von Lukas 1 und 2." Pp. 309–35 in *Intergerini Parietis Septum: Essays Presented to Markus Barth,* edited by Dikran Hadidian. Pittsburgh: Pickwick Publications, 1981.

Scott, Bernard Brandon. "A Master's Praise: Luke 16,1–8a." *Biblica* 64 (1983): 173–88.

Seccombe, David. "Luke and Isaiah." *New Testament Studies* 27 (1980–81): 252–59.

_____. *Possessions and the Poor in Luke-Acts.* Studien zum Neuen Testament und seiner Umwelt. Linz, 1982.

Sellin, Gerhard. "Komposition, Quellen und Funktion des lukanischen Reiseberichtes (Lk IX 51–XIX 28)." *Novum Testamentum* 20 (1978): 100–35.

Selvidge, Marla J. "Mark 5:25–34 and Leviticus 15:19–20: A Reaction to Restrictive Purity Regulations." *Journal of Biblical Literature* 103 (1984): 619–23.

Siegert, Folker. "Lukas–ein Historiker, d. h. ein Rhetor? Freundschaftliche Entgegnung auf Erhardt Güttgemanns." *Linguistica Biblica* 55 (1984): 57–60.

Sjöberg, Erik, and Eduard Schweizer. "Πνεῦμα, πνευματικός." Pp. 359–455 in *Theological Dictionary of the New Testament,* edited by Gerhard Kittel and Gerhard Friedrich, vol. 6. Translated by Geoffrey W. Bromiley. Grand Rapids: Wm. B. Eerdmans, 1968.

Sloan, Robert B., Jr. *The Favorable Year of the Lord: A Study of Jubilary Theology in the Gospel of Luke.* Austin: Schola, 1977.

Smalley, Stephen S. "Spirit, Kingdom and Prayer in Luke-Acts." *Novum Testamentum* 15 (1973): 59–71.

Sparks, H. F. D. "The Semitisms of St. Luke's Gospel." *Journal of Theological Studies* 44 (1943): 129–38.

Spengel, Leonhard von, ed. *Rhetores graeci.* Vol. 2. Bibliotheca scriptorum graecorum et romanorum Teubneriana. Leipzig: B. G. Teubner, 1854.

Stählin, Gustav. "Χήρα." Pp. 440–65 in *Theological Dictionary of the New Testament,* edited by Gerhard Kittel and Gerhard Friedrich, vol. 9. Translated by Geoffrey W. Bromiley. Grand Rapids: Wm. B. Eerdmans, 1974.

Steck, Odil Hannes. *Israel und das gewaltsame Geschick der Propheten.* Wissenschaftliche Monographien zum Alten und Neuen Testament 23. Neukirchen-Vluyn: Neukirchener-Verlag, 1967.

Steele, E. Springs. "Luke 11:37–54—A Modified Hellenistic Symposium?" *Journal of Biblical Literature* 103 (1984): 379–94.

Strathmann, H. "Λαός." Pp. 29–57 in *Theological Dictionary of the New Testament,* edited by Gerhard Kittel, vol. 4. Translated by Geoffrey W. Bromiley. Grand Rapids: Wm. B. Eerdmans, 1967.

Talbert, Charles H. "An Anti-Gnostic Tendency in Lucan Christology." *New Testament Studies* 14 (1967–68): 259–71.

——. *The Certainty of the Gospel: The Perspective of Luke-Acts.* DeLand: Stetson University, 1980.

——. "Discipleship in Luke-Acts." Pp. 62–75 in *Discipleship in the New Testament,* edited by Fernando F. Segovia. Philadelphia: Fortress Press, 1985.

——. *Literary Patterns, Theological Themes and the Genre of Luke-Acts.* Society of Biblical Literature Monograph Series 20. Missoula, MT: Scholars Press, 1974.

——. *Luke and the Gnostics: An Examination of the Lucan Purpose.* Nashville: Abingdon Press, 1966.

——. "Martyrdom in Luke-Acts and the Lukan Social Ethic." Pp. 99–110 in *Political Issues in Luke-Acts,* edited by Richard Cassidy and Philip Scharper. Maryknoll, NY: Orbis Books, 1983.

——. "Promise and Fulfillment in Lucan Theology." Pp. 91–103 in *Luke-Acts: New Perspectives from the Society of Biblical Literature Seminar,* edited by Charles H. Talbert. New York: The Crossroad Publishing Co., 1984.

——. "Prophecies of Future Greatness: The Contribution of Greco-Roman Biographies to an Understanding of Luke 1:5–4:15." Pp. 129–41 in *The Divine Helmsman: Studies on God's Control of Human Events, Presented to Lou H. Silberman,* edited by James L. Crenshaw and Samuel Sandmel. New York: Ktav Publishing House, Inc., 1980.

——. *Reading Luke: A Literary and Theological Commentary on the Third Gospel.* New York: The Crossroad Publishing Co., 1982.

——. "The Redaction Critical Quest for Luke the Theologian." Pp. 171–222 in *Jesus and Man's Hope,* edited by David G. Buttrick, vol. 1. Pittsburgh: Pittsburgh Theological Seminary, 1970.

——. "Shifting Sands: The Recent Study of the Gospel of Luke." *Interpretation* 30 (1976): 381–95.

——. "The Way of the Lukan Jesus: Dimensions of Lukan Spirituality." *Perspectives in Religious Studies* 9 (1982): 237–49.

Tannehill, Robert C. "Attitudinal Shift in Synoptic Pronouncement Stories." Pp. 183–97 in *Orientation by Disorientation: Studies in Literary Criticism and Biblical Literary Criticism Presented in Honor of William A. Beardslee,* edited by Richard A. Spencer. Pittsburgh: Pickwick Publications, 1980.

——. "The Composition of Acts 3–5: Narrative Development and Echo Effect." Pp. 217–40 in *Society of Biblical Literature 1984 Seminar Papers*, edited by Kent Harold Richards. Chico, CA: Scholars Press, 1984.

——. "The Gospel of Mark as Narrative Christology." *Semeia* 16 (1979): 57–95.

——. "Homiletical Resources: Gospel Lections for Advent." *Quarterly Review* 2,3 (1982): 9–42.

——. "Introduction: The Pronouncement Story and Its Types." *Semeia* 20 (1981): 1–13.

——. "Israel in Luke-Acts: A Tragic Story." *Journal of Biblical Literature* 104 (1985): 69–85.

——. "The Magnificat as Poem." *Journal of Biblical Literature* 93 (1974): 263–75.

——. "The Mission of Jesus according to Luke IV 16–30." Pp. 51–75 in *Jesus in Nazareth*, edited by Walther Eltester. Beihefte zur Zeitschrift für die neutestamentliche Wissenschaft 40. Berlin: Walter de Gruyter, 1972.

——. "A Study in the Theology of Luke-Acts." *Anglican Theological Review* 43 (1961): 195–203.

——. *The Sword of His Mouth: Forceful and Imaginative Language in Synoptic Sayings.* Semeia Supplements 1. Philadelphia: Fortress Press, & Missoula, MT: Scholars Press, 1975.

——. "Types and Functions of Apophthegms in the Synoptic Gospels." Pp. 1792–1829 in *Aufstieg und Niedergang der römischen Welt*, edited by Hildegard Temporini and Wolfgang Haase, II Principat, vol. 25,2. Berlin: Walter de Gruyter, 1984.

——. "Varieties of Synoptic Pronouncement Stories." *Semeia* 20 (1981): 101–19.

Theissen, Gerd. *The Miracle Stories in the Early Christian Tradition*. Translated by Francis McDonagh. Philadelphia: Fortress Press, 1983.

Tiede, David L. *Prophecy and History in Luke-Acts*. Philadelphia: Fortress Press, 1980.

Trites, Allison A. "The Prayer Motif in Luke-Acts." Pp. 168–86 in *Perspectives on Luke-Acts*, edited by Charles H. Talbert. Danville, VA: Association of Baptist Professors of Religion, 1978.

Trompf, G. W. *The Idea of Historical Recurrence in Western Thought: From Antiquity to the Reformation*. Berkeley: University of California Press, 1979.

Turner, Nigel. "The Quality of the Greek of Luke-Acts." Pp. 387–400 in *Studies in New Testament Language and Text*, edited by J. K. Elliott. Leiden: E. J. Brill, 1976.

Tyson, Joseph B. "Conflict as a Literary Theme in the Gospel of Luke." Pp. 303–27 in *New Synoptic Studies: The Cambridge Gospel Conference and Beyond*, edited by William R. Farmer. Macon, GA: Mercer University Press, 1983.

——. "The Jewish Public in Luke-Acts." *New Testament Studies* 30 (1984): 574–83.

——. "The Opposition to Jesus in the Gospel of Luke." *Perspectives in Religious Studies* 5 (1978): 144–50.

Untergassmair, Franz Georg. *Kreuzweg und Kreuzigung Jesu: Ein Beitrag zur lukanischen Redaktionsgeschichte und zur Frage nach der lukanischen "Kreuzestheologie."* Paderborner theologische Studien 10. Paderborn: F. Schöningh, 1980.

——. "Thesen zur Sinndeutung des Todes Jesu in der lukanischen Passionsgeschichte." *Theologie und Glaube* 70 (1980): 180–93.

Uspensky, Boris. *A Poetics of Composition: The Structure of the Artistic Text and Typology of a Compositional Form*. Translated by Valentina Zavarin and Susan Wittig. Berkeley: University of California Press, 1973.

Vanhoye, Albert. "Structure du 'Benedictus'." *New Testament Studies* 12 (1965–66): 382–89.

van Stempvoort, P. A. "The Interpretation of the Ascension in Luke and Acts." *New Testament Studies* 5 (1958–59): 30–42.

van Unnik, W. C. "Éléments artistiques dans l'évangile de Luc." Pp. 129–40 in *L'Évangile de Luc: Problèmes littéraires et théologiques*, edited by F. Neirynck. Bibliotheca ephemeridum theologicarum Lovaniensium 32. Gembloux: J. Duculot, 1973.

———. "First Century A. D. Literary Culture and Early Christian Literature." Pp. 1–13 in *Protocol of the First Colloquy of the Center for Hermeneutical Studies in Hellenistic and Modern Culture*. Berkeley: 1970.

———. "Luke-Acts, a Storm Center in Contemporary Scholarship." Pp. 15–32 in *Studies in Luke-Acts*, edited by Leander E. Keck and J. Louis Martyn. Nashville: Abingdon Press, 1966.

Via, E. Jane. "According to Luke, Who Put Jesus to Death?" Pp. 122–45 in *Political Issues in Luke-Acts*, edited by Richard Cassidy and Philip Scharper. Maryknoll, NY: Orbis Books, 1983.

Violet, B. "Zum rechten Verständnis der Nazareth-Perikope Lc 4.16–30." *Zeitschrift für die neutestamentliche Wissenschaft* 37 (1938): 251–71.

Völkel, Martin. "Exegetische Erwägungen zum Verständnis des Begriffs καθεξῆς im lukanischen Prolog." *New Testament Studies* 20 (1973–74): 289–99.

———. "Zur Deutung des 'Reiches Gottes' bei Lukas." *Zeitschrift für die neutestamentliche Wissenschaft* 65 (1974): 57–70.

Voss, Gerhard. *Die Christologie der lukanischen Schriften in Grundzügen*. Studia Neotestamentica 2. Brügge: Desclée de Brouwer, 1965.

Wainwright, Arthur W. "Luke and the Restoration of the Kingdom to Israel." *Expository Times* 89 (1977–78): 76–79.

Wanke, Joachim. *Die Emmauserzählung: Eine redaktionsgeschichtliche Untersuchung zu Lk 24,13–35*. Erfurter theologische Studien 31. Leipzig: St. Benno, 1973.

Weinert, Francis D. "Luke, the Temple and Jesus' Saying about Jerusalem's Abandoned House (Luke 13:34–35)." *Catholic Biblical Quarterly* 44 (1982): 68–76.

Wilckens, Ulrich. "Interpreting Luke-Acts in a Period of Existentialist Theology." Pp. 60–83 in *Studies in Luke-Acts*, edited by Leander E. Keck and J. Louis Martyn. Nashville: Abingdon Press, 1966.

———. "Vergebung für die Sünderin (Lk 7,36–50)." Pp. 394–424 in *Orientierung an Jesus: Zur Theologie der Synoptiker*, edited by Paul Hoffmann. Freiburg. Herder, 1973.

Wilson, Stephen G. *The Gentiles and the Gentile Mission in Luke-Acts*. Society for New Testament Studies Monograph Series 23. Cambridge: Cambridge University Press, 1973.

———. "Lukan Eschatology." *New Testament Studies* 15 (1969–70): 330–47.

———. *Luke and the Law*. Society for New Testament Studies Monograph Series 50. Cambridge: Cambridge University Press, 1983.

Wink, Walter. *John the Baptist in the Gospel Tradition*. Society for New Testament Studies Monograph Series 7. Cambridge: Cambridge University Press, 1968.

Winter, Paul. "Magnificat and Benedictus—Maccabaean Psalms?" *Bulletin of the John Rylands Library* 37 (1954–55): 328–47.

———. "Some Observations on the Language in the Birth and Infancy Stories of the Third Gospel." *New Testament Studies* 1 (1954–55): 111–21.

Wire, Antoinette Clark. "The Structure of the Gospel Miracle Stories and Their Tellers." *Semeia* 11 (1978): 83–113.

Witherington, Ben III. "On the Road with Mary Magdalene, Joanna, Susanna, and Other Disciples—Luke 8.1–3." *Zeitschrift für die neutestamentliche Wissenschaft* 70 (1979): 243–48.

———. *Women in the Ministry of Jesus: A Study of Jesus' Attitudes to Women and Their Roles as Reflected in His Earthly Life*. Society for New Testament Studies Monograph Series 51. Cambridge: Cambridge University Press, 1984.

Wrege, Hans-Theo. *Die Gestalt des Evangeliums: Aufbau und Struktur der Synoptiker sowie der Apostelgeschichte*. Beiträge zur biblischen Exegese und Theologie 11. Frankfurt: Peter Lang, 1978.

Zehnle, Richard. "The Salvific Character of Jesus' Death in Lukan Soteriology." *Theological Studies* 30 (1969): 420–44.

Ziesler, J. A. "Luke and the Pharisees." *New Testament Studies* 25 (1978–79): 146–57.

Zmijewski, Josef. *Die Eschatologiereden des Lukas-Evangeliums: Eine traditions- und redaktionsgeschichtliche Untersuchung zu Lk 21,5–36 und Lk 17,20–37.* Bonner biblische Beiträge 40. Bonn: Peter Hanstein, 1972.

Index

Authors

Primary Texts

Index

SUBJECTS